MW01053263

# The New England Gardener's Year

# The New England Gardener's Year

A Month-by-Month Guide for Maine, New Hampshire, Vermont, Massachusetts, Rhode Island, Connecticut, and Upstate New York

**Reeser Manley**
**and**
**Marjorie Peronto**

Distributed by University Press of New England
Hanover and London

The New England Gardener's Year: A Month-by-Month Guide for Maine, New Hampshire, Vermont, Massachusetts, Rhode Island, Connecticut, and Upstate New York



Library of Congress Control Number: 2012954444

ISBN 978-1-937644-14-7 (hardcover)
ISBN 978-1-937644-18-5 (eBook)

Cover and interior design by North Wind Design & Production,
www.nwdpbooks.com
Cover photos by authors

Cadent Publishing
9 Gleason Street
Thomaston, ME 04861
www.cadentpublishing.com

Printed in the United States of America

Distributed by University Press of New England
1 Court Street
Lebanon, New Hampshire 03766

# Contents

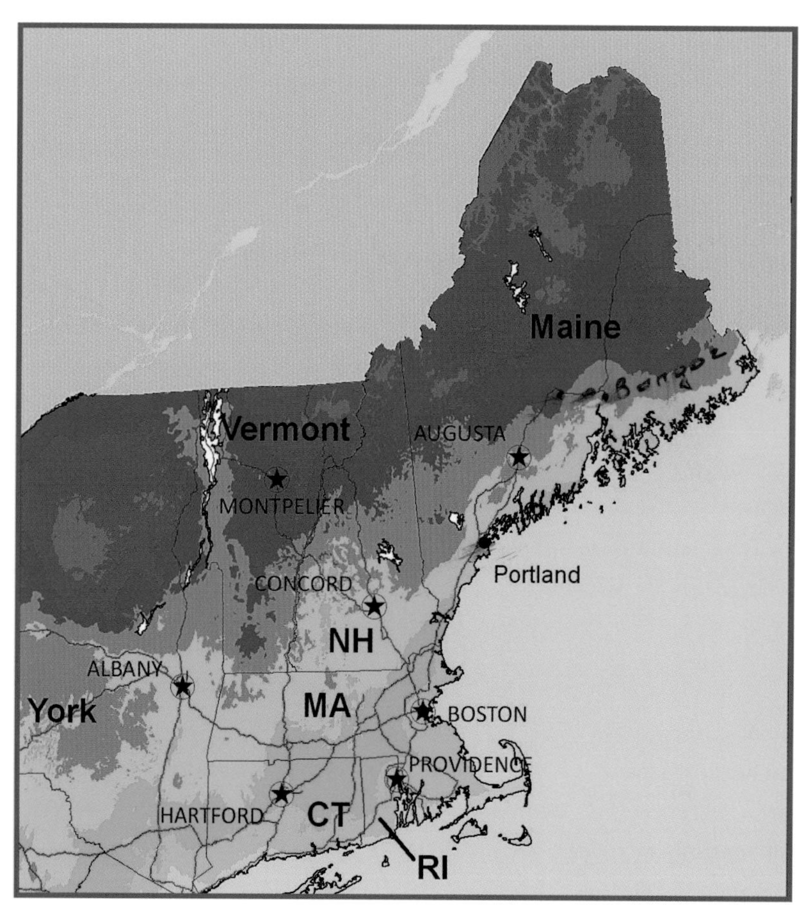
Maine
Vermont
AUGUSTA
MONTPELIER
Portland
CONCORD
NH
ALBANY
York
MA
BOSTON
PROVIDENCE
HARTFORD
CT
RI

**Average Annual Extreme Minimum Temperature 1976-2005**

| Temp (F) | Zone | Temp (C) |
|---|---|---|
| -40 to -35 | 3a | -40 to -37.2 |
| -35 to -30 | 3b | -37.2 to -34.4 |
| -30 to -25 | 4a | -34.4 to -31.7 |
| -25 to -20 | 4b | -31.7 to -28.9 |
| -20 to -15 | 5a | -28.9 to -26.1 |
| -15 to -10 | 5b | -26.1 to -23.3 |
| -10 to -5 | 6a | -23.3 to -20.6 |
| -5 to 0 | 6b | -20.6 to -17.8 |
| 0 to 5 | 7a | -17.8 to -15 |

For updates and tips, visit Reeser's gardening community on Facebook at:
http://www.facebook.com/negardener

# Chapter 1

# Garden Paths and the Path Through This Book

*"Everything that slows us down and forces patience, everything that sets us back into the slow circles of nature, is a help. Gardening is an instrument of grace."*

—May Sarton, *Plant Dreaming Deep,* 1968

***Early in the development of this book,*** my publisher and editor asked me, "Should you define 'garden'? Your examples of gardens include trees, shrubs, mown paths through fields, etc., so your definition of a garden is bound to be a broad one. Where, I wonder, is the distinction between a landscape and a garden?"

I had been writing my weekly garden column in the *Bangor Daily News* for five years, and it had never occurred to me to define what I mean by "garden."

The dictionary is of little help. "Garden" is more idea than object, and ideas of a garden are as diverse as the gardeners who cultivate them.

"You've got to come by and see my garden!" I never know what to expect when I get this invitation, but I seldom turn it down unless it comes from someone who really means, "you've got to see what my paid gardener has done with the space that I call *my* garden." I'm sorry, but it's not your garden if you are not the gardener.

Marjorie and I share a concept of garden that is as broad as the diversity of life within the boundaries of eye and ear. It begins at our doorway and extends to the old spruce snag we can see from the upstairs window. Our garden includes the early morning call of the loon flying high over the house on its way to the river.

As for the term "landscape," I think of our garden (which I call Marjorie's Garden for reasons that will become clear) as part of a larger landscape of other gardens and the roads that connect them, the Union River flowing through town on its way to the sea, the buildings of Ellsworth, Maine, the view of Cadillac Mountain on the horizon. The landscape is the larger view. I am one of the caretakers of a small piece of that landscape, Marjorie's Garden.

In his essay *The Idea of a Garden,* Michael Pollan suggests that the worldwide scourge of invasive plant species has rendered every place, no matter how wild, a garden—a place in need of cultivation to keep invaders out. This concept seems to fit one of the dictionary definitions of

*Facing page:* Along one of the many paths through her Cape Cod garden, Patricia Crow combines the bright yellows of lilies and hypericum with the purple flowers of lavender and the fine texture of hairgrass *(Deschampsia cespitosa)*. In the background is the glaucus purple foliage of a purple-leaved shrub rose *(Rosa glauca)*.

"cultivate": "to improve by labor, care, or study." Cultivation is the gardener's task, whether it be wrenching Norway maple seedlings from the forest soil, or growing vegetables and fruits, or caring for a collection of shrubs and trees that surround the home. In this book we will be talking about all these forms of cultivation, everything that provides richness, beauty, and utility to the place you call your garden.

Our book focuses on gardening in New England, a region that extends from USDA Hardiness Zone 3 in northern Maine to Zone 7 on the shore of Rhode Island Sound. If you are not sure which of these zones you garden in, refer to the USDA Hardiness Zone map in the front of this book or on the Internet. Or, you can enter the phrase "hardiness zone by zip code" in a search engine and discover a National Gardening Association site that will identify your gardening zone based on your zip code.

Beans ready for harvest from a Woodbury, Connecticut garden (Zone 6a) in late July. (Photo courtesy Charles Heaven)

Knowing your hardiness zone helps you set limits on what is likely to grow in your garden. For example, you may really like the glossy abelia *(Abelia* x *grandiflora)* that grew in your grandmother's garden on the southern shore of Massachusetts (Zone 7a), but it is rated as hardy only in Zones 5 through 9, and you live in Zone 4. Your garden would likely be too cold in winter for this shrub to survive.

But then again, maybe not. Within any garden, regardless of hardiness zone, there are microclimate pockets, small areas that are warmer or colder, wetter or drier, more or less prone to early frosts than the garden as a whole. You might be able to grow that abelia in a protected courtyard or in front of a warm, south-facing wall even though you live in Zone 4. Or your entire garden may be nestled within an extensive microclimate, perhaps bordering a large body of water that moderates temperatures for several miles inland, or in the "heat island" of a large urban area, where asphalt and concrete absorb and re-radiate the sun's heat, keeping the air warmer. Microclimates, small and large, do not typically show up on the USDA Hardiness Zone map.

I know gardeners who enjoy testing the hardiness limits of their gardens. They might try growing glossy abelia in Zone 4, or perhaps even okra! They know the microclimates within their gardens well enough to say, "This is a Zone 4 spot, but over there is Zone 5." That kind of knowledge comes from years of gardening in the same place, although scattering a few minimum-maximum thermometers around the garden can't hurt.

On August 20, 1811, Thomas Jefferson, then 68 years old, wrote the following to American painter Charles Willson Peale:

> *"I have often thought that if heaven had given me choice of my position & calling, it should have been on a rich spot of earth, well watered, and near a good market for the productions of the garden. No occupation is so delightful to me as the culture of the earth, & no culture comparable to that of the garden. Such a variety of subjects, some one always coming to perfection, the failure of one thing repaired by the success of another, & instead of one harvest, a continued one thro' the year. Under a total want of demand except for our family table, I am still devoted to the garden. But tho' an old man, I am but a young gardener."*

Jefferson's words are a message of encouragement to all gardeners. No matter how long you garden, you will make countless mistakes, and yet your garden will forgive and respond to your cultivation by growing ever more beautiful and welcoming.

Not a year in the garden passes without failures. I neglect to mention most of my failures in this book, allowing them to be repaired by the successes.

# Garden Paths

Let me introduce you now to Marjorie's Garden, and to several other gardens around New England that have provided inspiration for this book. Some of these gardens were carved from forest, swamp, or field. One was built on granite ledge, one was once a dairy farm. All of these New England gardeners and their gardens will be featured in more detail throughout the chapters that follow. Though wildly varied in size and style, the gardens all share one trait in common: they thrive in tune with nature.

## Marjorie's Garden

I have been a gardener for over four decades and a gardener in New England for the past seventeen years. For the last twelve years I have lived in Maine on the outskirts of Ellsworth with my partner in life, Marjorie Peronto, and her now 17-year-old daughter, Lynne. There has always been a cat, and early on we added two dogs. Our house sits in the middle of a one-acre garden surrounded by spruce forest.

The bones of this garden were here before me. Four years before we met, Marjorie laid out the lines of the garden and did the initial digging, raising the garden beds from a shelf of granite rock. The soil she began with was only a few inches deep in most spots, typical of many Maine landscapes.

The section of the garden devoted to growing vegetables and small fruits took form over two years of raising beds while digging pathways, framing the down-slope edges of the beds with unearthed rocks, bringing in topsoil when needed. The same process formed an island perennial bed positioned so that it can be viewed from the living room windows. Over time this island has become a tapestry of our favorite herbaceous perennials, small ornamental shrubs, and highbush blueberries.

Small fruits are Marjorie's garden passion. In addition to the blueberries growing with the flowering perennials, she grows more highbush blueberries, raspberries, and strawberries in beds adjacent to the vegetable beds. A small bed attached to the house holds her grape vine. Chokeberry shrubs have a spot of their own, and a young serviceberry tree grows across a narrow walkway from the perennial island. This little tree produced a double handful of berries last year, mostly for the birds.

From the start, I have referred to our garden in my weekly *Bangor Daily News* column as "Marjorie's Garden." Carved from a spruce forest, the garden was hers before it was ours, its lines of her making, a reflection of her idea of a garden. I fell in love with the woman who created this lovely spot and have spent the last twelve years helping her care for it.

I want to take you on an early July morning's walk through Marjorie's Garden.

Rhodora blooms throughout New England as April progresses. *See page 133.*

> *Walking up to the house in the rain after taking the dogs for their morning walk, I detour to the vegetable-and-small-fruits garden, wanting to check the beer traps for drowned slugs and the nearby pole beans for signs of fresh slug feeding during the rainy night. The Brittany, Reilly, and her partner in crime, Dixie, a lab-German shepherd mix, head straight for the dry porch, knowing that I will shut the garden gate in their faces. Edible-pod peas are ready for harvest, and both dogs love to do their own picking.*
>
> *There are pickled slugs in the beer traps and little new damage to the beans, so perhaps the skirmish is won, though certainly not the war. I'm not ready to let up, and I add more cheap beer to my mental shopping list.*

Of all the harvests in Marjorie's Garden, I think we look forward most to picking ripe blueberries.

*I become anxious as I look down on a bed of ten tomato plants, two each of five heirloom varieties chosen for their tolerance of short, cool summers. Here it is July, and the plants are well behind last year's schedule. This spring was cold and rainy and the tomatoes look as if they were transplanted only two weeks ago instead of Memorial Day, over six weeks ago. I recall the cool wet summer of 2009 when late blight hit like a sledge hammer and no gardener that I know ripened a tomato.*

*Nearby, cucumber and squash plants are still small and just starting to flower, all male blossoms so far. Across the garden, pole beans, direct sown in late June when soil temperatures finally crept above 55 degrees, can't grow fast enough to outpace the slugs. I can't help feeling anxious as these crops, tropical or warm temperate in origin, struggle through a cool, wet Maine spring and early summer.*

*But some crops are forging ahead. Thanks to native bumblebees, fruit set on the highbush blueberries seems record-breaking, although we are a month from the first ripe berry. Raspberries, just forming, are also abundant despite foliage under attack from a fungus that loves the rain and cool, cloudy days. Looking at the blighted leaves, I am again reminded of three years ago, the summer that never was, when raspberries grew gray beards as they ripened.*

*Welcome to gardening in Maine, I think to myself, as rain drips down the back of my neck. When Maine's weather closes one door in the garden, it opens another. We've been picking snap peas and snow peas for a week now with no end in sight. The strawberries somehow escaped the slugs (they were too busy working on the beans, I bet), lettuce lasted into late June before bolting, and the potatoes, sequestered under a row cover to thwart the Colorado potato beetle, have been hilled twice and are now three feet tall.*

*Who knows what the weather will be tomorrow, next week, or in August? We've done all we can. I close the gate behind me.*

Bumblebees, like this orange-banded species, are the hardest-working creatures in the garden.

*Just outside the gate, I stop to watch rain washing the broad leaves of the grape vine, rivulets running from the leaf tips. On the nearby perennial island, bumblebees forage on catmint blossoms. The bumblebee's willingness to work in the cold and rain never ceases to impress me; you would never catch a honeybee out in this weather.*

*I remember a bumblebee I found one chilly September morning atop a sunflower head. I took it for dead, but as I examined it closely, a ray of sunlight broke through overhead pine boughs to shine directly on its hairy body. Slowly its legs began to move. Soon it was back at work, crawling across the head with its pollen-laden flowers.*

*I walk across the garden to check the fruit set on one of our favorite native trees, a pagoda dogwood planted beneath the canopies of a yellow birch and a pin cherry. Each year its mid-June flowers brighten this shady corner of the garden for two weeks. The tiny flowers, borne in tight, flat-topped clusters, are a pollinator magnet, and fruit set is usually abundant. This year is no exception.*

*Turning back into the garden, I stop under the canopy of a red oak, the largest of several in the garden and the only one old enough to produce a crop of acorns in each of the last four years. This year will be no exception, judging from the abundance of developing nuts on a branch just over my head.*

*I've stopped to look at leaves that will be assaulted by feeding insects throughout the summer. By fall almost every leaf will be tattered, torn, or riddled with holes. At this point the attack is just starting.*

*The dominant herbivore at the moment is a small, almost translucent caterpillar, probably a moth larva. There is exactly one caterpillar per affected leaf and it lies in the center of a "windowpane," a section of the leaf in which the epidermal cells on the lower surface have been rasped away, leaving a colorless network of thin leaf veins visible from either side of the leaf. These necrotic windows will soon fall out, leaving holes in the leaves.*

A pagoda dogwood's white flowers brighten the shady corner of the garden for two weeks in June.

*About a third of the oak leaves have one of these caterpillars, easily spotted by the damage they do as they feed. I think, this is what bird food looks like.*

*Now I'm on an herbivore hunt. I visit the nearest pin cherry in the garden, remembering that cherries are second only to oaks as hosts to lepidopteran larvae. Sure enough, half the leaves bear holes in a shotgun pattern and the other half are rolled downward from the tip. Carefully unrolling a leaf, I find more bird food, a caterpillar even tinier than those on the oak, moving quickly to avoid the sudden sunlight. I wonder, has some bird species figured this out, learned how to unroll or peck open the leaf?*

*Nearby mountain maples, trees that we grew from seed ten years ago and that now have started to form their own winged samaras, show signs of herbivory, holes in some leaves, chewed margins on others. And the yellow birch leaves are under attack by inch-long greenish caterpillars with red heads. More bird food.*

*I finish my morning walk with a quick tour of the rest of the garden. The sun has come out and the dogs are with me again, noses to the ground as they read their morning paper.*

*Without losing stride, I notice that the winterberry hollies are flowering, as are the diervilla on both sides of the steps leading from the drive to the house. Bumblebees forage among the orange-yellow diervilla flowers, a good thing, since the garden's summer squash and tomato flowers together could not support a single bee at the moment.*

*I round the corner of the house and two chipmunks scamper into the woodpile under the porch, Reilly in hot pursuit. If one of them stopped, turned around and chortled, Reilly would jump out of her skin. For her, a long summer day in the garden is all about the chase.*

Two human gardeners, one teenage girl who we hope will become a gardener, two dogs, one cat. All the plants, birds, and insects.

We share our garden with white-tailed deer, although a deer fence went up around the vegetables and small fruits three years ago when resident deer more than nibbled the raspberry canes. We share the garden with raccoons and black bear, both seeming to know when we have forgotten to bring in the bird feeders at dusk. Dixie has been skunked twice in her life, Reilly once, and neither can resist a porcupine, resulting in two trips to the vet for quill removal. Every so often we see a red fox, one year at the bottom of the drive with her kits. We hear them more often than see them, and we hear the coyotes running along the banks of the Union River in the middle of the night, a hundred yards from the house, and the loon flying down to the river at dawn.

The pagoda dogwood is one of several native tree and shrub species that we grow for birds and insects as well as for their ornamental beauty. In early June we watch young wood thrushes feasting on the bright berries of red elders scattered about the garden, all bird-planted shrubs that Marjorie manages with careful pruning. The berries on one of these shrubs bring the young thrushes right up to the porch steps.

Common elderberries, a different species, flower in midsummer, their broad, flat-topped clusters of tiny bright white flowers like lace doilies attached to branch tips. Their fruits will ripen in August, and then it will be a race between birds and gardeners. What we get will end up in Lynne's elderberry muffins.

We share the highbush blueberry harvest with birds as well, and with resident chipmunks. We tried bird netting once, and it almost cost a chipmunk its life. I'll tell the whole story later, but suffice it to say we took down the bird netting and threw it away.

In late August through September, as butterflies forage on goldenrod flowers, white-throated sparrows eat the ripened fruits of mapleleaf viburnums growing just off the porch. We consider ourselves lucky to be able to enjoy this native viburnum's spring flowers and unique fall foliage in our garden. Nurseries don't grow it, garden centers don't sell it. The plants were salvaged seven years ago from an experiment conducted by one of my graduate students while earning her degree in horticulture at University of Maine. She dug them, with permission, from the wild, near Boothbay, replanted them to pots, and kept them in the research nursery until her project was done. I wasn't about to see them thrown away.

Birds benefit not only from what we plant, but also from what we choose to nurture among the wild plants that grow in Marjorie's Garden. Each year, a colony of wild roses grows broader and thicker. In July it sports pink flowers, each with a single whorl of pink petals surrounding a cluster of golden stamens, and in fall its hips turn dark red before birds and mice eat the seeds.

Birds benefit when we choose to leave a dead tree in the landscape. Pileated and downy woodpeckers, representing the extremes of woodpecker size in our garden, are year-long residents that hunt for beetle grubs and other insects under the bark of dead and dying birches left standing on the edge of the garden.

From our upstairs window we have visual ownership of a tall spruce snag used as a morning perch by crows, mourning doves, pileated woodpeckers, and various hawks. Sometimes there are two pileated woodpeckers—we like to think of them as a mated pair. She clings to the trunk several feet below the top, while he perches at the top, an extension of the snag's trunk, his head and long bill slowly turning from side to side as he surveys the distant horizon. No doubt he gets fantastic views of Frenchman's Bay and Cadillac Mountain.

When a hawk flies in to perch on the snag, the garden becomes still and quiet. Birds at the feeders sit motionless on their perches. Red squirrels freeze on the pine limbs and chipmunks dive underground. Sooner or later the predator moves on, often with a nudge from a crow or blue jay.

In summer, chickadees, goldfinches, and purple finches forage high in the birches, pecking seeds from catkins. And ruby-throated hummingbirds are everywhere, at the nectar feeders and in the trees where they find the insect protein they need, and even resting for a moment on the ground in the vegetable garden. They make a game of darting in and out of the hose spray when we water the garden.

Crows, jays, and mourning doves are conspicuous year-round, including winter when they rely in part on the cracked corn we spread in small patches of ground cleared of snow. When the snow gets too deep to scratch out an acorn, a flock of wild turkeys join the corn fest.

Other year-round residents include a pair of cardinals and flocks of juncos and white-throated sparrows. The juncos are a constant presence around the feeders, while the sparrows spend most of their time scratching out a living under a thick cover of spruce and fir seedlings.

Among the myriad insect species in our garden, most remain unidentified. I know many of the butterflies by name and have learned to recognize hoverflies, beneficial predator insects otherwise known as flower flies or syrphid flies. The larvae of many hoverfly species prey on aphids and other plant-eating insects; adults feed on pollen and nectar and can be encouraged in the garden by planting their favorite flowers.

Several species of solitary bee are abundant in the garden, attracted by nest boxes attached to the deer fence posts and by plantings that provide nectar and pollen throughout the growing season. These native solitary bees, along with bumblebees, are the chief pollinators of our strawberries, blueberries, and vegetable garden crops.

The pearl crescent butterfly is but one of the many butterfly species that frequent Marjorie's Garden.

We did not have a clue to the diversity of moths in the garden until we left the porch lights on a few summers ago and found over 30 species of moths on the porch wall at sunrise, among them a rosy maple moth. More colorful than many of the others, it has reddish-pink legs and antennae, a yellow body and hind wings, and pink forewings with a triangular yellow band across the middle. The males have bushy antennae.

We know that luna moths are around, but we seldom see one unless we forget to turn off the porch light.

We discovered the queen of all moths, a luna moth, hugging the porch wall at sunrise one June morning. Relying on two plants that are abundant in our garden, birch and sumac, as larval hosts, how can such a large and magnificent creature escape more frequent discovery?

We were not looking, it's that simple. The colorful adults fly only at night, while their far less conspicuous larvae spend their time on the undersides of leaves.

We've learned to spend more time looking under leaves. And every once in a while, we leave the porch lights burning through the night.

Like many gardeners, we measure success by the diversity of life sharing the garden with us, by our ability to create a garden that functions as part of nature. Yet ecologically functional gardens come in all sizes and all styles, each with its own personality, each reflecting the gardener's idea of a garden. Several distinctive New England gardens are featured throughout this book, each one representing an effort to garden in tune with nature. At this point, I want to introduce these gardens and their gardeners.

## Growing Vegetables in the Berkshires

Ron Kujawski and his daughter, Jennifer, care for a 6,000-square-foot vegetable garden in West Stockbridge, Massachusetts (USDA Hardiness Zone 5a). Ron is an old friend and colleague from my teaching days at the University of Massachusetts, Amherst, where he worked for 25 years as an extension educator for UMass Cooperative Extension. Like her father, Jennifer is a horticulturist, writer, and editor. When I visited recently, she was teaching children the joys of gardening at Berkshire Botanical Garden.

Now retired from university, Ron writes a syndicated garden column for three regional newspapers, and he and Jennifer have written a book, the *Week-by-Week Vegetable Gardener's Handbook* (Story Publishing), from which I have liberally poached many great gardening tips. Ron has always been an advocate of ecologically friendly gardening, and Ron and Jennifer's garden provides an ideal opportunity to broaden the regional focus of this book's major theme, gardening in tune with nature.

Jennifer and Ron Kujawski digging potatoes in their Berkshire garden.

## Gardening on the Southern Shores of Rhode Island and Massachusetts

Nate and Berta Atwater live and garden on fifteen acres in Little Compton, Rhode Island. When they purchased the property, part of a dairy farm, in 1945, it was all high and dry, but today—thanks to the rising sea level—their property line lies submerged in a marshy area along the edge of Rhode Island Sound. They garden in USDA Hardiness Zone 7a.

Nate and Berta Atwater admire one of the many native American hollies in their garden. Nate remembers when he barely missed mowing down the tiny seedling that, over the next half century, became this handsome tree.

The Atwater home, built in 1963–64, is surrounded by planted beds and rock gardens, many under the shade of large trees. The garden is noted worldwide for its carefully pruned trees and shrubs, including native American hollies *(Ilex opaca)*, kousa dogwoods *(Cornus kousa)*, seven-son flower *(Heptacodium miconiodes)*, and many other species from around the globe. Two rock gardens constructed from native rock are planted with rhododendrons, azaleas, hollies, hostas, dwarf conifers, ornamental grasses, and Japanese maples, many artfully pruned by Berta to accentuate their branching habits or bark character.

Nate's gardening passions include his vegetable garden, 1,500 square feet of sandy loam surrounded by sturdy fencing, and, beyond the fence, the large pyramidal American hollies, trees that at midday cast round shadows on the lawn beneath their broad bases. Nate selected these native trees as permanent members of the garden when they were seedlings only inches high. Now their tapered leaders tower 20 feet or more above their shadows.

Beyond the house and surrounding gardens are woodlands and open vistas to the seashore. American holly, black cherry *(Prunus serotina)*, and tall multi-trunked blueberries *(Vaccinium corymbosum)* dominate the woodland walking trail.

When I visited in late July 2012, I found Nate, "closer to 80 than 70," as he later put it, mowing the lawn around his vegetable garden. Wood-framed drying screens filled with just-harvested scallions were balanced across two wheelbarrows and across the corners of the garden fence.

From early spring through summer, Nate is in his vegetable garden, locally famous for its rows of spring lettuces. On this late July visit, summer crops were at or reaching their peak. Nate was quick to tell me, in response to my question about planting fall crops, that once the summer crops are harvested, he's had enough and is ready to hang up his gardening tools until next year, but he's pleased with the notion that "a lot of food comes from this little garden."

I made another visit in late August, when I had the privilege of also visiting Nate and Berta's daughter, Dora Atwater Millikin, and her husband, Trip, and seeing their vegetable garden on Westport Point, Massachusetts, just across the state line from Rhode Island.

Trip and Dora enjoy munching the tiny Emerite pole beans as they work in their garden.

Trip and Dora live and grow vegetables on the old Macomber Turnip Farm, noted for glacial soil that once grew a regionally favorite turnip, a cross between a yellow turnip and a white radish. "With good soil, you really don't have problems," Trip remarked as we approached his fenced garden of about 3,000 square feet. His garden echoed this statement with asparagus fronds 6 feet tall, hundreds of plum tomatoes ripening on the vine, okra fruiting, hops growing along the fence rail, wide clumps of lemon grass, and head-high pole beans dripping with small pods.

## Gardening for Wildlife on Cape Cod

In Orleans, Massachusetts (Zone 7a), on Cape Cod, is the garden of landscapte architect Patricia Crow. With the help of her husband, architect James Hadley, Patricia has used her training in landscape design (a BS at Rhode Island School of Design with a minor in painting) and landscape architecture (a MS at Harvard Graduate School of Design) along with her passion for

Patricia Crow stands among sunflowers and goldenrods, a favorite spot in her summer garden.

ecologically sensitive design to create a garden on two and a half acres of land that, seven years ago, was filled with invasive species.

In Patricia's own words, "we started the project by having invasive species removed, which left little but an existing pear, oak, and apple tree and some arrowwood viburnum, cedar, and cherry. We began a habitat restoration immediately, attempting to use local genotypes where possible and as great a variety as would suit the site. We are almost complete in the planting, which is mainly native species with a few non-native, non-invasive plants for the human habitat part. Little by little, the soil has been built up and most native plants are naturalizing at a very quick rate. We have otter, foxes, deer, turtles, frogs, and countless butterflies, bees, wasps, birds, and dragonflies, as well as many small mammals. In a sense we feel that, in our house, we are the zoo animals, and the animals are the citizens."

This is a garden I just had to include in this book!

## A Garden along the Penobscot River in Maine

Theresa Guethler's garden in Bucksport, Maine (Zone 5b) begins at the edge of a busy highway paralleling the Penobscot River. Containers and beds filled with flowering plants surround the house, and the front gardens are anchored by one of five Northern catalpa trees *(Catalpa speciosa)* scattered about. Paths the width of a tractor cut through fields of unmown grass into the woods, ending where Theresa keeps her beehives. Walking along these paths, a visitor will find a raised-bed vegetable garden; small collections of various trees, including osage orange *(Maclura pomifera,* native to Massachusetts, Connecticut, and Rhode Island but not Maine) and persimmon *(Diospyros virginiana,* native to southern Connecticut and points south); and a long border of flowering perennials backed by a rock wall reminiscent of traditional English borders.

I first met Theresa in her role as a Master Gardener Volunteer in Hancock County. Like most MGVs, she is an industrious and innovative gardener, always experimenting with new ways of growing plants. She introduced Marjorie and me to the concept of growing sweet potatoes in Maine. When not in the garden, she constructs native bee nest boxes, one of which is featured in Chapter 5, The Garden in March.

A corner of Theresa Guethler's garden combines goldenrod (back), swamp milkweed (middle) and purple coneflower, each in their season attracting pollinators to the garden. Attached to the fencepost is one of Theresa's hand-painted birdhouses.

A focal point of Tom and Jan McIntyre's garden is a pond that they dug and planted.

## A Garden Devoted to Wildlife Diversity

Tom and Jan McIntyre live in a log cabin on Mount Desert Island, Maine (Zone 5b). They built their home in a moss-covered spruce-balsam fir forest, surrounding it with flowering perennials, shrubs, and trees, many native to the region. They also created the focal point of the garden, a small pond fed by an adjacent fen.

Their garden is a registered National Wildlife Federation backyard wildlife habitat, providing food, water, and cover for insects, amphibians, birds, and mammals. Tom, a retired biology teacher who now spends some of his time peering through a microscope at drops of pond water, is quick to add pond microorganisms to the list of garden wildlife, pointing out that they form the foundation of garden biodiversity.

Jan's passion for gardening was kindled when, as a child, she helped her parents cultivate their perennial garden. She is a professional gardener and, as a Master Gardener Volunteer, serves as the Garden Coordinator for the historic Garland Farm in Bar Harbor, Maine. Her lifelong interest in herbaceous perennials is evident in the borders and beds that surround the pond and their home.

Both Jan and Tom enjoy telling stories about the wildlife that visit their garden. Since they are both gifted writers and photographers, I asked Tom to write about the life in his pond and Jan to contribute a photo essay of their garden to this book. You will find both of these essays in Chapter 13, Gardens in Tune with Nature.

Astilbes dominate the summer landscape in Dr. Charles Richards' coastal garden.

## A Garden Built on Ledge

In 1965, Dr. Charles Richards, the University of Maine's preeminent field botanist and plant taxonomist, looking ahead to a retirement spent gardening, purchased a secluded cottage and three acres of granite outcropping on Great Wass Island (Zone 5b), overlooking the Gulf of Maine. He immediately set to work, planting native trees among the sheep laurel and other coastal scrub wherever there was enough soil for roots to take hold.

Over time, he exposed the granite, saving the peat for soil amendment, and filled in the depressions among the rock with loam and compost to create the foundation of a garden. He hauled stones by boat from outlying islands to form garden paths.

In July 2012, Marjorie and I joined several other gardeners on a visit to Dr. Richards' garden. Richards, 92 years old, led us into the middle of an acre or more of garden beds filled with blooming astilbes, daylilies, rhododendrons, and other plants, some native, some exotic. The gardener's passion for plants was evident. "I enjoy just seeing what will grow here," he told us. "My goal is to integrate native vegetation with exotic species."

## A Garden Devoted to Feeding The Hungry

In 2010, Eva Eicher and Dorcas Corrow, owners of Sweet Haven Farm on Mt. Desert Island, Maine, began growing food for the hungry on a 1,800-square-foot garden plot. By the end of the growing season, they had delivered 500 pounds of food to several low-income housing facilities.

In 2011 they delivered 1,000 pounds of organically grown produce, including 100 pounds of potatoes, 30 pounds of frozen tomato sauce, 150 pounds of winter squash, and fall crops of broccoli, green beans, chard, and carrots. Thanks to a succession planting tactic, the string beans were available each week starting the first week of August until the last week of September.

In 2012, the project expanded to 4,000 square feet of garden plots and raised beds with the goal of providing 1,000 pounds of organically grown vegetables to seniors and others on limited incomes.

Eva and Dorcas, along with a well-organized army of volunteers, are providing fresh, healthy vegetables to members of their community in need. It is my hope that their success story will inspire other gardeners to share their harvest in similar fashion.

These raised beds of lettuce and green beans are part of Sweet Haven Farm's production of organic vegetables for community members in need.

## *The Path Through This Book*

This book's second chapter develops the idea of the garden as a functional ecosystem, as a local "hot spot" of biodiversity in an age of global decline in species diversity, both plant and animal. I suggest that gardens throughout New England can be beautiful, healthful, and functional without the use of toxic chemicals, without reliance on synthetic (factory-produced) fertilizers, and without the presence of non-native invasive plant species. We offer native alternatives to many invasive species and explain how the gardener can create insectaries, plantings of flowering annuals and herbaceous perennials that provide a season-long source of pollen and nectar for beneficial insects.

Chapter 3 emphasizes the importance of soil testing as an essential tool for managing nutrient levels in the garden and discusses the use of organic material in the form of compost and cover crops to build healthy soil. In Chapter 6, The Garden in April, I discuss how to start and manage a compost pile while Marjorie describes composting with worms (vermiculture), explaining how to set up a home worm bin.

To meet the current surge of interest in home vegetable gardening, Marjorie discusses vegetable garden design and planning in Chapter 4, providing advice on selecting varieties and offering a few tips for success. We hope it makes for good fireside reading as you plan for the coming year.

Chapters 5 through 12 cover gardening month-by-month, March through October. Marjorie takes the pen to cover everything dealing with small fruits and pruning. You will find in these chapters a strong bias toward growing native plant species and their cultivated varieties, a bias that is justified, we believe, by the lack of connection of non-native species with the garden ecosystem. We want to avoid being labeled purists in this regard, however. We do grow a few non-native small trees, shrubs, and flowering perennials in the garden, species systematically screened for invasive potential.

Chapter 13 presents photo essays of the gardens introduced earlier in this chapter.

Finally, Chapter 14 examines the garden and gardener in winter. There is more to both than you might imagine.

Take from this book what will serve you in your garden. Marjorie and I hope you find it a good read the first time through and a book that you take down from the shelf when you are planning for the next year's garden.

# Chapter 2

# Gardening in Tune with Nature

*"The gardener recognizes that he is dependent for his health and survival on many other forms of life, so he is careful to take their interests into account in whatever he does. He is in fact a wilderness advocate of a certain kind. It is when he respects and nurtures the wilderness of his soil and his plants that his garden seems to flourish most."*

—Michael Pollan, "The Idea of a Garden" *(Second Nature: A Gardener's Education, 1991)*

***The title of this chapter originated*** as the umbrella for my weekly newspaper columns when, in 2011, the *Bangor Daily News,* reading the handwriting on the wall, created an Internet blog site for its columnists. For several years I had been developing a personal philosophy of gardening that was aptly described as "Gardening in Tune with Nature." The title fit then and still defines my idea of a gardener's work and the relationship between gardener and garden.

Throughout this chapter, indeed throughout the book, I will invite you to think of the garden as an ecosystem. I believe that one very good measure of a gardener's success is the species diversity, or richness, of his or her garden—i.e., the number of species of plants, animals, and microorganisms that can be found living in the soil, rooted in the soil, and feeding on garden plants. The gardener is one species, but there are thousands of others. There is a direct relationship between a garden's species richness and the production of healthy, chemical-free food and stress-resistant ornamentals.

There are three key components of building a healthy garden ecosystem, a garden with high species richness. First, an ecologically functional garden comes from building and maintaining healthy soil without reliance on synthetic (factory-produced) fertilizers. The conversion of atmospheric nitrogen to forms of organic nitrogen that plants can utilize is the work of soil bacteria, work that is derailed when the gardener relies on synthetic fertilizers. Chapter 3, Nurturing Healthy Garden Soil, provides a complete discussion of managing soil fertility.

*Facing page:* A lone bumblebee forages a peony blossom.

Herbivores such as this monarch butterfly caterpillar are an integral part of garden biodiversity.

While adult hoverflies depend on a steady supply of pollen and nectar, their larvae are important predators in the garden, helping to control aphids and other herbivores. A garden with high species diversity will host several hoverfly species.

Second, the ecologically attuned gardener uses no toxic chemicals, no "-cides" of any kind: no insecticides, no herbicides, no fungicides. Even biorational pesticides such as Bt (*Bacillus thuringiensis*) and horticultural oils such as neem oil are used with extreme caution out of concern for loss of non-target organisms. Throughout the monthly chapters of this book, you will find ways to manage herbivore populations without using toxic chemicals.

Third, ecologically functional gardens are composed largely of regionally native plant species. While planting a non-native invasive species in your garden may increase plant species diversity by one, it will likely do little to sustain total garden diversity. Having no evolutionary link with non-native plants, native insects are unlikely to forage non-native plants for pollen or nectar. Thus a garden filled with non-native plants, invasive or not, will likely have lower species diversity that one planted with mostly native species.

## *What Does Garden Biodiversity Look Like?*

The term "biodiversity" is formally defined as the totality of genes, species, and ecosystems in a place. By this definition, species diversity is only one component of biodiversity, but it's the one that concerns us most as gardeners. The species diversity of a garden ecosystem, under the right conditions, is much greater than you might think.

Let's start with life in the garden's soil, a community of bacteria, fungi, nematodes, earthworms, and other often unseen creatures—the "little things that run the world," as eminent ecologist E.O. Wilson calls them. In fact, some of these soil organisms, such as bacteria and nematodes, cannot be seen without the aid of a microscope.

But let's not confuse size with importance. The most abundant microorganisms on Earth, cyanobacteria in the genus *Prochlorcoccus*, too small to be seen with conventional microscopes, were not discovered until 1988. As it turns out, these organisms are responsible for much of the photosynthesis occurring in our world's oceans.

So it is with soil organisms; the smallest are the most important. Soil scientists estimate that one gram of garden soil will contain about 6,000 species of bacteria, some of which are vital to our success as gardeners. One group of soil-borne bacteria, the nitrifying bacteria,

Mosses and lichens, often found growing together in the garden, are components of species diversity.

convert ammonium nitrogen, which is produced by bacterial decomposition of organic matter, into a form of nitrogen that garden plants can readily absorb. Other bacteria, the nitrogen fixers associated with the roots of legumes (peas and beans), are capable of converting atmospheric nitrogen into the molecules that compose soil organic matter.

Assume that your garden grows 99 species of plants—an ambitious garden! You, the gardener, bring species biodiversity to 100. But in healthy soil there are also thousands of bacteria species as well as numerous species of fungi, nematodes, and other forms of "hidden biodiversity." Above ground there are mosses growing in shady nooks and lichens growing on rocks, countless species of insects—including pollinators, herbivores, and beneficial predators—flying and crawling about, numerous species of birds, a few rodent species, and a handful of mammals other than the gardener, including, perhaps, a young black bear like the one that mooches sunflower seeds off our back porch. In other words, you and the garden plants make up less than 1% of your garden's species biodiversity.

I often stop while working in the garden, lean on my rake, and observe and listen to all the forms of life around me. My mind becomes boggled by the many different species present, most of them part of the warp and weft of the garden ecosystem, most performing a function vital to the garden's health.

This sense of wonder is not limited to the gardener whose garden is surrounded by natural area. Gardeners in all environments, including the most urban, can count a healthy garden's species diversity index in the thousands.

Red squirrels spend summer days gathering acorns from the garden's oak trees and sunflower seeds from the porch bird feeders. They have a huge impact on the garden, particularly when the blueberries are ripe.

## Synthetic Fertilizers Reduce Soil Biodiversity

Factory-produced fertilizers are chemical fertilizers with much of the nitrogen in chemical forms—primarily nitrate—that are immediately available to the plant. This chemical nitrogen may push plant growth, but it does little to build healthy populations of soil organisms. In addition, any nitrate nitrogen not immediately taken up by plant roots is quickly leached out of the root zone by rain or irrigation water.

Because chemical fertilizers are composed of high concentrations of mineral salts, they are capable, when used to excess, of killing many of the soil organisms that are responsible for decomposition and soil formation. If only chemicals are added, the soil gradually loses its organic matter and thus its microbiotic activity. The end result of reliance on chemical fertilizers is certain: The fertilizers must be used in ever-greater quantity until the "soil" becomes little more than an anchoring substrate in a hydroponic growing system.

Natural fertilizers, including compost, composted farm animal manures, and cover crops (green manure crops), nourish complex populations of soil organisms while improving soil structure and water-holding capacity. The organic nitrogen in these natural fertilizers is slowly broken down by soil life, resulting in a sustainable level of soil nitrate nitrogen for plant use.

## Consult the Genius of Your Place: Creating Gardens That Look and Function Like Nature

In the acronym HIPPO, E.O. Wilson identifies the five major causes of global biodiversity decline in order of relative impact. All are the result of human activity. The "H" stands for habitat destruction, including climate change; the "I" for invasive species; the first "P" for pollution of all kinds; the second "P" for human population growth; and the "O" for over-harvesting of resources, primarily excessive hunting and fishing.

Peas in the June garden.

Let's focus for a moment on the "I," invasive species.

Non-native invasive species, second only to habitat destruction as a leading cause of global biodiversity decline, are plant and animal species that outcompete native species for essential resources, including water, food (nutrients), and space. *Eighty percent of all woody invasive species in the United States were introduced as ornamentals for our gardens*, a statistic that should command the attention of gardeners and make us all feel complicit.

I know I do. As a young man just beginning what would turn out to be a lifelong passion for plants, both in gardens and in the wild, I wanted to grow everything, particularly exotic plants from other countries. I began my career in horticulture (in 1975, when a M.S. in botany plus a quarter would buy you a cup of coffee) working for a mail-order nursery that imported garden-worthy plants from all over the world. In my own garden or the gardens I designed for others I grew Japanese barberry in all its forms, burning bush, and other invasive species that we now see growing in the wild, displacing native plant species.

In other words, I was in the leading edge of invasive species introduction.

Fast forward two decades and you find me guiding graduate student research on the invasion of burning bush in a land trust area near Boothbay, Maine. I cringe when I think back on the days when I promoted the use of burning bush and other problem plant species.

Take Norway maple *(Acer platanoides)*, for example. Native to Europe and Western Asia, it was first introduced in this country (Western Pennsylvania) as an exotic ornamental in the 1700s. Nurseries found it easy to propagate and grow and relatively pest free. Today it is used as an ornamental tree in every region of the United States, perhaps in every city, due to its popularity as an urban street tree. Unfortunately, it can also be found displacing native trees and shrubs in natural areas throughout America.

How was it possible for Norway maple and other non-native plants introduced for our gardens, parks, and city streets to become invasives? Part of the explanation includes a suite of characteristics common to most invasive plants, including production of a large quantity of bird- or wind-dispersed seed. If you have a Norway maple in your yard, you have no doubt noticed all those maple seedlings growing in your flower beds. But another factor contributing to their invasive potential is that when we imported them to this country, we left their natural herbivores and pathogens behind. And the herbivores native to this country, with no evolutionary link to invasive plant species, tend to shun the imports—hence the "pest free" nature of many invasive plants. Left unchecked by natural controls, the invasives grow rampant.

Invasive plant species are helping to alter the American landscape, reducing biodiversity in natural areas while leading to a homogenization of landscapes throughout the country. Landscapes in Seattle look the same as landscapes in Atlanta or Boston or Bangor, Maine.

As gardeners, we have an opportunity to reverse these trends by creating landscapes that speak to a sense of place, a *terroir*, which is embodied in the use of mostly native plant species. Landscapes in Maine should look like Maine, not Washington or Georgia, and so it should be throughout the greater New England area.

"Consult the genius of the place," Alexander Pope advised landscape designers. In today's world, this advice can result in landscapes that not only look like nature but act like nature, preserving what remains of local biodiversity.

Creating gardens with native plant species does not mean sacrificing ornamental interest or beauty. In later chapters I discuss trees, shrubs, and flowering perennials that are native to Maine and provide year-round ornamental character. And in an appendix at the back of this book, I provide a list of the major invasive trees and shrubs to avoid using in your garden.

## Dropping "Pest" from the Gardener's Vocabulary

Humans have been working hard and creatively to eliminate insects and other arthropods, such as spiders, from planet Earth. Insecticides are the major weapon in this effort, inasmuch as few of them kill only the targeted insect. And the "H" in HIPPO, habitat destruction, is eliminating many other insect species. According to E.O. Wilson, human activity, if unabated, will result in the extinction or critical endangerment of one-half of existing insect species by the end of this century. One-quarter of existing insect species will be lost within the next five decades. Some of these lost species will be insects of benefit to our gardens and to our efforts to grow food.

You are never more than three feet away from a spider, especially in a garden in tune with nature.

If you have a wet area in your garden, capitalize on it. Including a small pool in the garden provides habitat for toads, frogs, and salamanders as well as the opportunity to grow plants that love wet feet.

Somewhere along the way, Marjorie said to me, "I've taken the word *pest* out of my vocabulary." This idea immediately took root in my own life, and I have not used the word since. You will not find it again in this book. Every garden creature is part of the garden ecosystem, part of a vital food web that includes soil organisms, plants, insects, birds, and other creatures, including the gardener.

This lofty idea has very practical application. To maintain high population levels of beneficial insect predators such as lady beetles, hoverflies, and parasitic wasps, there must be an ever-present population of herbivores such as aphids for the predators to eat.

In our garden, we have noticed that sudden explosions of herbivores are quickly dealt with by the predator insects. One day there are a hundred aphids, standing room only, sucking sap from the soft new growth of every red elder branch. A few lady beetle larvae take note and a week later the aphids are gone, the plants as healthy as ever.

This is why finding a few aphids on a garden plant will bring a smile to my face. I know the predacious insects will soon find them.

Goldenrod, shown here flowering with fall asters, provides a late-summer source of nectar and pollen for pollinators.

Predator insects in their adult stages are often pollen and nectar feeders, leaving predation to the larvae. Providing sources of pollen and nectar in or around the garden as early in the growing season as possible will ensure that the larval stages of lady beetles, hoverflies, and other predators will be plentiful when herbivore outbreaks occur.

Plantings created to attract beneficial insects, including both predators and pollinators, are called insectaries. No doubt they also attract herbivores—that is the point. Insectaries are balanced mini-ecosystems designed to ensure the presence of pollinators and beneficials when you need them in the garden proper.

Insectaries can also be created simply by leaving a section of your landscape wild. About a hundred feet from the vegetable garden, we leave a patch of grass and wildflowers for the insects. We never mow this patch and, as a result, there is a constant supply of nectar and pollen for the bees, from violets and dandelions in spring to goldenrod and queen anne's lace in summer and asters in autumn. In addition to the pollinators, hoverflies and other beneficial insects thrive in this spot, completing their life cycles undisturbed while frequently visiting the vegetable garden.

Two plant families, the Asteraceae (composites) and Apiaceae (umbellifers), dominate any list of insectary plants. Composites include cosmos, sunflower, dandelion, yarrow, artemisia, feverfew, tansy, marigold, zinnia, thistle, aster, goldenrod, and calendula; also artichoke and lettuce, if you let a few plants flower. These plants mature their flowers in heads over a long period of time, thus providing a long-term source of nectar.

Umbellifers include parsley, carrots, parsnips, lovage, angelica, and Queen Anne's lace. They produce large amounts of nectar over a short period of time.

In summary, the gardener in tune with nature views the garden as an ecosystem and manages that ecosystem to ensure the greatest possible biological diversity. Healthy vegetables are grown in healthy, organically enriched soil teeming with bacteria, fungi, nematodes, and other life forms. Ornamental plants are valued not only for their beauty but also as host plants for other life forms, including birds, small mammals, and pollinating insects.

The gardener's job becomes one of caretaker, of nurturing the garden's biodiversity. One of the gardener's rewards is the garden's resilience in the face of stress, the ability to withstand periods of drought or invasions of herbivores. Another is the increased depth of understanding and appreciation of the garden food web, the delight in finding aphids crowding a plant stem, knowing lady beetles are close at hand. And those caterpillars feeding on leaves of the oak tree? They are what bird food looks like.

Dandelion flowers provide early-spring pollen to native solitary bees (left) and bumblebees. Later in the spring, native flowering plants, such as diervilla (above), keep bumblebees and other native pollinators supplied with nectar and pollen.

# Chapter 3

# Nurturing Healthy Garden Soil

*"The soil is the great connector of lives, the source and destination of all. It is the healer and restorer and resurrector, by which disease passes into health, age into youth, death into life. Without proper care for it we can have no community, because without proper care for it we can have no life."*

—Wendell Berry, *The Unsettling of America,* 1977

***Successful gardeners nurture healthy soil.*** We recognize the soil as an ecosystem teeming with life. Plant roots explore a matrix of minerals and organic matter, the domain of bacteria, fungi, nematodes, earthworms, arthropods, and other life forms. The more I read and think about soil biodiversity, the less inclined I am to take a spade to a garden bed, to disturb the complex food web we call healthy soil.

There are about one billion bacteria in a single teaspoon of productive soil, the equivalent of a ton of bacteria per acre. They live in the water-filled pore spaces of the soil, on the moist surfaces of soil particles and decaying organic debris, and, most importantly from the plant's point of view, in the rhizosphere, a 2-millimeter-thick zone immediately surrounding each root. Exudates pumped out by the roots combine with teeming life to make the rhizosphere layer a viscous solution of sugars and other chemicals.

*Facing page:* Corn and winter squash make a compatible intensive planting. The spiny leaves of the squash help deter raccoons from robbing the ripe ears of corn. Add pole beans to climb the corn stalks and you have a three-sisters garden (see pages 119–120).

Many soil bacteria are decomposers, converting the energy held within the carbon-to-carbon bonds of organic matter into forms of energy useful to all organisms in the soil food web. Nitrogen and other elements essential to plants are retained by decomposers in their cells, preventing their loss from the root zone. When bacteria die, their stored nutrients can be absorbed by plant roots.

Nitrogen-fixing bacteria form mutualistic relationships with the roots of legumes such as peas and beans and trees such as alder. The plant supplies carbon-based energy sources to the bacteria, and the bacteria convert nitrogen from the air into a form the plant can use. When the host plant's leaves and roots decompose, soil nitrogen levels increase. This is why I chop up the pea vines when they have stopped producing, dig them into the soil, and wait a couple of weeks before planting a fall crop of spinach.

Other soil bacteria species, the nitrifying bacteria, convert ammonium produced by the decomposition of organic matter to nitrate, a preferred form of nitrogen for most garden crops. And the actinomycetes, a large group of bacteria that are responsible for the "earthy" smell of healthy soil, decompose a wide variety of organic materials including chitin and cellulose, the tough stuff of plant cell walls.

The billion bacteria in a teaspoon of healthy garden soil represent 6,000 known species of bacteria, a healthy population both in numbers and diversity. Scientists speculate that this number could be as high as 30,000 if all species yet to be discovered were included. This diversity keeps pathogens in check, perhaps outcompeted until they disappear. Beneficial bacteria can coat root surfaces so thoroughly that pathogens have no room to take hold.

Joining the bacteria as important decomposers of dead organic matter are the saprophytic fungi. That teaspoon of healthy garden soil will contain several yards of fungal hyphae, the threadlike strands of the fungal body that bind soil particles together to create stable soil aggregates. These soil aggregates help increase soil water-holding capacity and water infiltration. The fungal hyphae form nets or webs around roots, creating physical barriers to invasion by pathogens. And like bacteria, fungi are important in retaining nutrients in the soil.

Other fungi, called mycorrhizal fungi, colonize plant roots in mutualistic relationships. These fungi provide physical protection, water, and nutrients to plant roots in return for carbon-containing exudates secreted by the roots into the rhizosphere. You scratch my back, I'll scratch yours.

In addition to bacteria and fungi, a teaspoon of healthy garden soil contains several thousand nutrient-mobilizing protozoa and a few dozen beneficial nematodes (microscopic worms). Each square foot of healthy garden soil also contains up to 100 beneficial arthropods (insects, spiders, mites, and others) and between 5 and 30 earthworms. Earthworms are particularly important to maintaining healthy soil structure. Their tunnels provide aeration and drainage, and their excretions (worm castings) bind soil crumbs together.

A gardener can measure success by the number of earthworms in the soil.

It's an eat-and-be-eaten world in the soil. And since most organisms eat more than one kind of prey, food chains are not straight lines but rather complex webs of food chains linked and cross-linked to each other.

Plants control the rhizosphere food web, including the numbers and kinds of bacteria and fungi, by the kinds and volumes of exudate they secrete from their roots. A dynamic mix of bacteria and fungi compete for the carbohydrates and proteins in this exudate. These well-fed beneficial organisms in turn attract bigger microbes, including nematodes and protozoa, who eat the bacteria and fungi. Anything they don't need is excreted as waste, which plant roots absorb as nutrients.

From the gardener's point of view, the primary role of the soil food web is to pass nutrients through the web until they become temporarily immobilized in the soil in the bodies of bacteria and fungi and then converted to a form that plants can utilize. The most important of these nutrients is nitrogen, and the biomass of bacteria and fungi in the soil determines, for the most part, the amount of nitrogen readily available for plant use.

Many gardeners live their entire lives without appreciating the complex ecosystem beneath their feet or acknowledging its importance to their success. And that is why garden center shelves are still stacked with insecticides, herbicides, fungicides, and synthetic fertilizers.

This is a gardener's truth: Putting toxic chemicals into the soil destroys the soil ecosystem. Pesticides, fungicides, and herbicides kill off important members of the soil food web, destroying ecosystem function. And once the soil is dead, the gardener becomes totally dependent on the toxic chemicals, forever adding more and more synthetic fertilizer, more and more chemicals to deal with plant pathogens and herbivores. Some of these chemicals end up in the gardener.

The healthy alternative is to nurture the soil ecosystem, and a good place to start is with this precautionary principle: If you don't know what something will do to your soil, don't use it.

# A Nutrient Management Primer

Nitrogen (N), phosphorus (P), potassium (K), calcium (Ca), magnesium (Mg), and sulfur (S) are all considered major plant nutrients (macronutrients), not because they are more important than other essential elements but because they are used by plants in relatively larger amounts. Essential minor elements (micronutrients) include boron (B) and zinc (Zn), the two most likely to be needed as soil supplements, as well as molybdenum (Mo), copper (Cu), chlorine (Cl), iron (Fe), and manganese (Mn). All essential elements, major and minor, are needed by plants for healthy growth.

Summer squash in western Connecticut, late July. (Photo courtesy Charles Heaven)

The organic gardener's goal is to sustain nutrient levels in the soil, providing plants with adequate quantities of these essential elements. Sustaining soil fertility requires conserving nutrients in the soil in slow-release forms through maintenance of soil organic matter levels and promotion of soil microbial activity.

## Nitrogen

The gardener sustains soil nitrogen levels by choosing composted stable manure and fish emulsion as the primary sources of nitrogen rather than water-soluble nitrogen broadcast from a bag. The former release nitrogen slowly through microbial activity; the later provides some immediate nitrogen for plant use, but much of the nitrogen is leached out of the root zone by rain and irrigation.

Nitrogen, the "N" in the three major element group, N-P-K, that is printed on commercial fertilizer bags, is one element that the gardener must supply every year. Nitrate nitrogen, the form of nitrogen that plant roots absorb, is quickly leached below the root zone of most plants after it is applied. Composted manure, a rich source of nitrogen in organic slow-release form, when added to garden soil in late autumn, will be available for conversion to usable nitrogen by soil bacteria as soon as soil temperatures rise in spring.

## Phosphorus

After nitrogen, phosphorus is the major element most likely to be deficient in the soil. Sources of phosphorus for organic gardeners include composted stable manures, vermicompost (worm castings), and rock phosphate. Rock phosphate requires acidic soils for phosphorus release and should not be used in soils with a pH above 7.

## Potassium

Hardwood ashes were among the earliest sources of potassium for building soil fertility. Depending on the type of wood burned, the ashes contain between three and seven percent potassium. Because over-application of wood ashes can decrease soil acidity (raise the pH, making the soil more alkaline), annual applications should never exceed 20 pounds per 1,000 square feet. Never use wood ashes on blueberries and other acid-loving plants.

Greensand, powdered potassium silicate, contains up to 5% potassium, but only a small portion of the potassium in greensand is released each year. The rate of release depends on soil conditions; increases in temperature, moisture, acidity, and organic matter all increase the release rate. If a soil test (see below) shows an immediate need for potassium, it may be recommended that you apply wood ashes to correct the immediate deficiency and greensand as a longer-term potassium source. Greensand is also valued for its micronutrient content.

In his book *Four Season Harvest*, Eliot Coleman suggests applying both rock phosphate and greensand directly on the soil in the first year of a new garden plot, adding each at the rate of 10 pounds per 100 square feet. In subsequent years, he suggests lightly sprinkling both products on the green layer of the compost pile (a yearly total of one pound of each mineral per 100 square feet of garden space).

## Calcium, Magnesium, and Sulfur

Each of the three remaining major nutrients, calcium (Ca), magnesium (Mg), and sulfur (S), can be supplied in a number of ways, depending on your soil's specific needs as defined in a soil test. For example, if soil test results indicate a need to reduce the acidity (raise the pH) of your soil and also show a need for both calcium and magnesium, you should use dolomitic lime, which supplies both of these nutrient elements while raising the soil pH. On the other hand, if no magnesium is needed but calcium is deficient, you can use calcitic lime (calcium carbonate).

If there is no need to change the pH, magnesium needs can be met with Sul-Po-Mag, a mined rock often used as a potassium source in commercial fertilizers. Use Sul-Po-Mag only if you need both potassium and magnesium. To supply magnesium without adding potassium, use epsom salts (magnesium sulfate).

What if there is no need to change the pH, but calcium is deficient? Your best choice is gypsum (calcium sulfate) which supplies both calcium and sulfur without altering soil acidity. Gypsum can also improve the structure of clayey soils, binding the clay particles together to create more space for air and drainage.

The soil test report makes all of this simple by telling you exactly what you need to add to your soil to overcome nutrient deficiencies and, if needed, adjust the soil pH. It will also tell you how much of each recommended substance to use.

## Essential Minor Elements

The essential minor elements (micronutrients), including boron (B), zinc (Zn), molybdenum (Mo), copper (Cu), chlorine (Cl), iron (Fe), and manganese (Mn), tend to be present in adequate quantities and are often added incidentally along with sources of the major elements. For example, granite dust, used as a source of potassium, contains a wide range of minor elements. Greensand, in addition to adding phosphorus, also supplies iron and other micronutrients. And seaweed, while supplying organic matter, nitrogen, and phosphorus, also contributes a variety of micronutrients, especially boron, copper, iron, manganese, and molybdenum.

Boron, zinc, and other minor elements are seldom limiting in most New England soils, particularly if high organic matter levels are maintained. Occasionally, however, deficiencies do occur. Boron deficiency can cause water-soaked areas to form in the stems of broccoli and cauliflower and ultimately lead to browning of the flower heads. The recommended solution for this malady is to add one-half pound of Twenty Mule Team Borax per 1,000 square feet of soil. But be careful—too much and you end up with boron toxicity!

### Nutrient Management Produces High Garden Yields

Monitoring your garden's nutrient levels with soil tests and then following the recommendations on the test report are the foundation of garden success. Consider, for example, the garden of Ladonna Bruce and Stuart Hall in Stockton Springs, Maine. I visited their small garden in August 2011 and was amazed by the number of plants squeezed into each small bed. Tomato plants grew shoulder to shoulder, their lower branches removed to minimize leaf blight. Corn plants erupted from a ground-covering blanket of winter squash vines. Six-inch-long cucumbers dangled from leafy vines covering a wire trellis. In every small bed, the close spacing of plants acted as a living mulch, covering the soil, keeping it cool and moist.

Ladonna and Stuart garden intensively and break all the rules of spacing. By season's end in 2011, they had harvested over 900 pounds of produce from their small garden. When I asked Ladonna to explain this phenomenal success, she gave all the credit to soil nutrient management. Stopping at the cucumber trellis to crush cucumber beetles, she explained that they had followed recommendations from a recent soil test, adding lime to decrease the soil's acidity, and she had amended her soil with rock phosphate and greensand, mineral sources for the essential nutrients phosphorus and potassium, respectively. She is convinced that the increase in corn yields was due to addition of the rock phosphate.

In Ladonna and Stuart's garden, intensive planting of the beds produces high yields. They test the soil annually and follow recommendations on the test report

Because well-managed soils seldom lack minor elements in adequate amounts, the soils lab does not test for minor element levels. Often an analysis of the affected plant tissue is suggested as the best approach to isolating a minor element deficiency. Many university soils labs will perform this tissue analysis.

Sustaining soil fertility hinges on frequent soil testing. One approach is to have one or two specific beds (or rows) tested every year so that you can develop a profile of how your soil management strategy is working. Also, independently test new beds and any beds where you have intentionally changed soil management. Finally, test areas where plants have grown poorly.

## Soil Testing

One late summer weekend a few years back we created a new raised bed in Marjorie's garden, a bed formed with purchased loam on ledge covered with only a few inches of native soil. All of the existing beds had been started this same way, their soil depths increased over the years with generous top dressings of compost. In the oldest beds you can sink a spade up to its hilt before hitting rock.

Good soil is the garden's foundation. (Photo courtesy Charlies Heaven)

Weeds grew in the new soil, some from seeds that had been in the soil when we purchased it, others creeping in from the edges or sprouting from windblown seeds, and these were removed with the first turning of the soil the following spring. Several wheelbarrow loads of composted goat manure were then forked into the soil.

I wasted no time in planting the entire bed with cucumbers and sunflowers. At the end of the day, Marjorie found me leaning on the garden rake, content with my accomplishment, and announced that the results of a soil test on the loam should arrive any day. There was more than a hint of exasperation in her voice.

When the soil test report arrived two days later, we learned that levels of phosphorus and calcium were above optimum, no cause for alarm, but levels of potassium, magnesium, and sulfur were below optimum. And the pH of the loam was 7.1, well above the optimum, slightly acid pH of 6.5.

A short time later, the sunflower seedlings in the new bed looked good but the cucumbers were failing. In the harsh light of the soil test results, I started over, throwing out the declining cucumbers and transplanting the sunflowers to a holding area while I reworked the soil chemistry.

Instructions for correcting the nutrient deficiencies and high pH came with the soil test report and were geared to our desire for an organic garden. To correct the deficiencies in potassium, magnesium, and sulfur, we were told to apply Sul-Po-Mag, the commercial name of a naturally occurring mineral that contains significant quantities of sulfur, potash, and magnesium. Water-soluble, it can be broadcast at the recommended rate and dug into the soil.

To lower the pH, we were advised to apply elemental sulfur, digging it in well. Again, the report told us exactly how much to apply.

Taking into consideration a relatively high organic matter content, the report also advised that we bolster the new bed's nitrogen levels by working in either blood meal or soybean meal, both relatively fast-acting forms of organic nitrogen.

After following all of the report's suggestions, I waited two weeks for the soil chemistry to adjust before replanting the cucumbers. The plants responded with vigorous growth and plenty of late summer cucumbers. Apparently there are some lessons that I have to keep relearning. Have the soil tested first, then plant. I blame my failure to follow this rule on unbridled enthusiasm to be planting *something*.

### When and How to Test Garden Soil

Any new soil brought into the garden should be tested before any crop is planted. Ideally, purchased loam should be tested by the seller and you should be allowed access to the test results before you fork out the money. This seldom happens, however, in the "buyer beware" world of finding good garden loam.

Soil in your garden should be tested whenever poor plant growth signals that something is wrong, because it could be a change in soil pH or a nutrient deficiency causing the problem. And it is a good idea to have the garden's soil tested routinely every other year or so. I admit to being derelict in this regard, tending more toward letting the plants tell me when something is wrong.

For Maine gardeners, late autumn is a particularly good time to collect soil samples from your garden, since the Analytical Laboratory and Maine Soil Testing Service (University of Maine, Orono) offers fee discounts for samples received between January 1 and March 1. Simply take the samples in late October or early November, then let them air dry until January. For complete details, including instructions on how to take the samples and where to deliver them, visit their website: http://anlab.umesci.maine.edu/default.htm (see FAQs). If you tell the Analytical Lab that your garden is organic, they will respond with organic soil amendment recommendations.

For gardeners in other states, the following website should automatically connect you with your land grant university's cooperative extension website: http://www.extension.org/. Once there, follow appropriate links to the soil testing lab.

## Would You Like Red Ants or Horsetail with That Loam Order?

I cannot imagine life without a garden, yet there are many communities along the Maine coast where the joy of gardening is tempered by the presence of a tiny insect, the European red ant. Wherever this invasive nonnative insect has established its nests, some gardeners have given up the garden rather than suffer repeated stings.

Horticulture introduced the European red ant to Maine. Infested potted plants were brought from Europe to coastal Maine estates during the early half of the 20th century, and by 1950 the ants were established in two locations. By 2002, their presence was confirmed at more than 20 coastal sites. European red ants are now permanent residents of six Maine counties.

The greatest risk of importing unwanted insects or plants to your garden lies with the purchase of infested topsoil or bark mulch. Many persistent weeds, including horsetail, Japanese knotweed, Oriental bittersweet, and Norway maple, have been introduced to New England gardens in purchased soil or mulch.

There are several questions to ask when buying loam from a landscape contractor, and all are better asked on site. For example, how long has the loam been there? (If you see plants growing out of the pile, pass it by.) Where did the material come from? Has it been screened to eliminate debris such as rocks, bricks, and roots? Has a soil test been done, and if so, what were the results?

Find out if the loam has been blended with composted municipal waste. If so, do not use it for growing vegetables or fruits. It is fine for ornamentals and lawns as long as it does not have a disagreeable odor, an indication that the composting process is not complete. Finished compost of any kind should smell earthy, not like the raw products from which it is made.

If you are asking these questions on site, you can personally dig into the pile, looking for weeds and insects. At the same time, squeeze a fistful of soil, making sure that it is not too sandy (the sample does not hold together) and does not contain too much clay (the sample does not break apart when dropped). The gardener who orders a load of loam over the phone, sight unseen, is asking for trouble.

## *The Minimum-Till Garden*

It is a clear blue-sky day in early spring when the garden's life is waking from a long winter's sleep. The vegetable beds are bare, their dark soil soaking up rain one day, warmed by sunlight the next. At their surface or just below, signs of the garden's awakening abound.

Scarab beetles, tossed up in the digging of postholes for the garden's new gate, lumber sleepily over clods of damp clayey soil. Earthworms tunnel just below the soil surface while a stubby banded woolly caterpillar crawls lazily above them. All around, birds argue about nesting territory.

A bumblebee queen stirs in her underground winter's nest at the edge of the garden where she spent the long winter alone, the sole survivor of a teeming summer colony. In a week or so she will be seen flying over the garden in search of early nectar. She will be joined by adult solitary bees, awakened from a long winter's sleep in cramped cells stacked end-to-end in an old fence post, searching first for mates, then for dandelions in bloom.

And the life the gardener cannot see, but knows must be there, is waking. Single-celled and multicellular, these invisible soil-builders, bacteria and fungi, begin their work of breaking down organic matter into nutrients that the garden's plants must have to succeed. As the soil warms, their populations expand.

Into this community of life, this ecosystem called the garden, comes the gentle gardener. She treads lightly on paths made for walking, circling beds raised above the paths by years of topdressing with compost. She carries only tools that fit her hand, extensions of her hand. No plow, no tiller, has ever been in this garden.

She sows seeds and transplants seedlings with the least possible disturbance of the life around them, for it is this life that will feed the growing plants, enable them to mature, to bear leaves and fruit. Weeds, if they are troublesome, are pulled by hand. She has a helper, a partner, and between them the garden thrives.

I started gardening several decades ago, at a time when double-digging of garden beds was the prevailing paradigm. Now I know better, having arrived at a view of the gardener as caretaker of the life in the garden. In this view, deep tilling of the soil is anathema.

Marjorie and I have had some interesting discussions on the question of when, if ever, the soil should be invaded by a spade, considering the disruption of life that this act creates. (We never talk about using a tiller—we don't own one.) For example, is cover-cropping with winter rye worth the disruption of soil life caused by digging in the cover crop?

Perhaps not. There are other annual cover crops that do not need to be turned into the soil in order to plant a spring crop. And perhaps the same goal, increasing the organic matter content of the soil, can be accomplished by topdressing with composted manure. This was my thinking when I realized how many earthworms I kill when I turn over a cover crop of winter rye. (No, they don't grow back the missing half. They die.) Not to mention the disruption of microbial life in the soil caused by digging.

So, when I plant peas in early spring, I do it as non-invasively as possible, making furrows in the soil and covering the seeds by hand. I may relocate a worm or two, but I won't bisect any. Life below the inch-deep furrows will go on undisturbed. When I transplant tomato seedlings in early June, I will dig the planting holes by hand, throwing a handful of compost in the bottom of each hole as penance for the disturbance.

In my mind, no good can come from tilling or digging established garden beds. Each tilling or digging disturbs the natural growing environment of plant roots, breaks up fungal hyphae, kills worms and arthropods, destroys soil structure, and eventually reduces soil aeration. Tillage disrupts the complex cycling of nutrients through the soil food web. It brings dormant weed seeds to the surface where they will sprout.

Minimal-till gardens have fewer insect herbivores and plant diseases, likely due to the more balanced community of life in an undisturbed soil environment.

Nourishing life in the garden, treading lightly, providing habitat for pollinators and other wildlife, this is the gardener's work. Leave the deep tilling to the earthworms.

## Organic Mulches

Every spring, as soon as the soil has thawed and drained, we pick a sunny afternoon to plant peas and onions. Typically this first activity in the vegetable garden captures the attention of several crows, who watch from a nearby birch.

I feel the sun's warmth on my back and the soil's warmth in my fingers as I dig 2-inch-deep furrows down the length of a garden bed. Into each furrow I scatter pea seeds, plump with water just imbibed, then cover them with the warm soil, gently patting it down with the flat of my hand. All the while, the crows watch.

I push twiggy birch branches into the soil between the rows, forming a 4-foot scaffold for future pea tendrils and an immediate barrier to scheming seed scavengers. Defeated, the crows fly off as I soak the bed with a gentle shower.

Finally, I spread over the bed a thin blanket of shredded leaves, one handful at a time pulled from a bag stored in the basement since fall when we spread them in an open space on the drainfield and shredded them with a lawn mower. Dry leaf dust drifts downwind as I settle the leaf mulch into place with a final watering.

The vegetable gardener's reward. Now, who's going to eat all this chard? (Photo courtesy Charles Heaven)

We also use shredded leaves to mulch the onion transplants, just enough to cover the soil, hold in the moisture, keep the root run cool, and perhaps make it a little harder for weed seeds to get started. Later, after the plants are established and growing, we lay down a deeper mulch.

We also do a lot of mulching with composted goat manure, "nannyberries," applying it liberally around the highbush blueberries, raspberries, and our grape vine as these small fruit crops begin growth in early spring. Nannyberries have replaced straw as the mulch of choice for these crops; we learned from a small-fruits expert that mulching with straw can increase chances of root rot disease in raspberries.

Nannyberries are too coarse for use where vegetable seeds will be sown and often contain too much nitrogen to place in direct contact with tender transplants. We spread nannyberries over the soil of most vegetable beds in the fall, relying on shredded leaves as mulch for these beds after planting.

We mulch the potato bed with nannyberries in early spring. When it's time to plant seed potatoes, we rake this mulch aside to make furrows for the seed potatoes, then spread it back over the bed once the cut tubers are covered with soil. In two or three weeks, when the first potato leaves appear, the composted manure mulch will be well seasoned, its nutrients seeping into the soil with every rain.

Finished garden compost is another excellent mulch. A mixture of vegetable scraps from the kitchen, spent plants from the garden, shredded leaves, seaweed (when we can get it), and nannyberries, our compost pile decomposes through the summer and, by October, yields a modest amount of rich, crumbly mulch. We screen it first, eliminating tough stems and other coarse materials that need more time to break down, then spread it where it is needed most, often on the strawberry beds.

And we mulch with worm castings. Over the course of a year, the worm bin occupants transform pounds of banana peels, coffee grounds, and other kitchen vegetable waste into buckets of nutrient-rich castings. Blueberries and raspberries are the usual beneficiaries.

Organic mulches are the only fertilizer for our trees, shrubs, and perennials. In the vegetable garden, organic mulches supply sufficient quantities of nitrogen and other essential nutrients for sustained vegetable and fruit production, year after year.

Organic mulches should be in the final stages of decomposition. Wood chips, shredded wood, and sawdust are excellent mulches for garden walkways but should never be used where plants are grown. The wood in these products consists of large molecules, mostly lignin and cellulose, which must be decomposed by legions of soil bacteria into smaller molecules. The hard-working microbes utilize the bulk of the soil's nitrogen as they work, leaving the garden plants nitrogen-starved.

## Compost: The Search for Black Gold

If I am going to put something on or in my garden soil, I want to meet the manufacturers and, if possible, scratch their ears.

I recall a rainy morning one early spring when Marjorie and I found ourselves leaning over the top rail of a barn door, scratching goats behind their ears as they nibbled at our rain jackets. Raindrops dripped off the roof and down our necks while, inside the warm barn, 125 milk goats enjoyed the comfort of dry hay strewn about the floor. "They hate the rain," remarked Lynn Ahlblad, petting the head of another Seal Cove Farm goat as she talked to us about making cheese.

Seal Cove Farm, located in Lamoine, Maine, is run by Lynne Ahlblad and Barbara Brooks. They have been at it since 1976 when they adopted their first Saanen doe, and now they milk 125 goats every day. Seal Cove Farm produces prize-winning chevre and feta cheeses that are marketed throughout New England, including chevres filled with Maine blueberries and cranberries.

We came to buy a truck load of "black gold," the name any earnest gardener would give to the composted manure produced by Seal Cove goats and their goatherds. Lynn met us at the composting site, where a horseshoe-shaped compost windrow defined the perimeter of a cement pad. At one end of the row, fresh manure mixed with hay and stable litter had just been dumped. At the opposite end was finished compost, ready for the garden.

Lynn turns the entire pile once a week with a front-end loader to promote thorough heating. The result is very uniform compost. With each turning, developing compost is moved forward in the windrow as new material from the barn floor is added at the front. Mature, ready-to-use compost waits at the end of the line to be loaded into the bed of a gardener's truck.

As Lynn worked in the rain to load our truck, I took note of the effort taken to keep the perimeter of the pad free of weeds. Too often weed seeds make their way to the garden in loads of compost, but not in this case. Steam rose from the windrow along its length, an indication

## Nutrient Management Produces High Garden Yields

I can think of a couple of good reasons to rake autumn leaves into huge piles. Neither involves stuffing them into plastic bags left at curbside until trash day.

Most important when she was younger was Lynne's need to jump feet first from a running start into the pile, to hide perfectly still below the surface, breathing in the pungent organic odor, until routed out by Reilly's cold nose. I am too old to fly into the pile as Lynne once did, but I have memory of being ten years old on blue-sky October afternoons, my father heaping up the leaves after every flying leap. And I can still wrestle in the leaves with old Reilly.

And I pile them up to recycle their nutrients into leaf mold and compost for the garden. True, much of what leaves contain at the end of their life is transferred to roots and stems before the leaf dies. But those dry, brown remnants of summer have a surprisingly high nutrient element analysis. Fallen leaves of deciduous trees such as maple, beech, ash, and oak contain about 0.5 percent nitrogen, 0.1 percent phosphorus, and 0.5 percent potassium along with equally substantial amounts of calcium and magnesium, all essential nutrients for plant growth.

Because decomposition of leaves is a slow process, these nutrients are released gradually--nature's version of a slow-release fertilizer. Indeed, annual topdressing with decomposing leaves, or leaf mold, is all the fertilizer that trees, shrubs, and many perennials need for healthy growth. Even lawns are healthier for the nutrients released from fallen leaves by a mulching lawn mower.

Nutrients, however, are only part of the garden worth of autumn leaves; leaf mold also improves both the structure and the water-holding capacity of soil. While rich topsoil can hold 60 percent of its weight in water (compared with 20 percent for subsoil), leaf mold can retain 300 percent or more of its weight.

Shredded leaves make an excellent mulch for vegetable crops like these leeks.

The question then becomes not what to do with autumn leaves, but how to do it, how to make leaf mold? Start by shredding the dry leaves into small pieces that will break down quickly. This can be done with special grinders designed for the task or with a lawn mower. I know one gardener who puts his dry leaves in a trash can and shreds them with a weed whacker.

Some of the shredded leaves can be added to the compost pile, but only sparingly unless they are mixed with high-nitrogen materials such as fresh grass clippings or stable manure. Too many leaves will stall the composting process, but a mixture of five parts leaves to one part manure (by volume) will decompose quickly.

Reluctant to rob nutrients from the woodland garden, we rely on a willing neighbor for an endless supply of autumn leaves. We wait for a blue-sky Saturday afternoon to walk down the road, rakes in hand, to make the piles. We build them tall and broad for Lynne and Reilly, and only when they have had enough do we haul the leaves home and spread them out for the mower.

A mulch of shredded leaves on the surface of the soil will conserve water in pots, reducing the time spent watering containerized plants.

of internal temperatures high enough to kill weed seeds in the hay. Lynn regularly takes the temperature of the pile to make sure it is heating properly.

The rain leached from the compost a dark brown tea that ran in rivulets around our feet as we worked with shovels to level the load for travel. I imagined this nutrient tea saturating the garden soil, bathing the roots of blueberries, raspberries, and strawberries.

Before we left Seal Cove Farm we were introduced to Kel, the farm's working dog, and her companion, Sophie. Lynn whispered that Sophie had failed herding school, but what she lacked in herding skills she made up for in enthusiasm. We were also given the grand tour of the milking room and allowed a peek through the window of the cheese room door.

The sun came out on the drive home, and we spent the afternoon topdressing every bed in the garden with black gold, which we now call "nannyberries." We mulched the garden's trees and shrubs and spread a good layer on the vegetable beds. With a nutrient analysis of around 2 percent nitrogen in a slow-release form, this compost is the only fertilizer we need to apply.

My education as a gardener also includes Saturday mornings at Ellsworth Feed and Seed. If I don't have a reason to go there, I invent one. Maybe I need mulching straw, black oil sunflower seeds for the birds, a bale of potting soil, seeds of this or that vegetable variety, or to check if the seed potatoes are in yet. I always need something.

I drive my twelve-year-old Hyundai hatchback past the resident flock of mallards dabbling in the flooded field along the edge of the drive, navigate through a minefield of potholes filled with water deep enough to stock with trout, and park, usually between two pickups loaded with bales of hay or sacks of feed.

On one such trip, before I could open the car door there was Harvard, the store's manager, bearing down with a wide grin.

"Reeser, I've got to tell you," he called out as he approached, stopping at the nose of my car, inches from a pallet of composted sheep manure, slapping his hand on the top bag, "I've waited 30 months for this day, two and a half years, and here it is!" And so Harvard and I spent the next ten minutes talking manure.

It was early, 7:00 A.M., and Harvard had time to talk. Later, as he moved rapidly from loading dock to truck or car, carrying a 50-pound sack under each arm, he would have time for little more than a cursory nod.

When Harvard talks, I listen, and I always learn something new about gardening. I mentioned that I could not recall ever running across composted sheep manure for sale. Harvard told me that it was produced in Canada and that it was, in his opinion, unbeatable as a vegetable garden soil amendment.

Unfortunately, he went on, one reaction to the mad cow disease epidemic of a few years ago was a halt to importing sheep manure into the U.S. We both expressed dismay that the government can't distinguish between a cow and a sheep.

Harvard sells just about every brand of bagged compost you can name. They all have their following. So when he said that he thinks this sheep manure is the best, I knew I was getting the inside track on something extraordinary. I listened as he explained that he never had better crops than when he used this sheep manure, and this included his crop of towering tobacco plants.

That's right, Harvard grows tobacco in Maine—he loves the flowers of the tobacco plant. He also tried growing cotton, with less satisfying results. The man is always trying something new, always learning, always willing to share what he has learned.

Next thing I knew, we were loading six bags of composted sheep manure into the belly of my old rust bucket. As we loaded, Harvard told me that he had an exclusive on this sheep manure. At the moment he had plenty, but I knew it would go fast if Harvard told everyone what he had told me.

We went inside to settle up, and the conversation turned to organic sources of nitrogen. I learned that the cost of blood meal had soared to such heights that Harvard could not afford to stock it, but he had cottonseed meal and alfalfa meal, both just as good, he thought. One entire wall of the store was lined with organic soil amendments. What was conspicuous in its absence was synthetic nitrogen in any form.

"That's a thing of the past," he said. "I only sell it for fertilizing hay fields and such, not to home gardeners." Good news!

The parking lot was filling with earnest farmers and gardeners, and the line at the cash register curved around sacks of bird seed, past racks of garden seed, and clear back to the horse supplies. No one was in a hurry. Everyone knew someone in front or behind, and conversation ran the gamut. A sign on the wall said, "No Cell Phones Allowed".

Driving home, I couldn't wait to show Marjorie the sheep manure I'd bought, then realized that there was no cause for her to be as elated as I was; she hadn't been there to hear Harvard talk about it. There's a sheep on the front of the bag, but nothing to explain why this composted manure is better than the brand of compost blend that sat on a pallet to the left or the composted cow manure on the pallet to the right.

Harvard said it is better, an opinion constructed from experience in his own garden. Good enough for me.

Buying compost should be like buying produce at the farmer's market. There is a face and a name that goes home with the purchase, and often a whole lot more.

Garden as landscape: perennial border foreground, vegetable beds behind, and trees in background. (Photo courtesy Charles Heaven)

## Winter Cover Crops and Green Manures

Working garden soil is a meditative thing, best done in silence punctuated only by reports on the number of earthworms in a handful of soil. I will say how many, and Marjorie will respond, "Excellent!"

Gardening is about feeding earthworms and other soil creatures. Do all you can to nourish them and protect their environment; do nothing that disturbs their work.

In the vegetable garden, you can plant a cover crop in the fall to protect the soil over the winter when it would otherwise be bare, vulnerable to erosion by wind and water. Two popular cover crops used by gardeners and farmers in New England are oats and winter rye (also called cereal rye).

Oats, readily available and inexpensive, should be sown between mid-August and early September (not before mid-August or they could go to seed, leading to a volunteer spring oat crop). They produce good vegetative growth all fall and make an excellent catch crop, trapping soluble nutrients in the soil, keeping them in the top of the soil profile. The oat plants are killed by freezing temperatures, forming a dense mat of dead vegetation that holds the soil in place through the winter. This oat mulch can be easily incorporated into the soil in spring. Or, to avoid disturbing the soil and help with weed control, you can transplant seedlings directly through the mulch.

When a spot in the garden opens up in late September, too late to plant oats, consider sowing seeds of winter rye, although using this cover crop is not quite as easy. The most cold tolerant of commonly used cover crops, winter rye sown in late September grows rapidly, even into cold weather. It does not winterkill and puts on vigorous new growth the following spring, the extensive fibrous root systems preventing the leaching of excess soil nitrogen.

To use a bed cropped with winter rye you need to be able to turn it under early in the growing season. Otherwise its growth gets unmanageable. So, winter rye works best in gardens that warm up and dry out quickly in spring. It must be incorporated into the soil, which seriously disrupts soil life. Lastly, you should allow four weeks after turning it under before planting any vegetables or flowers. There are two reasons for this waiting period. First, the bacteria which decompose the fresh organic matter tie up available soil nitrogen as they grow in number. Once their job is done, most of these bacteria die, returning the nitrogen to the soil. The process of decomposition takes two to three weeks.

The second reason for waiting demands the fourth week. Winter rye has an allelopathic effect on many other plant species, releasing chemical compounds into the soil that can inhibit the growth of those sensitive species. These allelochemicals disappear during that additional week.

Alternatively, you can wait until the rye sends up a flower stalk in early summer and then mow or weedwack it back, which kills the plant. Wait one week after mowing and then turn it under. By then it is late June, and you still have time to plant most warm-season crops.

When a cover crop is grown and turned into the soil while still alive and green, it is also called a green manure. Sometimes a gardener will take a part of the garden out of production during the growing season just to grow a green manure. Green manures are grown for the same reason that livestock manure is applied; they condition the soil, building organic matter and adding nutrients. To get the full benefit of many green manure crops, they must be planted in the spring and not turned under until the following spring. The small-space gardener might consider conditioning a new garden bed with a year-long green manure crop.

An excellent summer green manure crop for building soil biomass is P.O.V., a mixture of field peas, oats, and hairy vetch in equal amounts. Both the peas and vetch are nitrogen-fixing plants, while the oats are an excellent catch crop. If sown in the spring, it should be cut back and turned under just after the peas flower, to prevent them from setting seed. If sown in mid to late summer, it can be left in place until the following spring. While the peas and oats will always winterkill, the vetch may resume growth in spring and need to be cut down.

POV is the crop of choice for gardeners who want to build a main-season green manure crop into their garden rotation plan. Each year a different plot can be taken out of vegetable production and sown to POV. The increased soil organic matter that develops from such a program will improve habitat for soil organisms while building nutrient reserves in the soil.

Nitrogen-fixing vegetable crops, such as beans and peas, will serve as green manures when you cut them down after they have stopped producing and allow two to three weeks for the leaves and stems to decompose, returning the fixed nitrogen back to the soil, before planting another crop through the residual mulch.

For example, when your spring-planted peas stop producing in early July, you can cut the vines at the soil level and lay them on top of the soil to dry and decompose. Wait two weeks, cover with compost or composted manure, and then pop in broccoli transplants for a fall harvest.

If your garden is overrun with annual weeds, consider growing a smother crop of buckwheat, a broad-leaved fast-growing summer annual. It has a very short growing season, reaching flowering stage in four to six weeks from sowing. At this point it should be cut down.

New beds with heavy weed seed loads should be sown to buckwheat immediately after last frost. This crop can be followed by POV to catch the nutrients released from the decomposing buckwheat.

Cover crops and green manures will be among the hardest working plants in your garden. They prevent erosion, suppress weeds, help build soil organic matter and nutrient levels. They feed the earthworms.

## Wood Ashes in the Garden

A lot of New England gardeners rely on wood-burning stoves and fireplaces to stay warm in winter, resulting in an abundance of wood ashes. An average cord of wood, depending on wood type and combustion efficiency, will yield a five-gallon bucket of ashes. Should these ashes be used in the garden?

There was a time when wood ashes were valued as a primary source of potassium for both field and garden as well as a means of raising the pH of acidic soils. While those days may be gone, home gardeners can still take advantage of a supply of wood ashes to add needed nutrients.

Wood ashes, used in moderation, can benefit most garden soils. They contain between 5 and 7 percent potassium and up to 2 percent phosphorus, both major plant nutrients. Hardwood ashes have higher potassium levels than softwood ashes.

Wood ashes also contain 25 to 50 percent calcium, another essential plant nutrient, along with a number of minor elements. They do not contain a significant amount of nitrogen, so you will need to supply this essential element from compost, green manures, and other sources.

There are two potential problems associated with use of wood ashes: excess soluble salts and alkalinity. Since wood ashes are up to 90 percent water-soluble mineral salts, excessive applications can result in a buildup of these salts in the soil, resulting in root injury and plant death.

Because ashes are alkaline, you should avoid using them in soils above pH 6.5. Also, avoid using them around rhododendrons, blueberries, and other acid-loving plants. Wood ashes act much faster than lime in raising soil pH, so you should have your garden soil tested at least every other year to make sure the use of wood ashes is not raising soil pH above the optimum level.

A safe application rate for most garden soils is 20 pounds per 1,000 square feet, the equivalent of a five-gallon pail of ashes. This is the equivalent of 6 pounds of ground limestone per 1,000 square feet, an amount considered appropriate for yearly applications without changing proper soil pH.

Wood ashes can be raked into soil in spring, three to four weeks before planting, or they can be side-dressed around growing plants. Apply the ashes evenly, avoiding lumps or piles. To avoid burning sensitive plant tissues, do not apply ashes over germinating seeds or young seedlings. Also, rinse applied ashes off foliage.

Store your wood ashes in a metal container to keep them dry. Potassium and other water-soluble nutrients are leached out of wood ashes that are left standing in the rain. This leaching not only reduces the nutrient value of the ashes but also leaves them more alkaline.

Never put coal or charcoal ashes on the garden! Coal ashes tend to be high in toxic heavy metals, while charcoal ashes contain sodium borate, a chemical toxic to plants.

A final caution: protect yourself when applying wood ash. Use the same precautions you would use when handling household bleach, another strongly alkaline material. Wear eye protection and gloves and, depending on the fineness of the ash and the direction of the wind, you may want to wear a dust mask.

In moderation, applications of wood ashes can be an effective part of garden soil management. And gardeners know from experience that the garden demands moderation in all things.

Crevices in the edging of large stones that frame each of our garden beds are favorite slug bedrooms. Left alone, these slimy creatures spend hot summer days in these cool niches, gliding around the garden at night munching on succulent stems and leaves. Wood ashes to the rescue! Imagine sliding on your belly over the micro-sharp particles. I think such thoughts as I fill each crevice with ashes.

A lovely perennial bed with a coastal inlet in the background.

## *Biochar: Part of the Future of Gardening*

Like most of us, Eastport, Maine, resident George Hoche waits for the thaw. Waiting, he thinks about his vegetable garden and his greenhouse. He thinks about the schoolyard food garden that he and other Master Gardener Volunteers are supporting. And he thinks about firing up a self-made oil-drum furnace that now stands buried under ice and snow across the drive in front of his home. George is anxious to make more biochar.

One morning last week, I stopped by George's home to drop off an article on biochar just published in the journal *Orion*. The article, "Plants Suck," written by Middlebury College scholar Bill McKibben, reminds us that plants suck carbon dioxide out of the atmosphere, storing it in their tissues in the form of cellulose and lignin, the primary molecules of wood, as well as starch and other compounds. When plants die and decay, or when wood or other plant tissues are completely burned, this carbon is returned to the atmosphere as carbon dioxide.

The incomplete combustion of these plant tissues, however, produces a form of carbon called biochar. Anyone who heats with a wood stove knows biochar, the small charcoal-like lumps found under the ashes where combustion is hindered by lack of oxygen. Lasting for years in the soil, biochar keeps carbon that would have been returned to the atmosphere out of circulation.

Golden daffodils in early spring are a sign of hope, a promise of the garden to come.

Handing the article to George, I pointed to McKibben's words, "If you could continually turn organic material into biochar, you could reverse the history of the last two hundred years." McKibben was talking about the last 200 years of human activity—the burning of fossil fuels, including gasoline, natural gas, and coal—that has caused the increase in atmospheric carbon dioxide levels responsible for Earth's current global warming crisis.

George calls his method of making biochar the "indirect method" because the feedstock, usually hardwood bark or wood chips, is never in direct contact with the flame. By minimizing the amount of oxygen reaching the feedstock, incomplete combustion produces plenty of biochar. George also equipped his furnace with an afterburner that returns waste gases back to the flame for their complete combustion. Recycling of the waste gases contributes to operation of the furnace.

The biochar is removed from the furnace and, after cooling, crushed to a fine granular texture before being used or stored. Hardwood bark crushes easier than other feedstocks.

As a gardener, George understands the importance of building healthy soil. Shelves in his work area are crammed with books, soil testing equipment, and samples of the biochar he has produced from various feedstocks. He views biochar as a soil amendment that can improve soil texture, hold essential plant nutrients in the soil, and increase soil populations of beneficial microorganisms. His views are echoed by research reports from universities around the world.

George has experimented with application rates and determined that lower levels, around two ounces per square foot of soil (125 pounds per 1,000 square feet) work best for soil nutrient levels and plant growth. Higher rates result in excessive nitrogen and potassium levels. He has also noticed improved soil structure with use of biochar.

What is the future of biochar? McKibben believes we can use biochar to sequester significant amounts of carbon in the soil, the first real attempt at "scrubbing the atmosphere." He envisions mobile biochar-producing furnaces patrolling forests devastated by storms or insect attacks.

George is planning additional field trials of his biochar. He also plans to use biochar this spring to improve the soil in the schoolyard garden project. He envisions a day when biochar is as common as peat moss at the local garden center.

## Breaking New Ground

*"Perhaps the most radical thing you can do in our time is to start turning over the soil, loosening it up for the crops to settle in, and then stay home and tend them."*
*—Rebecca Solnit*

As writer and gardener Rebecca Solnit points out in her article "The Most Radical Thing You Can Do" (*Orion*, November/December, 2008), the word "radical" comes from the Latin word for root. Gardeners rooted in the soil of their gardens have always worked diligently to keep it healthy and productive. Now, in times of escalating fuel and food prices, the quality of our lives may depend on staying home and breaking new ground.

When we break new ground in Marjorie's Garden, we typically start with the closest thing we have to "lawn," a mixture of grasses (mostly Kentucky bluegrass), wild strawberries, and dandelions. Before beginning the task of converting this weed patch to garden bed, we sample the soil for testing. The results typically come back from the university soils lab before we need them.

Taking advantage of a late autumn week's mild weather, we begin by mowing the patch as short as possible. We then cover the area with several layers of newspaper, followed by an 8-inch layer of seaweed and straw (not hay, which contains weed seeds).

Our future garden bed spends the winter under this cover and the snow that accumulates above it. In early spring, as the sun warms the soil and stimulates new growth, most of the plants buried beneath the cover quickly use up the food reserves stored through winter in their roots and die.

In early May, after snowmelt, we remove what is left of the cover, exposing bare ground to the sun. By this time, the newspaper has mostly disappeared, and what remains of the seaweed-straw mix is set aside to use as weed-suppressing mulch over the new bed.

After the soil dries out, we turn it over with a spade (one of the few times in gardening when spading is unavoidable), adding amendments recommended by the soil test as well as plenty of nannyberries. As we turn and rake the soil, we remove the remaining clumps of live grass and roots.

By the end of May, our new bed is ready for its first planting. For many years, the grasses and wild plants that were growing there functioned as a perennial cover crop, recycling nutrients, including those returned to the soil as clippings each time we mowed. Whatever we plant, we expect a good yield.

This is how we transform "lawn" into new garden beds in Marjorie's Garden. We like to begin in late autumn unless the snow falls early, in which case we cover the bed as soon as possible in spring and keep it covered until the end of May. This late start delays planting of the first crop until sometime in June, still early enough for a crop of summer squash, cucumbers, even tomatoes in a good year.

In hard times, gardeners turn to their gardens. We enlarge our gardens or begin new ones. We stay home, grow our own food, and perhaps discover, as Solnit writes, "a more stately, settled, secure way of living." We find richness rooted in our connection with healthy soil.

## Tips for Improving Your Garden's Soil

Does your soil dry and crack in the summer? Do azaleas, rhododendrons, and other shallow-rooted plants wilt in hot weather even when you water them frequently? Do your tomatoes suffer from blossom-end rot even when you add calcium to the soil? Are your potatoes scabby? Does water pool on the soil surface or drain slowly?

While not intended to replace recommendations on a soil test report, the following tips will help you solve these and other problems by improving your garden's soil.

If you have not been annually incorporating organic matter in your soil or mulching with organic matter, do not expect major changes in soil conditions to occur rapidly. However, you should expect to see improvement in soil tilth, as measured by ease of tillage, seedling emergence, and root penetration, every year.

Rhododendrons require acidic soil for healthy growth and abundant blossoms.

| Soil Condition or Plant Problem | Remedy |
| --- | --- |
| Soil is too clayey, drying and cracking during periods of drought, draining slowly. | Before planting in spring, dig or till in a 3-inch layer of compost or composted manure (1 cubic yard/100 square feet). Repeat annually. |
| Soil is too sandy, drying too quickly between waterings. Plants with shallow root systems, such as rhododendrons, azaleas, and blueberries, wilt in hot weather. | Add organic matter annually as described above. In addition, mulch with organic matter (straw, shredded leaves, compost) during the growing season. |
| Tomatoes are afflicted with blossom-end rot, a sign of excessive soil moisture fluctuations. | Ensure a constant supply of moisture by mulching soil with organic matter and irrigating when necessary for plants to receive 1 inch of water each week. |
| Harvested potatoes are scabby with raised, corky, circular lesions on their surface. | Soil pH is too high. Have the soil tested and apply elemental sulfur as instructed to reduce pH to 5.2. |
| A soil test indicates your soil is too acid. | Apply dolomitic lime or calcitic lime in fall or spring, following recommendations on soil test report for amounts to use. See discussion of "Calcium, Magnesium, and Sulfur" earlier in this chapter. |
| A soil test indicates your soil is too alkaline. | Apply elemental sulfur in fall or spring, following soil test report's recommendations. See discussion of "Calcium, Magnesium, and Sulfur" earlier in this chapter. |
| Rhododendrons, blueberries, and other acid-loving plants are growing poorly or not at all. Other garden plants are doing well. | This is likely a pH problem. Rhododendrons, azaleas, blueberries and other ericaceous plants need acidic soils. Have the soil around these plants tested separately and apply elemental sulfur as recommended to lower pH. |
| A soil test indicates your soil's organic matter content is too low. | Before planting in spring, dig or till in a 3-inch layer of compost or composted manure (1 cubic yard/100 square feet). Repeat annually. |

# Chapter 4

# Planning the Vegetable Garden

## *by Marjorie Peronto*

*"The most noteworthy thing about gardeners is that they are always optmistic, always enterprising, and never satisfied. They always look forward to doing something better than they have ever done before."*

—Vita Sackville-West

***In January, just when it seems the New England winter will drag on forever,*** the seed catalogs arrive in the mail. Weeks before the sap rises in the sugar maples and the first pussy willows appear, as sure as the imperceptibly increasing day length, seed catalogs are the first hopeful harbingers of spring. But leafing through their pages confronts you again with the annual question: What vegetable crops do you want to grow in your garden?

A better question to get the decision-making process going would be, what will your family eat? Have a family meeting and make a list. Which vegetables does everyone like best?

Next, what will grow in your garden? If in doubt, seek the opinions of experienced local gardeners. For example, you may love bell peppers, especially the sweet flavor of a fully ripe, deep red bell, but if you garden in northern New England, experienced gardeners will tell you that your plants will not see enough hot weather to fully ripen the fruits; you'll have to settle for green bells or decide not to grow bell peppers at all.

Does your garden get enough full sun to grow heat-loving crops such as peppers, tomatoes, and melons? Perhaps your garden, like ours, has some sections that receive full sun and others that get only a few hours of direct sun every day. A useful rule to follow is that a crop grown for fruit or root requires full sun, whereas one grown for leaves, stems, or buds will mature in partial shade. Crops that produce with three to six hours of sun per day include lettuce, spinach, broccoli, cauliflower, beets, Brussels sprouts, radishes, and Swiss chard.

Having decided what the family likes to eat and what your garden can grow, think about how much time you have to devote to the garden. Some crops require more maintenance than others.

*Facing page:* Lynne took great pride in the turnips she grew one summer.

For example, carrots require little more than sowing, thinning, watering, and weeding, while potatoes require planting, periodic hilling, watering, weeding, and protection from Colorado potato beetles, a chore that, in an organic garden, involves covering the crop with a floating row cover to exclude the beetle. Broccoli and other brassica crops also must be grown under cover to exclude the cabbage butterfly, the adult form of the imported cabbage worm, a devastating brassica herbivore.

Some crops, such as tomatoes, need staking or caging. Others, including many small fruit crops, need pruning. If you're in doubt, experienced gardeners can help you identify the high-maintenance crops.

Finally, consider the size of your garden. I often sit in front of the wood stove on snowy January evenings and browse the seed catalogs—Baker Creek Heirloom Seeds, Comstock Garden Seeds, Johnny's Selected Seeds, High Mowing Organic Seeds, and so many others—and I want to grow ten times as many vegetable crops as I have the garden space to plant. But I know better. A little of this and a little of that cannot compete with the need for daily handfuls of pineapple tomatillos or pounds of potatoes to last the winter. If space is limited, avoid growing crops such as corn, melons, and winter squash (including pumpkins) that produce relatively sparse yields per square foot of garden space. Consider buying such vegetables from a local farmer and saving your garden space for the high-value crops on your family's wish list (see the accompanying sidebar).

Once you choose your vegetables, you'll want to choose varieties. We'll return to this later in the chapter.

Finally, do set aside one small bed, or part of a bed, to try something new every year. It will lend a sense of purpose to those winter evenings spent poring over seed catalogs.

A pepper plant in a Connecticut garden in late July. (Courtesy Charles Heaven)

## Laying Out the Garden

When planning a vegetable garden, your first decision is where to site it. Think sun. Most vegetable crops require at least six to eight hours of direct sun each day. The only exceptions are the leafy greens, including lettuce and spinach, which can manage with a little less. If you are assessing likely garden sites in the winter, remember that surrounding deciduous trees will cast a far-reaching shade during the growing season.

Think excellent drainage. The soil in your vegetable garden should be loose and well-drained. Examine each possible site on the day after a soaking spring rain. Are there any soggy areas or puddles of standing water? If your favored site has poor or indifferent drainage once the ice is out of the ground, either eliminate it from consideration or build raised beds on the site as discussed below.

What about garden size? If you're a first-time vegetable gardener, you may want to start small, perhaps a garden of only 10 by 10 feet (100 square feet), and expand the garden over time. If you feel bolder and more ambitious, try a garden of 20 by 20 feet (400 square feet), which will grow a wide range of crops including those such as corn and winter squash that hog space. Even a garden of 12 by 16 feet (nearly 200 square feet) will grow a lot of food, particularly if you train vining crops, such as cucumbers, to grow on trellises. Of course, the requirements for lots of sun and excellent drainage may limit the garden's size or result in two or more smaller vegetable gardens in a larger landscape.

Before making final decisions about garden size, read the sections below on raised beds and intensive gardening. Both of these gardening systems are designed for maximum production in limited space.

Once your garden's location, size, and growing system have been determined, make a plan for the garden, a scale drawing on graph paper. Use paper with ¼-inch squares, each square

### High-Value Vegetable Crops

Which crops provide the most dollar value per square foot of garden space? The top fifteen high-value vegetables are listed below. Value is based on harvested pounds per square foot, the retail value per pound at harvest time, and length of time in the garden:

- Tomatoes
- Green bunching onions
- Leaf lettuce
- Turnips
- Summer squash
- Edible-pod peas
- Storage onions
- Beans
- Beets
- Carrots
- Cucumbers
- Peppers
- Broccoli
- Head lettuce
- Swiss Chard

representing one square foot of garden space. For best sun exposure, orient the garden so that the beds run east to west.

In spring, as soon as the soil can be worked, you will translate your plan into a real garden, driving wooden stakes into each of the four corners, then rototilling or digging the area by hand, turning over the soil and removing existing vegetation before creating the growing areas.

## The Case for Raised Beds

There are several good reasons for raised-bed gardening. Raised beds help compensate for less-than-optimal drainage after hard rains, and they dry out quickly in spring, allowing an early start for cool-season crops such as peas, lettuce, and spinach. They also hold the sun's warmth longer at day's end and in the fall—a real boon to northern gardeners trying to grow heat-loving vegetables

Most of the raised beds in our vegetable garden are framed with stones unearthed when the beds were made. The walkways are mulched with wood chips.

Raised beds at the Berkshire Botanical Garden (Stockbridge, Massachusetts) offer visitors ideas on vertical gardening and on vegetable varieties suitable for small spaces.

The 4-foot by 8-foot raised beds in this schoolyard community garden in Eastport, Maine, were constructed from hemlock timbers that will last for 10 or more years. Each bed is 2 feet high in order to accommodate gardeners of all ages and sizes, including wheelchair-bound students and elderly members of the community who serve as volunteers. Because a 12-inch-deep root zone is sufficient for most vegetable crops, the bottom half of each bed is filled with dead sand, which is much cheaper than loam. The top half is filled with loam amended with plenty of composted manure.

such as tomatoes, melons, and summer squash. And finally, in many places in New England the garden may sit on barely buried ledge, leaving the gardener with little topsoil in which to grow. This is the case in our garden; in most spots we can't drive a stake more than a few inches into the ground before striking a shelf of stone. When you can't dig down, you have to build up.

A few of the raised beds in our garden have wooden frames, while the rest are buttressed with large rocks, which are abundant on our property. The beds average about 3 feet in width and vary in length from several yards to just a few feet, their top surfaces slightly narrowed to minimize erosion. The adjacent pathways are about 2 feet wide.

You can be creative when framing raised beds, using logs, stones, cinder blocks, corrugated tin, or wood. You can also leave them freestanding with no frame. Start construction by cultivating the entire garden area, then mark out each bed with stakes and string or with the framing materials. Shovel the topsoil from adjacent pathways onto each bed, adding screened loam if needed, then dig in 2 inches of compost and rake the top of the bed level. Then define the walkways around your beds with a mulch of straw or wood chips. When finished, each bed should rise about 8 inches above its adjacent pathways. Children and pets can then easily tell the walkways from the growing beds.

You should be able to plant, fertilize, weed, and harvest each bed from the walkways. Since you won't have to step on the beds once they are established, you won't be compacting the soil in the growing areas. If your beds are unframed, some of the soil inevitably slides back into the walkways over time. Just shovel this errant soil back where it belongs each spring.

## Gardening Intensively for Maximum Harvest Yield

Intensive vegetable gardening in beds can increase a small garden's harvest up to fifteen times over that of conventional row gardening. Instead of planting in a single row separated by wide walkways, crops are planted in blocks that span the width of a bed. The "in-row" spacing on the seed packet is used between plants within the block so that when they are mature, their leaves just barely touch. This creates a "living mulch" over the soil, keeping weed growth to a minimum. A 3-foot by 2-foot bed of carrots thinned to a final spacing of 3 inches between plants will produce as many carrots as a single 24-foot row.

In one long bed, you might plant a block of carrots next to a block of beets, followed by a block of lettuce and so on. It is easy to reach into each bed from the adjacent walkways, and the intensive plant spacing reduces weed competition.

The higher plant densities in intensive gardening demand fertile, well-drained soil that is enriched annually with organic matter. Extra attention must be given to watering.

Here is a list of popular direct-sown garden vegetables and their recommended final wide-row spacing:

- Beets: 4 to 6 inches
- Carrots: 2 to 3 inches
- Garlic: 4 to 6 inches
- Kohlrabi: 7 to 9 inches
- Leeks: 4 to 6 inches
- Lettuce (head): 10 to 12 inches
- Lettuce (leaf): 7 to 9 inches
- Onions (dry): 4 to 6 inches
- Parsnips: 5 to 6 inches
- Radishes: 2 to 3 inches
- Spinach: 4 to 6 inches
- Swiss Chard: 7 to 9 inches
- Turnips: 4 to 6 inches

In this raised bed, carrots thinned to a final spacing of 2 to 3 inches between plants create a living mulch over the soil.

In his West Stockbridge, Massachusetts, garden, Ron Kujawski trellises cucumbers to save space.

For crops started with transplants, use the following final spacings between plants in the bed:

Asparagus: 15 to 18 inches
Cole crops (broccoli, cabbage, cauliflower): 18 inches
Eggplant: 18 to 24 inches
Peppers: 15 inches
Seed potatoes: 12 to 15 inches
Summer squash: 18 to 24 inches
Winter squash: 24-36 inches (a single row down the middle of a 4-foot-wide bed)

To save garden space, many vegetables, including tomatoes and cucumbers, can be grown vertically on trellises, nets, strings, cages, and poles. Trellised tomatoes should be planted on a 24-inch spacing, and climbing cucumbers should be planted 12 inches apart. Remember that vertically grown plants cast more shade and should not be planted in front of sun-loving plants. Instead, grow shade-tolerant crops such as summer lettuce in the shade of trellised vegetables.

The exceptions to such intensive crop spacing are bush beans and peas. Both are easier to pick and less disease prone if planted as double rows in a 3- or 4-foot-wide bed.

## Choosing Vegetable Varieties

After the decision of which crops to grow comes the more daunting task of choosing the right variety of each vegetable. Of the forty tomato varieties listed in the seed catalog, which should you grow in a New England garden? Or should you simplify the decision, narrowing the choices to the half-dozen varieties of tomato transplants offered at the local garden center? What loaded

### Intensive Cropping in Small Raised Beds by Reeser Manley

In 2012, Marjorie and I expanded our vegetable garden by constructing several small raised beds. Most were 3 feet by 5 feet, and because they were located outside the deer fence that surrounds the main vegetable garden, we fitted each bed with three PVC hoops to support a cover of polyfabric fencing material.

In one of these small raised beds we grew an early crop of spinach. After one good cutting, the plants bolted, so we dug them into the soil, waited two weeks, and planted 60 basil transplants.

Sixty basil plants in 15 square feet translates to four plants per square foot. That's intensive gardening! But that little bed produced the best basil crop we have ever grown. As I write this in mid-August 2012, Marjorie has converted two cuttings of basil leaves into pesto with the certainty of another cutting before frost.

Another raised bed of the same size was planted to pineapple tomatillo, normally a sprawling vine that you might plant on at least 2-foot centers. Feeling bold, we planted the 15-square-foot bed with fifteen young transplants, one per square foot. As the plants grew, I staked those on the outside to keep them from spilling over the bed edges.

With little room to sprawl, the plants grew upright, eventually getting so tall that I had to remove the deer cover. The deer left them alone for the rest of the season--either the bed was too close to the house or deer are not fond of the pineapple taste--and we enjoyed a bumper crop of the tasty little fruits.

Intensive cropping in raised beds requires more frequent watering, particularly as the plants grow larger and dry spells last longer. The soil in both of the beds discussed above was amended liberally with composted manure before planting each crop. I also top-dressed the basil with organic fertilizer one week after the second cutting.

By the end of the season, this little bed will have produced an early spinach crop and three cuttings of summer basil. This photo was taken a week after the second cutting of basil leaves.

By mid-August, these tomatillo plants were dropping dozens of husked fruits on the ground every day.

Sungold cherry tomatoes are a variety with almost universal appeal. No other tomato comes close to matching their sweetness, particularly when you pop one in your mouth right after you pick it.

questions! Ask ten gardeners and you're likely to get ten different answers, each gardener biased by his or her reason for growing tomatoes or even for gardening at all.

Yes, there are published lists of recommended varieties of tomato and every other vegetable that can be grown in a New England garden. But in planning our garden, if we really want to know which variety will grow trouble-free or which variety has real flavor, we rely on the experience of local gardeners.

For example, when Harvard Jordan at the Ellsworth Feed and Seed says that nothing beats Kennebec potatoes, we are likely to plant Kennebecs. Or when a reader of Reeser's weekly column suggests the Bolero carrot as the best variety for winter storage, a recommendation based on twenty years of gardening, we pay close attention. The same reader put us onto a softball-size kohlrabi variety that keeps all winter in her root cellar.

For new gardeners there is a decision-making process that begins with deciding which crops to grow, followed by careful winnowing of the many varieties available for each crop. My advice is to start with the seed catalogs to pick varieties of both direct-sown crops and crops transplanted as seedlings. With one or more current seed catalogs in hand, go through the following decision-making process and then, if the local garden center offers transplants of varieties that fit the bill, you still have that option. On the other hand, you can produce your own transplants from seed for crops such as tomatoes, peppers, brassicas, and cucurbits (see *"Growing Your Own Vegetable Transplants"* on page 63).

Begin the variety selection process by deciding if you will be growing for fresh consumption only or for preserving some of the harvest by storing, freezing, or canning. If the latter, you may want to grow two varieties of a crop, one for eating fresh, the other for preserving. Again, tomatoes serve as an example. There are paste varieties for making and preserving tomato sauces and scores of varieties for fresh eating. When it comes to storing onions, braided together and hung in a corner of the kitchen, we have always considered Copra to be one of the best varieties.

We like the summer squash variety 'Magda' both for its nutty flavor and because it has a compact growth habit perfect for close spacing in tight quarters. There are five plants in the 10 square feet of this bed.

Next, study the different growth habits found in different varieties of each crop. In gardens with limited space, pole beans that make use of vertical space make more sense than bush beans that tie up a lot of ground. And the compact-growing form of Delicata winter squash takes up far less room than the vining form of the same variety, although you get more squash fruits from the vining form.

Your garden's soil texture may influence variety selection of root crops such as carrots. For heavier soils, tapered carrot varieties such as the Chantenays or Danvers types grow best, wedging their way through the soil. In loose sandy loam or silty soils, most types will grow well.

Disease resistance is another consideration in variety selection. Many catalogs will identify varieties that have been selected for resistance to certain diseases. For example, beans are susceptible to root rot fungi, mildew fungi, and several viruses, all of which can be avoided to some extent by cultural measures such as never handling or harvesting when the foliage is wet and planting with enough space between plants to ensure ample air circulation for rapid drying of leaves. (Fungal diseases spread more quickly when plants are wet.)

## Heirloom Vegetable Varieties

Recently I re-read Barbara Kingsolver's book *Animal, Vegetable, Miracle*, a chronicle of a family's effort to eat only locally produced food for an entire year. Early on, in her third chapter, Kingsolver makes a strong case for growing heirloom vegetables in the family garden.

The bottom lines are flavor and nutrition. Most vegetable varieties found in the produce section of the grocery store (the exceptions being those stores willing to give space to local growers) are hybrid varieties bred for pest resistance, ease of packaging, and ability to survive long-distance transport from a factory farm in California, Florida, or points south, all at the expense of flavor and nutrient value. Anyone with a home garden in New England knows that those shiny, blemish-free green peppers on the grocer's shelf in February are tasteless replicas of the real thing. The same can be said for tomatoes, cucumbers, and all the rest. Flavor is sacrificed for shelf life, and nutrients are lost during storage and shipping.

A hybrid, the one-time product of a cross between two dissimilar varieties, will not come true from seed, instead producing a spectrum of characteristics. Hybrid seeds have to be purchased every year from the companies that create them. Growing hybrid varieties in the home garden eliminates the possibility of saving seed for use in next year's garden. Growing hybrids nixes seed sharing.

Heirloom vegetable varieties are the champions of flavor. Passed down from one generation to the next in the form of seed saved from the garden's best performers, their names reflect their origin, history, or something of their character: Cherokee Trail of Tears Pole Bean, Boothby's Blonde Cucumber (from Livermore, Maine, where the Boothby family grew it for several generations), Chadwick's Rodan Lettuce (developed by Alan Chadwick, the English leader of the organic movement), Early Hanover Melon (first introduced to Virginia in 1895), Sweet Chocolate Pepper, Collective Farm Woman melon—the list goes on.

And while heirloom vegetables have been selected primarily for flavor, they have also stood the test of time with respect to disease resistance, performing for generations in organic gardens where proper cultural methods trump the use of chemicals. I would not rule out a flavorful heirloom variety that meets all other criteria just because it has not been specifically bred for disease resistance.

After reading Kingsolver's book the first time, I resolved to include more heirloom varieties in our family's vegetable garden. We grew Black Prince tomato, an heirloom from Siberia, thinking that any tomato that grew in Siberia would produce fruits in the coolest Maine summer. Sure enough, through July and August we picked dozens of purple-black tomatoes with a rich fruity flavor.

The following season I increased the number of heirloom tomato varieties in our garden to include Amish Paste, a deep-red oxheart variety often used for tomato paste; Pink Brandywine, with large, potato-leaved foliage and pink beefsteak fruits; Principe Borghese, an Italian heirloom producing clusters of red, plum-shaped paste tomatoes; Cosmonaut Volkov, a Ukrainian tomato with high yields in cool summers; and Caspian Pink, a mild and sweet Russian tomato.

And I added Boothby's Blonde cucumber to one of my seed orders. This is a relatively short, stout cuke with creamy white skin at the picking stage, yellow skin when older and seedier. It is very prolific and very tasty.

## A Vegetable Crop Planting Guide for New England Gardeners

The autumn of 2011 was characterized by above-normal temperatures and many December days that were more like September. On October 5, however, we cut the garden's last three summer squash. They came from a small bed of plants sown in early August, plants that produced double handfuls of yellow crooknecks in late September, enough for the family with extra to give away. A hard frost hit that early October night, and by mid-morning the huge spiny leaves lay wilted on the ground, the dark green of cooked spinach. Small yellow finger-length fruits leaked from ice-ruptured cells.

The same freeze took out most of our tomatoes as well. Yes, we saw it coming and could probably have saved the plants with row covers, but I am not inclined toward such efforts. I prefer to garden with the seasons, letting the first hard frost bring an end to tender crops.

Late-summer plantings of tender vegetables are a gamble, but the odds of success seem to be increasing; some years you can get away with it. New England's climate is changing, and the hallmark of that change is unpredictability.

Vegetable crops can be sorted into four hardiness groups: very tender, tender, half-hardy, and hardy. In addition to summer squash and most tomato varieties, very tender vegetables, those likely to be killed by even a light frost, include cucumbers, melons, eggplants, and peppers. Some may be severely damaged when night temperatures suddenly dip below 40 degrees Fahrenheit but stay above freezing, a response called chilling injury.

Tender crops—including beans, corn, winter squash, and tomato varieties that originate from cooler climates—are not frost tolerant but can handle cool night temperatures. It may still make sense, however, to pull them up in late summer as their productivity wanes and replace them with fast-growing hardy crops such as broccoli or edible-pod peas.

Half-hardy vegetables—those that can take a light frost (but not a hard freeze)—include beets, carrots, cauliflower, potatoes, and lettuce. The truly hardy crops, those that will withstand a hard frost, include broccoli, cabbage, peas, onions, radishes, turnips, and spinach. Together, these two groups are the mainstay of the spring and fall gardens.

Begin the garden year by sowing peas as soon as the soil can be worked. The exact date will vary from southern to northern New England, from coast to inland uplands, and from year to year, depending on temperature and the combination of snowmelt and spring rains. I like to wait until the weather settles somewhat, and I typically get my peas in the ground in the first week of May. Many of my gardening friends beat me by at least two weeks, but some years, when the spring turns wet and chilly in late April, the peas in those earliest sowings never germinate.

The rest of the hardy and half-hardy crops are planted as spring advances, some direct sown, others, such as broccoli and cabbage, transplanted in early May as seedlings that were started indoors in early April or purchased from local garden centers.

Tender and very tender crops should not be planted until soil temperatures are consistently above 60 degrees F. I place a soil thermometer in one of the garden beds and hold off on planting these crops until the temperature registers 60 degrees for several consecutive days. This is the hardest waiting period, often extending well into June, but experience has shown me that jumping the gun leads to poor or no germination for direct-sown crops and poor growth of transplants.

I typically transplant cucurbits—including cucumbers, melons, and squashes (both summer and winter)—as seedlings. I have been successful with direct-sowing summer squash in early August for fall harvest, keeping the young plants under a row cover to protect them from slug damage. The row cover should be removed when the plants start flowering.

Use the above information as a guide, but remember that these are only guidelines and that no two gardens are alike. New lessons are learned every year as you fine-tune your sense of place.

## Rotating Families through the Garden

Whether you're cultivating a hundred acres or a handful of raised beds, you should rotate crops from year to year so that no two vegetable crops of the same family are growing in the same soil two years in a row. Why? Because this practice minimizes the damage caused by insects and plant pathogens that overwinter in the soil. Insect pests and plant diseases that plague tomatoes are also problems for the other nightshades. All cucurbits suffer from the same pests and diseases, and so forth. Crop rotation is a vital management strategy for the gardener who chooses not to use pesticides.

To accomplish this feat of planning, you need to be able to place any vegetable crop into one of six "families."

The brassica family (named after the botanical family to which they all belong, the Brassicaceae) includes broccoli, cauliflower, cabbage, Brussels sprouts, and kohlrabi. If these vegetables do not seem all that closely related, it is because botanists work mainly with reproductive structures when grouping plant species into families. If you were to let all these crops flower in the garden at the same time, you would see the family relationships. We typically miss the flowering stages of these plants, harvesting them for their leaves, stems, or flower buds before they bloom.

Chard in late July. (Photo courtesy Charles Heaven)

Tomato, pepper, potato, eggplant, and tomatillo belong to the nightshade family, technically the Solanaceae, a family that also includes belladona, the deadly nightshade, and petunia. Again, the family connections become more obvious if you let a potato vine flower and fruit.

The Cucurbitaceae, or "cucurbits," include cucumbers, squash (summer and winter), pumpkins, melons, and gourds. Several superficially different cucurbits, including acorn squash, field pumpkins, yellow summer squash, and zucchini, are all the same species, *Cucurbita pepo*, their fruits being very similar.

Peas and beans are legumes, members of the Fabaceae, a family once called Leguminoseae. These are the plant species famous for their ability to fix atmospheric nitrogen into nodules on their roots. Peanuts, alfalfa, and even a tree, the mimosa, belong to this family.

Onions, chives, garlic, and leeks are common vegetable garden members of the Amaryllidaceae family. Other members of this family are cultivated as ornamentals.

Finally, the catch-all group, which we'll call the "Otheraceaea," is a mixed bag of root crops such as carrots and turnips, and leafy vegetables such as spinach. Corn belongs to this group, too.

If you grew tomatoes in the bed by the gate last year, don't grow tomatoes in that bed this year—and don't grow potatoes, peppers, eggplants, or tomatillos there either. It's that simple—or that complicated if you don't remember what was growing where last year.

Ideally, we'd put our beds on a four-year rotation schedule, with no member of the same family growing in the same soil for the next three years. Most of us don't have that much room, however. If a frog had wings. . . .

Another way to put your knowledge of plant families to good use is by growing members of the same family together, taking advantage of their similar management needs. While root crops and leafy vegetables (the "Others") do not constitute a botanical family, they do have similar growing needs and thus can be grouped together in the garden. These groupings also make the planning for crop rotation much easier.

## Leaving Room for Annuals in the Vegetable Garden

No life form is more important to the vegetable gardener's success than pollinating insects such as the small and solitary native bee and the tireless bumblebee. If these creatures are not there when we need them, the ovaries of winter squash wither on the vine, while only a fraction of the potential tomato harvest is realized. Providing essential pollen and nectar sources, as well as nesting sites, will enable bumblebees to build colony strength in early spring and will keep solitary bees close at hand in the garden.

Why not plant a little pollinator insurance, a few annual flowers among the vegetables? The idea is appealing, a vision of orange and yellow calendula blooms poking through the dark green leaves of winter squash, bees and beetles swarming over the blossoms of both. But would it really work that way? Would the same pollinators that visit the calendula also service the squash? Would another species of annual flowering plant be a better choice?

These are not well-researched questions, and many authorities suggest that gardeners concentrate on perennials for attracting native pollinators. There are a few annuals, however, that are known to attract pollinators, particularly the native bees.

In general, native bees prefer annual flowers in shades of purple, blue, and yellow. The lilac flowers of verbena *(Verbena bonariensis)*, for example, attract not only native bees but also butterflies, while the deep violet blue blooms of heliotrope *(Heliotropium arborescens)*, with their strong vanilla fragrance, are always covered with bees in search of nectar.

Some bee-attracting annuals also provide leaves and/or flowers for human consumption and thus are excellent candidates for integration into the vegetable garden. As the purple flowers of anise hyssop *(Agastache foeniculum)*, an annual herb or tender perennial in New England, provide nectar for bees from June to August, the gardener can harvest the aromatic leaves for their sweet, licorice-mint flavor. Fresh or dried, they add flavor to salads, teas, and garnishes. And the hundreds of small blue flowers of borage *(Borago officinalis)*, a tall annual herb (18 to 30 inches high), do double duty, providing both nectar and pollen to foraging bees while adding a mild cucumber flavor to salads and garnishes.

Nasturtiums growing in pots become a moveable feast for native solitary bees.

Nasturtiums *(Tropaeolum majus)* are excellent container plants for attracting native bees to the vegetable garden. Every year we grow several pots of climbing nasturtiums, moving them about the garden, placing them among the vegetables in bloom.

Calendulas *(Calendula officinalis)* do make the cut, but only the single varieties. The gardener interested in attracting pollinators should avoid annuals with double flowers (varieties in which the pollen-bearing stamens have been replaced with petals), since the pollen production will be greatly reduced or eliminated entirely. As calendulas are self-sowing annuals, coming back from seed each year, their location in the garden is managed by weeding out the unwanted seedlings. This means a little more work, another reason to linger late in the garden at the end of the day, and it makes for delightful plant combinations that you would have never thought of yourself!

Finally, there is comfort in realizing that the yellow flowers of broccoli and other brassicas will bring native bees to the garden. This is great solace for those of us who experience bolting of these crops every spring. We can leave them be, along with a few radishes left in the ground to flower.

### A Suggested Crop-Rotation Schedule

Since vegetable crops can be divided into six groups, each subject to common diseases and herbivores and each with common management needs, it makes sense to divide your garden into six areas and rotate crops according to the following table. If your garden is too small to divide into six sections, divide it into as many sections as feasible and rotate crops so that none from the same group are grown in the same section two or more years in a row.

| Section A | Section B | Section C | Section D | Section E | Section F |
|---|---|---|---|---|---|
| Year 1 | | | | | |
| Brassicas | Tomatoes, Potatoes, Peppers, Eggplants, Tomatillos | Carrots, Beets, Parsnips, Spinach, Lettuce | Onions, Leeks, Garlic | Beans, Peas | Cucumbers, Squash, Melons |
| Year 2 | | | | | |
| Cucumbers, Squash, Melons | Brassicas | Tomatoes, Potatoes, Peppers, Eggplants, Tomatillos | Carrots, Beets, Parsnips, Spinach, Lettuce | Onions, Leeks, Garlic | Beans, Peas |
| Year 3 | | | | | |
| Beans, Peas | Cucumbers, Squash, Melons | Brassicas | Tomatoes, Potatoes, Peppers, Eggplants, Tomatillos | Carrots, Beets, Parsnips, Spinach, Lettuce | Onions, Leeks, Garlic |
| Year 4 | | | | | |
| Onions, Leeks, Garlic | Beans, Peas | Cucumbers, Squash, Melons | Brassicas | Tomatoes, Potatoes, Peppers, Eggplants, Tomatillos | Carrots, Beets, Parsnips, Spinach, Lettuce |
| Year 5 | | | | | |
| Carrots, Beets, Parsnips, Spinach, Lettuce | Onions, Leeks, Garlic | Beans, Peas | Cucumbers, Squash, Melons | Brassicas | Tomatoes, Potatoes, Peppers, Eggplants, Tomatillos |
| Year 6 | | | | | |
| Tomatoes, Potatoes, Peppers, Eggplants, Tomatillos | Carrots, Beets, Parsnips, Spinach, Lettuce | Onions, Leeks, Garlic | Beans, Peas | Cucumbers, Squash, Melons | Brassicas |

## The Humble Bumblebee *by Reeser Manley*

One out of every three bites of food you eat depends on insect pollination. In the garden, you depend on pollinators, mainly bees, for success with tomatoes, peppers, eggplants, summer and winter squash, cucumbers and melons, peas and beans, strawberries, blueberries, and other small fruits.

I can count on one hand the number of honeybees that we see in Marjorie's garden, while native bee species, mason bees and various bumblebees, are abundant. In summer the catnip stems sway from dawn to dusk as bumblebees dance among the flowers. At first light we find bumblebees sleeping on sunflower heads where they spent the chilly night dusted with golden pollen. I gently stroke their hairy bodies and think them dead, then watch them come to life in the warmth of the first sunbeam.

Bumblebees live in underground colonies during the summer, the number of bees per colony being far less than the population size of a honeybee hive. In winter, new bumblebee queens hibernate underground alone to start new colonies come spring.

Providing homes for bumblebees is a matter of keeping a portion of your garden out of cultivation. While there are several styles of bumblebee nest boxes available commercially, they are rarely used if there is an old mouse or vole hole nearby, or an underground cavity in a clump of grass. If you want to attract bumblebees, be less tidy in the garden. In Marjorie's garden where the catnip grows, an old tree stump slowly rots, each year sinking a little deeper into the earth, the holes left by decayed roots providing perfect nests for the bumblebees. They live where they work, a perfect arrangement that reminds me of my graduate school days.

As you plan for the upcoming season in the garden, here are some steps you can take to ensure that these all-important pollinators will be there with you:

- Leave part of the garden wild. About a hundred feet from the vegetable garden, we leave a patch of grass and wildflowers for the insects. We never mow this patch, and are rewarded with a season-long supply of nectar and pollen for the bees, including violets and dandelions in spring, goldenrod and Queen Anne's lace (wild carrot) in summer, and asters in autumn. In addition to the pollinators, hoverflies and other beneficial insects thrive in this spot, completing their life cycles undisturbed while frequently visiting the vegetable garden.

In Theresa Guethler's garden (Bucksport, Maine), goldenrod grows wild in August along the garden fence. There is no shortage of pollinators for the vegetables flowering in the garden. Theresa sculpted the metal frog on the fence post.

- Plant for the bees. A large patch of catmint (*Nepeta*) in the perennial bed provides bumblebees with a nectar source that lasts for weeks and doubles as a bumblebee playground, the flower scapes swaying to and fro under their weight. Unlike honeybees, bumblebees do not think twice about leaving one nectar source for another. I have watched the same bumblebee move from catmint to allium to summer squash, all in the course of a few minutes. Honeybees tend to forage monocultures, large fields of a single species, and thus are not reliable small garden pollinators.
- Weed selectively. What a gardener might consider weed, a bumblebee considers food, either nectar or pollen. Volunteer calendulas and other flowering weeds are left to flower at the feet of pea plants and in the sunny spaces between squash leaves, attracting a variety of native bees to pollinate the garden plants.
- Provide nest sites for the bumblebees. In our garden, an old stump slowly rots at the edge of the catmint patch mentioned above. The bumblebees took to this stump, building an underground nest beneath it. I often sit near the stump and watch bumblebees disappear down a hole in the ground. Bumblebees are finicky about their nest sites and do not always appreciate the gardener's efforts to help, although I still want to try burying an old teapot, leaving the spout at ground level as an entrance hole. It is better to leave natural nesting sites, like the old stump or an abandoned mouse hole, for them to use. In other words, don't be too tidy around the garden—what looks like a pile of sticks to you might cover the entrance to a bumblebee nest.
- Do not use any toxic chemicals. Period.

We value the bumblebees that share our garden. Every tomato we harvest will likely have been pollinated by one. Tomatoes are self-pollinating, but only after the bumblebee shakes the pollen from the anther by a unique technique called "buzz pollination in which the bee grasps the flower and moves its flight muscles rapidly, causing the anther to vibrate and release the pollen.

Bumblebees know how to enjoy life.

An old stump left rotting in the garden can serve as a bumblebee nest for years.

# Chapter 5

# The Garden in March

*"Now is that sweet unwritten moment when all things are possible, are just begun."*

—Donald Culross Peattie, *An Almanac for Moderns*, 1935

***Just knowing that February is gone*** gives me hope. By the first of March I have had enough of shoveling snow, sanding icy steps, entering and leaving the schoolhouse in the dark, making treacherous pre-dawn treks down slushy county roads. I know better than to think winter is over, but a day will come in early March in which the air carries a certain quickening softness and I whisper to myself, "The back of winter is broken."

Not that February is entirely dismal. I remember a flock of redpolls that came for an extended visit one February. A single redpoll showed up at our porch feeders early in the month, and for several days he dined alone. (A splash of red on the heavily streaked breast identified "it" as a "he.") And then the rest of the flock caught up with him.

Suddenly there were fifty redpolls dining at the porch feeders, a sign that winter in the far north must have been truly severe. These little birds seldom winter as far south as Ellsworth, Maine, unless driven there by lack of food in the woodland edges and weedy fields of northern Canada.

Canada's loss was our gain, for redpolls are among the most colorful and tamest of winter songbirds. They lined the porch rails, pecking at black oil sunflower seeds, their red forehead feathers ruffled by winter winds, oblivious to the dogs and allowing us to approach within arm's reach. After a short period of feeding, they departed en masse to nearby branches, only to reappear at the feeders a while later.

I wondered about this behavior and checked the bird books, discovering that each redpoll has a pouch within its throat where it can store food for up to several hours, allowing it to feed in a frenzy in the open and then digest the food over a long period in a sheltered spot, sequestered from predators. Such are the adaptations that must accompany life in the far north.

These tiny, restless birds—just a bit larger than their cousins, the pine siskins and the goldfinches, all in the same genus—gave February a facelift, and we hated to see them leave, wondering how many winters would pass before they visited us again.

*Facing page:* Serviceberry in the March garden. (See page 105 for a discussion of shadblow serviceberry, *Amelanchier canadensis.*)

Marjorie and I also enjoy our February morning walks down the snow-covered dirt road with the dogs, watching Dixie, our mostly black lab with a touch of German shepherd, chomp off mouthfuls of snow from roadside banks while Reilly, the Brittany, plows into the woods, following her nose. They converge in the middle of the road ahead, snapping playfully and barking at each other, Dixie's muzzle covered to the ears in snow, Reilly's feathered legs caked with ice balls.

But I am always ready for March, for daytime highs steadily pushing toward 50 degrees, the hills of snow outside my windows gradually shrinking to puddles. I want to see the green tips of winter rye rising through the last few inches of snow covering the garden's beds.

March brings visions of bare soil warming in sunlight, the needle on the soil thermometer slowly rising. Soon it will be time to sow pea seeds.

In March the soil awakens from its long winter's sleep with a slow but sure increase in the number and variety of micro- and macroscopic organisms, which, along with plant roots, make up the soil ecosystem. Earthworms rise into the root zone. The gardener spreads composted goat manure over the surface of the soil, feeding the biotic explosion.

The seed orders have been mailed and should be arriving soon. By the end of March the germination table will be covered with flats of seedlings, fluorescent tubes just inches above their leaves. Just the early-season crops, mind you, and only those such as onions and leeks that need several weeks to reach transplant size. Paper packets sporting colorful drawings of bean pods, trellised cucumbers, and bright red tomatoes lie in a nearby box, their contents, dreams of the summer to come, still dormant.

Phenological events in the garden, such as the opening of serviceberry buds, can be accurately predicted from records of past observations linked to growing degree days.

## Monitoring Growing Degree Days in the Garden

Over time, gardeners learn the sequence of phenological events such as flowering and fruiting in their garden plants, but the exact date for each such event cannot be predicted by the calendar. Plant development—at least for woody plants—is controlled largely by the number of accumulated *growing degree days* (GDDs).

You can track growing degree days in your garden and, over time, accurately predict developmental changes in woody plants. All you need is a garden thermometer that measures daily high and low air temperatures, or you can use the temperatures reported in the newspaper or online. There are several variations of GDD methodology; the method I use is one I learned from researchers at University of Massachusetts. This is the method that nursery industry professionals in Massachusetts have been using to scout for herbivores in their Integrated Pest Management System since I was working there over 12 years ago.

To calculate GDDs for any day, begin by averaging the day's high and low temperatures. A low temperature below 50° F is recorded as 50; a high temperature greater than 86° F is recorded as 86. (The assumption here is that 50 degrees is too cold and 86 degrees too hot for most plants to grow.) From the resultant average you subtract 50, and the result is the number of GDDs for that day. If the average is less than 50°, there are no GDDs for that day—there are no negative GDDs, because plants cannot reverse developmental changes.

As an example, consider an early April day in which the high temperature was 54° and the low 40°. Setting the low to 50, the average would be 52°. Subtracting 50 gives a total of 2 GDDs for the day.

In addition to governing stages in the life cycles of garden plants, accumulating GDDs also control the emergence and development of insects that feed on those plants. Thus the hatching of viburnum leaf beetle eggs is synchronized with viburnum leaf development.

By tracking GDDs in your garden, you will develop a keen sense of when to expect woody plants to break

Flowers of the mapleleaf viburnum and the tiny insects that pollinate them appear together in spring thanks to their synchronized responses to accumulating growing degree days.

dormancy and when they should be flowering and fruiting. At the same time, you can predict when certain insects, friend and foe, should be around. For example, silver maple reaches full bloom when 42 GDDs have accumulated, while PJM rhododendron does not reach full bloom until 147 GDDs accumulate. First hatch for the viburnum leaf beetle occurs at 210 GDDs, and the Japanese beetle adult does not emerge until 970 GDDs. Begin monitoring for specific herbivores (and the effectiveness of their predators) when the accumulated GDDs tell you they should be active.

At the first of March, few if any growing degree days have accumulated, but in June, with daytime highs in the 80s and lows around 60, GDDs accumulate by leaps and bounds. Tracking these changes every year makes a splendid activity for gardeners and their children.

## Growing Your Own Vegetable Transplants

For gardeners interested in growing transplants of heirloom vegetables—those flavor-rich varieties found only in specialty seed catalogs—and for those who believe that home-grown transplants of any ilk are far superior to nursery-grown, the gardening season starts in March. There may be three feet of snow outside, but on a table somewhere in the house (or in a greenhouse if you're lucky) will be an array of soil-filled plastic trays under fluorescent lights, with only 2 inches of space between the bulbs and the damp soil.

In the schoolhouse where I teach, the lights are hung from chains on frames made of PVC pipe. We raise the lights as the seedlings grow, maintaining a 2-inch separation between lights and developing leaves.

So begins three months of indoor gardening—watering, fertilizing, transplanting, adjusting lights, moving trays of plants to and from the outdoors—until finally the sturdy little transplants are set out into the garden beds. When asked why you are going to all this effort when the garden centers will soon be filled with ready-to-plant seedlings, you give the only honest answer: Either start gardening indoors in March or go insane.

*Note: I am not a big fan of using row covers and cold frames as season extenders, because there has been no research that I can find on the impact of season extenders on soil life, and also because I worry about the disposal of plastic row covers in communities without recycling. I do use cold frames to harden seedlings before transplanting them, however, as discussed in Chapter 6.*

### Scheduling

Growing your own transplants begins with backward planning. Estimate the last likely frost date for your garden site and then schedule the seed sowing date for each crop based on the pace of seed germination, the time required for seedling development, and, for summer crops that require warm soil temperatures, the date on which you will actually plant.

For our garden in Ellsworth, I assume May 31 as the zero frost date, the date by which there is little chance for a frost. With this date in mind, I sow seeds according to the table below (typically on the weekend closest to the date shown). The sowing dates in this table take into account the tolerance of some crops for a light frost after planting and the requirement of other crops for warm soil temperatures. Let's look at a couple of specific examples.

Seeds of onions and leeks need between 9 and 10 weeks after sowing to reach transplant size. Adding another week for hardening brings the total time between sowing and earliest planting to 10 or 11 weeks. Started on March 1, the transplants can go in the ground in the last week of May, a little before the zero frost date of May 31. Properly hardened, they can tolerate a light frost after transplanting.

Like onions and leeks, peppers also need between 9 and 10 weeks after sowing to reach transplant size. The week of hardening brings the total time between sowing and earliest planting to 10 or 11 weeks, the same as for onions and leeks. Peppers, however, can be damaged by chilling temperatures (below 40° F) and they need a soil temperature above 65° for optimum growth. A May 1 sowing date results in transplanting to the garden in early July. This is why gardeners in northern New England focus on pepper varieties that produce fruits in a relatively short period of time!

Table 5.1
Sowing Schedule for Growing Vegetable Transplants from Seed

Ellsworth, Maine, is in USDA Hardiness Zone 5. Gardeners in Zone 3 should add two weeks to the earliest sowing date, those in Zone 4 should add one week. In Zones 6 and 7, subtract one and two weeks, respectively.

| Crop | Earliest Sowing Date | Time from Seeding to Germination (days) | Optimum Soil Temperature (°F) for Germination | Time from Germination to Transplanting (weeks) |
|---|---|---|---|---|
| Basil | Apr 26 | 10 | 65 | 5-7 |
| Broccoli | Mar 26 | 7-10 | 50-85 | 5-7 |
| Cabbage | Mar 12 | 4-10 | 50-85 | 5-7 |
| Celery and Celeriac | Mar 30 | 9-21 | 55-70 | 10-12 |
| Cauliflower | Mar 26 | 7-10 | 50-85 | 5-7 |
| Cucumber | May 15 | 6-10 | 65-85 | 4 |
| Eggplant | May 1 | 6-10 | 65-85 | 6-9 |
| Kale | Apr 1 | 4-10 | 50-85 | 5-7 |
| Kohlrabi | Mar 12 | 4-10 | 50-85 | 5-7 |
| Lettuce | Mar 19 | 6-8 | 50-65 | 3-5 |
| Melons | May 15 | 6-8 | 65-85 | 3-4 |
| Onions and Leeks | Mar 1 | 7-10 | 55-75 | 8 |
| Parsley | Mar 15 | 12-28 | 50-75 | 8 |
| Peppers | May 1 | 9-14 | 65-85 | 6-8 |
| Pumpkins | May 15 | 4-6 | 65-85 | 3-4 |
| Squash | May 15 | 4-6 | 65-85 | 3-4 |
| Swiss Chard | Mar 26 | 7-14 | 55-75 | 5-6 |
| Tomatoes | May 1 | 6-12 | 65-85 | 5-7 |

Despite the incipient insanity, don't start too early. You will end up holding garden-ready plants under the lights, waiting for warmer weather, and the end result will be pot-bound, leggy plants with reduced vigor in the garden.

## Sowing Seeds

Seeds can be sown in any 2- to 3-inch-deep container with drainage holes. I prefer to use small plastic trays sold at garden supply stores. They are typically 5 inches wide by 7 inches long, and six of them fit snuggly in a 10-inch by 20-inch plastic tray (called a "10-20 flat" by growers) without drainage holes. This system allows you to carry six seed trays at a time and to water them from below simply by lifting one seed tray and pouring water into the flat to a half-inch depth.

With careful handling and storage, the seed trays and flats will last several years. They are easily cleaned after each use with soap and water, then sterilized with a 10% solution of household bleach. This sterilization step helps prevent seedling diseases.

Seeds planted in cold, wet soils tend to germinate slowly if at all. To maintain soil temperatures in the optimum range (see the table), invest in a heating mat or cable to place under the flats. Heating mats and soil thermometers are available from mail-order garden supply houses or from your local garden center.

Fill each seed tray with a sterile growing mix that includes a starter nutrient charge. I use either Fafard #2 potting soil or Pro Mix. Wet the mix ahead of use to the moisture content of a wrung-out sponge.

Sow seeds in rows running the length of the tray, planting the seeds at a depth equal to twice the seed's width. Typically I make three evenly spaced rows down the length of each 5-inch-wide tray, spacing the seeds within each row according to seed packet instructions.

After placing the seeds in each row, cover them to the required depth with a thin layer of fine-textured germinating mix such as Ready-Earth. Particles in the coarse growing mix can impede germination when used to cover small seed. After covering the seeds, water each tray with a gentle spray until the soil is saturated.

Label each seed tray and cover each flat with a loose layer of clear plastic (plastic wrap works well) to maintain uniform moisture in the seed trays. Once the seeds have germinated, remove the cover and the bottom heat.

## Growing Seedlings

Provide supplemental lighting as soon as the seedlings emerge; window light alone is too low in both duration and intensity. Standard fluorescent tubes are adequate, although some growers prefer using one cool white and one warm white bulb in each fixture. Keep the lights on for 14 hours each day, maintaining the tubes 2 to 4 inches above the growing seedlings.

Water the seed trays gently and thoroughly on sowing day, then as often as necessary to avoid excessive drying. Be careful, however, not to keep them too wet; let the soil surface dry between waterings. When you do water, use a half-strength solution of water-soluble fertilizer to provide essential nutrients.

Once the seedlings have germinated, watch for development of the "seed leaves," the first leaf-like structures produced by most seedlings. These seed leaves, typically rounded and fleshy, are not true leaves. They contain nutrients that were stored within the seed prior to germination, and their function is to provide early nourishment to the developing seedling. Wait until the seedlings have produced two sets of true leaves before transplanting them to individual pots.

I prefer to transplant into cell packs, a set of small plastic pots linked together in sheets that will fit the "10-20" flat. When the plants are ready to be transplanted into the garden, they can be lifted easily out of their individual cells.

When transplanting seedlings from the seed tray, lift and handle them gently by their leaves, never by their tender stems. A seedling can survive the loss of part of a leaf, but cannot survive a crushed stem.

While plants are growing in their pots or cell packs, keep them under the lights, watered and fertilized in the same manner as the seedling trays. Do not overwater! This is the most common cause of seedling diseases and can be avoided by allowing the surface of the soil to dry before watering. Use a fine spray when watering or else water from below to avoid damaging the tender young seedlings.

I prefer watering from below, especially when growing in cell packs. I place the cell pack strip in a "10-20" flat that does not have holes in the bottom, and I add about ½ inch of water to the flat. This can be done by lifting the corner of the strip to add the water. Typically, this much water will be absorbed by the pots within a few hours, eliminating the risk of overwatering. Do not add more

Basic materials for sowing seeds and growing seedlings indoors include (left to right) "10-20" flats for holding seed trays and cell packs, seed trays, and cell packs.

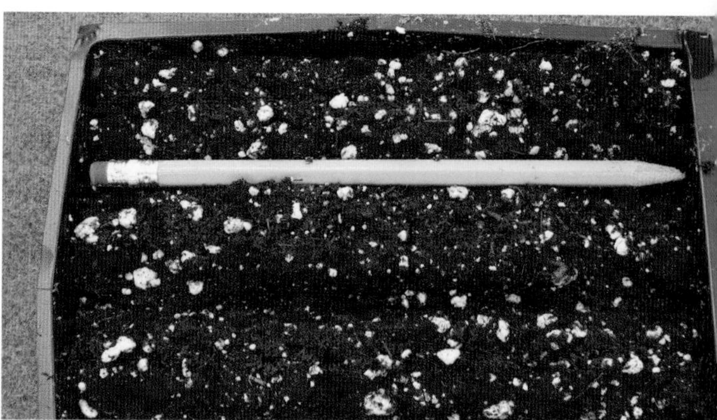

After filling a seed tray with germinating mix, make shallow furrows with a pencil, finger, tongue depressor, etc.

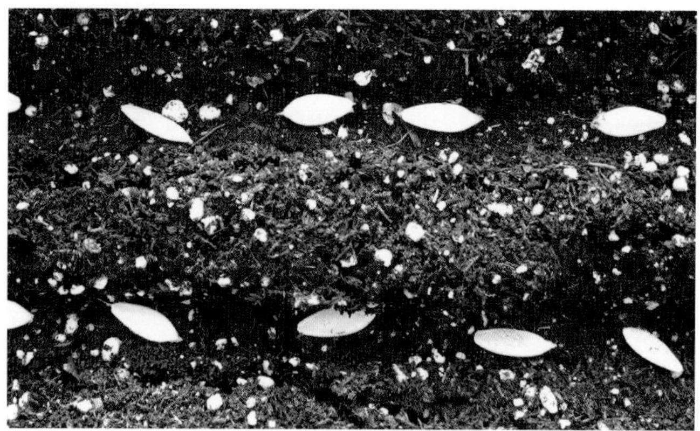

Seeds (such as these cucumber seeds) should be sown as evenly spaced as possible in each furrow and covered with a thin layer of fine-textured germinating mix.

After sowing, the seed trays should be covered to prevent drying out. A heating mat under the flat will maintain optimum soil temperature for uniform germination.

Remove the cover and turn off the heating mat as soon as seeds germinate.

As soon as seedlings emerge from the soil, the lights should be turned on for 14 hours each day.

## Sowing Schedule for Transplants of Flowering Annuals

Since you are already set up to grow vegetable transplants, why not use the same equipment and procedures to grow transplants of your favorite flowering annuals? Doing so will allow you to have blossoms much earlier than direct sowing in the garden. And, as with vegetables, growing your own allows you to decide which varieties will be growing in your garden, rather than delegating that decision to your local garden center.

The accompanying sowing schedules are set up for transplanting to the garden on June 1 in USDA Zone 5. Gardeners in Zone 3 should add two weeks to the earliest sowing date, those in Zone 4 should add one week. If you garden in Zone 6 or 7, subtract one or two weeks, respectively.

Some annuals require light for germination, others require dark, and some will germinate in either light or dark. To meet the dark conditions, simply cover the seed flat with aluminum foil until the seeds germinate, then remove the foil.

| Flowering Annual | Earliest Sowing Date | Time from Seeding to Germination (days) | Optimum Soil Temperature (°F) | Light Requirement |
|---|---|---|---|---|
| Ageratum | Apr 1 | 5-10 | 70 | Light |
| Alyssum | Apr 1 | 5-10 | 70 | Either |
| Aster | Apr 15 | 5-10 | 70 | Either |
| Balsam | Apr 15 | 5-10 | 70 | Either |
| Begonia | Mar 1 | 10-15 | 65-70 | Light |
| Browallia | Mar 1 | 15-20 | 70 | Either |
| Celosia | Apr 1 | 5-10 | 70 | Either |
| Centurea | Apr 15 | 5-10 | 65 | Dark |
| Coleus | Apr 1 | 5-10 | 65 | Light |
| Cosmos | May 1 | 5-10 | 70 | Either |
| Dahlia | Apr 1 | 5-10 | 70 | Either |
| Dianthus | Mar 15 | 5-10 | 70 | Either |
| Geranium | Mar 1 | 10-20 | 70 | Light |
| Impatiens | Mar 15 | 15-20 | 58-60 | Light |
| Larkspur | Mar 1 | 5-10 | 55 | Dark |
| Marigold | Apr 15 | 5-10 | 70 | Either |
| Nasturtium | May 1 | 7-14 | 65 | Light |
| Nicotiana | Apr 1 | 10-15 | 70 | Either |
| Pansy | Mar 1 | 5-10 | 50-55 | Dark |
| Petunia | Mar 15 | 7-10 | 75-80 | Light |
| Phlox | Apr 1 | 5-10 | 65 | Dark |
| Portulaca | Mar 15 | 5-10 | 65-70 | Light |
| Snapdragon | Mar 15 | 7-12 | 65 | Light |
| Stock | Mar 15 | 10-15 | 70 | Either |
| Verbena | Mar 15 | 15-20 | 65 | Dark |
| Vinca | Mar 1 | 10-15 | 70 | Either |
| Zinnia | Apr 15 | 5-10 | 70 | Either |

Table 5.2 Sowing Schedule for Growing Selected Flowering Annuals from Seed

## Sowing Schedule for Transplants of Herbaceous Perennials

Growing your own herbaceous perennials from seed, perhaps seed that you collected from the wild or from a friend's garden, is the ultimate challenge in seed propagation. Germination periods are longer, often measured in months, and some species require pre-germination treatments such as stratification (cold treatment). Still, growing your own may be the only way to come by some species or varieties. The following table, far from comprehensive, will give you an idea of what it takes to produce seedlings of a few perennials mentioned elsewhere in this book.

Sowing schedules are set up for transplanting to the garden on June 1 in USDA Zone 5. Gardeners in Zone 3 should add two weeks to the earliest sowing date, those in Zone 4 should add one week. If you garden in Zone 6 or 7, subtract one or two weeks, respectively.

Table 5.3 Sowing Schedule for Growing Selected Herbaceous Perennials from Seed

| Perennial Crop | Earliest Sowing Date | Time from Seeding to Germination (days) | Optimum Soil Temperature (°F) | Notes |
|---|---|---|---|---|
| Lady's Mantle *(Alchemilla sp.)* | Mar 15 | 21-28 | 60-70 | Lightly cover seeds. |
| Beard Tongue *(Penstemon sp.)* | Mar 15 | 14-35 | 55-65 | Germinate under lights. |
| Milkweed *(Asclepias incarnata)* | Mar 15 | 30-90 | 55-75 | Plant in peat pots, covering seeds lightly. Chill seeds in the fridge for 3 weeks, placing pots in plastic bags. Germinate under lights. |
| Campanula *(Campanula sp.)* | Mar 15 | 14-28 | 70 | Sow seeds on surface and provide light for germination. Keep moist. |
| Catmint *(Nepeta sp.)* | Mar 15 | 7-21 | 60-70 | Sow seeds on surface and do not cover. |
| Rudbeckia *(Rudbeckia fulgida)* | Mar 1 | Variable | 70-72 | Press seed into surface of mix—do not cover. Place seed tray in a plastic bag and store in refrigerator for 4 weeks, then place in warm spot (70–72 degrees) until seeds germinate. Once germinated, seedlings should be grown in a cool, bright location. |

water until the surface of the soil in the pots is dry. From my experience growing seedlings in my classroom, I have learned that watering seedlings in this fashion will keep them sufficiently watered over a weekend.

Before transplanting your seedlings to the garden, they must be hardened with a slow transition to outdoor conditions. Begin by setting them outside (temperature above 45 degrees) in partial shade for 1 or 2 hours per day, gradually increasing both the light and the length of exposure over a one-week period. Return them to the artificial-light regimen when not outdoors.

## A Moveable Feast

When the vegetable garden's beds, as outlined on the coming season's planting plan, are all spoken for, and you wish there was just a little more space for a pepper plant or two or a small patch of that new lettuce variety, think pots. Vegetables in pots are a moveable feast. The pot that this year grows lettuce in a shady corner of the perennial bed was used last summer to grow basil on the sunny porch steps.

Potted veggies are a feast for the eye as well as the table. We are not fond of eggplant's texture or flavor, but in 2012 we grew the variety 'Hansel' for its bright purple miniature fruits and lovely lavender flowers, both summer-long features of this slender, "little finger" eggplant. And who knows, perhaps we'll learn to enjoy eating eggplants.

Extend your garden to the porch steps with pots of vegetables and herbs. Shown here are 'Hansel' eggplants, peppers, cherry tomatoes, rosemary, and basil.

These two plants, a summer squash and a cucumber, both left over from spring planting, were almost tossed in the compost bin. Then I remembered one pot still not planted. I put these leftovers together, and this is the scene that greeted me on my stroll through the garden one summer morning, by no means the first time that the least-planned event in the garden has turned out to be one of the most beautiful.

| Vegetable | Container Size | Number of Plants |
|---|---|---|
| Broccoli | 2 gallons | 1 plant |
| Cucumber | 1 gallon | 1 plant |
| Eggplant | 5 gallons | 1 plant |
| Green Onions | 1 gallon | 3-5 plants |
| Leaf Lettuce | 1 gallon | 2 plants |
| Parsley | 1 gallon | 3 plants |
| Peppers | 5 gallons | 1 or 2 plants |
| Radish | 1 gallon | 3 plants |
| Spinach | 1 gallon | 2 plants |
| Summer Squash | 5 gallons | 1 plant |
| Tomato | 5 gallons | 1 plant |
| Turnip | 2 gallons | 2 plants |

Table 5.4 Recommended Container Sizes for Vegetables

Almost any container will work, provided it has drainage holes in the bottom and suitable capacity. Use the table on page 69 to determine the container size needed for various vegetables.

## Growing Medium

There was a time when container gardeners had to make their own growing media, mixing horticultural-grade vermiculite, peat moss, perlite, and various mineral nutrients to produce a soilless mixture that would provide physical support for the plant yet drain well (garden soil drains poorly in containers). The only other options were packaged soil mixes that were generally too tight, held too much water, and thus drowned plant roots. Thank goodness those days are over!

These days there are some excellent soilless media for container vegetable production. I use either ProMix or one of the Fafard mixes, adding composted cow manure or worm compost as a nutrient source (one part compost or castings for every four parts soilless mix) and wetting the mixture thoroughly before seeding or transplanting.

## Fertilizing

I like to give all of my containerized veggies a shot of liquid fish emulsion once a month during the growing season, beginning a week or so after potting. My thinking is that the frequent watering necessary for container production rapidly leaches nitrogen out of the pot, and it needs to be replaced regularly. Too much nitrogen can delay flowering and fruiting, so I use half the recommended amount of the fish emulsion concentrate unless the plants tell me there is a definite nitrogen deficiency (yellowing foliage or no new growth).

## Watering

Most importantly, avoid wetting the foliage of plants when watering, since moisture on the leaves encourages plant diseases. When to water will depend on the container size, plant size, and weather conditions, so you should check each pot every day. Use your index finger to see if the soil is dry about an inch below the surface; if so, water the pot slowly, letting the water seep into the soil, until you see some water emerging from the drainage holes at the bottom of the pot. This will ensure thorough watering.

I put our pots on large rocks or other surfaces that will allow excellent drainage of excess water. The drainage holes of pots placed directly on the ground can become plugged with soil or roots that grow out of the container and into the surrounding soil. Elevated pots are also less likely to attract slugs, which like to spend the day beneath objects resting on the ground.

Mulches can be placed on the surface of the container's soil mix to reduce water loss. Keep in mind, however, that you may be providing another hiding spot for slugs.

Container gardening is a rapidly growing avocation. Indeed, for many urban gardeners, containers are the only option. Pots filled with vegetables as well as flowering plants are becoming a common sight on the balconies and patios of apartment dwellers. And parents are discovering that container gardens are a great way to introduce children to the joys of gardening.

# *Stalking the Cultivated Asparagus*

In her book *Animal, Vegetable, Miracle,* the story of her family's move from the factory-farm pipeline of Tucson, Arizona, to a farm in southern Appalachia where they eat only from their own garden and those of local growers, Barbara Kingsolver writes about asparagus:

> *"From the outlaw harvests of my childhood, I've measured my years by asparagus. I sweated to dig it into countless yards I was destined to leave behind, for no better reason than that I believe in vegetables in general, and this one in particular. Gardeners are widely known and mocked for this sort of fanaticism. But other people fast or walk long pilgrimages to honor the spirit of what they believe makes our world whole and lovely. If we gardeners can, in the same spirit, put our heels to the shovel, kneel before a trench holding tender roots, and then wait three years for an edible incarnation of the spring equinox, who's to make the call between ridiculous and reverent?"*

I love asparagus, yet stop short of buying it at the grocers when I read the fine print on the rubber band that binds the spears: "Product of Peru." I know spears with that many food-miles behind them cannot compare in flavor with the locally grown, just-picked asparagus sold in early May at the local farmers' market. What I don't know is what may have been sprayed on that Peruvian asparagus.

Why should we want to eat asparagus every month of the year? It should be the first fresh taste of spring, a celebration of surviving winter and the start of another season in the garden, a taste soon to be displaced by so many others.

## Varieties

If you want to avoid the major fungal diseases of asparagus, rust and fusarium, your best variety choices are 'Jersey Knight' and 'Jersey Supreme,' both fruits of research conducted at Rutgers University. They yield almost twice as many spears as the old heirloom variety 'Mary Washington,' and both are male strains (asparagus plants are either male or female), making them more productive. As a Maine gardener, I lean toward Jersey Supreme because of its greater tolerance of cold springs.

Yes, for once I am straying from my passion for heirloom varieties, largely because asparagus is a perennial crop. Once planted, the same plants may remain productive for 30 or more years, a longevity that depends on disease resistance.

One-year-old asparagus crowns (plants) should be purchased in February or early March for planting in late March. You can purchase them from most vegetable seed companies and, possibly, from a local garden center. Twenty-five crowns will plant about 40 linear feet of bed.

## Planting

Hopefully by late March you have had the soil tested for pH. Asparagus does not grow well in acid soils, so you may need to add limestone to raise the pH to 7.

Begin by digging one or more trenches, each about 12 inches wide and 8 inches deep (a little deeper if your soil is sandy, a little shallower if the soil is heavy). Crowns should be spaced 18 inches apart in each trench with 5 feet between trenches, center to center.

Before planting the crowns, add a 2-inch layer of compost or aged manure to the bottom of each trench, along with a dusting of rock phosphate and wood ash. Then place the crowns in the bottom of the trench, spreading the roots out. Cover them with several inches of soil. As the plants grow, continue to add soil to cover the shoots until the trench is completely backfilled.

## Growing

During the first year, water the asparagus bed deeply once a week unless there has been a good rain. Once established, the plants are more drought-resistant and supplemental watering will be necessary only during extended dry periods.

One year after planting, and every year thereafter, you should fertilize the asparagus bed with an organic fertilizer such as fish meal, blood meal, cottonseed meal, soybean meal, fish emulsion, aged manure, or compost. The manure or compost can be spread an inch deep over the ground. Follow label instructions for any of the others.

## Harvesting

In the second year after planting, you will be able to harvest a few tender spears from your asparagus bed over two or three weeks. In following years the harvest can go into the third week of June before you stop cutting and allow the remaining spears to develop their fernlike shoots. Harvesting involves cutting or snapping off the spears at ground level, taking care not to leave above-ground stubs that can attract asparagus beetles.

# *Recommended Varieties of June-bearing Strawberries*

If you are planting your first strawberry bed this year or replacing a waning bed in its last season of production, March is the month to order the plants while supplies are plentiful. Consider growing at least two varieties, particularly if one is an early-ripening variety that will be more susceptible to late frost injury to the flowers, resulting in reduced yield in some years. And before placing your order, make sure that the plants you are buying are from "certified virus-free stock."

While all June-bearing strawberries are harvested over a relatively short period of time in early summer, the group can be divided into early-, mid-, and late-season varieties. By selecting two or three varieties from the following list, the gardener can extend the season over several weeks.

Disease resistance is an important factor in selection of strawberry varieties. Red stele, a root-rot fungus, is a common disease organism in many soils, particularly those with poor drainage, and resistant plants are the best

| Variety | Harvest Period | Berry Size | Flavor | Resistance |
|---|---|---|---|---|
| Wendy | Early Season | Large | Excellent | Red Stele |
| Annapolis | Early Season | Large | Good | Red Stele |
| Sable | | | | |
| Cavendish | Early Mid-Season | Large | Excellent | Red Stele, Verticillium Wilt |
| Allstar | Mid Season | Large | Good | Red Stele |
| Mesabi | Mid Season | Large | Excellent | Red Stele |
| Sparkle | Late Mid-Season | Medium | Excellent | Red Stele |
| Valley Sunset | Late Season | Large | Good | Leaf Diseases |

way to combat this problem. Non-resistant varieties can experience a total crop loss in wet years.

Verticillium wilt is another potentially devastating strawberry disease carried over in the soil from previous susceptible crops such as tomato and potato. The disease organism can persist in wet soils for several years.

For my taste, and for Marjorie's, flavor is the primary factor. We grow Sparkle, not the largest of berries but definitely one of the sweetest. The distinction between "Excellent" and "Good," when it comes to flavor, is sugar content.

## *March Pruning of Raspberries and Blueberries*

by Marjorie Peronto

Raspberries and blueberries need to be pruned every year to remain healthy and vigorous. Enjoy this task on a crisp, sunny day in March after the coldest days of winter have passed, but while the plants are still dormant.

### Pruning Raspberries

Raspberries do best when grown in a hedgerow that is no more than 2 feet wide. Although the crowns and roots of raspberry plants are perennial, each individual cane lives only two years. Every year, the plant sends up new canes from the base.

A cane in its first year of growth, called a *primocane,* does not produce fruit. In its second year it becomes a *floricane,* developing side shoots that flower and bear fruit. Once the cane has yielded a crop, it dies.

When you prune your dormant raspberry planting, the first step is to remove all the dead canes that fruited last year, the spent floricanes. These are easy to identify, as their bark is gray and peeling and they have multiple side shoots. Take these out at the base with a pair of loppers. These canes can be brittle and unwieldy, so wear long sleeves, thick gloves, and eye protection to keep from getting scraped or jabbed.

Once you've removed the spent floricanes, take out any additional canes that have sprouted up outside the 2-foot-wide hedgerow. If you don't do this, your planting will become a dense thicket the center canes of which are shaded, inaccessible, and disease-prone. Keep your rows narrow to assure good sun exposure and air circulation through the whole planting, which will give you a better yield.

Your third and last step is to thin the remaining canes within the row to three or four per linear foot. Take out weak, short and spindly canes and keep the strong, thick, taller ones. When warm temperatures arrive, their buds will break and give you lateral shoots that will bear this year's crop of berries.

To keep your fruit-bearing canes from falling over, set up a T-shaped trellis. Begin by installing a sturdy post at each end of the row. Attach a 3½-foot-wide cross arm to each post at a height of 4 feet. String a heavy-gauge wire along the length of the row on each side of the cross arms and attach the canes to these wires with baling twine. This will spread the canes out, creating a V effect, which allows for good sunlight penetration and air circulation. New canes that will provide next year's crop will grow up in the center of the row, and this year's fruit crop will be on the outside edges, easy to harvest.

One last note: "everbearing" red raspberries give you a late-season crop on the tips of the canes in their first year and another crop on the lower part of the same canes in the second summer. If you prune these in the same way, they will bear two crops per season: one in the summer on the second-year canes, and one in the fall on the first-year canes.

## Pruning Highbush Blueberries

We've grown several varieties of highbush blueberries in our garden for the last twelve years. They vary in mature height and breadth, but they all have the same growth pattern. Highbush blueberries send up sturdy canes from the crown and bear fruit on one-year-old lateral shoots growing on the upper portions of these canes, in the shrub canopy. The most productive canes tend to be between three and six years old.

Here is the ideal: your blueberry plant sends up one or two healthy new canes (also called suckers) each year. After six years, your shrub consists of six to twelve vigorous canes coming up from the base, none of which are more than six years old. In the seventh year, and from then on, you remove one or two of the oldest canes at the base, allowing vigorous new canes to replace them. You can tell which ones are the oldest, as they are thickest at the base, have gray bark, and are sometimes lichen-covered. As a cane ages beyond six years, its fruiting potential declines, and its fruiting shoots become short, weak, and spindly. This is the time to remove it, leaving a new cane to fill its place.

Once you've done this, move to finer pruning in the shrub canopy. Look for and keep the long, healthy shoots that developed last year. These shoots should contain both flower buds and vegetative buds. The flower buds are on the distal half of the shoot and have a plump, teardrop shape. Each of these buds will break in the spring and provide you with a cluster of six to eight flowers. The smaller, pointed buds farther down on the shoot will grow into vegetative shoots that will be next year's fruiting wood. Snip off any small, weak shoots that only have a couple of fruit buds and a couple of vegetative buds. In doing so, you may take out between 50 and 75% of the fruiting potential of the shrub. This seems severe, but it is best for the long-term health of the shrub. If you don't remove the weak-fruiting wood, the shrub will become too dense and prone to disease, and the fruits will be smaller and slower to ripen. By taking out the weaker shoots, you open up the canopy and allow sunlight to

Witch's broom is a common rust fungus of highbush blueberries wherever fir trees grow nearby.

penetrate to the center of the shrub. This is crucial for all fruiting plants, as it helps keep diseases to a minimum and promotes vigorous, healthy new growth each year.

### *A couple of notes*

Some highbush blueberry varieties are much less apt to produce new canes than others. In fact, one of my favorite varieties, 'Patriot,' has grown only five or six canes in the 12 years we've had it. In this case, I don't remove entire canes, as there are no new ones there to replace them. Instead, I work strictly in the canopy. If a branch attached to a cane is producing nothing but weak shoots, I remove it at its point of origin, leaving other branches that are producing stronger shoots. If I find branches that are producing both strong and weak shoots, the weak ones get taken off and the strong ones stay.

In Maine, and wherever fir trees abound, it is not uncommon for blueberry plants to develop dense broom-like clusters of twisted, spongy branches. This occurs when the plant has been infected by a rust fungus whose alternate host is balsam fir; it is a perennial, systemic fungus that is very difficult to eliminate.

These "witches' brooms" sap energy from the plant and decrease the plant's ability to flower and fruit. If you see a witch's broom developing on a branch, prune it out right away by cutting off the branch several inches below the broom, and get rid of it. Our garden is surrounded by fir trees that we are not willing to remove (the recommendation is no fir trees within 1,200 feet of your blueberry plants), so we keep a watchful eye for brooms. With careful and diligent pruning, we've been able to keep our blueberries fruiting prolifically for several years despite the persistent infection.

## Pruning the Old Apple Tree *by Marjorie Peronto*

You have an apple tree, it's been there for decades, and you can't remember the last time it was pruned. It is tall, with a thick canopy of branches growing every which way. The fruit it produces are abundant, scabby, dimpled, and small. Trees like this have personality and purpose. They give us fragrant spring flowers and cool summer shade; they are alive with insects and songbirds; and they provide sweet fruit to deer and smaller mammals.

When it comes to pruning, there are some things you can do to enhance the health of your tree. For safety's sake, get in there and remove the dead branches. This may have to be done in pieces, as they are most likely tangled in the canopy. (Wear good eye protection and rugged clothing!) You can remove deadwood at any time of year.

An old crabapple in need of pruning (top) and the same tree after pruning (above).

If you are hoping to renovate the tree so that it will produce market-size fruit, think about planting another tree or two instead. A young semi-dwarf tree will give you good-sized fruit within three years and will be far easier to maintain for production.

Getting back to your big old tree, the next steps can be done over a period of several years, always when the tree is dormant. If you are working on a smaller tree such as an old crabapple, however, this work can be accomplished in a single year. Once you've removed the deadwood, take a good look at the canopy from all angles. Identify the limbs you want to keep – those that have a slight upward angle and are not directly above one another. The candidates for removal are:

- vigorous vertical branches (these "water sprouts" congest the canopy and bear little to no fruit)
- branches growing in a downward direction
- damaged or diseased branches
- one of any two branches that are crossing and rubbing or are competing with one another for light.

The long-term goal is to thin out the tree canopy so that sunlight will penetrate to all the remaining branches. This will improve flowering and the size and quality of fruit and will reduce the likelihood of diseases. However, if you remove too many branches in one year (over one-third of the canopy), the tree will respond by producing an overabundance of water sprouts the following season, negating the work you've done. Don't shock the tree. Take your time.

When you do this kind of restorative pruning on an old, neglected tree, start with the branches at the top, where pruning will have the most benefit. Once you decongest the top, you'll find you have to remove less as you make your way down the canopy.

When you remove a limb or branch, take out the whole thing. Don't leave stubs or partial branches, because water sprouts will arise from these with gusto. Taking a branch out at its point of origin is called a thinning cut. Look for the ring of wrinkled bark where the branch joins the trunk or limb. Leave that ring, or branch collar, intact, and make your cut just outside it. Doing so will promote the fastest healing of the pruning wound.

Apple trees respond to heavy pruning by producing abundant water sprouts in the following growing season. These should be removed when first noticed.

Make any thinning cut just outside the branch collar (left). This allows the tree's natural healing process to seal off the wound properly. (bottom)

## Forcing Branches of Flowering Trees and Shrubs

By early March, gardeners are aching to be in the garden. Why not get a headstart on pruning trees and shrubs and, at the same time, bring a touch of early spring into the house? Branches of many woody plants can be forced into early flower or leaf in late winter, providing a glimpse of the season ahead. Trees and shrubs that lend themselves to forcing are described in the table on pages 77–78.

Take cuttings on a mild afternoon when the temperature is above freezing and the stems are soft and pliable. This will ease the transition from the cold outdoors to the warm indoors. As you prune to shape the tree or shrub—removing competing, crowding, and crossing branches—set aside cuttings of younger shoots at least 12 inches long with abundant flower buds, distinguished from leaf buds by their larger size and rounder shape. If in doubt, cut open a few buds to look for leaf or flower parts inside.

Select only branches that are well budded. Also, remember that many fruit trees, such as apples, crabapples, and cherries, bear flowers on short shoots called spurs.

Once inside with your collection of cuttings, fill both the sink and a bucket with warm (100° F) water. Many experts suggest adding a floral preservative (see page 78 for recipes) to the water to promote hydration and retard bacterial growth.

Holding the stems underwater in the sink, cut them at a sharp angle an inch or two above the original cut. Split the stem in half on larger branches (more than a half-inch in diameter) with an inch-long lengthwise cut that exposes more of the water-conducting tissue to the forcing solution. Making these stem cuts underwater prevents entry of oxygen that could block uptake of water.

Immediately place the stems in the bucket of warm water and set it aside in a cool place where the temperature stays between 60 and 65° F, then arrange the stems for display as the buds begin to show color. Alternatively, you can immediately create an arrangement and place it on display in a cool location for all to watch as the buds slowly swell and open. High temperatures speed up bud development but reduce the size, color, and keeping quality of the blooms. Keep the arrangement away from direct sunlight and away from any direct heat source, such as a heating vent or woodstove, that would dry out the buds. A cool location with bright indirect light is best.

Change the water and add new preservative each week. If the surrounding air is dry (often the case in rooms with a woodstove), mist the arrangement with water several times a day to keep the bud scales moist until flowers or leaves emerge. Once the buds open, a process that can take two to three weeks, the blooms should stay fresh for at least a week. Branches forced for their foliage will last even longer.

For a succession of forced blooms and foliage throughout the month of March, cut a variety of branches at various times. Treat yourself to an early spring!

The staminate (male) catkins on alder branches can be forced to bloom in March, often accompanied by last year's female catkins.

Table 5.5 Flowering Trees and Shrubs Suitable for Forcing (continued next page)

| Plant | Bloom or Leaf | Comments |
|---|---|---|
| Forsythia (*Forsythia* sp.) | yellow flowers | one to three weeks to force<br><br>Cut as early as mid-January in northern New England, late January in southern New England.. |
| Cornelian Cherry Dogwood (*Cornus mas*) | yellow flowers | two weeks to force<br><br>Cut as early as mid-January in northern New England, late January in southern New England. |
| Poplar (*Populus* sp.) | long lasting, drooping catkins | three weeks to force<br><br>Cut as early as mid-January in northern New England, late January in southern New England |
| Willow (*Salix* sp.), including Pussy Willow | catkins | |
| Red Maple (*Acer rubrum*) | pink to red flowers followed by leaves | two weeks or less to force<br><br>Cut in early February in northern New England, mid-February in southern New England. |
| Swamp Alder (*Alnus rugosa*) | long yellow male catkins | three weeks to force<br><br>Cut in early February in northern New England, mid-February in southern New England |
| Birch (Betula sp.) | long lasting catkins | two to four weeks to force<br><br>Cut in early February in northern New England, mid-February in southern New England. |
| Flowering Quince (*Chaenomeles* sp.) | red to orange flowers | four weeks to force<br><br>Cut in early February in northern New England, mid-February in southern New England.. |
| Cherries (*Prunus* sp.) | white to pink flowers on short spurs | two to four weeks to force<br><br>best cut in March |
| Rhododendrons and Azaleas (*Rhododendron* sp.) | many colors | four to six weeks to force<br><br>best cut in March |
| Hawthorns (*Crataegus* sp.) | white, pink, or red flowers | four to five weeks to force |
| Apples and Crabapples (*Malus* sp.) | white, pink, or red flowers on short spurs | two to four weeks to force<br><br>Double-flowering forms take longer to force but last longer. (*Continued*) |

Table 5.5 Flowering Trees and Shrubs Suitable for Forcing (*continued from previous page*)

| Plant | Bloom or Leaf | Comments |
|---|---|---|
| Oaks (*Quercus* sp.) | catkins | two to three weeks to force |
| Lilacs (*Syringa* sp.) | many colors | four to five weeks to force |
| Spirea (*Spiraea* sp.) | white flowers | four weeks to force |
| Serviceberries (*Amelanchier* sp.) | white flowers | two to four weeks to force |
| Horse Chestnut (*Aesculus hippocastanum*) | umbrella-shaped leaves and pyramids of flowers | four weeks to force<br>best cut in March |
| Beech (*Fagus americana*) | flowers in long drooping spikes | three weeks to force |
| Tamarack (*Larix laricina*) | green needle-like leaves | Branches have an oriental line, beautiful alone or in combination with other species. |
| Japanese Andromeda (*Pieris japonica*) | evergreen foliage with clusters of small while flowers | Flowers develop in less than two weeks. |
| Beauty Bush (*Kolkwitzia amabilis*) | small clusters of pink flowers | best cut in March<br>five weeks to force |
| Deutzia (*Deutzia gracilis*) | white flowers | five weeks to force |
| Mockorange (*Philadelphus coronarius*) | clusters of white fragrant blooms | best cut in March<br>four weeks to force |
| Spicebush (*Lindera benzoin*) | fragrant pinkish-white flowers | two weeks to force |

### Homemade Floral Preservatives

You can purchase floral preservatives or make your own. Here are a couple of recipes.

2 cups lemon-lime carbonated beverage
2 cups water
½ teaspoon household chlorine bleach

2 tablespoons fresh lemon juice or white vinegar
1 tablespoon sugar
½ teaspoon household chlorine bleach
mix with 1 quart water

## Get Those Native Bee Nest Boxes Ready

Native bee species such as the Maine blueberry bee (*Osmia atriventris)* are important pollinators of both wild and cultivated plants. Unlike non-native honeybees, which live together in hives, many native bee species are solitary. Each female bee needs her own nest site, and unlike ground-nesting bumblebees, native female solitary bees lay their eggs in hollow plant stems, such as raspberry canes, or in the holes made by other insects in dead trees and fence posts. Because the population of solitary bees is limited by lack of natural nesting sites, placing nesting boxes built from wooden blocks around the garden can increase the numbers of gentle bees at work there.

Building bee nest boxes can be a fun March garden project for the entire family. The boxes can then be placed in the garden in April. Solitary bees start searching for nest sites in May.

A single female may lay up to 35 eggs, with each tunnel of the box containing up to 16 egg cells. Within each cell, the female bee lays a single egg on a loaf-shaped provision of nectar and pollen. She then seals the cell with a thin partition of masticated plant material or mud. For the Maine blueberry bee, it takes up to 20 trips to blueberry flowers to complete one cell.

The eggs hatch into larvae (grubs) that feed on the nectar-pollen provision. They then go through a nonfeeding pupal stage. By late fall, they have become adult bees that remain dormant through the winter, emerging the following spring.

Solitary bee nest boxes are easy to make. Adults and older children can do the sawing and drilling while the younger children personalize each box with a drawing done in water-based paint or markers.

### Materials

- Pine or spruce 2 x 6 cut into 5- to 6-inch lengths
- Metal ¾-inch strapping tape (also called plumber's tape) cut into 3-inch pieces
- Screws for attaching the plumber's tape to the back of the box
- Nails to attach boxes to stakes
- Drill with 5/16-inch and 7/16-inch drill bits
- Saw
- Water-based paints or markers

Native bee nest boxes in the garden—like this one made by Theresa Guethler of Bucksport, Maine—help ensure that pollinators will be there when you need them.

### Construction

Drill 12 to 14 holes in the front of each block (see photo). Make half of the holes 5/16-inch in diameter, the other half 7/16-inch, a mix of sizes that will provide nesting sites for more than one species of solitary bee.

Each hole should be about 5 inches deep. Adult female bees will not nest in tunnels that are open at both ends, so be careful not to drill completely through the block.

Screw the piece of plumber's tape 1-inch from the top on the center of the back of the block. The tape should extend 2 inches above the top of the wooden bee nesting block. Take care not to screw through a tunnel!

Let the children have fun decorating the sides of the box using water-based paint or markers.

### Placement in the Garden

Mount the bee nest 3 feet from the ground on a stake or tree trunk by nailing through the exposed top end of the metal tape. Bees prefer boxes that face the morning sun. Angle the front slightly downward to avoid flooding by rain.

Old Man's Beard, a common lichen found hanging from tree branches, is an indicator of pollution-free air.

## The First Green of Spring: Lichens in the Garden

I recall a day in my sixtieth year when I sat in my doctor's examination room waiting for my annual physical to commence. I shivered in my skivvies and tried to shake off the memory of an old *New Yorker* cartoon in which a patient sitting on the exam table says to the doctor, "You're going to keep looking until you find something wrong, aren't you?" Something like that.

I had been worrying about a couple of mole-like growths, one at my left temple and the other at the base of my throat, that seemed to be slowly enlarging and turning darker. Their existence was bothering me more than the cranky knee, the aching shoulder, and the acid reflux that has increased exponentially since freshman physics took over both ends of every teaching day.

Imagine my relief when the doctor pronounced these moles to be harmless, giving them a long technical name, and my further delight when he added, "They're like lichens on an old tree."

This is as it should be, I thought. I'm aging like an old tree, taking on passengers in the process.

What are lichens? In the strictest sense, they are not plants at all, but two organisms – a fungus and algae—living intimately together in a symbiotic relationship. As one of my students eloquently described this arrangement, "The photosynthetic algae provide the food, the fungus provides a place to hang out."

I've developed a fondness for lichens since moving to Maine. Along with mosses, they are the first green of spring, emerging from the melting snow in early March looking as if they have spent the winter in active growth. In the middle of winter I have found clumps of bright green lichens attached to slender, snow-covered hardwood branches, apparently photosynthesizing at below-freezing temperatures while the tree sleeps.

I spend winter hours exploring granite surfaces exposed by the sun's warmth, constantly amazed at the diversity of lichens growing there: crusty lichens that cover sections of rock in intricate patterns of gray, green, and orange; colonies of brown leafy lichens that trail down the sides of a rock; pillow-like masses of silver-gray lichens that branch like miniature shrubs. All seemingly active and growing, despite the cold.

Lichens also grow on the trunks and branches of the garden's trees, and I am often asked if they harm the tree,

Wherever lichens appear in the garden—on rocks, garden benches, or in trees—they should be embraced as signs of a healthy environment, of a garden in tune with nature.

Lichens on birch bark.

if they are parasitic, or if they mark a diseased or dying tree, all misconceptions arising from the abundance of lichens on dead branches or declining trees. In fact, lichens increase their growth rate in full sun and are thus more abundant where lack of foliage admits more light. They do the living tree no harm.

The presence of some lichens in the garden, whether growing on trees or rocks, is an indicator of pollution-free, moist air. The shrubby and leafy lichens are the "canaries in the coal mine"—they will not grow where the air is polluted—while the crusty lichens, the ones that cover the surface of rocks and pavement, are more tolerant of sulfur dioxide and other pollutants.

Old Man's Beard (*Usnea* sp.) is a reliable indicator of a pollution-free garden. This gray-green lichen hangs in long tresses from the branches of coastal spruces and deciduous trees, reminding me of Spanish moss, an epiphyte related to pineapples that festoons the knobby horizontal branches of old live oaks growing in Charleston, South Carolina, an old stomping ground.

The crusty lichens that cover granite boulders are pioneers in soil genesis, secreting organic acids that weather the granite surfaces, eventually forming a pocket of mineral soil deep enough for grass. All the while, moisture trapped by the lichen at the surface of the rock cycles through freezes and thaws, slowly expanding tiny cracks in the rock, making way for the roots of a tree or shrub seedling. It is part of the education of a gardener to sit atop a granite outcrop and survey these stages of soil formation.

Lichens hang out on rocks or the old headstones of cemeteries. And they hang from the branches of trees. They are remarkably tough, enduring exposure to freezing temperatures in winter and extreme desiccation during summer droughts.

The gardener cannot cultivate lichens; we can only make room for them. They are an important part of the rock garden and xeriscaping because they are not dependent on a constant supply of moisture. Their ability to survive alternating periods of drought and abundant moisture give them an advantage in colonizing stressful environments.

Moss and lichens after snowmelt in the March garden.

# The New England Garden in March, Zone by Zone

For most of New England, March is the month to start indoor production of garden transplants. Look for the date to start seeds of brassicas, leafy greens, onions, leeks, and other vegetable crops, as well as some flowering annuals and perennials. March is also the month to prune small fruits such as highbush blueberries and raspberries. And in your spare time, get a headstart on spring by forcing branches of some of your favorite spring-flowering woody plants.

| IN THE GARDEN | March | Date by USDA Hardiness Zone | | | | | Notes |
|---|---|---|---|---|---|---|---|
| | | 3 | 4 | 5 | 6 | 7 | |
| **GENERAL MAINTENANCE** | Make native bee nest boxes.<br>Put out bird-houses. | | | | | | Both bumblebees and native solitary bees are key garden pollinators. Providing nesting sites will ensure their abundance in your garden. See Chapters 4 and 5 for more information.<br>Bluebirds and other bird species feed on herbivores, helping to keep populations of these insects in balance. |
| **VEGETABLE CROPS** | | | | | | | |
| Asparagus | Order crowns | | | | | | Order crowns in early March. |
| | Plant crowns in garden.<br>Fertilize existing plants. | Apr 9 | Apr 2 | Mar 26 | Mar 19 | Mar 12 | See Chapter 5 for details on planting crowns and first-year growing. For established beds, fertilize with an organic fertilizer such as fish meal, blood meal, cottonseed meal, soybean meal, fish emulsion, aged manure, or compost. The manure or compost can be spread an inch deep over the ground. Follow label instructions for any of the others. |
| Broccoli | Start seeds indoors. | Apr 9 | Apr 2 | Mar 26 | Mar 19 | Mar 12 | Optimum germination temperature range is 50-85° F. Once seeds have germinated, keep the seedlings uniformly moist. Water with a half-strength solution of an organic fertilizer such as fish emulsion or liquid seaweed |
| Cabbage | Start seeds indoors. | Mar 26 | Mar 19 | Mar 12 | Mar 5 | Feb 26 | Optimum germination temperature range is 50-85° F. Once seeds have germinated, keep the seedlings uniformly moist, as soil crusting from drying out can lead to poor germination. Water with a half-strength solution of an organic fertilizer such as fish emulsion or liquid seaweed. |

| IN THE GARDEN | March | Date by USDA Hardiness Zone | | | | | Notes |
|---|---|---|---|---|---|---|---|
| | | 3 | 4 | 5 | 6 | 7 | |
| Cauliflower | Start seeds indoors. | Apr 9 | Apr 2 | Mar 26 | Mar 19 | Mar 12 | Once seeds have germinated, keep the seedlings uniformly moist. Water with a half-strength solution of an organic fertilizer such as fish emulsion or liquid seaweed. |
| Celery | Start seeds indoors. | Apr 13 | Apr 6 | Mar 30 | Mar 23 | Mar 16 | During germination and seedling development, soil temperature must be kept between 55 and 70° F. This is vital to success. |
| Celeriac | Start seeds indoors. | Mar 15 | Mar 8 | Mar 1 | Feb 22 | Feb 15 | During germination and seedling development, soil temperature must be kept between 55 and 70° F. This is vital to success. |
| Chard, Swiss | Start seeds indoors. | Apr 9 | Apr 2 | Mar 26 | Mar 19 | Mar 12 | |
| Garlic | When shoots are showing, remove half of the winter mulch. | | | | | | Keep the removed mulch in the walkways just in case temperatures below 28° F are forecast. If so, put the mulch back in place until temperatures settle above freezing. |
| Kohlrabi | Start seeds indoors. | Mar 26 | Mar 19 | Mar 12 | Mar 5 | Feb 26 | Optimum germination temperature range is 50-85°F. Once seeds have germinated, keep the seedlings uniformly moist. Water with a half-strength solution of an organic fertilizer such as fish emulsion or liquid seaweed. |
| Leek | Start seeds indoors. | Mar 15 | Mar 8 | Mar 1 | Feb 22 | Feb 15 | Optimum germination temperature range is 55-75° F. Once seeds have germinated, keep the seedlings uniformly moist. Thin seedlings to ½-inch apart in the seed flat. Keep tops trimmed to 3 inches for stockier transplants. Water with a half-strength solution of an organic fertilizer such as fish emulsion or liquid seaweed. (Photo by Björn König) |
| Lettuce | Start seeds indoors. | Apr 2 | Mar 26 | Mar 19 | Mar 12 | Mar 5 | Sow 3-4 seeds per inch of row in seed flat. Water seedlings with a half-strength solution of an organic fertilizer such as fish emulsion or liquid seaweed. Plan to transplant individual plants to cell packs or pot in 2-3 weeks after emergence. |

| IN THE GARDEN | March | Date by USDA Hardiness Zone | | | | | Notes |
|---|---|---|---|---|---|---|---|
| | | 3 | 4 | 5 | 6 | 7 | |
| Onions | Start seeds indoors. | Mar 15 | Mar 8 | Mar 1 | Feb 22 | Feb 15 | Optimum germination temperature range is 55-75° F. Once seeds have germinated, keep the seedlings uniformly moist. Thin seedlings to ½-inch apart in the seed flat. Keep tops trimmed to 3 inches for stockier transplants. Water with a half-strength solution of an organic fertilizer such as fish emulsion or liquid seaweed. |
| Parsley | Start seeds indoors. | Mar 29 | Mar 22 | Mar 15 | Mar 8 | Mar 1 | Optimum germination is between 50 and 75° F. The seeds must stay wet during germination. Parsley likes a lot of nitrogen, so water with a half-strength organic fertilizer solution. |
| Rhubarb | Order crowns. | | | | | | |
| **SMALL FRUITS** | | | | | | | |
| Highbush Blueberries | Prune | | | | | | |
| Raspberries | Prune | | | | | | |
| Strawberries | Order bare-root plants. | | | | | | Select varieties with resistance to red stele and root rot. Dependable New England Varieties include Earliglow, Wendy, Cavendish, Jewel, Allstar, and Sparkle. (Photo by Kai-Martin Knaak) |
| **FLOWER BEDS AND BORDERS** | Keep an eye out for perennial plant crowns that may have heaved out of the ground during recent thaws. Replant these perennials as soon as possible.<br><br>At the end of March, begin removing winter mulch on perennial plantings as the temperatures rise. | | | | | | (Photo by Bturner) |
| **CONTAINER GARDEN** | Make plans for growing vegetables in pots. | | | | | | |
| **FLOWERS** | | | | | | | |
| Begonia | Start seeds indoors. | Mar 15 | Mar 8 | Mar 1 | Feb 22 | Feb 15 | Seeds are tiny, dust-like, and young seedlings are very fragile. Plan on watering from below after sowing. Do not cover the seeds—leave them where they fall on the soil. Cover the seed flat with a sheet of plastic wrap to avoid loss of moisture; remove wrap when seedlings start to press against it. Transplant only when the seedlings have four leaves. (Photo by Wayne Ray) |
| Browallia | Start seeds indoors. | Mar 15 | Mar 8 | Mar 1 | Feb 22 | Feb 15 | |

| IN THE GARDEN | March | Date by USDA Hardiness Zone | | | | | Notes |
|---|---|---|---|---|---|---|---|
| | | 3 | 4 | 5 | 6 | 7 | |
| Campanula | Start seeds indoors. | Mar 29 | Mar 22 | Mar 15 | Mar 8 | Mar 1 | Sow seeds on surface and provide light for germination. Keep moist. |
| Catmint *(Nepeta)* | Start seeds indoors. | Mar 29 | Mar 22 | Mar 15 | Mar 8 | Mar 1 | Needs light to germinate, so do not cover the seeds. |
| Geranium | Start seeds indoors. | Mar 15 | Mar 8 | Mar 1 | Feb 22 | Feb 15 | Cover seed flat with plastic wrap during germination to ensure uniform moisture. |
| Impatiens | Start seeds indoors. | Mar 29 | Mar 22 | Mar 15 | Mar 8 | Mar 1 | Cover seeds lightly. |
| Lady's Mantle *(Alchemilla mollis)* | Start seeds indoors. | Mar 29 | Mar 22 | Mar 15 | Mar 8 | Mar 1 | Lightly cover seeds. |
| Larkspur | Start seeds indoors. | Mar 15 | Mar 8 | Mar 1 | Feb 22 | Feb 15 | Pre-chill seeds in refrigerator (35° F) for 7 days. Sow in peat pots to avoid transplant stress. Germinate in dark. Keep soil temperature at 55° F during both germination and growing on. (Photo courtesy Duke University) |
| Milkweed *(Asclepias)* | Start seeds indoors. | Mar 29 | Mar 22 | Mar 15 | Mar 8 | Mar 1 | Plant in peat pots, covering seeds lightly. Chill seeds in the fridge for 3 weeks, placing pots in plastic bags. Germinate under lights. |
| Pansy/Viola | Start seeds indoors. | Mar 15 | Mar 8 | Mar 1 | Feb 22 | Feb 15 | Grow at cool temperatures after germination. |
| Penstemon (Beard Tongue) | Start seeds indoors. | Mar 29 | Mar 22 | Mar 15 | Mar 8 | Mar 1 | Germinate under light. |
| Petunia | Start seeds indoors. | Mar 29 | Mar 22 | Mar 15 | Mar 8 | Mar 1 | Seeds are very fine. If possible, use pelletized seed. Press seed gently into moist soil, then cover with plastic wrap until germination. Transplant to cell packs when plants have three true leaves. Fertilize weekly with half-strength organic fertilizer. |
| Portulaca | Start seeds indoors. | Mar 29 | Mar 22 | Mar 15 | Mar 8 | Mar 1 | Grow at cool temperatures after germination. |

| IN THE GARDEN | March | Date by USDA Hardiness Zone | | | | | Notes |
|---|---|---|---|---|---|---|---|
| | | 3 | 4 | 5 | 6 | 7 | |
| Rudbeckia (Black-eyed Susan) | Start seeds indoors. | Mar 15 | Mar 8 | Mar 1 | Feb 22 | Feb 15 | Press seed into surface of mix—do not cover. Place moist sown seed in a plastic bag and store in refrigerator for 2 weeks. Once germinated, seedlings should be grown in a cool, bright location. |
| Stock | Start seeds indoors. | Mar 29 | Mar 22 | Mar 15 | Mar 8 | Mar 1 | Grow at cool temperatures after germination. |
| Verbena | Start seeds indoors. | Mar 29 | Mar 22 | Mar 15 | Mar 8 | Mar 1 | Chill seeds in refrigerator for 7 days before sowing. |
| Vinca | Start seeds indoors. | Mar 15 | Mar 8 | Mar 1 | Feb 22 | Feb 15 | Grow in warm temperatures. |
| Woody Plants | Force branches of flowering trees and shrubs. (Photo by Avicennasis) | | | | | | |

The sight of bursting willow buds, triggered by only 14 growing degree days, is bound to make the gardener smile, for the back of winter is surely broken and sowing peas is just around the corner.

# Chapter 6

# The Garden in April

*"No occupation is so delightful to me as the culture of the earth, and no culture comparable to that of the garden. Such a variety of subjects, some one always coming to perfection, the failure of one thing repaired by the success of another. . . . Under a total want of demand except for the family table, I am still devoted to the garden. But although an old man, I am but a young gardener."*

—Thomas Jefferson, 1811

***It is a warm night in April,*** and as I write lesson plans at my desk in Eastport, Maine, rain drips from the eaves just beyond the near window. Suddenly it dawns on me: This is it, the first warm rain of spring. Tonight could be Big Night, the night when thousands of wood frogs and salamanders migrate from woodland winter shelters to local mating pools filled with snowmelt and rain. Spawning will be fast and furious, each species in its own way, and the adults will leave the pools as quickly as they arrived, abandoning their offspring to a race against dryness. The vernal pools will be dry holes come early summer.

Twenty minutes later I am standing beside a roadside ditch, my feet surrounded by scores of salamanders and wood frogs on the last leg of their journeys. It would be a perilous trek if not for the small clusters of people, mostly children, stopping traffic from both directions, allowing the amphibians to reach their mating pools in safety. Car headlights illuminate yellow spots on some of the salamanders.

Intent on spawning, this wood frog makes the last leg of its April journey from woods to vernal pool.

*Facing page:* A red oak greets April with scarlet leaves that turn to green.

The same warm rain will melt the last of the crusty ice covering the ground as it seeps into the soil. For the first time in months I will be able to see the garden's beds, and though it will be another month before I can go to the garden with a digging fork, my spirit soars with thoughts of planting.

During April I make frequent visits to a local rain garden, chronicling the native plants, both woody and herbaceous, that are growing there. This garden absorbs a tremendous volume of water from snowmelt and rainfall, water that otherwise would flow into storm drains and nearby surface waters, diminishing groundwater while enhancing the potential for erosion, water pollution, and flooding.

The rain garden is a planted depression off one corner of a flat-roofed building. During each rainfall, water from the roof falls onto a gravel bed at the base of the building wall and is carried to the garden through perforated pipe buried in the gravel. Immediately after a rain, the garden is flooded, but within a short time, a few days at most, the standing water has drained into the surrounding ground and the clayey soil begins to dry. In midsummer, this can be a very dry garden.

Some of the plants in this garden are old friends, including rhodora *(Rhododendron canadense),* a native rhododendron common both to seasonally flooded areas and to arid granitic outcrops. Others, particularly the herbaceous perennials, I did not know well or at all until I started these annual spring visits.

For example, while I have often encountered marsh marigolds (*Caltha palustris*) in the shallow water of hardwood swamps, the rain garden provided my first opportunity to observe them in a managed landscape. They are always the first herbaceous plant to flower in this garden, thriving in the full sun of early spring, blooming in mid-May with waxy bright yellow flowers that take center stage for two weeks.

Rhodora, a native rhododendron and true harbinger of spring, flowers in New England wetlands before the leaves emerge.

Bloom time for marsh marigolds overlaps the appearance of rhodora's purple flowers, and through most of May this dominant combination of bright yellow and purple is punctuated by the fresh green emerging leaves of *Iris prismatica*, the slender blueflag iris. By the end of May, the rain garden is a sea of green, the rounded leaves of marsh marigolds, their flowers gone by, surrounded by broad clumps of slender sword-shaped iris leaves, 3 feet tall and swaying in every gentle breeze.

Native to saltmarshes and wet near-coastal meadows —and often found in the company of sweetgrass, wild rose, and bayberry—slender blueflag thrives in seasonally flooded gardens. It is a rare iris in the wild of Maine, listed in the state as a threatened species due to habitat destruction (filling of wetlands) at the northern limit of its range, but common in other states and still available from growers of native perennials.

The rain garden's carpet of green continues to expand through early June, and by June 12 the slender blueflags have burst into bloom. And just in time, because the leaves of marsh marigolds (a summer-dormant perennial) are falling apart, edges curling as they turn to brown in the summer heat, and another player is needed on the stage. The iris flowers, blue-purple with heavily streaked falls, are still in flower at the end of June.

Marsh marigolds are the first herbaceous perennials to flower in a New England rain garden. Note the emerging outflow pipe that delivers water collected off the roof to the rain garden.

By mid-June, slender blueflag iris have burst into bloom in midcoast Maine gardens.

Meanwhile, in late June, a clump of giant sunflower *(Helianthus giganteus)* waits in the wings. Already 5 feet tall and buttressed with stout stakes at all four corners, this towering sunflower bursts into bloom in late July and continues to flower into October, reaching a final height of up to 12 feet. The yellow flower heads, up to 3 inches in diameter, are borne at the top of each plant in loose multi-branched clusters.

The flowers of the giant sunflower tower over other garden plants from late July into October.

Another player in the late summer is the swamp milkweed *(Asclepias incarnata)* with its tight clusters of pink to mauve flowers on plants up to 6 feet tall. The flowers are followed by seed pods (4 inches long) that split open at maturity, releasing silky-haired seeds on the wind. Butterflies use swamp milkweed as a nectar source, while the foliage is a food source for monarch butterfly larvae.

My frequent spring visits to this rain garden have taught me that a wet corner of a garden planted with native plants can be both functional and beautiful. The plant species discussed above can be grown in any seasonally flooded landscape site, including the edges of vernal pools and ponds that swell with snowmelt and April showers.

Instead of filling wet areas of our gardens—which have important ecological roles to play—we should take advantage of them. We should learn to think of them as opportunities to grow the many herbaceous plants that love wet feet, plants that will enrich our lives and the diversity of life in the garden.

A true pollinator magnet in the rain garden, swamp milkweed blooms in late summer in central Maine.

# April in the Vegetable Garden

The first warm rain of April is the gardener's assurance that ice will soon be out of the garden beds and that the perennial shoots of winter rye sown last fall will green and grow for one more month before being gently turned under to decay and feed the soil, making way for summer crops of tomatoes and beans. A warm rain in April shifts garden planning into high gear.

## Hardening Transplants in Cold Frames or on the Back Porch

Vegetable seedlings grown indoors must be hardened—i.e., gradually conditioned to withstand the cooler temperatures, brighter light, and stiff breezes of the April garden. For years, Marjorie and I have accomplished this by slowly lengthening the time each day that seedlings spend on the back porch. On the first day, we leave them out for just a few hours in the early morning. We lengthen the exposure time each consecutive day until, by the end of the week, they are spending both day and night outside unless a sudden late frost forces them back inside for a night or two. In heavy wind or rain, we relocate them to a more sheltered spot on the porch.

All this moving around does get old, and it also incurs the stress of worrying about the seedlings when we are away and a storm suddenly comes up. Each year, in the midst of all this moving and worrying, I vow to build cold frames for hardening our seedlings.

A cold frame is simply a wooden frame set onto the ground (or on top of a raised bed) and topped with a transparent lid, called the "light," that is often slanted downward at a 45-degree angle toward the south to maximize exposure to the sun, and is hinged on its back (top) edge. The effect is to create a mild microclimate using passive solar energy and insulation.

Veteran gardener Elisabeth Curran inspects lettuce hardening in her cold frame.

Gardeners often use old storm windows or discarded shower doors for lights. A corrugated polycarbonate sheet mounted on a lightweight wooden frame also makes a durable light, lasting 15 years or more. A hinged light can be opened for ventilation on warm, sunny days, either manually or with a temperature-sensitive automatic vent opener.

In early spring, cold frames are the preferred method to harden seedlings produced indoors. A week in a cold frame will acclimate the seedlings, bridging the gap between indoor warmth under fluorescent bulbs and the garden's chilly nights and full-sun days.

## Direct Sowing in Rows or Blocks

Cool-season vegetables, including beets, carrots, Chinese cabbage, lettuce, onions and shallots, parsnips, peas, radishes, spinach, Swiss chard, and turnips, are often sown directly in the garden as soon as the soil can be worked (see the monthly to-do list at the end of this chapter). For the leafy greens in this group, small quantities of seed can be sown every two weeks through May to provide a continuous harvest. Sowing dates for summer crops, on the other hand, are based on soil temperature, and there is a list of their minimum soil-temperature requirements for direct sowing in Chapter 7.

Root crops such as carrots, beets, radishes, and turnips are always direct-sown because their seedling taproots are too easily damaged by transplanting seedlings grown indoors. Most gardeners also direct-sow beans, peas, and corn, although I know a few who try to get a jump on spring by sowing corn and beans indoors. They sow the seeds in peat pots because the sides and bottom of a peat pot can be carefully torn away at planting time with minimal disturbance of the root system. (Peat pots are sold to be planted with the seedlings, but there are two problems with this concept. First, any portion of the pot that is left above ground serves as a wick that rapidly dries out the soil around the seedling's roots. Second, roots will often circle the inside of the pot rather than growing out of the pot and into the surrounding soil.)

Other crops—such as lettuce, cucumbers, and summer squash—are often grown from transplants at the beginning of the garden season (as described in Chapter 5), then grown from direct-sown seed later in summer for fall harvest. This is a matter of not wanting to keep the indoor seedling-production program going through the summer. Also, filling in those small patches of empty garden space that open up as main crops are harvested is quickly accomplished by direct sowing without a lot of prior planning. Just keep a supply of fresh seeds on hand.

Direct sowing requires a well-prepared seed bed. This need not involve deep tilling, which disrupts the soil food web, but rather shallow raking to remove soil clods, stones, anything that would interfere with emergence of tender shoots. There is never a need to go deeper than the tines of a garden rake.

If you are a fan of no-till gardening, you may be sowing seed in a bed covered with mulch or remnants of the last crop. This material will have to be removed or raked into the space between rows before sowing.

Pay close attention to the seed packet for instructions on depth of sowing and spacing, both between seeds in each row and between rows. With these instructions in mind, make furrows in the bed if you are a straight-row kind of gardener. I usually look around for the nearest bamboo stake to make these furrows or use the handle of the rake or my fingers. Actually, I prefer the latter, relishing the feel of sun-warmed soil on my hands.

After the furrows are made, you are ready to sow seeds. For large seeds such as beans, peas, and corn, sowing at the proper within-row spacing is quick and easy. For small seeds such as those of carrots, lettuce, and spinach, it can be totally aggravating. While holding the open seed packet in your hand, you attempt to vibrate the seeds out the open end, one by one, tapping the packet with your index finger while moving the packet down the row at a uniform pace. The end result is an erratic pattern of 2 inches between seeds in some sections of the furrow and twenty seeds per inch in other sections. I usually settle for sowing thickly, followed by extensive thinning. (See page 94 for a couple of tricks to reduce thinning time.)

If you prefer to sow seeds in blocks that span the width of the bed rather than in rows, you need to rake enough soil aside to scatter the seeds within the block, then carefully pull the soil back over the seeds. For really small seeds, like those of lettuce and spinach, I've had good results just scattering the seed over the surface of the soil and then gently pulling the tines of a leaf rake over the soil a few times in both directions. Some seeds probably go too deep, but most do germinate. (For more information on intensive planting in raised beds, see the Chapter 4 sidebar, "Gardening Intensively for Maximum Harvest Yield.")

Cucurbits, including cucumbers, squash (both summer and winter), and melons, should be sown

This seed bed, sown with pea seeds, was cleared of large clods and stones prior to making the furrows.

in hills, mounds of soil about 2 feet in diameter with flattened tops. Five or six seeds should be planted in each hill, evenly spaced and at a depth recommended on the seed packet. Once these seeds germinate, thin to the most vigorous two or three seedlings, gently pulling the others from the soil.

After sowing in rows, blocks, or hills, you should gently firm the soil over the seeds, either by hand or with the back side of a spade, then soak with a fine spray. Water until you know the soil is damp several inches deep. Until the seeds germinate and send down roots to explore the soil, you will need to keep the soil moist with frequent gentle watering. Seeds of many crops (carrots being notable among them) will not germinate uniformly or at all if the seed bed is allowed to dry out. A very light mulch of straw (so thin that you can still see the soil) will help conserve moisture yet still allow the soil to stay warm enough for quick germination.

Root crops, such as these carrots and turnips, begin with direct sowing of seeds in the April garden.

### Is the Garden's Soil Workable?

Digging and walking on soil that is too wet will destroy its structure, compacting it to the point that plant roots will not grow. How do you know when your garden's soil is workable?

Pick up a handful of soil from one of the garden's beds and squeeze it in your hand. If the soil remains in a tight clump after you release your hand, or if you can actually squeeze water out of the soil, it is still too wet to work. If the soil falls apart with just a little gentle prodding, grab a spade or fork and get to work, but keep your feet in the walkways. Walking on soil in which plants will be growing is never a good idea, as even dry soils are compacted by foot traffic.

## April in the Strawberry Patch

To encourage flower formation in established strawberry beds, remove the mulch in early April, tucking it under and around the plants and moving the excess into the walkways, keeping it handy for protecting plants from a late frost. Strawberry buds and flowers will be killed by a hard frost if left exposed.

After removing the mulch, you should fertilize very lightly, applying six ounces of organic nitrogen per 1,000 square feet of bed. And start your weed control in early spring.

## An Old Gardener Discovers Rhubarb

Each year in Marjorie's Garden, I like to grow something new. In 2012, one chosen plant was rhubarb, and I found myself wondering, why this sudden interest in a perennial vegetable crop? My only experience with rhubarb at the time was the dessert that gives it the nickname of "pie plant," so I wasn't sure if I even liked the unadulterated taste of those bright red stems.

I did like the idea of a crop that I would not have to replant every year, one ideally suited to Maine's frigid winters and mild summers, a plant that can be propagated simply with an ax every few years. Something really different.

I made a serious study of this vegetable that thinks it's a fruit. As with celery, you eat the petioles, the leaf stalks. But you don't even think about eating the leaves, as they contain high concentrations of toxic oxalic acid crystals. And yet the leaves make fine garden compost, the oxalic acid breaking down during decomposition.

As for the unadulterated taste, I learned that popular rhubarb recipes in this country call for a good bit of sugar to offset the tartness of rhubarb stalks used in pies, tarts, cold soups, and jams. The English, on the other hand, add ginger to their rhubarb recipes.

As with asparagus, rhubarb crowns need their first year to get established, and only a week or two of harvest will be possible the second year after planting. By the third year, however, the harvest season will run from April through June.

### Tips for Sowing Small Seeds

Whenever I sow the tiny seeds of lettuce, carrots, or spinach, I always mix a handful of fine sand with the tiny vegetable seeds, then add a pinch or two of radish seeds that will germinate quickly and mark the rows. While not eliminating the need for thinning after germination, this technique does produce more uniform spacing of seedlings. The radishes are harvested long before plants of the main crop need the space.

Another technique that I plan to try is mixing the tiny vegetable seeds with a soft gelatin, then using a plastic mustard bottle to squeeze the seeds into the planting furrow. The trick here, as I understand it, is to get the gelatin soft enough to be forced through the squeeze bottle. Start by mixing one-half of a gelatin packet with slightly more water than recommended. If the gelatin sets too firmly, stir in additional warm water until you get the desired consistency. Add the seeds and shake to mix, then squeeze the seeds into the furrow. I like the sound of this technique, but I suspect it takes some practice.

Many seed companies offer pelletized seeds, each tiny seed encased in a pellet of clay. While I have yet to try these, they certainly should make sowing easier.

## Planting Rhubarb in Early April

There are two ways to get started with rhubarb: order a few dormant one-year-old crowns from a garden seed company, or latch on to someone about to divide an old rhubarb plant growing in their garden, something that you will be doing a few years after planting your first rhubarb crowns. In either case, you will be planting in early April, as soon as the garden's soil can be worked.

Let's assume you have purchased crowns. Pick a spot in your garden where you can grow three or five rhubarb plants spaced about 3 feet apart. For each crown, mix a shovelful or two of compost, aged manure, or worm compost into the soil where it will be planted. Make a hole slightly wider than the crown and deep enough so that it will be 1 to 2 inches below the soil surface. Put the crown in the hole and bury it, buds up.

Mark the location where each new crown is planted until the new shoots appear. And remember, let these new plants grow for the first year without harvesting any stems.

Whenever you need more rhubarb plants, or when old plants become too large and crowded with stems (usually five to eight years after planting), grab a sharp spade or an ax and start dividing. Rhubarb lends itself to this kind of garden math as long as it is done in early spring, before new growth begins.

First, dig up the entire plant with a garden fork or spade, trying to keep as many roots intact as possible. Then, using the spade or ax, divide the crown into pieces, each with at least one bud and a portion of the roots. Plant these new divisions as described above.

### Heeling in Early Arrivals

The rhubarb crowns arrive in the mail before construction of their raised bed is finished. What do you do?

If kept in the shipping container, dormant perennial crowns, including rhubarb, asparagus, and herbaceous perennials, will lose water and their buds may die. To store them temporarily, I use a technique called *heeling in*. After digging a shallow trench in one of the garden beds and propping the crowns, buds up, against the side of the trench, I cover the crowns with soil so that the buds are just below the soil surface. They will keep just fine for a week or two.

These rhubarb crowns arrived early from the grower and were heeled (temporarily stored) in a garden bed for a week or so while their planting bed was under construction. After placing them in this shallow trench, buds up, they were covered with soil so that the buds were just below the soil surface.

## Growing Rhubarb

Rhubarb grows best on fertile, well-drained soil that is high in organic matter and slightly to moderately acid (pH 6.8 to 6.0). Given these conditions, it is a relatively trouble-free crop with no major herbivore or disease problems.

Rhubarb demands relatively high levels of nitrogen for maximum yield. This can be supplied by annual fall applications of well-rotted stable manure spread over the surface of the soil between the plants. Do not cover the plants with manure, as this will lead to rotting of the crowns. In addition to providing needed nitrogen, the manure helps conserve moisture in the soil, preserves soil structure, and makes nutrients readily available to plant roots.

## Harvesting Rhubarb

Harvest begins in early May. Two-year-old plants can be harvested for two weeks, then remaining stems should be allowed to stay on the plant for the rest of the growing season. Beginning in the third year, stalks can be harvested well into June, stopping when new stalks are noticeably thinner.

When harvesting the stalks, pull them off rather than cutting them. Pulling the leaf stems causes less damage to the plant and avoids the large cutting wounds that can lead to entry of a fungal disease.

Should any flowering stems appear from your plants, cut them off. Their appearance may mean that the plant is ready to be divided or that you need to enrich the soil with rotted manure or compost.

When you start harvesting more than you can eat fresh, you can freeze the surplus. Simply chop it into half-inch pieces and spread them on a cookie sheet. Place the sheet in the freezer, and when the rhubarb pieces are frozen, transfer them to freezer bags.

## The Compost Pile

I once joined a group of adults, all students in a Master Gardener Volunteer training course, to construct a compost pile in 30 minutes. It was impressive and made me think of community members gathering together to raise a barn in a day.

Everyone arrived with a key ingredient in the recipe for compost: dry straw, stable manure, seaweed, vegetable and fruit peelings, coffee grounds, eggshells, grass clippings, and dried leaves, whole and shredded. The bin, a closed wire fence measuring 3 feet in all three dimensions, was the minimum size for a successful compost pile. I worked in amazement as something that takes most gardeners months to build was accomplished in half an hour.

We began by turning over the soil beneath the bin to provide easy access to the pile for earthworms, ground beetles, and microbial agents of decomposition. Because a compost bin in full sun will easily dry out, slowing down decomposition, we located our bin in a well-drained spot with partial shade.

We started with a 12-inch layer of fluffed straw—not hay, which is full of weed seeds. Dry straw, the hollow stems of harvested grain, is used as the initial layer because it is stiff enough to resist compaction and will allow air to enter the pile from the bottom. Like dry leaves, straw is also an excellent source of carbon, the primary energy source for the bacteria and fungi that decompose organic matter.

Six inches of fresh grass clippings were added next, providing the compost-manufacturing bacteria with nitrogen essential for reproduction. Grass clippings are not the only source of nitrogen, however, and many gardeners prefer to leave them on the lawn. Livestock manures are excellent nitrogen sources, as are coffee grounds, vegetable and fruit waste, and seaweed collected from above the high tide line.

Layer by layer the pile grew, shredded leaves being followed by garden weeds that had been chopped into small pieces with a digging spade, then dry whole leaves. At this point, with the bin about one-third full, we mixed everything together with a garden fork and thoroughly watered the pile.

Next came layers of chopped seaweed, straw, alpaca manure, shredded leaves, chopped kitchen wastes, more leaves. Last, we once again thoroughly stirred and watered the pile, then topped it off with final layers of seaweed and leaves.

Chopping bulky ingredients such as garden weeds, vegetable and fruit peelings, and seaweed increases the surface areas of these ingredients. Bacteria and fungi work at the surfaces of decaying materials.

Decomposition occurs quickly when the pile's carbon to nitrogen ratio (C:N) is approximately 30:1. We accomplished this by mixing high-carbon materials (C:N of 50:1), such as straw and dry leaves, in roughly equal amounts with high-nitrogen materials such as manure, seaweed, and grass clippings (C:N of 15:1).

Success in composting is measured with a compost thermometer. A well-constructed compost pile heats up as bacteria do their work, reaching a peak between 90 and 150° F, and then starts to cool. When the pile returns to ambient temperature, it should be turned so that the least decomposed material on the cooler outside of the pile is moved to the middle. While turning, water the pile to the consistency of a wrung-out sponge. Within a day or so, the temperature in the middle should start to rise again.

One week after building our pile, its temperature was a healthy 149°. Four months later, the finished compost was dark brown with a crumbly texture, none of the original ingredients recognizable. Chocolate cake for the garden.

Bringing together everything needed to build a compost pile in half an hour takes either a captive audience of eager students or a lot of space for stockpiling essential ingredients. Most gardeners fill compost bins at a much slower rate, adding materials as they become available but always remembering the need to mix materials high in carbon with those high in nitrogen. A neighbor who would love to have someone rake their autumn leaves for free, a local dairy farmer or horse owner with a growing pile of stable litter (straw and manure), a friend with ready access to seaweed—these are goldmines for the gardener who composts.

### Piles and Bins

Any productive compost pile must meet certain characteristics. It should be large enough to retain heat but small enough to allow air and water to penetrate to its center; three feet in all directions satisfies this requirement. It should be constructed to maximize air and water penetration throughout the pile. Beyond these features, however, compost piles take many forms.

Tom and Jan McIntyre, gardeners on Mt. Desert Island, Maine, have perfected the pallet system of composting. On the edge of their garden a row of wooden pallets presents a time line in the creation of compost from a mixture of vegetable scraps, garden weeds, and stable litter. On the pallet at one end of the row, the elements of the mixture are still recognizable. Looking down the row, the contents of the pile become more and more homogeneous until, on the final pallet, sits a mound of dark crumbly compost. When finished compost is removed from the end pallet, each pile is pitchforked one pallet forward.

Simple in construction, the pallet system ensures frequent turning of each pile as it is moved down the line. It also provides maximum exposure of each pile's contents, including the bottom layer of the pile, to air and water.

Nate and Berta Atwater care for a beautiful coastal garden in Little Compton, Rhode Island. Berta's passion is trees, and her garden is an arboretum that attracts horticulturists from around the world. Nate loves to grow vegetables.

Berta calls their four-bin composting edifice her folly. I disagree: It is large, but it is also functional. And it is constructed to last for generations. Built from redwood timber, each of the four connected bins has removable front panels that are ventilated, as are the side, back, and internal walls. The roof shades the compost piles, preventing rapid drying, but also reduces the amount of rain falling on the piles, so Nate adds water with the garden hose as needed.

Composting in Marjorie's Garden is conducted in two simple wire-frame bins, each measuring 3 feet in all dimensions with side panels that separate for easy moving and storage. We operate what could be called a continuous composting program. Some might call it the "lazy man's composting operation."

We start out the gardening year with one of the bins half full of garden waste, most of it accumulated in late autumn as we cleaned up the garden beds for winter. On top of this, we add layers of composted goat manure, green grass clippings, shredded leaves, and seaweed collected above the tide line at a local public beach. When we're done, the compost thermometer thrust into the middle of this pile will read above 100 degrees in a few days.

Tom McIntyre inspects the contents of a palleted compost pile.

"Berta's Folly" is the name that Berta Atwater has given this large yet very functional four-bin composting facility in their seacoast garden. It seems like anything but folly to me.

Whenever the kitchen compostables bucket is full, we bury its contents in the supercharged pile. Garden clippings and weeds (except for perennial weeds such as quackgrass that will survive thermonuclear explosions) get tossed on top. When the pile's temperature drops below 90 degrees, we transfer the contents to the second bin, adding grass clippings and/or composted manure in layers. Again, things get hot quickly.

Back and forth through the summer, the compost pile changes bins. If we need a little compost, we simply take

The compost bins in Marjorie's Garden

it from the lower half of the old pile as we change bins, screening it through one-quarter-inch hardware cloth to remove anything that has not fully decomposed. Coconut shells, corncobs, and pinecones take forever to rot!

I know gardeners who are hooked on composting. They keep records of the pile's temperature and know the carbon:nitrogen ratio of every ingredient that goes into the bin. They have a hose dedicated to watering the pile. They insulate their piles in winter to keep them cooking longer. They claim bragging rights to the quickest turnover in converting raw materials to black gold. I'm pretty sure I could be one of these gardeners if I had more time on my hands.

And I know gardeners who build their compost piles on top of the ground, no bin. If the kitchen waste on top of the pile is too tempting to skunks, they take the time to turn the pile or at least throw some straw on top. The pile gets watered when it rains. They don't own a compost thermometer.

Most gardeners compost between these two extremes. The mixture of materials may not be precise, the bin may not be elaborate, but sooner or later, there's compost.

## Winter Composting

Composting kitchen vegetable waste during a Maine winter requires ingenuity and strong legs! Our compost piles are 200 feet from the kitchen, no big deal in summer but a real workout when the snow is packed 4 feet high in the path that you shoveled out a week ago. And, of course, the compost piles are frozen solid.

I use a three-pail system to handle kitchen waste, a system that is particularly useful during winter, reducing the number of trips to the frozen compost pile to one or two per month.

Three 5-gallon pails sit side by side on the back porch, their covers tight. One contains potting soil mixed with an equal volume of perlite and a handful of lime. The other two are the composting pails. I cover each deposit of kitchen scraps (no meat or cheese, as they draw raccoons and skunks) with a layer of the potting soil mixture, continuing this process until the first pail is full, then set it aside and start on the second pail. When both pails are filled, I dump the partially decomposed contents of the first pail onto the compost pile at the back of the garden and cover the exposed material with a layer of mulch straw. I store straw bales under the porch to keep them dry for this purpose.

In summer, by the time both pails are full, the contents of the first pail are well on their way to finished compost. Little composting happens in winter, but I don't have to shovel that long path as often.

## *Composting Indoors with Worms*

by Marjorie Peronto

Our cat and two dogs are an important part of our family, and the thought of adding worms to the menagerie was intriguing. Also, I thought, if worms could process our kitchen scraps indoors in the winter, nobody would have to trudge out to dump them on the frozen compost pile. (No matter what the season, I can't bring myself to throw compostable food scraps in the trash. I just can't.)

Red wigglers (*Eisenia fetida*) process kitchen scraps into nutrient-rich castings that can be added to potting soil or used as organic fertilizer in the garden.

Your completed worm bin should have drainage holes in the bottom (top). It should also have holes for air exchange along the upper edge (above). Nest the bin in a shallow plastic tray to catch drips.

I'm not someone who dives headfirst into the unknown. I like to pilot a new endeavor on a small scale and expand as I learn. It was fun. It worked. I graduated to bigger and bigger bins and more and more worms.

The first worm bin I tried was a simple 10-gallon Rubbermaid tub. I drilled eight ¼-inch holes in the bottom for drainage and nested it in a shallow plastic tray to catch any drips. I drilled a few ½-inch holes along the upper edge of each side for air exchange. I cut old newspapers (not the glossy pages) into half-inch-wide strips, enough to fill the tub when fluffed. Once moistened, this was to be the worms' bedding, the medium in which they would crawl around and in which I would bury their food. The worms eventually would consume the newspaper as well.

I started out with about 4 ounces of worms (about 150 to 200 worms), which I bought from a local supplier. The type of worm that works best for vermiculture is *Eisenia fetida*, the red wiggler. Don't try to do this with the large earthworms you find in your garden—they create extensive burrows deep in cool soil and won't survive when confined in a box. Red wigglers are much smaller than earthworms and are often found in manure piles. They can process large amounts of organic material, reproduce quickly in confinement, and don't mind being disturbed. When you get your worms, place them on top of your moistened bedding and close the lid. They will quickly burrow down and hide.

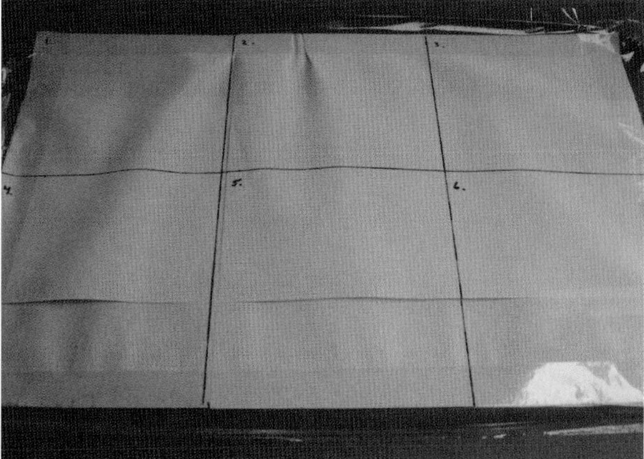

Keep track of your worms' feeding schedule with a grid taped to the bin's lid.

Red wigglers can easily consume half their weight in food every day. It's helpful to have a small kitchen scale when you get started. With 4 ounces of worms, I fed them 2 ounces of food scraps a day (about ½ cup). I know it doesn't seem like much, but the worm population does grow over time. Two years after I started, I now have over two pounds of worms, and a much larger bin. They can comfortably process a pound of food scraps per day, year-round. In our house, we generate a LOT of banana peels and broccoli stems, which the worms love.

Tape some paper on top of the lid of your bin and draw a grid, dividing it into eight equal blocks. Each time you put food in the bin, put it in a different block, noting the date and the weight on the grid. Add food in a clockwise pattern around the bin, burying the food shallowly in the moist bedding. The worms will follow the food source. By the time you get back to where you started, there should no longer be recognizable food in the first block. If there is, wait until it disappears before adding more.

What can you feed your worms? Just as in your outdoor composting system, put in fruit and vegetable scraps, grains, coffee grounds, and tea bags. Don't add meat or dairy products, as these take much longer to break down and can generate unpleasant odors. Keep cat litter out of your worm box too. Try not to overload

Fruit and vegetable scraps, along with coffee grounds, make up the bulk of worm fodder in our house.

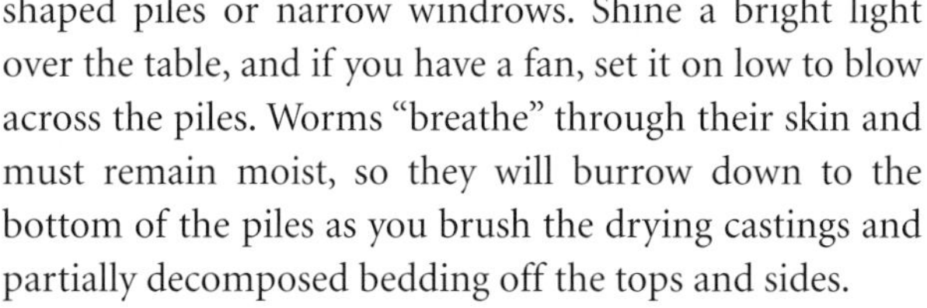

Bury the food scraps shallowly in the bedding.

your worm bin with too much of any one ingredient. The worms seem to process the food more quickly when there is variety, and when it is chopped up. When I put in nothing but apple peels for several days (after making applesauce), the worms' rate of food processing slowed way down. The same thing happened with potato peels and cornhusks.

Worm droppings (castings) will accumulate over time as the food and bedding are consumed. These castings are the nutrient-rich material that you can put in your garden or add to your potting soil. Once every three or four months, you'll want to harvest the castings from your bin and put in new, fresh bedding. The worms don't do well if the castings become very concentrated.

To harvest the castings, lay a big sheet of plastic on a table. Scoop material out of the bin and create cone-shaped piles or narrow windrows. Shine a bright light over the table, and if you have a fan, set it on low to blow across the piles. Worms "breathe" through their skin and must remain moist, so they will burrow down to the bottom of the piles as you brush the drying castings and partially decomposed bedding off the tops and sides.

Once you've separated out the partially decomposed material, you can put the worms back in the bin with fresh bedding. Learn to recognize baby worms (white or translucent) and eggs (tiny, round, translucent to brown),

Over time, food scraps and bedding are converted to worm castings.

Windrows of this mixture, including the worms, are dried with a fan. The worms hunker down in the bottom of each pile, allowing you to harvest the bedding and castings from the top.

as these can go back in the bin too. You can put the partially decomposed material on your garden as is (after removing any recognizable food scraps and big pieces of bedding) or you can sift it through a screen. We made a simple screen from ¼-inch-mesh hardware cloth and a wooden frame that fits right over another tub. What falls through the screen is the finer compost that can be mixed into potting soil or spread at the base of seedlings in the garden. The larger material gets put back in the worm bin for further processing.

### A little math

How big does your worm bin need to be? First, your bin should be no more than 18 inches deep so that the material doesn't become too compacted, which is unhealthy for the worms. Second, the other dimensions of your bin (length and width) depend on how much compostable waste you typically throw away in a week. There should be 1 square foot of surface area for each pound of food waste you generate per week. So, if you average 6 pounds of food waste per week, a bin that is 3 feet long, 2 feet wide and 12 to 18 inches deep will be perfect.

Now, what quantity of worms do you need to process your food scraps? Remember that worms can process about half their weight in food per day. So if you average 1 pound of food scraps per day, you'll need 2 pounds of worms in your bin.

### A few tips

Your worm bin must have drainage holes in the bottom. Worms will drown if there is standing water in the bin. Worms don't try to escape through the drainage holes or aeration holes. They'd rather stay in the bin (unless something is very wrong there).

Bedding should be light, moist, and fluffy. After experimenting with shredded newspaper, my favorite bedding now is shredded autumn leaves mixed with a little peat moss (two handfuls for a 10-gallon bin) for moisture retention. We run a lawn mower over the dry leaves in the fall, then bag them up and store them for future use. You can also use shredded computer paper, strips of corrugated cardboard, wood shavings, or composted manure.

Keep your worm bin at room temperature. If it goes below 50° F or above 86° F, your worms may die.

If you put eggshells in your worm bin, they'll stick around for a long time, and the worms will use them as a place to congregate, which is interesting! They'll do the same in orange and grapefruit halves. If you pulverize eggshells in a plastic bag using a rolling pin, you'll provide the worms with grit that helps them process food. Worms don't have teeth, and they break down food particles by muscle action in their gizzards. If you cannot add pulverized eggshells as a source of grit, then throw a handful of soil into the bedding.

If you mistakenly overload your bin with more food than the worms can process, you might develop a fruit fly problem. They will fly out in a cloud whenever you remove the lid. Put about ½ inch of cider vinegar in an open jar or cup and cover it with plastic wrap secured with a rubber band. Poke small holes in the plastic wrap with the tip of a pencil and set the jar near your bin. The fruit flies are drawn like magnets to the vinegar. They will crawl in the tiny holes and down into the vinegar where they drown.

It is normal to see other organisms in your bin. Expect to find tiny mites, fungi, and other microorganisms. They are all part of the worm bin food web!

## *Formative Pruning of Young Trees*

A few years ago, I spent a Saturday morning helping a small group of gardeners learn more about the formative pruning of young trees. We spent an hour working on a collection of Japanese tree lilacs in the parking lot of a local business, then left the pruning tools behind and took a walk down the main corridor of town, closely examining a line of street trees that had been planted the previous summer.

Our tour began with a ginkgo tree, its 3-inch-diameter trunk rising from its tiny planting hole for about 3 feet before the first branch. Within the next 2 feet of trunk height were twelve branches spaced between 1 and 2 inches apart, some already crossing and rubbing over others, others making a narrow angle with the trunk, growing up rather than out.

Tree after tree, ginkgos and tree lilacs, looked the same, with too many closely spaced scaffold branches, a result of pre-pruning trees in the nursery. In this industry-wide practice, small unbranched tree seedlings, "whips," are headed back to encourage a proliferation of lateral branches. The problems associated with nursery pruning

Nursery-pruning of young trees results in closely spaced lateral branches (left), most of which must be removed for the future health of the tree. For small trees like this streetside crabapple (right), the space between scaffold branches after pruning should be at least 6 inches.

occur as the crowded branches grow larger in diameter, exerting pressure on each other while becoming weak and susceptible to breakage when loaded with ice or snow.

I asked my pruning class to think down the road a few years, to imagine each branch increasing in diameter, reminding them that the space between branches remains the same as the tree grows. Surely something would have to give!

Pre-pruning is done to sell trees. Most people, unaware of the future problems associated with such closely spaced branches, will select a young tree with crowded branches over one with fewer, widely spaced branches. But while scaffold branches 2 inches apart may look nice in miniature, they are going to be overcrowded and poorly attached after they become a foot thick.

Pre-pruning is the standard in production—you are not likely to find trees that are otherwise. Your only recourse with a nursery-butchered tree is to do the necessary formative pruning to thin crowded branches, allowing the remaining scaffold limbs sufficient room to develop along the trunk.

Branches on large trees should be at least 18 inches apart in a spiral arrangement up the trunk, with about 3 feet between branches on the same side of the trunk. For smaller tree species, such as crabapples, the space between branches should be at least 6 inches, with a foot between branches on the same side of the trunk.

When should this formative pruning be done? I normally recommend little pruning during the establishment period of a tree, defined as one year after planting for every inch of trunk diameter. This delay in pruning allows for retention of maximum foliage to nourish the developing root system. But when I see trees such as these street trees, I want to reach for the loppers immediately and do the formative pruning while the branches to be removed are still small, rather than making larger wounds down the road. Of course, this is the strongest argument for buying small trees that will establish in a single year, trees no more than 1 inch in diameter.

It is a sad fact that the average street tree lives only ten years. There are a lot of reasons for this, but chief among them is putting large pre-pruned trees in small planting holes and walking away.

# Pruning Spring-Flowering Shrubs

## Forsythia and Most Other Spring-Flowering Shrubs

In early spring, beneath the soft and subtle golds of willow and oak, the bright yellow of forsythia *(Forsythia* x *intermedia)* covers the New England landscape. I believe states must be offering tax breaks to homeowners who grow this herald of early spring, for few properties are without at least one shrub, and some citizens compete with the highway department for the largest colony.

One year, on an April journey across Massachusetts, Marjorie and I documented the many forms that forsythia assumes in home landscapes. We photographed wild and woolly hedges that had not been pruned in decades, a few slender flowering branches twisting into the light from a tangle of old woody stems. Other informal hedges, open and airy and far more floriferous, reflected the care of annual pruning. And there were all of the tortured forms, meatballs lined up along the property line, hot-air balloons flanking the entrance drive, and flat-topped plants that might be used as garden benches.

For my taste, the best forsythias are those managed to enhance their natural growth habit, slender branches that grow upward and outward, stiffly arching down to earth under the weight of spring flowers. This can be accomplished with a single plant, a small grouping, or a long informal hedge.

Forsythia flower buds form during the summer on one-year-old branches that grow out of older branches or from ground level. As a branch ages, its flowering potential is reduced, and plants with an abundance of old branches thicker than an inch in diameter often bear few flowers. Also, shearing plants into unnatural forms removes many flowering stems and shortens the length of others, thus reducing the total number of flowers.

The gardener's task is to enhance the proportion of young, floriferous branches, and this can be accomplished with a three-year cycle of pruning. Each spring, as soon as the plants stop flowering, prune one-third of the branches, choosing the oldest and thickest. Cut some branches back to the ground, others a few to several inches above the ground, varying the height of the cuts to maintain a natural form. Make each above-ground cut just above an outward-facing bud. New stems will then grow outward

Pruning forsythias should enhance their natural growth habit (top). Turning otherwise graceful landscape plants into parachutes (middle) and meatballs (above) is a form of plant butchery best avoided. Annual shearing of forsythias to produce these unnatural forms will reduce the flowering potential of the shrub as scaffold stems age without replacement.

from lateral buds, stems that will grow vigorously during their first year and flower profusely in their second and third years.

While pruning each plant, you should also remove any dead, damaged, or diseased stems, again making each cut either just above an outward-facing bud or at ground level. Pruning for these "three D's" should be done throughout the year, whenever they are noticed.

Pruning forsythias, even informal hedges, should be done with hand-pruners, loppers, and a small pruning saw. Under no circumstances should any form of pruning shears be used! Shears lop off stems at indiscriminate points—you want to make each cut just above an outward-facing bud.

Forcing forsythias into unnatural shapes is plant butchery. A narrow hedge with a flat top and straight sides is about as unnatural for forsythia as you can get. So are meatballs and hot-air balloons.

Other spring-flowering shrubs that should be pruned immediately after flowering include beautybush *(Kolkwitzia amabilis)*, bridal wreath spirea *(Spiraea x vanhouttei)*, mockorange *(Philadelphus coronarius)*, mountain laurel *(Kalmia latifolia)*, slender deutzia *(Deutzia gracilis)*, weigela *(Weigela florida)*, and lilac *(Syringa vulgaris)*. These can be pruned like forsythias with the exception of lilacs, which are handled somewhat differently. We'll look at lilacs next.

## Pruning Lilacs

Lilac flower buds are formed in early summer, right after the shrub flowers, so if you wait too long after flowering to prune, you will be removing next year's flowers. This may not matter if you are renovating an old lilac that only produces flowers 25 feet above the ground. In that case, you can do your renovation work in summer, knowing that you will be sacrificing a year of blooms in order to get future flowers down to nose level. More on this later.

Annual pruning of a lilac should begin when the shrub is between 6 and 8 feet tall. The goals of annual pruning are to keep the plant within this height range, to keep it flowering profusely, and to maintain the plant with eight to twelve stems of varied ages, none more than 2 inches in diameter. Also, you should prune to keep the center of the shrub open to air circulation. (Old-timers advise that you should be able to throw a cat through the middle of the shrub.)

As you work toward accomplishing these goals, you should never remove more than one-third of the shrub wood in a single year. Lilacs, some varieties more than others, are overstressed by removal of too much wood at once. Or so we are told. The truth is, no one has ever been able to tell me which varieties are likely to succumb to overzealous pruning, so I treat them all with deference.

Begin by removing dead, damaged, and diseased stems. When removing diseased or damaged branches, make the pruning cuts through healthy wood, not through the diseased or damaged portion of the stem, and make each cut ¼ inch above an outward-facing bud, if visible. This will direct new growth outward, helping to keep the shrub open. Buds are not often visible on the thicker stems because they are buried beneath the bark, so go ahead and make the cut—you can always rub out any inward-directed new growth.

After taking care of the three "Ds," remove *crossing wood*, branches that are rubbing against other branches. Often you will see the wound made by a crossing branch as it rubbed the protective bark from another branch. One of these stems must go. Use a *thinning cut* to take out the wounded branch at its point of origin, making the cut through the wood of the branch you are removing, not through the wood of the branch from which it grew. At the same time, do not leave more than a ¼-inch stub. Thinning cuts are not likely to promote new growth.

Next, prune out stems thicker than 2 inches in diameter, which are targets for the lilac borer. By removing these largest stems you are keeping your lilac

### Deadheading Lilacs

Deadheading, the removal of spent flowers or, if you wait a while longer, the removal of seed heads, is probably not essential to the health or future flowering of mature lilacs. During the first few year of growing, however, deadheading seems to help shrubs bloom. The theory is that removing the spent flowers immediately after blooming allows the plant to put more energy into setting next year's buds rather than maturing seeds. Once the plant matures, however, allowing the seeds to mature on the plant does not seem to affect the abundance of flowers. And this is good news, since removing all the spent blossoms from a large lilac would be a full-time summer job!

free of this damaging herbivore, and larger stems are also less floriferous.

Stems selected for removal should be cut as close to the ground as possible if they are closing up the center of the shrub. Otherwise, you can prune them back to within a foot or so of the ground with expectations that they will produce new lateral branches. In either case, you are using a *heading cut*, which will promote new growth.

Finally, remove any twiggy growth on the remaining branches and any pencil-thin suckers originating at ground level. At this point, if you want your lilac to fill in more and become shrubbier, prune the remaining younger stems to an outward-facing bud. This will cause more branching.

Now, about that old neglected lilac tree that looms over the roof of your house, the one that your grandmother planted and that you would never consider removing despite the fact that you haven't seen it bloom in years. What can be done?

You can rejuvenate an old lilac in about three years. Each year, prune one-third of the oldest branches all the way to the ground, starting with the thickest stems first. Do this in the spring, before leaf buds break, even though you might be removing some flower buds. It is easier to see what you are doing while the branches are naked.

After the third year, new stems dominate the plant and it should begin to produce abundant blooms. Thereafter, you can do maintenance pruning as described above.

Alternatively, if you like to live dangerously, take the more drastic approach and cut the entire plant back to 6 or 8 inches from the ground in early spring. New shoots will emerge throughout the growing season. The following spring, prune out the weaker shoots and keep the healthiest ten to twelve stems, pruning them back to just above an outward-facing bud to encourage branching. Thereafter, stay on the annual maintenance pruning.

## The Blooming of Shadblow Serviceberry: A Link with Maine's Past

In mid-April, shadblow serviceberries on the coast of Maine signal the true arrival of spring, the loosening of winter's grip on their pointed buds. Roadsides from Cape Elizabeth to Eastport are adorned with these small multi-stemmed trees in full bloom, bright white clouds come to earth.

When I see these trees festooned with their delicate white flowers, I try to imagine how it was to live in Maine when the blooming of *Amelanchier canadensis* (shadblow serviceberry or shad bush) signaled the alewife spawning run in the Penobscot, Dennys, Pleasant, and other Maine rivers and their tributaries. Of all the migratory fish that ascended Maine's rivers to spawn, the alewife, close relative of the American shad, was the most abundant.

Shadblow serviceberries signal the true arrival of spring, bright white clouds come down to earth.

One historical account, written in 1852, relates that alewives were once so plentiful in Maine streams "that bears, and later swine, fed on them in the water. They were crowded ashore by the thousands." Alewives were once so common that Maine farmers used them to fertilize their fields.

The alewife fishery in Maine is four centuries old. In the beginning, the bulk of the harvest was for human consumption; alewives provided a critical source of fresh food at a time of year when winter food supplies were low.

Lobster fishermen prefer alewives for bait, when they can get them. In the past, the alewife harvest provided 30 to 50 percent of lobstermen's bait during the spring. With decreased returns of adult alewives in recent years, only about 1 percent of lobstermen's bait needs can be filled with alewives.

A granite outcrop adorned by the red autumn foliage of lowbush blueberry *(Vaccinium angustifolium)*.

Although alewife populations have plummeted during the past two centuries due to dam construction, pollution, and overharvesting, spawning runs still occur. Each spring, when the shadblow serviceberries are in full flower, the adult alewives, guided by their sense of smell, migrate upstream from the ocean to rivers, streams, ponds, and lakes. While a single female alewife produces between 60,000 and 100,000 eggs, only a few survive to the juvenile stage, and sometimes only as few as three juveniles survive to adulthood. Some adults die after spawning, but the majority make their way back to the ocean—and many return the following spring to spawn again.

I think about all of this when I see the shadblow in bloom, about how the phenological event of a tree's flowering carried such weight in the lives of past generations and gave this beautiful native tree its common name. If efforts to restore the Penobscot and other Maine rivers are successful, perhaps the sight of shadblow in bloom will once again send us scampering to the nearest shore to watch alewives in their spawning frenzy, to see ospreys and eagles taking their share, to eat smoked alewife, and to feel connected to the past.

## Rock Gardening New England Style

Lucky are the New England gardeners who can count among their garden niches a granitic rock outcrop, who can step gingerly between patches of crusty lichen for a closer view of the life that colonizes shallow pockets of newly formed soil. Such garden spots are maintenance-free islands of natural beauty, and they are worthy of protection. The plants that grow there are true pioneers, eking out a living in the thinnest and poorest of soils. In August, they know the meaning of drought. Yet they survive.

The early pioneers on granitic outcrops are herbaceous plants. Mosses and wildflowers, such as the white-flowered three-toothed cinquefoil *(Potentilla tridentata)* that blooms in early June, flourish in long narrow rock fissures holding an inch or less of coarse, sandy soil formed from lichen-weathered rock.

As the cracks widen and soil layers deepen and become enriched with decaying organic matter, woody plants take hold. In June, look for shallow-rooted lowbush blueberries bearing their white bells just above the gray crustose lichens. And in pockets of deeper soil, the swales between boulders, you'll find colonies of native rhodora *(Rhododendron canadense)*, their spindly stems festooned with lovely rosy purple blooms.

In even deeper pockets, larger shrubs such as the wild raisin *(Viburnum nudum* var. *cassinoides)* and small trees struggle for survival, their roots penetrating every subterranean crack and fissure for purchase and moisture. In August, if you walk quietly, you may run across a wood thrush perched within the heart of a viburnum, feasting on wild raisins, too heavy to fly away.

## Remembering the Trees of Our Youth

The flowers of the northern catalpa have an exotic beauty similar to those of the horse chestnut. (Photo courtesy Robert H. Mohlenbrock @ USDA-NRCS PLANTS Database)

We love the trees of our childhoods. I spent my boyhood in western Alabama in the summer shade of a southern catalpa *(Catalpa bignoniodes)*, a tree very similar to the catalpa that will grow in New England, the northern catalpa *(C. speciosa)*. I have vivid memories of a large tree with crooked branches growing at the intersection of our driveway with the road. I was intrigued by the long slender "beans" that hung from its branches in late summer. We called it the cigar tree, and I wondered if people really did smoke the bean pods as some of my older friends claimed. I never worked up the courage to try.

This tree was a source of summer income for my two sisters and me. Spurred into action by the presence of frass covering the leaves and ground, we would grab the longest cane poles from the shed and vigorously beat the foliage, forcing the "catalpa worms" down to the ground. Each spotted, 6-inch-long caterpillar (larva of the catalpa sphinx moth, *Ceratomia catalpa*) was worth a penny at the local bait store. These caterpillars had a worldwide reputation as the best large-mouth bass bait in existence, particularly if you turned them inside out before threading them on the hook. I always kept a few dozen for myself.

Today, catalpas are often classified as "weed trees," and few are sold for landscape use. This is unfortunate, as catalpas combine toughness with exotic beauty. Indeed, "speciosa" is Latin for beautiful or showy, a reference to the large, white, bell-shaped flowers that appear in late spring in upright pyramidal clusters. These flowers are speckled on the throat with yellow and purple and have been likened to those of the horse chestnut *(Aesculus hippocastanum)*. The large, heart-shaped grass-green leaves can provide textural interest in the landscape. The leaves of the northern catalpa may turn canary yellow in fall.

The native range for northern catalpa is limited to a small river bottom area defined by the confluence of the Wabash, Ohio, and Mississippi rivers, from the Memphis area northward into southeastern Illinois. The tree's adaptability, however, encouraged its use in forestry plantings throughout the eastern United States. When the woods were cleared for farming, the catalpas were often left standing in the fields to provide welcome shade on hot summer days. Now you see these old trees standing lonesome in old fields gone to pasture throughout New England.

In April, northern catalpas in New England can be recognized by irregular open crowns and unfolding heart-shaped leaves. The flowers open in June throughout New England and are soon followed by the long, bean-like seedpods.

# *The New England Garden in April, Zone by Zone*

Across New England, April is a busy month in the garden. Seedlings started in March are ready for hardening and transplanting, while seeds of cool-season crops such as spinach, turnips, lettuce, kohlrabi, and carrots can be sown directly in the garden as soon as the soil is workable. Rhubarb and asparagus crowns go in the ground, and the winter mulch is removed from the strawberry bed. And April is the time to put up nest boxes for native bees, to rekindle the compost pile or start a new one, and to start weeding.

| IN THE GARDEN | April | Date by USDA Hardiness Zone | | | | | Notes |
|---|---|---|---|---|---|---|---|
| | | 3 | 4 | 5 | 6 | 7 | |
| **GENERAL MAINTENANCE** | Set out native bee nest boxes. Provide nesting sites for bumblebees. Build a raised bed. Heel in early-arriving perennial crowns. | | | | | | Mount the bee nest 3 feet from the ground on either a stake or tree trunk, angling the front of the box slightly downward to avoid flooding by rain. Bees prefer boxes that face the morning sun.<br><br>Be less tidy in the garden; leave a portion of the garden wild. |
| **THE COMPOST PILE** | Start a new compost pile. Consider setting up a worm bin. | | | | | | See "The 30-Minute Compost Pile," Chapter 6. See "Composting Indoors with Worms," Chapter 6. |
| **VEGETABLE GARDEN** | Spread wood ashes over the garden.<br><br>Add organic matter to garden soil.<br><br>Start weeding.<br><br>Sow seeds of early-season crops in containers. | | | | | | Apply wood ash at the rate 2½ pounds (½ gallon) per 100 square feet. Do not apply to soils growing blueberries and other acid-loving crops or to soils with a pH 7 or higher.<br><br>If soil is still wet, wait a while before applying organic matter. If soil is dry, topdress with 1-2 inches of aged manure or compost.<br><br>See Chapter 5, "A Moveable Feast," for tips on growing early-season vegetable crops in containers. |
| **VEGETABLE CROPS** | | | | | | | |
| Asparagus | If not done yet, plant crowns as soon as soil can be worked. | | | | | | |
| Beets | Sow seeds outdoors if soil is workable. | Apr 26 | Apr 19 | Apr 2 | Mar 26 | Mar 19 | See "Direct Sowing in Rows or Blocks," Chapter 6 |
| Broccoli | Harden-off transplants. | May 7 | Apr 30 | Apr 23 | Apr 16 | Apr 9 | Harden-off with a week in the cold frame or in a protected outdoor area. Bring exposed seedlings inside if a freeze threatens. |

| IN THE GARDEN | April | Date by USDA Hardiness Zone | | | | | Notes |
|---|---|---|---|---|---|---|---|
| | | 3 | 4 | 5 | 6 | 7 | |
| Cabbage | Harden-off transplants. | May 1 | Apr 23 | Aprl 6 | Apr 9 | Apr 2 | Harden-off with a week in the cold frame or in a protected outdoor area. Bring exposed seedlings inside if a freeze threateans. |
| | Set out transplants. | May 7 | Apr 30 | Apr 23 | Apr 16 | Apr 9 | Set transplants 18-24 inches apart in soil amended with aged manure or compost. If planting in rows, space rows 2-4 feet apart. DO NOT apply excessive fertilizer as high nitrogen levels result in poor head shape and reduced yields. For uninterrupted growth, the planted area should receive one inch of water per week from rain and/or irrigation. |
| Carrots | Sow seeds outdoors if soil is workable. | Apr 16 | Apr 9 | Apr 2 | Mar 26 | Mar 19 | See "Direct Sowing in Rows or Blocks," Chapter 6 |
| Cauliflower | Harden-off transplants. | May 7 | Apr 30 | Apr 23 | Apr 16 | Apr 9 | Harden-off with a week in the cold frame or in a protected outdoor area. Bring exposed seedlings inside if a freeze threatens. |
| Chard, Swiss | Sow seeds outdoors if soil is workable. | Apr 16 | Apr 9 | Apr 2 | Mar 26 | Mar 19 | See "Direct Sowing in Rows or Blocks," Chapter 6 |
| Garlic | Remove the rest of the winter mulch if weather is mild. | | | | | | Keep the removed mulch in the walkways just in case temperatures below 28° F are forecast. If so, put the mulch back in place until temperatures settle above freezing. |
| Green Onions | Sow seeds outdoors if soil is workable. | Apr 16 | Apr 9 | Apr 2 | Mar 26 | Mar 19 | See "Direct Sowing in Rows or Blocks," Chapter 6 |
| Kale | Start seeds indoors. | Apr 15 | Apr 8 | Apr 1 | Mar 25 | Mar 18 | Optimum germination temperature range is 50-85° F. Once seeds have germinated, keep the seedlings uniformly moist. Water with a half-strength solution of an organic fertilizer such as fish emulsion or liquid seaweed. |
| Kohlrabi | Sow seeds in garden if soil is workable. | | | | | | See "Direct Sowing in Rows or Blocks," Chapter 6 |
| Lettuce | Set out transplants. | May 7 | Apr 30 | Apr 23 | Apr 16 | Apr 9 | Before transplanting, harden off for 2-3 days by reducing water and placing outside during the day in a sheltered location. Plant in soil amended with aged manure or compost. |
| Lettuce, Leaf | Sow seeds outdoors if soil is workable. | Apr 16 | Apr 9 | Apr 2 | Mar 26 | Mar 19 | See "Direct Sowing in Rows or Blocks," Chapter 6 |

| IN THE GARDEN | April | Date by USDA Hardiness Zone | | | | | Notes |
|---|---|---|---|---|---|---|---|
| | | 3 | 4 | 5 | 6 | 7 | |
| Onions | Shear seedling tops if they are getting floppy. | | | | | | Keep top growth to 4 inches. |
| Peas | Sow seeds outdoors if soil is workable. | Apr 16 | Apr 9 | Apr 2 | Mar 26 | Mar 19 | See "Direct Sowing in Rows or Blocks," Chapter 6 |
| Potatoes | Plant a few seed potatoes early. | | | | | | Try planting a small crop as soon as the soil can be worked, planting the seed potatoes about six inches deep. See Chapter 6 for more information on growing potatoes. |
| Radish | Sow seeds outdoors if soil is workable. | Apr 23 | Apr 16 | Apr 9 | Apr 2 | Mar 26 | See "Direct Sowing in Rows or Blocks," Chapter 6 |
| Rhubarb | Plant new crowns as soon as soil can be worked.<br><br>Divide overgrown crowns and replant, as soon as soil is workable. | | | | | | See Chapter 6 for details. |
| Spinach | Sow seeds outdoors if soil is workable. | Apr 16 | Apr 9 | Apr 2 | Mar 26 | Mar 19 | See "Direct Sowing in Rows or Blocks," Chapter 6 |
| Turnips | Sow seeds outdoors if soil is workable. | Apr 23 | Apr 16 | Apr 9 | Apr 2 | Mar 26 | See "Direct Sowing in Rows or Blocks," Chapter 6 |
| | | | | | | | |
| Strawberries | Pull off mulch from established plants and place in walkways.<br><br>Fertilize established plants lightly with 6 oz of organic nitrogen per 1,000 sq. ft. of bed. | Apr 30 | Apr 23 | Apr 16 | Apr 9 | Apr 2 | Rake back over plants during late frosts. (Photo by Marc Ryckaert) |
| **HERBS** | | | | | | | |
| Basil | Start seeds indoors. | Jun 10 | Jun 3 | Apr 26 | Apr 19 | Apr 12 | Scatter seeds thinly over the surface of the seed flat and cover lightly with fine vermiculite. Keep fluorescent lights within 2 inches of germinating seedlings to avoid leggy growth. Water seedlings with a half-strength solution of an organic fertilizer such as liquid seaweed or fish emulsion. |
| **FLOWERS** | | | | | | | |
| Ageratum | Start seeds indoors | Apr 15 | Apr 8 | Apr 1 | Mar 25 | Mar 18 | Do not cover seeds; they need light to germinate. |
| Alyssum | Start seeds indoors | Apr 15 | Apr 8 | Apr 1 | Mar 25 | Mar 18 | |

| IN THE GARDEN | April | Date by USDA Hardiness Zone | | | | | Notes |
|---|---|---|---|---|---|---|---|
| | | 3 | 4 | 5 | 6 | 7 | |
| Aster | Start seeds indoors | Apr 29 | Apr 22 | Apr 15 | Apr 8 | Apr 1 | Cover seeds only lightly. |
| Balsam | Start seeds indoors | Apr 29 | Apr 22 | Apr 15 | Apr 8 | Apr 1 | |
| Celosia | Start seeds indoors | Apr 15 | Apr 8 | Apr 1 | Mar 25 | Mar 18 | If you suspect a late spring, postpone sowing so that transplants can be set out no later than 4 weeks after germination. Germination occurs in 7-14 days. Sunflowers need warm soil, 70-75° F, for germination. |
| Centaurea | Start seeds indoors | Apr 29 | Apr 22 | Apr 15 | Apr 8 | Apr 1 | |
| Coleus | Start seeds indoors | Apr 15 | Apr 8 | Apr 1 | Mar 25 | Mar 18 | Provide warm temperatures, 80-85° F, for fast and even germination. A heat mat is ideal. |
| Dahlia | Start seeds indoors | Apr 15 | Apr 8 | Apr 1 | Mar 25 | Mar 18 | |
| Marigold | Start seeds indoors | Apr 29 | Apr 22 | Apr15 | Apr 8 | Apr 1 | Tall types require more time from sowing to transplanting. |
| Monarda | Start seeds indoors | Apr 23 | Apr 16 | Apr 9 | Apr 2 | Mar 26 | |
| Nicotiana (Flowering Tobacco) | Start seeds indoors | Apr 15 | Apr 8 | Apr 1 | Mar 25 | Mar 18 | Needs light to germinate. |
| Phlox | Start seeds indoors | Apr 15 | Apr 8 | Apr 1 | Mar 25 | Mar 18 | Direct seed into containers such as peat pots. |
| Snapdragon | Start seeds indoors | Apr 26 | Apr 19 | Aprl 2 | Apr 5 | Mar 29 | Needs light to germinate. Grow cool. |
| Sweet peas | Start seeds indoors | Jun 10 | Jun 3 | Apr 26 | Apr 19 | Apr 12 | Nick the seed coat or soak seeds 24 hours before planting. |
| **ROSES** | Remove mounded soil and mulch from around plants. | | | | | | |
| **WOODY PLANTS** | Remove trunk wraps from trees. | | | | | | |

# Chapter 7

# The Garden in May

*"I think that no matter how old or infirm I may become, I will always plant a large garden in the spring. Who can resist the feeling of hope and joy that one gets from participating in nature's rebirth?"*

*—Edward Giobbi*

***In the beginning, more than a decade ago,*** sweet peas arrived as summer gifts from Marjorie's Garden, small vases of nodding slender-stemmed flowers, bouquets of red, pink, purple, and white. I would set them in a sunny window of the house where I lived alone and enjoy the smell of orange blossoms and honey for days.

We cut sweet peas together now, often at the end of a summer day when their colors glow in the garden's last light. Or one of us will awake at dawn to walk about the garden with the dogs, returning with a fistful of blooms for the other. For days on end, the rooms we share are filled with the scent that can only come from sweet peas.

Sweet peas from Marjorie's Garden get their start in early May when we fork composted goat manure into the cold soil of a full-sun bed. We sow the seeds 1 inch deep and 2 inches apart in double rows only a few inches apart, each pair of rows separated by about 18 inches. After sowing, we push birch stems into the soil, spacing them about 2 feet apart down the middle of each pair of rows. Ranging in height from 4 to 5 feet, with lateral branches in the upper half, these pea stakes provide a scaffold of overlapping stems for the sweet pea vines to climb.

When the plants are several inches tall, we thin them to a final spacing of 5 inches, and when seedlings have three or four pairs of leaves, we pinch out the top pair to promote branching. Sweet pea transplants purchased from a local grower are used to fill in gaps within each row.

Gaps there will be, for germination is never better than about 80% and there are always a few dormant seeds, nature's insurance against a late hard freeze. By soaking the seeds for no more than eight hours before sowing, we can identify the ones most likely to germinate, planting only the ones that swell.

Our summer garden would be incomplete without the fragrance of sweet peas sown in May. It's orange blossoms and honey. It's how it all began.

Sweet peas sown in May will grace the garden all summer with colorful flowers and sweet fragrance.

*Facing page:* Volunteer Shirley poppies provide color wherever they're allowed to bloom.

# May in the Vegetable Garden

In early May, the vegetable garden is a blank canvas. Just-thawed beds of dark brown soil give off an earthy aroma as they warm in the sun. In the crevices of stones that frame the beds, the first volunteer pansies greet the gardener with outrageous color. The gardener waits impatiently for delivery of onion plants and for the soil temperature to rise.

## Planting by Soil Temperature

For gardeners in USDA Zone 5,Memorial Day weekend at the end of May is a popular time to plant tomatoes and other summer vegetables. Gardeners along New England's southern coastal zone, USDA Zone 7, reserve Mother's Day weekend in the middle of May for planting these same summer crops. There seems to be a wide consensus on these dates among a lot of calendar planters in both zones, although the reasoning is unclear.

Other gardeners believe that summer vegetables grow faster and larger when planted by a full moon. They hang onto this believe because it has produced admirable results in prior years, not because it has any support from plant scientists, many of whom believe it to be pure lunacy.

I think that New England gardeners came up with the idea of planting by moonlight because blackflies feed only during daylight hours.

When the full moon comes in early May, and it is obviously too damp and cold to plant summer crops, Moonlight Planters have to wait until early June. This may be the best of choices, not because the moon will be full, but because soil temperatures may have finally settled above 60 °F by then.

Soil temperature is the most important factor in transplanting seedlings of tomatoes, peppers, cucumbers, squash, and other summer crops. Many of these vegetables are tropical in origin and will not grow well until the soil has sufficiently warmed (see sidebar).

When I consider that the average end-of-May soil temperature in Maine's Zone 5 at a 6-inch depth for the period 1997 to 2010 was 55° F—and that in some years, according to University of Maine records, we lag about 10° F below that average, I understand why the survival of transplants and germination rate of direct-sown vegetables is higher for gardeners who exercise a little patience.

Soil temperature is the best indicator of sowing and planting times

For direct-sown crops, such as beans, we can ask not only what is the *minimum* soil temperature for germination, but also what is the *optimum* daytime soil temperature (at a 2-inch depth) for maximum seedling production in the shortest time. For the vast majority of summer vegetable crops, the answer is 77° F. For cucumbers and eggplant, however, it's even higher, 86° F. At soil temperatures of 60° F and below, seedling production drops dramatically. Clearly, direct sowing of summer vegetables when soil temperatures are still in the mid-40s to mid-50s makes no sense.

### Minimum Soil Temperatures for Planting Summer Crops

Minimum soil temperature (at a 4-inch depth) for transplants:

60° F – tomatoes, tomatillos, cucumbers
70° F – peppers, squash (both summer and winter)
75° F – cantaloupe, sweet potatoes

Minimum soil temperature (at a 2-inch depth) for direct-sown vegetables:

50° F – onions
50° F – beets, Swiss chard
60° F – snap beans and dry beans
60° F – sweet corn
70° F – lima beans

Where soil temperatures will be by Mother's Day or Memorial Day in any given year is anyone's guess and will depend entirely on the weather and on soil type. It may make sense to hold off until mid-June to sow beans or plant peppers. On the other hand, home-grown tomato seedlings that are getting leggy under the fluorescent lights need to go in the ground. Better to plant these sooner than later, holding off on the mulch so that the sun can warm the soil as quickly as possible.

Those of us who plant by soil temperature have one or two soil thermometers in the tool shed or in a garden bed. These thermometers have a large round dial, much like some cooking thermometers, but with a long probe (at least 8 inches) that can be pushed deep into the soil. A combined soil/compost thermometer with a 19-inch probe can be used to monitor both compost pile and soil temperatures.

There is an old saying that fits: "You pays your money and you takes your chances." You live with the consequences. Over the years, from Georgia to Washington State, I've been a Calendar Planter and a Moonlight Planter, but New England springs are something else. My money is on the soil thermometer.

## Selective Weeding of Garden Volunteers

Some of the garden's most striking scenes are the result of selective weeding of volunteers, plants that show up each year without effort on the gardener's part. Two examples always appear in Marjorie's Garden, beginning in May: Shirley poppy *(Papaver rhoeas)*, a self-sowing annual, and mullein *(Verbascum thapsus)*, a self-sowing biennial.

Several autumns ago Marjorie scattered a handful of tiny Shirley poppy seeds, a gift from the garden of a friend, in a small corner of a perennial bed. The seeds germinated the following spring and the resulting plants grew to 3 feet in height, their slender stems clad with blue-green leaves. In July, each stem was topped with a blossom, a single row of pink petals with the texture of crinkled tissue paper.

These first plants scattered their own seed, and the following spring there were poppy seedlings growing throughout the garden, easy to recognize by their unique foliage. Most were weeded out, but a few were allowed to grow and blossom.

These poppies have been with us every summer since, growing among the strawberries, winding through the branches of blueberry shrubs, circling the compost bin. And there are still poppies in the corner of the perennial bed.

Throughout the summer day, these few poppies are among the first plants to catch the eye as you stroll through the garden. I have been in the garden at first light to watch the poppies greet the day, to see them swaying

Self-sown Shirley poppies favor the vegetable garden with their translucent petals and unique seed pods.

A mullein plant is a woolly mammoth with a stout spike of yellow flowers that open sequentially, bottom to top.

with the slightest breeze, the low-angled light casting stamen-shadows inside curved petals. At dusk the flowers glow, reluctant to give up the last rays of sunlight.

We don't know the origin of the mullein in Marjorie's Garden, but each May we begin culling out most of the volunteer seedlings. Only a few are allowed to continue growing vegetatively through their first summer, waiting to flower until the following year. Such is the nature of biennials.

Unlike the slender poppy, a mullein plant in its second summer is a 6-foot-tall woolly mammoth. Densely hairy frost-green leaves clasp the lower two-thirds of the main stem, those nearest the ground more than a foot in length. The upper third of the stem develops into a stout spike of one-inch yellow flowers that open sequentially, bottom to top.

Although a single mullein plant can produce over 150,000 seeds, only a few will germinate and even fewer will make it to the second year. Mullein seedlings are not strong competitors, thriving only in the margins of the garden and along the bed edges. In a typical summer we have a few flowering plants on the edge of the strawberry beds where they stand in strong contrast to the creeping berry plants, and a few selected first-year plants scattered around the vegetable and small fruit beds. Their flowers bring native bees and other pollinators to the garden; their late-summer seed heads bring goldfinches. On summer mornings the large felted leaves covered with dew are an arresting sight.

## Edible Flowers

There is a blurred line between edibles and ornamentals in Marjorie's Garden. Take as an example the self-sown calendulas that pop up each year among the garden peas. They do double duty, their flowers adding a spot of color to the garden as well as to our summer meals. When I harvest peas and lettuce, I gather a few heads of calendula, also called Poor Man's Saffron, and pepper their petals over our supper salad, adding a subtle flavor ranging from bitter to spicy.

I cut flowers from a trailing nasturtium growing in a pot by the garden gate, its stems snaking through the onion bed, and add them to the same salad. After quick scrutiny for hiding insects, the golden blossoms are tossed in whole, providing a sharp peppery taste, much like the flavor of radishes. Nasturtium leaves are also edible, and the seed pods can be pickled as an inexpensive substitute for capers.

## Self-Sowing Annuals and Biennials to Scatter through the Vegetable Garden

In addition to Shirley poppies and mullein, many self-sowing annuals and biennials will become permanent residents of your vegetable garden, but only if you get them started by scattering their seed. Over the years, we have established populations of calendula, pansies, and nasturtiums in this way. The hawkweeds, on the other hand, were there before us.

Volunteer calendulas grow along the edges of strawberry and raspberry beds.

Volunteer pansies pop up everywhere, offspring of potted plants scattered about the garden the previous year.

### Calendula

This self-sowing annual grows in drifts and patches throughout our vegetable garden, its orange and yellow flowers serving as magnets for native bees. Every few years, when the seedling populations seem sparse, we scatter a few fresh seeds along bed edges, but in most years there are more than enough volunteers popping up everywhere. Calendulas are easy to transplant if you need them somewhere else in the garden.

### Violas (pansies)

We always grow pansies in pots on the porch railings. Despite efforts to keep them floriferous by snipping off fading blooms, a few seed pods ripen on these plants, the seeds winding up in the beds beneath the porch. Each May, new seedlings appear in these beds beneath the spreading arms of elderberry shrubs, and, as the season progresses, these self-sown pansies bloom in colors totally unlike their parents. Volunteer pansies also populate the vegetable garden, introduced from the compost pile.

A volunteer nasturtium in the onion patch.

### Nasturtiums

One year I placed pots of nasturtium *(Tropaeolum majus)* among the vegetables to create a movable feast for bumblebees. The following year, nasturtium seedlings were popping up in beds where the pots had rested, evidence that their seeds can survive the winter. Yet there are years when there are no self-sown nasturtiums and we have to start with pots again. Perhaps winter survival of seeds is dependent on depth of snow cover.

### Meadow Hawkweed

I selectively weed meadow hawkweed *(Hieracium caespitosum)*, leaving some to flower on the fringes of the garden, even though I know it to be a non-native invasive weed in pastures of the western U.S. I didn't plant the hawkweeds in Marjorie's Garden—they were there before there was a garden. I manage them in the same manner that I manage their cousins, the dandelions, and for the same reason: native bees forage them.

Meadow hawkweed volunteers, perfect companions for nearby catmint, colonized this old stump in Marjorie's Garden.

Edible flowers that can be collected from the garden include (clockwise from top left) calendulas, nasturtiums, pansies, and daylilies.

On my way to the kitchen, I snap off a few bright yellow daylily *(Hemerocallis* sp.) flowers, popping a crisp petal in my mouth to melt on my tongue and release a flavor much like buttery lettuce but sweeter, a combination of zucchini and asparagus. While some people detect unique flavors among daylily flowers of different colors, I've sampled the several varieties in our garden and find differences mainly in texture.

A porch pot of johnny-jump-ups *(Viola tricolor)* provides small flowers with yellow, white, and purple petals. Adding a touch of color as well as a mild wintergreen flavor, these flowers are often used in drinks, soups, and desserts as well as salads.

Flowers of pansies, related to johnny-jump-ups, are also edible. Eaten alone, the petals have a very mild green or grassy flavor, while entire flowers have a much stronger grassy taste. Pansy flowers can be used in desserts, soups, and salads.

To our harvest of flowers, lettuce, spring onions, yellow zucchini, and young carrots, we add a few leaves from basil scattered in pots about the garden. Marjorie is diligent about keeping the basil plants from flowering—she wants to keep them producing new leaves throughout the summer—and so we seldom see them produce the spikes of white blossoms that are milder but similar in flavor to the leaves.

As gardeners interested in eating the flowers of these and other plants, we follow three important rules: First, we never use pesticides, even organics, on any plants. Second, we never assume that all parts of a plant with edible flowers are edible. For example, elderberry *(Sambucus canadensis)* flowers are edible, but all other parts of the plant, including its uncooked berries, are poisonous. Once cooked, however, the berries are harmless and are often used in making jams, jellies, and elderberry wine.

Third, we use flowers sparingly in salads and other recipes. Large quantities often lead to digestive disorders. For example, you should use daylily petals sparingly as they can act as a laxative when eaten in excess. And johnny-jump-ups should always be eaten in small amounts, primarily as a garnish, as they contain saponins, which in large quantities can be toxic.

Combining edible flowers with traditional vegetables, gardeners can enjoy colorful and delicious summer salads throughout the gardening year. Each meal will be unique in the novelty of its creation, a combination of whatever is available in both traditional vegetables and edible blossoms.

## Growing Sweet Corn in a Small Garden

When Lynne was around 10 years old, she grew a small patch of sweet corn in the garden as a 4-H project. When all was said and done, in response to the prompt on the project report form, "What did you learn?," she wrote, "I learned that raccoons really like corn."

In spite of the raccoons, she did harvest a few ears and was able to experience the flavor of homegrown sweet corn just minutes from stalk to pot. It's unbeatable. Still, sweet corn has not been an every-year crop in our garden because of the amount of space it requires. Then last year I saw the success that Ladonna Bruce and Stuart Hall have growing corn in their Stockton Springs garden. They convinced me that sweet corn can and should be a part of every home garden, no matter how small.

Ladonna and Stuart use a modified version of a three-sisters garden to thwart the raccoons. They grow winter squash at the feet of their corn plants, letting the prickly leaves and stems keep the tender-footed raccoons at bay. Last year they harvested about four dozen ears from 25 plants, the raccoons absconding with only the few ears that could be reached from the walkways.

According to Native American legend, corn, squash, and beans are three inseparable sisters that only grow and thrive together. Planting these three crops together in the same garden space is a widespread tradition among many Native American farming societies, a sustainable system

Two of the three sisters are interplanted in Ladonna Bruce and Stuart Hall's garden.

that provides both long-term soil fertility and a healthy diet. The corn stalks provide a natural pole for the bean vines to climb, while the beans fix atmospheric nitrogen on their roots, improving the fertility of the entire plot. The beans also help to stabilize the corn plants against root and stem lodging. The squash vines form a living mulch over the soil, slowing weed emergence and preventing evaporation of soil moisture, and the spiny squash leaves and stems discourage predators, including the masked bandits.

## Planting a Three-Sisters Garden

Sweet corn grows best in loose, rich soil with a pH between 6.0 and 6.5; heavy soil inhibits rooting. Wait to plant your three-sisters garden until soil temperatures have settled above 60° F, since corn kernels will not germinate in cold soil.

After incorporating decomposed stable manure or compost into the soil, make mounds spaced about 3 feet apart, each 12 inches high and 24 inches across. To enhance wind pollination, group the mounds in a block rather than in one long row if possible.

Flatten the tops of the mounds, then plant five or six corn seeds in a small circle within the center of each mound. Plant the kernels 1 inch deep in heavy soil, 2 inches deep in light, sandy soil.

When the corn seedlings are about 5 inches high (about two weeks after sowing), plant seven or eight pole bean seeds in a circle about 6 inches away from the corn seeds. Wait another week, then sow seven or eight squash seeds around the edge of each mound, about 12 inches from the beans.

As the plants grow, thin the corn in each mound to the sturdiest two or three seedlings. Also thin the beans and squash, removing weak seedlings and keeping three vigorous seedlings of each evenly spaced around the mound. Help the bean seedlings to start climbing the corn stalks by gently propping their growing points against the stalks.

## Sweet Corn Types

Sweet corn is a genetic mutation of field corn, producing kernels with mostly sugar rather than starch. In the older sweet corn varieties, the sugar rapidly converts to starch after the prime harvest stage. Recent hybrids, however, have even higher sugar concentration and slower conversion of sugar to starch.

In seed catalogs you will find sweet corn varieties separated into genetic groups, the best of which, in tenderness and sweetness, are the "Sugar Enhanced" types (se and se+ genes). Some gardeners are high on Trinity sweet corn, a bicolor sugar-enhanced variety with excellent flavor that matures in 68 days. It grows to 5 feet tall, not so tall as to be prone to blow over in high winds.

Harvard Jordan, owner of the Ellsworth Feed and Seed, sings the praises of Ambrosia, another sugar-enhanced bicolor variety that matures in 75 days and grows to 6½ feet tall. He did mention that it toppled in a strong wind storm one year.

## Sweet Corn Growing Tips

Don't be in a rush to get your corn seeds in the ground. Planting corn too early results in poor stands and retarded growth. And start with fresh seeds rather than leftovers from last year. Even under ideal storage conditions, corn seed is short-lived.

Sweet corn is a heavy feeder. In addition to digging in the decomposed manure or compost at planting, apply additional nitrogen when the corn plants are 8 inches tall and again when the plants are tasseling. This can be accomplished with a variety of organic products, including blood meal, soy meal, fish meal, and alfalfa meal. All of these are dry materials that can be broadcast directly over the soil between the plants, followed by washing the dust from the leaves to avoid burning. Follow label directs carefully when calculating the correct amount to apply.

## Peas

Gardeners are anxious to get started at the beginning of May, if only the frost would leave the soil. It is hard to temper such enthusiasm, and mistakes will be made, turning soil still too cold and too wet, would-be seed beds that turn to muddy clods in the wake of the spade. Even experienced gardeners have been known to jump the gun for the sake of planting early peas.

Planting peas is an inaugural event in Marjorie's Garden, an early-spring ritual that starts with spreading composted goat manure over the surface of a sunny well-drained bed, forking it in, then raking the bed level.

I sow the seeds an inch apart and an inch deep in double rows down the length of the bed, each row about 3 inches from its mate and each pair of rows about

Edible-pod peas ready for harvest.

### Three Types of Garden Peas

There are three types of garden peas: English peas, snow peas, and snap peas. All three require the same growing conditions but differ in time of harvest and how they are eaten.

- English peas are allowed to ripen fully in the pod before the plump, round peas are shelled and cooked without the pod. Snow peas are harvested while the peas inside the pod are immature, and the entire pea pod is steamed or stir-fried.
- Snap peas, my favorite, can be harvested when immature and eaten raw or cooked inside the pod. Or they can be allowed to mature and then can either be shelled and eaten like English peas or be eaten pod and all, raw or cooked, with the mature peas inside, still tender and tasty.
- Sugar Snap was the original snap pea variety, winning a Gold Medal in the 1979 All-America Selection trials. It is still a popular variety among gardeners. In recent years our favorite snap pea variety has been Sugar Ann, ideal for small gardens. The vines are short and bushy and can be grown without support, although a birch-branch pea fence makes harvesting easier. Sugar Ann produces about 10 days earlier than other snap peas.

18 inches apart. This is intensive planting! Within a month of sowing, the vines will be so thick that a mouse couldn't crawl through them. Most of the growth is upward, however, and the bed is narrow enough to allow harvesting from the edges.

Between rows I construct pea fences of birch branches, pruning the lateral shoots from the bottom half of each branch so that it can be pushed deep into the soil but leaving the long, thin twigs on the upper half and placing the branches close enough to form a lattice for pea tendrils to grasp as the plants vine upward. I cut the branches from young yellow birch saplings, shaping the saplings in the process, and the smell of wintergreen at the cut ends is yet another sign of spring.

After covering the seeds with soil and watering well, I scatter a thin mulch of dry straw over the entire bed. The seeds germinate in 7 to 10 days, and the lush seedling growth quickly shades the ground, preventing weed seeds from germinating and keeping the soil cool.

Peas are essentially pest free unless you count Reilly, our Brittany, who several years ago discovered the pea patch to be a source of tasty treats. Lacking the ability to pinch a pod from the vine with one paw while grasping the vine with the other, she will pull an entire plant from the bed for a single plump pod. I've learned to do the picking for her.

Like Reilly, Marjorie and I love the sweetness and crunchy texture of raw snap peas; many pods never make it out of the garden. Those that do are tossed into garden salads or eaten as healthy snacks. High in carbohydrates but low in calories, peas contain nutritious amounts of essential vitamins, fiber, folic acid, amino acids, and proteins.

In some years, early May arrives with snow still a foot deep over the pea bed, and once it does finally melt, we must wait for the soil to dry out enough to dig before we plant. This is the hardest part of spring for me, waiting to plant peas.

## Onions

Sweet onions are a must-grow crop in our vegetable garden, an essential ingredient in Apple-ring Chicken, Lynne's all-time most favorite dinner, and in the Gingered Squash and Apple Soup that I cook up in double batches on winter weekends, making several hearty meals for the coming week (see Chapter 12, the Garden in October, for recipes). I like reaching into winter storage for onions that only get sweeter with time.

Copra onions drying on a sunny porch. Once cured, they will keep through the winter.

We grow Copra onions, which are medium-sized (3 to 4 inches, round), dark yellow, pungent but sweet and excellent for cooking. Copra is one of the highest in sugar content of all onion varieties, becoming milder with time in storage. It will keep for a year.

You can try growing other varieties, of course, but make sure they are long-day varieties like Copra that can be planted in April and grow leaves until June, when 14-hour days trigger the transition from leaves to bulbs. Vidalia onions and other short-day varieties, if planted in New England around the first of April, try to bulb up as soon as day length reaches 12 hours, long before leaf growth is sufficient to produce a large bulb.

The New England growing season is not long enough, even in Zone 7, to produce a good-quality onion from direct-sown seed. You can start seeds indoors in any zone, but the length of time required to produce a sizable transplant deters most people from doing so. It is far easier to plant transplants, and you are likely to grow larger onions from transplants. We transplant field-grown starter plants of Copra rather than trying to grow our own from seed. The transplants, grown in the South (but ordered from Johnny's Selected Seeds in Maine), will have a several-week jump on our season and on weeds, advantages that will hopefully promote production of large bulbs. (Note that these are transplants, not sets. Sets are small bulbs, essentially second-year onions. We do not plant sets in Marjorie's Garden.)

This works, however, only if the young transplants arrive on time, at least four weeks before your last frost date. Specify this need when you place your order, requesting the week that you want your plants to arrive. If they do arrive late, expect the average bulb size at harvest to be smaller than in years when the plants have more growing time before the critical day length is reached.

For immediate use, not for storage, try Walla Walla, a Washington State variety described by Johnny's as a "juicy, sweet, regional favorite." In Washington the seeds are sown in August and the plants overwinter in the ground; bulbs form the following spring and are harvested in early summer. In New England, we have to settle for transplants that don't grow as big a bulb but are still sweeter than many other spring-planted varieties.

Plant onion transplants as early as possible, four to six weeks before the date of the last expected spring frost. Onions can take cool soil and light frosts and require protection only from hard freezes. If you see a hard freeze coming after planting, water the plants thoroughly and cover them with a straw mulch. In exceptionally frigid weather, cover the mulch with burlap as well.

You should certainly be ready to plant the transplants as soon as they arrive, but if you have to hold them for a day or two, take them out of the box and keep them in a well-ventilated, cool location until you can plant them. Keep the plants dry; do not put them in soil or water.

For producing the largest bulbs, weed control and regular watering are the most critical factors. Onions survive periods of drought by using water stored in the developing bulbs, thereby reducing bulb growth, and weeds are serious competitors for available water.

Irrigation during dry periods is essential for production of large bulbs. Use the knuckle rule to determine when to water during the season. If you can feel moisture when you stick your finger in the ground up to your first knuckle, the onions are wet enough. Use drip irrigation if possible, rather than an overhead sprinkler system, which may promote the spread of disease. We often let the hose trickle over the soil surface, moving it as we work in the garden, a make-shift form of drip irrigation.

Mulching helps reduce competition from weeds while maintaining uniform soil moisture levels. Weeds that manage to grow through the mulch should be pulled by hand; a hoe will nick the young bulbs.

This business of keeping onions weed-free is a challenge that I readily accept—it is another excuse to be in the garden. We select our onion bed early in the season, a bed in full sun with excellent drainage, and keep it free of weeds, pulling them by hand or hoeing them out as they appear. Hand-weeding the onion bed is the first and last chore of every gardening day; we try never to let a weed grow beyond the seedling stage.

Onions are harvested in late summer, typically August or early September in most New England gardens. See Chapter 10 for details.

## Leeks

Think of leeks as a milder-tasting, more frost-tolerant member of the onion family. Many varieties, such as 'King Richard,' have large, dark blue-green leaves, an attractive ornamental feature in the edible landscape. Their upright, non-spreading habit makes leeks ideal plants for intercropping with other vegetables.

Cooked or uncooked, leeks are as versatile in the kitchen as onions. They can be used in soups, quiches, stews, casseroles, and salads, often as an onion substitute when a more subtle flavor is desired. They can also be prepared alone, as a winter vegetable.

Leeks are long-season plants that are best planted in the garden as seedlings that you grow yourself or purchase from commercial growers. I've been successful with both approaches but prefer to buy transplants, ordering them at the same time that I order my onion transplants. Grown in Southern fields, these starter plants are much larger than any I could produce under the lights at home.

Dark blue-green leaves make many leek varieties, such as 'King Richard,' ideal choices for the edible landscape.

Leeks grow best in full sun. They need a garden soil with high fertility, plenty of organic matter, and a soil pH between 6.2 and 6.8. The soil must hold plenty of moisture during the growing season but be well-drained in winter to prevent ice encasement of plants left in the soil to be harvested as needed. To avoid insect and disease problems, avoid planting leeks where they or any other member of the onion family have been grown in the past three years.

Transplants should be planted in the garden in late April or early May, as soon as daytime temperatures settle into the mid-40s. One approach to planting is to set the plants in holes that are 4 to 8 inches deep, leaving only a few inches of leaf above the soil. If you are planting in rows, leave 4 to 6 inches between rows.

Do not return the soil to the holes; they will be gradually filled with soil by rain or irrigation. Covering the plants all at once can result in rotting. As the leeks grow, hill or mound soil around them periodically to blanch the stems.

Many gardeners prefer to plant leeks in a 4-inch-deep trench, again setting them several inches deep. As the plants grow, the excavated soil removed is incrementally mounded around the stems to blanch them.

### Leek Varieties for All Seasons

By growing at least one variety from each of the following groups, the gardener can harvest fresh leeks throughout the year, even in winter. In areas where the ground freezes, covering the leek bed with a blanket of straw or shredded leaves will allow you to dig leeks in even the coldest months provided the soil is well-drained.

*Varieties for Summer Harvest:*

- 'King Richard,' 'Lincoln,' 'Rikor,' 'Kalima,' 'Titan'

*Varieties for Fall and Early Winter Harvest:*

- 'Varna,' 'Imperial,' 'Tadorna,' 'Falltime'

*Varieties for Overwintering:*

- 'American Flag,' 'Blue Solaise,' 'Giant Musselburgh,' 'Siegfried,' 'Winter Giant'

During summer, mulch the soil around the plants with straw or shredded leaves. This will lock in moisture, prevent weed growth, and blanch more of each plant's stem.

Leeks grown for use in late summer and fall can be harvested as needed beginning in early September. See Chapter 11 for details.

## Potatoes

A few years ago, I planted potatoes for the first time in Marjorie's Garden. They take up so much space in a garden, particularly if you are planting enough for winter meals, that I decided to plant them in a bin made with straw bales, a technique I had read about in numerous gardening magazines over the years. I constructed the bin over compacted soil on the outskirts of the garden where ropy tree roots, heaved by granite just beneath the surface, covered the ground.

I planted the seed potatoes an inch deep in a layer of compost at the bottom of the bin, and every time the plants grew a foot, I added 6 inches of compost and straw. I added bales as needed to increase the depth of the bin and kept the top of the bin covered with a lightweight fabric cover to thwart the Colorado potato beetle.

It all seemed like such a good idea at the time. I kept envisioning a wheelbarrow filled with softball-size potatoes.

It was an exceptionally cool and wet summer, and late blight ran rampant through Maine gardens, wiping out tomato crops and threatening potatoes as well. While my potatoes escaped the blight and the beetle, they were a magnet for the slugs that spent sunny days within the straw walls of the bin and rainy days and nights eating the leaves and stems of the potato plants. I estimated their numbers at a zillion. I surrendered in late July with a handful of egg-size potatoes, smaller than the original seed potatoes, to show for my effort.

In early May of the following year, defeated but not destroyed, I planted my Prairie Blush seed potatoes in the conventional fashion, in hilled rows. In one of our sunny raised beds I dug two trenches, about a foot apart and a foot deep, in soil amended with compost. I then laid the seed potatoes in the trenches at intervals of about 12 inches and covered them with about an inch of soil. Three weeks later, when the shoots were about a foot tall, I used a shovel to scoop soil from between the rows and mound it against the stems, burying them halfway. As the plants grew, I repeated this process, using either soil or compost.

In the conventional hilled row, seed potatoes are planted in trenches (top), about 12 inches apart and 12 deep, then covered with an inch of soil (center). As soon as shoots emerge, the potato bed is kept under an insect barrier, and the plants are hilled with soil (above) as they grow.

From early June, when the shoots first emerged from the bottom of the trenches, until mid-July I kept the potato plants covered with a fabric insect barrier. The fabric covered the entire bed, wide enough to be weighted down on all sides with large stones. There was no way that a Colorado potato beetle was going to fly or crawl onto the leaves of my potatoes.

In late August we dug the first of a respectable crop of potatoes, harvesting the last in mid-September. They were gone by early October. We discovered that digging potatoes and eating them the same day is among the most gratifying garden experiences available, worthy of the space they demand.

*Organic Gardening* magazine compared several methods of growing potatoes in test plots near Emmaus, Pennsylvania: hilled rows, straw mulch, raised beds, grow bags, and wire cylinders. The conventional hilled rows method worked well, as might be expected from a proven method that potato farmers have used for generations. This method will not work in places where the soil is badly compacted or low in organic matter, however.

Of the alternatives, raised beds yielded the largest harvest. In this method the soil is loosened in the bottom of a half-filled raised bed and the seed potatoes are spaced about 12 inches apart in all directions, then covered with 3 inches of soil. As the potatoes grow, more soil is added until the bed is full. If the bed is constructed with removable sides, harvesting is simple.

The yield from the straw-mulch method was slightly less than with hilled rows. The study report mentions problems with field mice in the straw, but never discusses slugs!

## Sowing Cucurbits Indoors

Cucurbits, including cucumbers, squash (summer and winter), pumpkins, and melons, can be direct-sown in the garden (early June) or, if you want to get an early start, sown indoors in May (see the zone-by-zone schedule at the end of the chapter for sowing dates in your zone). If the latter, sow the seeds in peat pots; cucurbit seedlings quickly develop extensive root systems that do not tolerate lifting from a seed tray. Sow two or three seeds in each pot, then thin to the most vigorous seedling when the first true leaves appear, about a week after germination. When planting the potted seedling in the garden, peel off as much of the peat pot as possible—particularly the bottom—to ensure continued healthy root growth.

Gardeners can choose from several types of summer squash that vary in color and shape. Most familiar are yellow fruits that are thinner at the stem end than the blossom end. These "constricted neck" squash can be straight-necked or crook-necked, with several varieties to choose from in both categories.

Scallop or patty pan varieties are round and flattened like a plate with scalloped edges. They may be white, yellow, or green, depending on the chosen variety.

Summer squash varieties include (left to right) patty pan, the Middle Eastern variety Magda, and zucchini, both yellow and green.

Zucchini are usually green and vary in shape from cylindrical to club-shaped.

## Rhubarb

Newly planted rhubarb crowns should not be harvested in the first year, but by the second year you can harvest stems for one or perhaps two weeks beginning in early May. Starting in the third season after planting, the harvest can continue for up to 10 weeks.

To harvest rhubarb stems, pull them off. Don't cut them, because cutting produces a large wound that can be invaded by a disease-causing fungus. Remove and discard the leaves, as they contain a toxic chemical and should never be eaten. They're fine for the compost pile, however.

If a flower stem should appear on a rhubarb plant, cut it off and take it as a sign that either the plant should be divided next spring or it is nitrogen-starved. In the latter case, topdress the soil around the rhubarb plants with compost, aged manure, or worm compost.

## Planting Strawberries

Like asparagus and rhubarb, strawberries are a perennial crop started from bare-root plants that are planted in early May or as soon as the soil can be worked. The strawberry bed will produce a good crop of berries in the second season after planting and will go on producing for two to four additional years before the plants begin to decline, at which point the bed should be replanted. A bed of 100 plants will provide about 100 quarts of berries, enough to provide a family of four with plenty of fresh berries and a surplus for freezing.

If you are new to growing strawberries, be prepared to spend an entire growing season selecting the perfect site, having the soil tested, and adequately preparing the soil for planting. Remember, you are preparing a home for plants that will reward you with delicious fruits every spring for several years.

### Site Selection

Strawberries are particular about their growing conditions, preferring a deep sandy loam that is rich in organic matter and well drained. The site should receive at least six hours of direct sun every day, and it should have a gradual slope that allows cold air to drain away from the plants on those frosty spring mornings after growth has begun. Also, strawberries must be irrigated during the growing season, so the chosen site should be near a source of water.

Avoid planting strawberries in beds where solanaceous crops—including tomatoes, peppers, eggplants, and potatoes—have grown in the previous four years. The soil-borne fungus that causes root rot in these crops, *Verticillium*, will turn its attention to the roots of strawberries. Also, do not plant strawberries where grass sod was recently turned under. White grubs (beetle larvae) that once fed on the grass roots will devour the strawberry roots.

### Soil Preparation

After selecting the site, have the soil tested. Strawberries grow best at a pH of 5.8 to 6.2, and you should follow the soil-test recommendations to ensure that your soil pH is in this range. Also, if the test indicates that soil organic matter is low, you can make repeated applications of decomposed barnyard manure or compost for a full season before planting. In spring of the planting year, apply the following nutrient amendments to each 1,000 square feet of bed: 8 bushels (10 cubic feet) of decayed manure, 1 pound of nitrogen (as cottonseed meal, fish meal, or soybean meal), 1 pound of phosphate (as rock phosphate), and 1 pound of iron chelate.

### Planting Bare-Root Strawberries

Plant bare-root strawberries in early May or as soon as the soil can be worked. In the traditional matted-row system, plants are spaced 2 feet apart with 4 feet between rows. If you garden in raised beds, you can plant a single row of transplants on 18-inch centers down the middle of each 2-foot-wide bed, with a narrow walkway between beds.

Do your planting in the late afternoon to minimize stress on the bare-root transplants. Using a trowel or your hand, make each planting hole wide enough to spread out the roots and deep enough to position the midpoint of the crown at the soil surface after planting. Remove all flower buds, runners, and damaged leaves from a plant, set it in its hole, spread out the roots, and backfill with soil. After all plants are in the ground, give the entire bed a thorough but gentle watering.

Throughout the month, pinch off any blooms that appear on your new strawberry plants. This is far more painful for the gardener than for the plants, but necessary to ensure bumper crops in the seasons to follow.

## Native Groundcovers

I am frequently asked to recommend a native plant species to grow as groundcover for shady sites. Behind this question is often the desire to grow a continuous carpet of a single species. My response is to plant a tapestry of shade-tolerant species. Growing conditions beneath a canopy of tall trees will vary from spot to spot, influenced by the extent of competition for water and nutrients and by the amount of sunlight received during the day, so it is unlikely that a single plant species will carpet an extensive area.

Following Alexander Pope's advice, we should "consult the genius of the place"; in other words, we should mimic what happens in nature. Take a walk through a local wooded area with an eye to the ground. In many places in Maine, for example, you will find a tapestry of bunchberry *(Cornus canadensis)*, lowbush blueberry *(Vaccinium angustifolium)*, and ferns. Here the bunchberry will thrive, there the blueberry, and so on, each species occupying the spots most suitable to its needs.

## Foamflower

I often find foamflowers *(Tiarella cordifolia)* growing in small patches along stream banks. They are native to the woodlands of Maine, growing 6 to 8 inches tall and 11 inches wide with slightly hairy heart-shaped leaves and foliage that is often marked with maroon patches. They spread vegetatively by runners. In spring the plants give rise to spikes of starry white or pink flowers that move in a gentle breeze like foam on a sea of green.

Many of the foamflowers we find in commerce are the products of intense hybridization and selection to produce varieties with foliage of various coloration and degrees of leaf dissection. In Marjorie's Garden, for example, we are growing the white-flowered 'Running Tapestry,' its dark green leaves boldly marked by deep maroon veins. We were sold on this evergreen variety when we saw the coppery tones of foliage in early spring as the plants emerged from under the snow.

Foamflowers are easily grown in well-drained soil in partial to full shade. They prefer humus-rich, moisture-retentive soil that does not dry out; wet soils, particularly in winter, can be fatal. You may want to remove the spent flower stalks after the blooming period to fully enjoy the summer foliage.

Foamflowers brighten a shady corner of Marjorie's Garden.

## Canada Mayflower

Natural colonies of Canada mayflower *(Maianthemum canadense)* grow in Marjorie's Garden, their glossy green oval leaves soaking up dappled sun beneath white pines and spruces. They seem to thrive in the thin acidic soils beneath these trees. Growing from 3 to 6 inches tall, the plants in some colonies have mostly infertile shoots and seldom flower, while those in other colonies send up 2-inch-high flowering stalks each May, the tiny white flowers arranged in pairs along the stalks on slender pedicels. Small native bees collect pollen from the fragrant flowers.

The flowers are followed by quarter-inch round berries, green at first, speckled pale red at maturity. The berries are eaten by ruffed grouse, white-footed mice, and chipmunks, all of which help spread the seed around.

Starflowers (flowering in center) often pop up in Marjorie's Garden among colonies of Canada mayflower in the dappled sun beneath tall spruces.

## Starflower

Starflowers *(Trientalis borealis)*, dainty plants rising only 4 to 8 inches from the ground, are always a joy to find blooming in Marjorie's Garden during May. They often mingle with the Canada mayflowers, developing open colonies from slender rhizomes. The star-shaped white flowers, about one-half inch across, often have seven petals, but sometimes as few as five or as many as ten. While tolerant of thin acidic soils, they also thrive in cool wooded areas with peaty soils.

We are lucky to have starflowers as part of the native flora in our garden. They can, however, be planted. The New England Wildflower Society (Framingham,

Massachusetts) recommends transplanting seed-germinated plants from containers in spring or planting dormant rhizomes into a moist acidic soil in late summer.

## Bluets

Bluets *(Houstonia caerulea)* occur throughout New England in deciduous woods, old fields, and roadsides but are noticeable only when they flower in spring at the same time dandelions are in bloom. I love to find them flowering in lawns, dense spreading clumps of tiny flowers with pale blue petals and yellow eyes (see photo page 137). A single patch of 6-inch-tall plants can spread over a large area of the lawn while it is still dormant. They are quick to produce seed, then disappear with the first mowing.

Other New England native ground covers that can be brought into the garden include bearberry *(Arctostaphylos uva-ursi)*, creeping wintergreen *(Gaultheria procumbens)*, creeping juniper *(Juniperus horizontalis)*, partridgeberry *(Mitechella repens)*, and the three-toothed cinquefoil *(Sibbaldiopsis tridentata)*. Readers interested in learning more about these and other garden-worthy native groundcovers should visit the New England Wildflower Society, either on line (www.newfs.org) or at Garden in the Woods in Framingham, Massachusetts.

Remember, one should never collect native wildflowers from the wild. These and other native groundcovers can often be purchased from growers, but you may have to do some research to find a grower in your area. Local garden centers may carry some species and know where you can purchase others.

# *May-Flowering Trees and Shrubs*

Some Mays the pace of the garden year slows to that of a slug gliding up a dandelion stalk. We wait patiently, holding space in our vegetable garden for summer crops, for heirloom tomatoes with exotic names like Cosmonaut Volkov, Caspian Pink, Amish Paste, Principe Borghese, Pink Brandywine; for a tomatillo called Pineapple that drops its ripe pea-size fruits on the ground to be scooped up and eaten like popcorn while we pull weeds; for an old Maine cucumber, Boothby Blonde; and for sprawling vines of summer squash such as yellow crooknecks and patty pans.

When that happens, we bide our time walking among the native plants in Marjorie's Garden, enjoying the subtle beauty of spring flowers on trees and shrubs that we have planted over the years. The cold and rain work to slow the advance of these plants from bud to bloom, allowing mature flowers to endure.

## Red Oak

A red oak grows at the edge of Marjorie's Garden. Twenty-five feet high and nearly as broad through its longest branches, it has more than doubled in size since I first met it more than a decade ago. Now, each year at the end of May, it raises its golden spring leaves to the sun in celebration of a new season.

Still a young tree, still slick-barked, this oak is flowering for the third consecutive year. Golden staminate

Young leaves of red oak in May morning sunlight.

The red oak's staminate catkins release pollen to the wind.

Each of the red oak's leaves begins (left) and ends its year in russet red (right).

catkins release their pollen to the wind, some grains no doubt coming to rest on the stigmatic surfaces of future acorns.

This oak has transformed the garden. A nearby perennial bed once considered suitable only for full-sun plants gets shadier each year. We have encouraged the transformation, removing spruce and fir that crowd the oak. Everything that can be done to enrich the future of this oak, we do.

This red oak is a playground for scampering red squirrels and chipmunks, a feeding ground for songbirds. Writing by a window that looks out on the tree, I watch birds feeding on insect eggs and larvae, blue jays hopping among the branches, chickadees darting in and out of the canopy, nuthatches creeping upside-down on the trunk in search of bugs, black-and-white warblers in the topmost branches nipping—what?—from the surfaces of leaves.

Late in a spring afternoon, thousands of crepuscular insects swarm in the canopy of our red oak, crawling over its new leaves. Many of the flying adults are tiny moths laying eggs. Many of the crawling larvae are leaf-eating caterpillars. Some of the insects are adults or larvae of predator species that will help control plant-eating insects throughout the garden.

In spite of the birds and predacious insects, by midsummer most of the oak's leaves will be riddled with holes, ragged with chewing, punctuated with galls. But the oak will have leaves to spare. Acorns will grow to full size, then disappear.

Who eats the acorns? Certainly the red squirrels and chipmunks, but possibly the wild turkeys, raccoons, deer, black bear, and mice that share the garden with us, creatures that visit the garden at night or in our absence during the day, leaving only tracks. All we know for sure is that it takes only a week or two for the acorns to go.

In late October, after the sugar maples have shed their technicolor leaves, red oaks like this one will paint the hills in rich earthy tones of yellow-brown and russet red. And then one night a strong wind will break the already-weakened connection between petiole and twig, and rain-soaked leaves will fall to earth.

Winter winds will drive snow against the trunk of our oak, while calmer snows will trace its strong horizontal limbs. Crows will greet frigid sunrises from the highest branch. But in May we watch young red squirrels chasing one another around the bole and through the branches. No doubt it was a squirrel that started it all.

## Native Cherries

After the red of early maple flowers and the soft gray-green of aspen tassels, clouds of white fill New England's woods and gardens as native cherries bloom. They are part of a spring parade of white-flowering trees and shrubs that starts in April with the serviceberries and continues through May and into June as our native pagoda dogwood and viburnums flower.

Of the three native cherries, the chokecherry *(Prunus virginiana)* is the least garden worthy and is best left to the truly wild landscape, to sunny clearings along the woodland edge and fence rows. Often more of a multi-stem shrub than a tree, it has a colonizing habit, producing thickets of genetically similar stems all sprouted from a common root system. It will quickly outgrow its allocated space in any managed landscape. Chokecherry is also highly susceptible to black knot fungus, a parasite that gives the tree a tumor-infested appearance, particularly in winter when the persistent warty growths are not hidden from view by foliage.

The remaining two species, bird cherry *(P. pensylvanica)* and black cherry *(P. serotina)*, do deserve a place in the garden, both for ornament and for attracting wildlife. Both are tall trees, but they differ markedly in growth rate and longevity. Bird cherry—often called fire cherry because it is one of the pioneer trees that quickly occupy a burned woodland area—is a short-lived tree, eventually giving way to native birches and other hardwoods.

Black cherry, while slower growing, can live for up to 200 years. The fact that we do not see many large black cherry trees, particularly with straight trunks, can be attributed to the harvest of their beautiful smooth-grained wood for furniture. Most old black cherries found in the wild today have contorted trunk growth that makes them worthless to hardwood buyers.

Where Marjorie's Garden meets the woodland edge, bird cherries of various ages come into bloom in May. For a week or so they become clouds of white, their branches filled with simple five-petaled flowers swarming with bees. As the season advances, their leaves provide food for numerous species of butterfly and moth caterpillars and, later in the year, the berries feed ruffed grouse, woodpeckers, cedar waxwings, thrushes, and grosbeaks. Cherries that make it to the ground will be quickly taken by black bears, red foxes, chipmunks, rabbits, mice, and squirrels.

Bird cherries grace our garden in May, their branches clothed in white, swarming with native bees.

Black cherry's white blossoms are borne in drooping clusters just after the new leaves have appeared. The purple-black, pea-sized cherries ripen in late summer and are quickly taken by the same assortment of birds and small mammals that eat the fruits of bird cherry. I remember students grabbing handfuls of ripe black cherries from trees on the Orono campus, a quick snack between classes. I found them slightly bitter, barely palatable, but am told that with the addition of a little sugar they make an excellent jelly.

Black cherry has a handsome bark, dark with scaly patches that curl horizontally away from the trunk at their edges.

We are lucky to have a black cherry growing at the edge of the drive up to the house, a tree that we greet every morning as we walk the dogs. We admire the rugged texture and rich color of its bark in winter and its snow-white flowers in May.

## Native Honeysuckle

The first shrub to flower each spring in Marjorie's Garden is the American fly honeysuckle *(Lonicera canadensis)*. The common name will never sell it, but its early May flowers and summer fruits, hidden among the leaves, possess a unique, understated beauty.

One of two native honeysuckle species found in New England, *L. canadensis* grows slowly in the dry shade of open canopies to a maximum height and width of 6 feet, but honeysuckle shrubs of this size are rare in the wild, where competition for nutrients and water often limits growth. They reach their full potential under a gardener's care. Planted six years ago beneath the canopy of mountain maples at the edge of Marjorie's Garden, our three shrubs took three years to establish themselves, growing slowly, but now seem to have picked up the pace. The largest is perhaps 3 feet tall and half as wide.

The first flowers open in the first week of May, small, pale-yellow trumpets dangling in fused pairs from long, slender stalks. New flowers open each day for two weeks, each pair of blooms lasting a day or two before being transformed into a pair of green, egg-shaped berries that will slowly ripen to bright red.

The fruiting plant is a bird magnet. The entire shrub shakes with the frantic movement of cedar waxwings and other songbirds as they quickly devour the small ripe fruits in early summer.

The pale yellow flowers of native honeysuckle dangle in fused pairs from long, slender stalks.

## Hobblebush

It has been over a decade since Marjorie and I were invited to dig a few hobblebush *(Viburnum alnifolium)* from private wooded property where mature plants had produced hundreds of offshoots from underground stems. We planted them along the edge of the driveway under the canopy of yellow birches.

The bright red fruit display of native honeysuckle is a magnet for birds.

After seven years, one of these hobblebush finally produced a single cluster of snow-white flowers. The inflorescence is of the lace-cap type, a cluster of tiny fertile flowers surrounded by a halo of showy white bracts. We watched it develop from an April bud cluster into a small bouquet that brightened its corner of the garden for the first two weeks of May.

Hobblebush gets its common name from its low-growing horizontal branches that catch you just above the ankle as you walk through the woods. This seems to be more a feature of young seedlings and offshoots than of older plants that send their flowering branches upward. In the wild, I usually meet the flowers of hobblebush at eye level, but our still youthful garden plant produced its first inflorescence 2 feet off the ground.

Hobblebush blooms in a lace-cap arrangement of tiny fertile flowers surrounded by snow-white bracts.

## Maple-Leaf Viburnum

Although never an advocate for transplanting native plants from the wild to the garden, I did come by the maple-leaf viburnums *(Viburnum acerifolium)* in Marjorie's Garden by such means, at least indirectly. Back when I was at university, this native viburnum grew alongside an invasive burning bush *(Euonymus alatus)* in a Boothbay, Maine, research site. My graduate student was studying the invasion of burning bush in this natural area and needed to do a greenhouse study that required both the invasive plant species and a native shrub species for a look at the effect of each on soil pH, so two dozen maple-leave viburnums were dug, transplanted to pots, and moved to the greenhouse. A year later, the study concluded, I rescued a dozen of these viburnums from the compost heap and transplanted them to our garden.

Fast-forward a decade, and the maple-leaf viburnums in Marjorie's Garden are thriving, the largest over 5 feet tall. This is one of the most shade-tolerant flowering shrubs. Ours grow in the shade of a tall white pine, nearby birches, and several common elderberries, yet they bloom and fruit profusely every year. The species is also known for its tolerance of dry soils, enabling it to compete successfully with surrounding plants in the understory.

In May, particularly when temperatures stay on the cool side, these shrubs grace our garden with tight bundles of pink flower buds that slowly transform into rounded clusters of tiny white blossoms with extruding stamens. These flowers, often not fully formed until early June, attract swarms of pollinating insects, mostly tiny beetles that crawl flower to flower, munching pollen.

As autumn approaches, the leaves, looking much like those of red maple but with a noticeable pubescence, begin to lose their chlorophyll, revealing hidden shades of salmon-pink flecked with purple, autumn leaf colors not found in any other plant in my experience. We have found it to be a durable shrub, even with the viburnum leaf beetle around, and enjoy the clusters of tiny white flowers in spring as well as the heavy fruit set—a favorite of birds—in summer.

## Pagoda Dogwood

Pagoda dogwood *(Cornus alternifolia)* is an understory tree, best grown in the shade of taller trees. In late May to early June, it brightens the corner of Marjorie's Garden with large flat clusters of white flowers. In late summer, birds feast on its purple-black berries. And in October, its leaves are colored with a mix of yellow, red, and purple.

One note of caution for gardeners growing this tree concerns a fungal disease called "golden canker," so named for the yellow discoloration of infected stems. The fungus attacks trees under stress, so growing pagoda dogwood in the garden must include siting the tree in the shade of taller trees and avoiding drought stress. On the other hand, pagoda dogwood is much less susceptible to the anthracnose fungus that in recent years has curtailed the use of flowering dogwood *(C. florida)* in New England landscapes.

Spreading beneath the shade of elderberries, maple-leaf viburnums bring early color to the May garden with clusters of pink flower buds.

Large clusters of pagoda dogwood flowers, layered on horizontal branches, brighten shady nooks in the May garden.

The red elders in Marjorie's Garden bloom in late April and early May (left). Their flowers (center) are quickly followed by clusters of bright red berries in June (right).

## Red Elder

Red elder *(Sambucus racemosa* var. *pubens)* is the true harbinger of spring in Marjorie's Garden, the plant that defies the cold dampness of early April to open its buds ahead of all others. When the thrush-planted seedling appeared a few years ago beneath the back porch steps, we discussed transplanting it to a more open spot, but then forgot about it. Over time it leaned more and more outward, until now it grows on crooked stems into the light.

By mid-April this red elder, protected against the damp cold by the nearby warm wall, has unpacked leaves and flowers, the latter beginning as rounded clusters of tight green buds, a reddish-purple blush over each cluster's upper surface. They look like small heads of broccoli nested within unfolding leaves that are tiny replicates of the large, pinnate, compound structures they will soon become.

Several other red elders, planted years ago by mice or birds, encircle the stout trunks of old yellow birches in a relatively dry and sunny site away from the house. Marjorie has pruned them into small multi-trunk trees bearing gnarly branches that grow at all angles with the trunks. All winter we enjoy their picturesque architecture.

The red elders are in full flower by the middle of May each year, their branches bent nearly to breaking with the heavy clusters of off-white flowers. Insect pollinators of all descriptions are attracted to these flowers, ensuring an abundance of bright red berries in June. (Berries of red elder are not edible—leave them for the birds!)

## Rhodora

Rhodora *(Rhododendron canadense)* is the earliest-flowering of New England's native rhododendrons. It is deciduous, flowering in May on leafless stems (see Chapter 6 photo on page 90), the purple flowers often sharing space with last year's orange-brown woody seedpods. After the flowers fade, I enjoy the blue-green foliage of rhodora through the summer, particularly as the new rosy-tipped seedpods develop among the leaves. On winter woodland walks, I look for the persistent pods at the branch tips, hoping to find them dusted with new snow.

Rhodora forms dense colonies of 4-foot-tall shrubs in lowland woods, often in seasonally flooded soils. In the swales between granite outcrops, where moisture is more limited, it grows to half that height.

I wish I could say that rhodora is widely available from local nurseries, but sadly, it will take some effort. I called around, asking garden centers and nurseries in central Maine if they had this plant. Most do not; indeed, most do not even know the plant, and have to look it up.

But perhaps that's for the best. I am certainly not advocating the use of rhodora the way we use other rhododendrons, as foundation plantings or specimens in the landscape. I am suggesting that it belongs in the wild garden, along the woodland path, or pondside. If you are fortunate enough to garden among granite outcrops, plant it in the swales, in pockets of deeper soil.

# *Planting Trees*

When is the best time of the year to plant a tree? Early spring, as soon as a hole can be dug, while temperatures are still cool and rainfall is typically abundant, will work. But then so will later in the spring or even in summer, provided you don't set off for a two-week vacation

## Two Non-Native Shrubs Worth Growing

The redbud's pea-like blossoms appear in early May (top), with the rosy-purple flowers clustered tightly around naked branches (above).

### *Eastern Redbud*

I grew up in Georgia, where small understory redbuds *(Cercis canadensis)* are native harbingers of spring and where large old specimens grow along the riverbanks, some 30 feet tall, their short main trunks dividing low to the ground into several stout ascending branches. In March these gray leafless branches, most spreading outward, a few curving back downward as if remembering the weight of a past winter's ice, are covered with pink flowers and gray Spanish moss. The efforts of earnest gardeners to bring pink and gray together are no match for what nature accomplishes on such fine spring days!

Redbud flower buds are often freeze-killed in Maine winters, and entire trees are sometimes lost to ice and snow. The species is listed as hardy to USDA Zone 5 and to protected sites in Zone 4. While teaching at the University of Maine in Orono, Maine, I was excited to find a few saplings of an Illinois population, the northernmost native range of the species, growing in the Littlefield Garden nursery, and to learn that these plants had actually flowered there.

One of these saplings made its way to Marjorie's Garden in 2000 and died back to the ground the first winter, probably the result of root loss during transplanting. But it regrew in the spring of 2001 and has prospered since, flowering every spring for the past several years.

In early May, pea-like flowers, rosy pink with a bluish or purplish tint, appear on naked branches. The short-stalked blooms literally cover the naked branches. The blossoms in turn become the summer fruits, small dry pods that often persist on the tree into winter. The genus name, Cercis, is derived from the Greek "kerkis," a shuttle, in reference to the resemblance of the pod's shape to that of a weaver's shuttle.

Unlike other members of the pea family, redbud leaves are simple rather than compound and heart-shaped, about 4 inches across, lustrous green in summer and turning yellow in the fall. Our tree, like many of this species, is multi-trunked and forms a lovely summer umbrella of cordate leaves.

Check with local nurseries and garden centers about the availability of cold-hardy redbuds. If you do find a source and decide to try one in Zone 5 or even Zone 4, plant it in a spot protected from desiccating winter winds. Gardeners in Zones 6 and 7 should have no problem growing the cold-hardy form of this lovely small tree, even in less protected areas.

In late May or early June, the red-vein enkianthus in Marjorie's Garden bursts into bloom.

### *Red-Vein Enkianthus* (Enkianthus campanulatus)

The red-vein enkianthus in Marjorie's Garden, now in its tenth year, flowers in late May or early June, depending on the weather, its clusters of creamy yellow bells with deep red veins hanging below the whorl of leaves at each branch tip. The flowers are slightly larger than those of highbush blueberry but have the same drooping habit.

We have pruned this naturally shrubby plant into a small multi-trunked tree, highlighting its layered branches. Now about 8 feet tall, it may eventually grow to 12 feet, the perfect small garden tree. Kept in shrubby form, red-vein enkianthus makes a beautiful informal hedge.

Native to Japan and hardy to USDA Zone 5, red-vein enkianthus is recommended by the University of New Hampshire Cooperative Extension service and by Massachusetts nurseries as a replacement for the non-native invasive burning bush *(Euonymus alatus)*, a shrub valued by home owners solely for its bright red fall foliage. Even in autumn, a burning bush can't hold a candle to the beauty of red-vein enkianthus.

immediately after planting, leaving the newly planted tree to wither on its limited root system in the hot sun.

Fall, too, is fine for planting, the return to shorter days and cooler temperatures giving the tree a chance to replace absorbing roots that were lost during harvest and handling in the nursery as well as roots lost during planting. Trees planted in spring must establish a new root system while supplying emerging leaves with water and nutrients. Fall planting, on the other hand, provides time for development of new roots after the leaves have dropped. Many tree species, such as sugar maple, continue producing new roots until the soil freezes. A tree planted in September may have six or more weeks of new root development before winter closes in.

Still, in May, the sap rises in gardeners as well as trees. Garden centers beckon, and many heed the call. So plant when the urge strikes, but to ensure the long-term health of your newly planted tree, follow these guidelines.

Purchase a small tree, one that is 1 to 2 inches in trunk diameter at most. Research has shown that the establishment time for a tree—the time required for the tree to replace roots lost during harvest and handling and thus regain a normal root:shoot ratio—averages one year for each inch of trunk caliper. During this time, the tree is especially sensitive to damage from drought and heat stress. Small trees establish adequate root systems more rapidly than large trees and ultimately catch up in trunk diameter with initially larger transplants.

Your new tree should show an obvious trunk flare, a widening of the trunk as it approaches the soil surface. Soil is often piled around the trunk during harvesting and handling of ball-and-burlap trees, so before planting a ball-and-burlap tree, completely remove the burlap and this excess soil until you can see the trunk flare. Better still, ask to do this in the nursery or garden center, before you purchase the tree, just to make sure there is a trunk flare and no hidden trunk damage.

Avoid purchasing a container-grown tree that does not show an obvious trunk flare. It may have been planted too deep in its pot, a situation that can lead to tree decline in the future.

Once home with your new tree, dig the planting hole at least twice as wide as the tree's root ball. Do not dig it deeper than the root ball, or the loosened soil under the tree will settle and so will the tree.

Do not amend the backfill soil with organic matter; use only the native soil that came out of the hole. The only exception is when the native soil is almost totally sand or clay, in which case up to 25% by volume of compost should be added to the backfill.

Do not use peat moss as a soil amendment! It dries out quickly, leading to pockets of dry soil around the roots. Use composted stable manure or aged compost from the bin.

Before placing your tree in its new home, carefully tease any roots circling the root ball to an outward-growing direction. Then center the tree in the hole, spreading the roots outward and making sure that the base of the trunk flare will be at the soil level when you finish planting.

Do not stomp on the soil as you return it to the hole! This breaks or damages tree roots. Instead, settle the soil with water. Once the hole is half full of soil, gently add water to settle the soil around the roots, eliminating air pockets. Water again after the hole is completely filled.

Mulch with compost (again, not peat moss) at least out to the drip line, starting a few inches from the trunk. Do not pile mulch at the base of the trunk! This all-too-common form of mulching is appropriately called "volcano mulching"—the tree looks as if it is erupting from a volcano. Moisture becomes trapped within the trunk-mulch interface, resulting in bark rot and slow death of the tree.

Minimize pruning at planting. Healthy root growth depends on chemicals transported from an abundance of leaves to the roots. Remove only dead, damaged, and diseased branches, delaying other pruning until after the establishment period (one year for each inch of trunk diameter).

Do not fertilize your newly planted tree. In fact, ask yourself, who fertilizes trees in the forest? Somewhere along the way—and I have to think this was the work of fertilizer-industry advertising—homeowners have been led to believe that trees in the garden must be annually fertilized for good health and adequate growth. Nothing could be farther from the truth.Research has shown that pushing tree growth with nitrogen leads to a reduction in tissue defense chemicals, the chemicals responsible for insect herbivore and disease resistance. In other words, excess nitrogen increases insect and disease problems.

When a tree receives a heavy shot of nitrogen in the form of applied fertilizer, it shifts its metabolism toward growth at the expense of defense chemical production. Insect herbivores such as the Japanese beetle love nitrogen-rich tissues, so herbivory of a fertilized tree increases even as its ability to build up herbivore-deterring chemicals decreases. A similar scenario has been established between high levels of nitrogen and disease pathogens.

When soil nitrogen levels are lower, metabolism favors defense chemical production over growth. And this is where we want our trees to be, growing relatively slowly in response to low soil nitrogen levels. In fact, trees fed annually by mulching with compost receive all the nitrogen necessary for a modest rate of growth. These trees will also be healthier, less damaged by herbivores and pathogens.

Follow these same procedures when planting a shrub. The only real difference is in estimating the establishment period, since many shrub species have multiple trunks. I define the establishment period for a shrub as one year for each gallon of container size when purchased. So, again, you are wise to buy smaller plants in smaller pots.

## Dandelions

The dandelions are in bloom in Marjorie's Garden during May. On warm sunny mornings, each of the dozens of flower heads lining the path from porch step to vegetable garden entertains a native bee, a fat bumblebee or slender solitary bee that can be seen crawling slowly across a plain of bright yellow flowers as it forages for nectar and pollen. Later, in June and July, some of these same bees can be found pollinating our tomatoes and cucumbers.

Most of the dandelion plants grow in places that we mow every two weeks or so, but only after the dandelions have gone to seed. We want to keep dandelions around the garden because we value the pollinators that they attract, and I cringe whenever I see someone mowing them down when still in bloom. How many bees get killed by those mower blades?

Bees need dandelions as an early source of nectar and pollen, but dandelions do not need bees. They can reproduce by a process called apomixis, the seeds developing without pollination. Each new dandelion is thus genetically identical to the parent plant.

Dandelions brighten the early spring landscape. Together with the carpets of bluets that flower at the same time, dandelions turn otherwise uninspiring expanses of lawn into mosaics of color and texture.

And who can resist picking a dandelion clock, the term used for the head of single-seeded fruits, each

A native solitary bee dives into a dandelion head.

attached to its own parachute, and blowing the seeds to the wind? So what if some of those seeds find their way into the strawberry bed? These you pop out of the ground as you wander around the garden on sunny April mornings, making grand plans for the season at hand.

And consider the impact of dandelions on garden biodiversity. A wide expanse of lawn, managed to exclude all weeds, has a biodiversity of one: the grass species. The chemicals used to control weeds (and insects) have further reduced surrounding biodiversity. On a small scale, such a lawn reminds me of another tiresome grass monoculture, the never-ending cornfields of Iowa.

The presence of dandelions in the lawn increases plant diversity by at least one species, insect diversity by the number of different nectar and pollen feeders, and other wildlife species diversity, including birds, through the absence of toxic chemicals.

Yes, I know, dandelions are not native to New England, or to North America for that matter, at least not the most regionally common species of dandelion, *Taraxacum officinale*. Native to Eurasia, this non-native species has followed humans around the world and can even be found in Alaska.

But is dandelion an invasive species? In Alaska's Denali National Park, dandelions can be found in roadside ditches and cut banks, both human-disturbed areas, and there are concerned citizens who would call them invasive. But experts there believe that dandelions do not have what it takes to move from those disturbed areas into wilder areas where they would outcompete native species for essential resources, the hallmark of an invasive species.

A publication by the Maine Organic Farmers and Gardeners Association (MOFGA), "Bee-Friendly Farming Increases Crop Pollination," recommends dandelions for attracting native bees to the garden. Dandelions are also recommended by the University of Maine Cooperative Extension service as an important pollinator plant. Their list includes the statement that "no plants listed here are invasive exotic species."

Wherever humans have roamed, dandelions have become naturalized in disturbed areas—such as our front lawns—their seeds hitching rides on car tires and shoes. Let's acknowledge which species is the true invasive species. Let's appreciate dandelions for the service they provide in the garden ecosystem and for brightening the otherwise desolate landscapes in front of many homes.

Keep the lawn mower in the garage until dandelion seeds fill the air!

If you let your dandelions grow, your reward may include a carpet of bluets like this one.

## The New England Garden in May, Zone by Zone

May is filled with every sort of garden task from sowing to thinning, planting to harvesting. Early in the month, transplants of broccoli and cauliflower are planted under row covers to thwart the cabbage butterflies. Lettuces and other leafy crops also go in the ground. Seeds of carrots and spinach are direct-sown in the garden, while earlier sowings get their first thinning. Peas are starting to wrap their tendrils around supporting twigs or twine, and the first spears of asparagus are harvested. Meanwhile, seedlings of heat-loving cucurbits, as well as tomatoes, are just getting started under indoor lights.

| IN THE GARDEN | May | Date by USDA Hardiness Zone | | | | | Notes |
|---|---|---|---|---|---|---|---|
| | | 3 | 4 | 5 | 6 | 7 | |
| **GENERAL MAINTENANCE** | | | | | | | |
| **THE COMPOST PILE** | | | | | | | |
| **VEGETABLE GARDEN** | Use cutworm collars around all transplants.<br>Year round, avoid working around garden plants when the leaves are wet.<br>Plant by soil temperature, not by calendar date or phase of the moon.<br>Plant a three-sisters garden.<br>Make plans to include edible flowers in your summer garden. | | | | | | We make our cutworm collars from 2-inch-wide strips of rolled newspaper. Wrap them around the stem so that half of the collar is below the soil line.<br>Diseases are easily spread from plant to plant by the gardener working when the leaves are wet.<br>See Chapter 7 for minimum soil temperatures for sowing and transplanting.<br>See Chapter 7 for details. |
| **VEGETABLE CROPS** | | | | | | | |
| Asparagus | Begin harvesting spears (not from 2-yr.-old plants). | | | | | | Snap off the spears at ground level, avoiding aboveground stubs that attract asparagus beetles and promote entry of diseases. |
| Beans, Bush | Sow in garden. | June 11 | June 4 | May 28 | May 21 | May 14 | Wait until soil temperature has settled above 60° F. |
| Beans, Pole | Sow seeds next to trellis or poles. | June 11 | June 4 | May 28 | May 21 | May 14 | Wait until soil temperature has settled above 60° F. |
| Beets | Thin direct-sown seedlings. | May 15 | May 8 | May 1 | Apr 24 | Apr 17 | To reduce need for thinning, see the sidebar "Tips for Sowing Small Seeds" in Chapter 6. |
| | Direct-sow seeds if not done yet. | May 15 | May 8 | May 1 | Apr 24 | Apr 17 | Wait until soil temperature has settled above 50° F. See "Direct -Sow in Rows or Blocks," Chapter 6. |
| | Protect plants from leaf miners with row covers. | May 22 | May 15 | May 8 | May 1 | Apr 24 | Use lightweight row covers and leave them on for the entire crop period. |
| Broccoli | Set out transplants under row cover. | May 22 | May 15 | May 8 | May 1 | Apr 24 | Broccoli can be grown under a row cover for the entire season, since pollination is not an issue. |
| | Make a second sowing indoors for a continuous supply. | May 15 | May 8 | May 1 | Apr 24 | Apr 17 | |

| IN THE GARDEN | May | Date by USDA Hardiness Zone | | | | | Notes |
|---|---|---|---|---|---|---|---|
| | | 3 | 4 | 5 | 6 | 7 | |
| Cabbage | Make a second sowing indoors for a continuous supply. | May 15 | May 8 | May 1 | Apr 24 | Apr 17 | |
| Carrots | Thin direct-sown seedlings. | May 15 | May 8 | May 1 | Apr 24 | Apr 17 | To reduce need for thinning, see the sidebar "Tips for Sowing Small Seeds" in Chapter 6. |
| | Direct-sow seeds if not done yet. | May 15 | May 8 | May 1 | Apr 24 | Apr 17 | See "Direct Sowing in Rows or Blocks," Chapter 6. |
| Cauliflower | Set out transplants. | May 22 | May 15 | May 8 | May 1 | Apr 24 | |
| Chard, Swiss | Set out transplants. | May 22 | May 15 | May 8 | May 1 | Apr 24 | Wait until soil temperature has settled above 50° F. See "Direct Sowing in Rows or Blocks," Chapter 6. |
| | Direct-sow seeds if not done yet. | May 15 | May 8 | May 1 | Apr 24 | Apr 17 | Use a lightweight row cover and leave it on for the entire crop period. |
| | Protect plants from leaf miners with row covers. | May 22 | May 15 | May 8 | May 1 | Apr 24 | To reduce need for thinning, see the sidebar "Tips for Sowing Small Seeds" in Chapter 6. |
| | Thin direct-sown seedlings. | May 29 | May 22 | May 15 | May 8 | May 1 | |
| Corn, Sweet | Make first sowing. | Jun 5 | May 29 | May 22 | May 15 | May 8 | Wait until soil temperature has settled above 60° F. |
| Cucumbers | Start seeds indoors. | May 29 | May 22 | May 15 | May 8 | May 1 | Sow seeds in peat pots that can be planted directly in the garden. |
| Eggplant | Start seeds indoors. | May 15 | May 8 | May 1 | Apr 24 | Apr 17 | |
| Garlic | Water regularly through July unless rainfall is frequent. | | | | | | |
| Green Onions | Thin direct-sown seedlings. | May 15 | May 8 | May 1 | Apr 24 | Apr 17 | To reduce need for thinning, see the sidebar "Tips for Sowing Small Seeds" in Chapter 6. |
| | Direct-sow seeds if not done yet. | May 15 | May 8 | May 1 | Apr 24 | Apr 17 | See "Direct Sowing in Rows or Blocks," Chapter 6. |
| Kohlrabi | Set out transplants. | May 15 | May 8 | May 1 | Apr 24 | Apr 17 | Use a lightweight row cover to deter the cabbage butterfly. |
| Leek | Set out transplants. | May 22 | May 15 | May 8 | May 1 | Apr 24 | |
| Lettuce | Thin direct-sown seedlings. | May 15 | May 8 | May 1 | Apr 24 | Apr 17 | To reduce need for thinning, see the sidebar "Tips for Sowing Small Seeds" in Chapter 6. |
| | Direct-sow seeds if not done yet. | May 15 | May 8 | May 1 | Apr 24 | Apr 17 | See "Direct Sowing in Rows or Blocks," Chapter 6. |
| Muskmelon | Start seeds indoors. | May 22 | May 15 | May 8 | May 1 | Apr 24 | Sow seeds in peat pots that can be planted directly in the garden. |

| IN THE GARDEN | May | Date by USDA Hardiness Zone | | | | | Notes |
|---|---|---|---|---|---|---|---|
| | | 3 | 4 | 5 | 6 | 7 | |
| Onions | Set out transplants. | May 22 | May 15 | May 8 | May 1 | Apr 24 | |
| | Irrigate as needed. | | | | | | |
| | Weed often. | | | | | | |
| Parsley | Set out transplants. | May 29 | May 22 | May 15 | May 8 | May 1 | |
| Peppers | Start seeds indoors. | May 15 | May 8 | May 1 | Apr 24 | Apr 17 | |
| Potatoes | Plant seed potatoes in the garden. | May 15 | May 8 | May 1 | Apr 24 | Apr 17 | |
| | Cover with row cover when shoots emerge. | Jun 5 | May 29 | May 22 | May 15 | May 8 | |
| | Hill plants. | | | | | | |
| Pumpkins | Start seeds indoors. | May 29 | May 22 | May 15 | May 8 | May 1 | Sow seeds in peat pots that can be planted directly in the garden. |
| Radishes | Thin direct-sown seedlings. | May 15 | May 8 | May 1 | Apr 24 | Apr 17 | To reduce need for thinning, see the sidebar "Tips for Sowing Small Seeds" in Chapter 6. |
| | Direct-sow seeds if not done yet. | May 15 | May 8 | May 1 | Apr 24 | Apr 17 | See "Direct Sowing in Rows or Blocks," Chapter 6. |
| Rhubarb | Begin harvesting stems from 2-year-old and older plants. | | | | | | Grab each stem by the base and pull it off, rather than cutting it. Use only the stem, not the leaf. |
| Spinach | Thin direct-sown seedlings. | May 15 | May 8 | May 1 | Apr 24 | Apr 17 | To reduce need for thinning, see the sidebar "Tips for Sowing Small Seeds" in Chapter 6. |
| | Direct-sow seeds if not done yet. | May 15 | May 8 | May 1 | Apr 24 | Apr 17 | See "Direct Sowing in Rows or Blocks," Chapter 6. |
| | Protect plants from leaf miners with row covers. | May 22 | May 15 | May 8 | May 1 | Apr 24 | Use lightweight row covers and leave them on for the entire crop period. |
| Squash, Summer | Start seeds indoors. | May 29 | May 22 | May 15 | May 8 | May 1 | Sow seeds in peat pots that can be planted directly in the garden. |
| Squash, Winter | Start seeds indoors. | May 29 | May 22 | May 15 | May 8 | May 1 | Sow seeds in peat pots that can be planted directly in the garden. |
| Tomatillo | Start seeds indoors. | May 15 | May 8 | May 1 | Apr 24 | Apr 17 | |

| IN THE GARDEN | May | Date by USDA Hardiness Zone | | | | | Notes |
|---|---|---|---|---|---|---|---|
| | | 3 | 4 | 5 | 6 | 7 | |
| Tomatoes | Start seeds indoors. | May 15 | May 8 | May 1 | Apr 24 | Apr 17 | |
| Watermelon | Start seeds indoors. | May 22 | May 15 | May 8 | May 1 | Apr 24 | Sow seeds in peat pots that can be planted directly in the garden. |
| **SMALL FRUITS** | | | | | | | |
| Strawberries | Plant bare-root plants.<br><br>Pinch off flowers on new plants. | May 22 | May 15 | May 8 | May 1 | Apr 24 | See Chapter 7 for planting details.<br><br>Removing flowers in the first year will encourage runner growth, resulting in better yields the following year. |
| **FLOWER BEDS AND BORDERS** | | | | | | | |
| **CONTAINER GARDEN** | | | | | | | |
| **FLOWERS** | | | | | | | |
| Calendula | Scatter seeds about the vegetable garden. | | | | | | A handful of seeds scattered about the vegetable garden will start a resident population of this self-sower. |
| Cosmos | Start seeds indoors. | May 15 | May 8 | May 1 | Apr 24 | Apr 17 | |
| Monarda | Set out transplants. | Jun 5 | May 29 | May 22 | May 15 | May 8 | |
| Morning Glory | Start seeds indoors. | May 22 | May 15 | May 8 | May 1 | Apr 24 | |
| Nasturtium | Sow seeds indoors.<br><br>Scatter seeds in vegetable garden. | May 15<br><br>Jun 5 | May 8<br><br>May 29 | May 1<br><br>May 22 | Apr 24<br><br>May 15 | Apr 17<br><br>May 8 | A handful of seeds scattered about the vegetable garden will start a resident population of this self-sower. |
| Pansy | Scatter seeds about the vegetable garden. | | | | | | A handful of seeds scattered about the vegetable garden will start a resident population of this self-sower. |
| Rudbeckia (Black-eyed Susan) | Set out transplants. | Jun 5 | May 29 | May 22 | May 15 | May 8 | |
| Snapdragon | Set out transplants. | Jun 5 | May 29 | May 22 | May 15 | May 8 | |
| Sweet peas | Set out transplants. | Jun 5 | May 29 | May 22 | May 15 | May 8 | |
| **WOODY PLANTS** | If buying a tree, select one with trunk caliper of 2 inches or less. | | | | | | See Chapter 7 for details. |

# Chapter 8

# The Garden in June

*Pulling weeds and pickin' stones*
*Man is made from dreams and bones.*
*Feel the need to grow my own*
*'Cause the time is close at hand.*
*Grain for grain, sun and rain*
*Find my way in nature's chain.*
*Tune my body and my brain*
*To the music from the land.*

— from "The Garden Song," written by David Mallett
(sung in my mind by John Denver and the Muppets)

***I do not strive for a weed-free garden.*** In fact, I encourage certain "weeds"—a word, like "pest," that I try to avoid—in some garden spots, calling each plant by name before I decide whether it's a plant worth nurturing or one growing where I do not want it. This scrutiny of every plant slows down the work and demands that doomed plants be pulled by hand, not by a weapon of mass destruction, mechanical or chemical.

Purslane *(Portulaca oleracea)*, for example, is a common exuberant plant in New England gardens. Seeds produced last year germinate in June's warm soil, and the soil-colored seedlings go unnoticed until suddenly one day they have become red-stemmed rosettes of succulent, paddle-shaped, dark green leaves. Everywhere. The rosettes coalesce into large colonies that, left alone, will quickly fill every open spot of cultivated soil.

Purslane is an easy plant to pull or hoe out of existence, but before you decide to annihilate it, give it a taste. It has been used as a tasty and nutritious warm-weather salad green for hundreds of years. Native American tribes were fond of the greens and used the seeds for cereal and bread. And recently, due to development of cultivated forms by European breeders, purslane has achieved gourmet status.

There are numerous recipes available on the Internet, but you might start with Henry David Thoreau's 1854 recipe from *Walden*:

*Facing page:* Foamflower's spikes of starry white flowers wave in a gentle breeze like foam on a sea of green.

*"I learned from my two years' experience that it would cost incredibly little trouble to obtain one's necessary food, even in this latitude; that a man may use as simple a diet as the animals, and yet retain health and strength. I have made a satisfactory dinner . . . simply off a dish of purslane which I gathered in my cornfield, boiled and salted. . . . Yet men have come to such a pass that they frequently starve, not for want of necessaries but for want of luxuries."*

The wild type suits my taste as well, with a flavor that resembles the best lettuce, perhaps a bit more peppery. And the nutritional value is greater in wild plants. Purslane is rich in vitamins E and C and beta-carotene, quite high in protein, and considered a better source of essential omega-3 fatty acids than any other leafy plant. I wonder how many of us are paying high prices for sources of these nutrients in pill form while waging war against the purslane in our gardens?

Knowing this, I manage the purslane in Marjorie's Garden, pulling it out where it competes with the planted crops, encouraging and harvesting it where it colonizes open space. It makes an attractive groundcover, particularly growing along the edge of a stepping stone.

June begins the weeding season, for sure. And I suspect that there are as many approaches to this task as there are gardeners. For me, weeding is a leisurely start and satisfying end to every summer day in the garden, and the punctuation necessary for completion of every garden task.

Before pulling it, give purslane a taste. It has a flavor that resembles the best lettuce, perhaps a bit more peppery.

Bent over, fingers in the soil, I sing my version of "The Garden Song" while the bumblebees wing theirs.

## *June in the Vegetable Garden*

In June, everything seems to happen at once. As the soil temperature rises and butterflies find the first chive blossoms, potato plants demand a second hilling, transplants of summer crops need hardening and then planting, and carrots must be thinned—all while slugs and weeds usurp their share of the gardener's time. The gardener begins and ends each day in the garden.

### Tomatoes

Use the first week of June to harden tomato transplants for the garden. Whether home-grown or purchased from a greenhouse grower, transplants will need gradual acclimation to the full sunlight and wind that they will soon experience.

We use our sunny porch railings and steps for this task. On the first day, in the morning, we move the flats of seedlings from under the fluorescent lights to the porch and give them an hour of angled light as well as exposure to wind. If the wind is hard and constant, we either delay hardening by a day or place the plants where the wind is buffered.

Each day we extend this outside time by an hour, so that by the end of the week the plants are able to remain outside until planted in the garden. Moisture loss from the pots increases outdoors, and we adjust the frequency of watering as needed.

In the garden, the bed has already been prepared, the soil amended with aged compost. On planting day, at the bottom of each hand-dug hole, I add two handfuls of worm compost, an extra dose of slow-release nitrogen for the growing plant.

I make each hole deep enough to set the plant a few inches deeper than it was growing in the pot. New roots will form along the buried portion of the stem, and the resulting transplant will be better anchored in the soil and less likely to bend or break in stiff winds. Before completely backfilling the hole, I wrap a newspaper cutworm collar around the stem so that it is an inch below and above the soil line after the hole is filled.

If you have purchased greenhouse-grown plants in plastic pots, you may need to deal with a mat of circling roots surrounding the soil, a sign that the plant has

Transplanted tomato seedlings should be fitted with a cutworm collar made from rolled newspaper. Wrap the collar around the stem so that it is an inch below and above the soil line

been in the pot too long and has become "potbound," a condition that will limit its vigor after planting. Gently pull the circling roots away from the soil ball with your fingers, spreading them outward. Circling roots at the bottom of the pot should also be pulled loose and spread out before planting. Even cutting away this bottom root layer is preferable to leaving it intact. If you purchase plants in fiber (peat) pots, tear the pot completely off the pot before planting.

## *The Tomato Grower's Dilemma: Cage or Stake?*

Tomato plants must by supported off the ground, particularly where slugs are part of the food web. Upright plants take up less garden space, and the enhanced air circulation reduces foliar and fruit disease.

There are two common methods of support, stakes and cages. While both have their merits, I recommend cages for two reasons: less maintenance (minimal pruning), more (if slightly smaller) tomatoes, and less sunscald.

Staked tomatoes require extensive pruning, the removal of lateral or side shoots that appear in the leaf axils between the stem and the leaves. If not removed, these shoots compete directly with the main stem, weakening it, and strong side shoots loaded down with fruits can easily break their attachment to the main stem. But removal of the side shoots also reduces foliage cover, increasing the chances of fruit sunscald.

Staked tomatoes with lower branches removed. When flowering begins, prune off all side branches below the lowest flowers with sharp pruning shears, cutting through each branch just ahead of where it meets a main stem. Keep an eye on the plants through the growing season and remove any non-fruiting side branches that bend down and allow leaves to touch the ground.

Cages made of concrete reinforcement mesh can be used to support tomatoes in the ground (top) and in containers (above). For in-ground plants, stabilize the cage by tying it to a strong stake driven into the ground.

Caged tomatoes do not require removal of all lateral shoots. The fruit-bearing side shoots are supported by the cage wire, while the abundant foliage cover protects the fruit from sunscald injury. The heavier fruit load will delay ripening a bit and result in somewhat smaller fruits.

To minimize foliar diseases such as fungal blights, I do recommend removal of lateral shoots below the fruiting zone of the plant. Wait until the first flower buds are formed, then remove all the side shoots below them. Do not do this before flowering, however, when the plant needs all its leaves for maximum photosynthesis.

If you decide to go with cages, you can build your own out of concrete reinforcement mesh. The openings are wide enough (6 inches) to reach through and harvest tomatoes with ease. And they will last forever. Other tomato cages are flimsy by comparison.

A cage 5 feet tall will support most tomato varieties. A 5-foot length of 5-foot-wide mesh can be rolled into a cylindrical cage with an 18-inch diameter, while a 6-foot length will produce a 21-inch diameter. Form the cylinder by hooking the two cut ends of the mesh together, then cut away the bottom rung to leave prongs to push into the soil. For stability, tie the cage to a strong stake driven into the ground.

With a little practice and a bolt cutter, you can make a cage in about 15 minutes. Don't be surprised if the mesh comes with an exterior layer of rust, the result of storage outside at the builder's supply store. The tomatoes won't mind.

### Flower but No Fruits

One of the most frequent questions I receive from readers of my *Bangor Daily News* garden column goes something like this: "I have plenty of flowers on my tomato plants, but no tomatoes. What's wrong?" Really observant gardeners may note that the flower stems turn yellow just before the flowers drop to the ground.

The diagnosis is not easy, since there are several possible causes of blossom drop in tomatoes. It is often the result of extreme temperatures during the day or night. Development of the pollen tube, a post-pollination event essential to fruit development that must occur within 24 hours of pollination, is inhibited in many tomato varieties by daytime temperatures above 85° F, nighttime temperatures above 70°, and, most often, nighttime temperatures below 55°. The latter is a possibility in any summer month for northern New England.

Also, if nighttime temperatures are less than 55° or greater than 75°, or if daytime temperatures are greater than 85°, recently deposited pollen may become tacky and non-viable. And fruits that do develop are more likely to be misshapen or cat-faced (scarred and puckered) when night temperatures are below 55°.

These temperature-related causes of poor fruit set can be minimized by selection of tomato varieties that are suited to cool summers. When perusing seed catalogs, choose varieties with the shortest number of days to maturity, an indication of suitability for gardens with cool, short summers. But don't believe the actual number, as ripening will happen more slowly in a cool summer.

Blossom drop may also result from lack of pollination, the transfer of pollen from the male part of the flower (the anther) to the female part (the stigma). Tomato flowers must be vibrated or shaken for this transfer to occur, and this is normally done by wind or bumblebees. If both are lacking in the garden, frequent gently shaking of the flowers by hand may improve pollination.

Other causes of blossom drop include nitrogen levels that are too high or too low. Given too much nitrogen, the plant diverts most of its energy to vegetative growth; given too little, it may be too spindly and weak to sustain many developing fruits.

Lack of water will also lead to blossom drop. Tomato plants have deep roots, some as deep as five feet. Shallow watering stresses and weakens plants. Tomatoes respond best to deep irrigation once each week, a task you should skip only if the garden gets a soaking rain.

## Peppers Sweet and Hot

To get off to a good start, peppers need warmer soil temperatures than tomatoes and most other summer crops. For this reason, peppers are not transplanted to the garden until mid-June at the earliest in Zone 5. If you are monitoring soil temperatures, wait until you've seen a week of temperatures above 65° before you transplant peppers.

Harden and transplant your pepper plants as described above for tomatoes, including the use of worm compost in the bottom of the planting hole and rolled newspaper cutworm collars around the stems. You do not need to plant peppers deeper than they are growing in their pots, however, and peppers do not need staking or caging like tomatoes. Heavy fruit load should be supported by tying each plant to a bamboo stake as it grows.

The requirement for very warm soil may mean a delay in planting peppers should June remain cool and wet, as it often does in northern New England. In this case, the plants can become potbound and lose vigor. The best remedy for this is transplanting them into larger pots *before* their roots start to circle within the original pot. Go ahead and put these potted peppers in the sun, even during cool days, as the pot will absorb solar energy and keep the root system warm. Be sure to bring them inside at night, however.

## Eggplants

Eggplants belong to the Solanaceae, the tomato family, along with tomatillos and peppers, and they should be hardened and transplanted as described for tomatoes but planted only as deep as they are growing in their pots. As with peppers, support the heavy fruit load on eggplants by tying each plant to a bamboo stake as it grows.

Petite Yellow Sweet is a perfect pepper for pot culture. (Photo courtesy Ron Kujawski)

'Hansel' eggplant is a popular variety for the garden and for container gardening. The slender dark-purple fruits are best when picked small, about 6 inches long.

### Protecting Young Plants from Wind

Even fully hardened transplants need protection from strong winds during the first week or two after planting. Their minimal root systems cannot keep up with the rate of water loss on a windy day.

Covering a bed of transplants with a row cover will help, or you can protect each plant by inserting a cedar shake or other thin board into the soil on the windward side of each plant. Cedar shakes can also be used to shelter transplanted seedlings from direct sunlight.

Use cedar shakes or other thin boards to protect newly transplanted seedlings from wind and direct sunlight.

Each tomatillo fruit grows in a husk suspended from the stem beneath a canopy of leaves (top). The fruits (above), still in their husks, fall to the ground and continue to improve in flavor. Fruit size varies from ¼ to ½ inch in diameter.

## Tomatillos

This relative to the tomato, commonly found in Mexican dishes, is overlooked by the authors of many gardening books. The green immature fruits, enclosed in a papery husk (the calyx of the flower) like ground cherries, contribute a citrusy taste to green salsas and other cooked sauces. Ripe fruits are yellow or purple.

We grow the small pineapple tomatillo, named for its distinct pineapple flavor. It can be used for making salsa, but Marjorie and I eat the little fruits like popcorn (they are about the size of a popped kernel), often while working in the garden. Fruits are at the peak of flavor after they have dropped to the ground, where they will keep for days hidden among the sprawling plants until discovered, husked, and eaten.

Easy to grow, tomatillos thrive under the same conditions as tomatoes but with greater tolerance for cool weather. During cool wet summers, the tomatillos in our garden prosper as the tomatoes lose leaves to blight. Tomatillos should be grown, hardened, and transplanted on the same schedule with tomatoes. Give them plenty of room to sprawl if you have the room, or they can be staked when young to develop an upright growth habit.

## Potatoes

Potatoes planted in April will need hilling by late May (Zones 6 and 7) or early June (Zones 4 and 5). New potatoes form on thin stolons (underground stems) that emerge from the main stems, and these stolons should

These potato plants, grown in Marjorie's Garden from seed potatoes planted on April 18, were hilled for the first time on June 11. Soil was mounded against the plants to bury the lower half of each stem.

be covered with soil to protect the young potatoes from sunlight. Do the first hilling when the plants are about a foot tall, mounding soil against the lower half of each plant. Repeat once or twice more during the growing season as the plants grow taller.

Red admiral butterflies are frequent foragers on chive blossoms.

## Chives

In the second week of June in Marjorie's Garden, at the end of a small vegetable garden bed once devoted to an assortment of herbs but recently turned over to rhubarb, a clump of chives is in full flower. It survived the transition because both Marjorie and I are fond of its June flowers. Garden seasons go by without harvesting any of the leaves, but we are drawn to the lavender-pink flower clusters and the pollinators they attract. Bumblebees and red admiral butterflies are frequent foragers.

Chives *(Allium schoenoprasum)* are among the easiest of plants to grow. All they need is plenty of sunlight and a slightly acid (pH 6.2 - 6.8) soil with plenty of organic matter. The latter requirement can be easily met by annual mulching with compost or aged manure and by digging in more organic matter when dividing the clumps. Established plants should be dug, divided, and replanted every three to five years.

Overfertilizing chives to push growth is detrimental. Slower, compact growth leads to stronger flavor in the leaves and healthier plants.

When we do harvest the leaves, we cut them back to an inch or two above the soil. A new plant should only be harvested once in its first year; in subsequent years, the leaves can be harvested monthly.

There is only the one clump in our garden, so most of the leaves are used as they are cut, spicing up salads (along with a few chive flowers, also edible) or dressing up baked potatoes. Extra leaves, pre-washed and chopped into small pieces, are frozen.

As an edible crop, chives are a good source of dietary fiber, thiamin, and vitamins A, C, and B-6. They also contain significant amounts of riboflavin, folic acid, calcium, iron, magnesium, potassium, phosphorus, and copper.

Chive plants are available at many garden centers in pots, ready for planting at any time during the garden season. In addition to the lavender-pink-flowered species, there are two cultivars, 'Forescate' (with rose-red flowers) and 'Corsica' (with white flowers). The variety *albaflorumn* also has white blooms.

## Cucumbers

Cucumbers, like all members of the cucurbit family, need warm soil. Maine growers who want to be first to market with cucumbers will set out transplants in late May or early June in beds covered with black plastic to

A trellis made of nylon twine, such as this long cucumber trellis (top) in Ron and Jennifer Kujawski's West Stockbridge, Massachusetts garden, is easy to install and will last several seasons. In addition to saving space, trellising makes finding and harvesting the fruits much easier (above).

warm the soil. I wait until mid-June to set out hardened transplants, planting them in hills to enhance warming of the soil immediately around the roots. I dig a spadeful of worm compost into each hill, even though the entire bed was amended earlier with composted goat manure, then plant the transplants at the same depth they were growing in their pots. I wait a couple of weeks for the soil to warm even more before mulching.

Cucumbers can also be direct-sown in warm June soils, and direct-sown seedlings can quickly catch up and even outgrow transplants, so why bother with transplants? I can think of one reason: the older stems of transplants are tough enough to deter cutworms from mowing them down, as often happens with direct-sown seedlings. Cutworms will devour the stem of a small cucumber seedling before it breaks the soil surface. (See the discussion of cutworms and their control at the end of this chapter.)

Cucumbers adapt easily to a trellis, saving space in the garden. Commercial trellising for cucumbers is quick to install and lasts several seasons, but I prefer sturdy 8-foot-tall poles that stand 6 feet tall once set in the ground 6 feet apart. Horizontal runs of jute twine, spaced about a foot apart from the ground up, are tied securely to the poles and then interlaced with vertical runs, also about a foot apart. As the cucumber vines grow, I carefully weave them into the base of the trellis and then let their tendrils take over. At the end of the season, spent vines and jute can all be tossed on the compost pile.

## Spinach

Spinach plants grown from seed sown in early May are likely to start flowering in northern New England by mid-June, a process called "bolting." Even the most bolt-resistant varieties, such as Bloomsdale Long Standing, will eventually respond to increasing daylength by flowering and setting seed, putting an end to the harvest.

We do manage to get one good spring harvest of young spinach leaves before the plants bolt, then it is out with the spinach and in with the summer crop of basil.

This early end to the harvest of spring-sown spinach is why many gardeners in New England wait until August to sow spinach. Late-summer-sown spinach will continue to produce leaves until the plants succumb to freezing temperatures. (See Chapter 9 for recommended varieties of spinach for fall harvest.)

Even bolt-resistant varieties of spinach, such as this Bloomsdale Long Standing, will produce only one cutting of young leaves before bolting in northern New England gardens.

### Sex in the Vegetable Garden

I teach a high-school course called "Sex in Plants," and once or twice each year I give a lecture to Master Gardener Volunteers on the same topic. In each case, we dissect flowers to examine their sex organs and I explain that the process of sexual reproduction in plants is, at one level, essentially like that in animals, including humans: sperm and egg unite to form the first cell of the next generation. I enjoy the astonishment on students' faces, young and old, when they discover that plants produce sperm and eggs, and that zucchini fruits and watermelons are really ripened ovaries.

I think it means more to the Master Gardener Volunteers. They can apply their new knowledge in numerous ways, unraveling garden mysteries such as why tomatoes flower but do not produce fruits (see "Flowers but No Fruits" earlier in this chapter) and why the early zucchini and cucumber flowers never produce fruits.

All cucurbits, including zucchini and other summer squash, winter squash, pumpkins, cucumbers, and melons, are monoecious plants with imperfect flowers, meaning both sexes can be found on the same plant but in different blossoms. The first flowers of the season are all male, incapable of producing fruits.

Once you know what to look for, you can easily sex a squash blossom. Female flowers have a slightly swollen ovary at the base of the petals; if both pollination and fertilization occur, this ovary will swell and become the familiar squash fruit. Male flowers lack this conspicuous feature.

So why would a plant invest energy in producing only male flowers? I've never heard or read an explanation, but I have a theory. Cucurbits depend on bees to transfer pollen (the sperm-producing structure) of male flowers to the stigma (gateway to the ovary) of female flowers. Perhaps production of the early pollen-loaded flowers serves to attract a resident population of pollinators before the plant invests energy in producing flowers that must be pollinated.

Female squash flowers (top) have a conspicuous ovary that resembles a small fruit. Male flowers (above) lack this feature, of course.

## Summer Squash

Given warm, well-drained soil high in organic matter, summer squash is easy to grow and prolific, each plant producing dozens of small immature fruits, the stage at which they should be picked. I like to start the early summer crop from transplants, then sow seed in late August for a fall crop that will stay productive until the first frost.

You cannot have too much organic matter in the soil for summer squash, so I always add more when planting, either worm compost or composted stable manure. I also mulch the soil in the squash bed with organic matter that will rapidly decompose, such as composted manure or shredded leaves.

Again, a newspaper cutworm collar should be wrapped around the young succulent stems of transplants. And because squash seedlings, with their large seed leaves (cotyledons), are a favorite of slugs, I keep a continuous ring of wood ashes around the plants (adding more after a heavy rain) until each plant has several true leaves and the stem is toughened. The leaves and stems develop spines as they mature, and when that happens the slugs leave them alone.

## Hand-Pollinating Sweet Corn

An old adage among sweet corn growers is that you need a block of corn at least 20 rows long and 20 rows wide for wind pollination of every ear shoot. Actually, even a block this large may have plants on the edges that do not receive enough pollen, depending on the direction and velocity of the wind during the pollen-shedding period. Certainly the home gardener who plants three rows spaced a foot apart, each only 4 feet long, should rely on some hand pollination to ensure filled ears.

The simplest hand-pollination technique involves cutting a tassel (the pollen-producing structure at the top of the corn plant) when it is shedding pollen and dusting the silks of each ear with the pollen. Work your way upwind so that pollen caught by the wind will move through the block, settling on other silks. One tassel will probably dust several ears, so some tassels can be left on the plant and allowed to throw their pollen to the wind. The end result should be filled ears at harvest time, well worth the investment of time.

### A Mailbox in the Garden

I don't want to leave the garden in summer, not even to pick up the mail, so I've attached a mailbox on the inside of the garden gate post, one of those really large mailboxes. Since I have yet to convince the mail carrier to drive down our potholed road with the daily delivery, I'm using the mailbox to store often-used small tools and supplies such as a dandelion wrench, a short-handled three-tined cultivator, a ball of twine, the velcro tape we used to tie tomatoes and cucumbers to their supports, a carpenter's pencil and pencil sharpener, a garden journal, and the soil thermometer. The mailbox has cut my daily trips from garden to basement in half.

A mailbox in the garden cuts down on those trips to the basement for hand tools and other often-used garden supplies.

## Carrots

Carrots are often listed among the cool-season crops, but carrot seeds germinate best when the soil temperature has settled above 50° F. Also, carrot seed germination is inhibited in waterlogged soils, often a characteristic of May in Marjorie's Garden, especially in the past few years. We often put off sowing carrots until the first of June.

Once conditions are right, I prepare a seed bed, repeatedly raking it to a depth of the rake tines while removing any clods of manure, pebbles, sticks, or other debris that could obstruct emergence of the tiny carrot seedlings. Once this is complete, I lay a slender bamboo stick, about the diameter of a pencil, across the bed and press it into the soil to make a shallow furrow no more than ¼ inch deep. I repeat this process, spacing furrows about 6 inches apart.

It will take two to three weeks before the carrot seeds germinate, so I begin by sowing a healthy pinch of radish seeds down each furrow. The radish seeds will germinate in a matter of days and clearly mark the rows, making weeding a lot easier. The emerging radishes also loosen the soil, making it easier for the carrot seedlings to emerge. A week or two after the carrots emerge, I begin harvesting the radishes, leaving room for the carrots to grow.

Carrot seeds are tiny and therefore difficult to space ½ inch apart in the furrow as instructed on the seed packet. I just do the best I can and don't worry, knowing that I will be thinning the seedlings once they put on a little growth. At some point the thinned carrots are large enough to eat.

Once the carrots seeds are sown, I cover them with a commercial seed-sowing mix that is largely peat and ground bark. I prefer this to covering with soil that still, despite my efforts, contains material coarse enough to impede germination. I use only enough of this mix to fill the seed furrow, then lightly mist the entire bed to saturate the mix and surrounding soil. A hose-end attachment that creates a fine mist is perfect for keeping the carrot bed uniformly moist until the carrot seedlings are up and growing.

An effective alternative to sowing carrot seeds in rows is broadcasting the seed over the entire bed and gently raking the seeds into the soil with a leaf rake. Some seeds end up too deep, and others wind up on top of the soil, but most of the seeds germinate. A light mulch of straw, thin enough to leave the soil visible, will help keep the seed bed moist between frequent waterings.

### Brassicas for Fall Harvest

Seeds of broccoli, cabbage, kale, and cauliflower should be sown indoors under lights in the second week of June to produce transplants for the July garden. (See Chapter 9 for a summer sowing schedule for Brussels sprouts.)

## *June-Flowering Native Shrubs*

You do not need to be a native-plant purist to understand the importance of including native plants in an ecologically functional garden. The native shrubs discussed below provide colorful flowers and fruits for the gardener's enjoyment as well as food and shelter for wildlife, including pollinators and birds. See this book's appendix for a further listing of woody invasives and suggested native alternatives.

### Diervilla

Few other native shrubs are as ornamental, stress tolerant, and ecologically functional as diervilla *(Diervilla lonicera)*, a beautiful flowering shrub with the most unfortunate common name of northern bush honeysuckle. It is not a honeysuckle and should not be confused with the non-native invasive shrubby honeysuckles. Ask for it by scientific name, not by common name.

A small deciduous shrub typically growing to 3 to 4 feet tall (occasionally to 6 feet), diervilla has an upright arching and spreading habit. The new light-green leaves emerge in mid-May, gradually turning dark green as the weather warms. If the weather stays cool and wet, the newest summer leaves display a unique pattern of light green and auburn. In autumn, the leaves turn first to yellow, then orange, and finally red. Diervilla is one of our loveliest fall shrubs.

Diervilla's first flowers appear in late June—clusters of funnel-shaped bells about a half-inch long in the leaf axils—and blooming continues through July. Pale yellow at first, the flowers slowly turn to orange or purplish-red as they mature. They provide steady forage for native pollinators, particularly bumblebees, during a time of the year when few other plants are flowering.

Thriving in sun or shade, diervilla is extremely drought tolerant and will grow in soils ranging from coarse sands to heavy clays. It is not tolerant of flooding, however, so do not plant it in low areas where snowmelt and early spring rains create seasonal ponds.

We purchased our diervilla plants in one-gallon

#### Irrigate without Wetting Leaves

The best way to avoid blighted tomato leaves and mildewed raspberries is to avoid wetting foliage when you irrigate. Ditch the sprinkler, and apply water to the soil, not to the plants.

One of my favorite high-tech irrigation techniques is to turn the hose on to a dribble and place it on the soil between plants while I pull weeds or turn compost. I move it around every 15 minutes or so while working, and when my work is done, I finish watering with a nozzle attached to a wand. I can just stand in one place, watching bumblebees buzzing tomato flowers while water soaks into the ground.

I keep promising to install a drip irrigation system in the raspberry beds and maybe some soaker hoses here and there in Marjorie's Garden. Both would work to direct water onto the soil rather than wetting leaves.

One area where we did install a soaker hose was the new strawberry bed. It was a plant saver in what turned out to be a very dry summer.

From late June through July, bumblebees are a constant presence on diervilla.

Native to New England, the Virginia rose *(Rosa virginiana)* has lovely flowers (top), provides fodder for native pollinators (center), and ends the year with a beautiful display of deep red hips (above).

containers, well-established plants that had already developed rhizomes, and planted them 3 to 4 feet apart on both sides of the steps leading up to the house. After a single growing season, shoots from the underground stems had emerged to fill in the spaces between plants. By the end of the second summer we had what we had envisioned, a continuous thicket of foliage and flower that not only holds the soil together but provides ornamental beauty from May to November. Even the plant by the driveway that gets whacked by the snow plow every winter is quick to recover.

## Native Roses

You will not find rugosa rose *(Rosa rugosa)*, often called beach rose, on a list of plants native to New England. Many people believe it to be native and are astonished when they learn that it is a non-native invasive species. And I've heard otherwise sane folks say that the invasion of beach rose is over, that it now occupies every possible coastal site where it can grow, and therefore we need not worry over it anymore.

Not true! Over my dozen years in Maine, visits to the island village of Vinalhaven have revealed a continuing encroachment of beach rose into the surrounding native landscape. In the open fields bordering the rocky coastline, I see colonies of beach rose expanding, swallowing up space previously occupied by native plants such as northern bayberry, meadowsweet, sweet fern, and native rose. No doubt this invasion began when seeds from garden plants in the village were dispersed by birds.

Despite its beauty, beach rose should be viewed as a serious threat to the integrity of all coastal plant communities. There are still areas of New England that can be protected from the invader and other areas that can be reclaimed, but only if we stop growing beach roses in our gardens.

There are beautiful alternatives. Chief among them are two very similar native rose species, *R. carolina* and *R. virginiana.* No, they are not as fragrant as beach rose nor as long-flowering, and they have simpler flowers, a single row of pink petals surrounding bright yellow stamens. But their autumn display of burgundy-red foliage and deep red hips more than compensates.

## Black Chokeberry

Blooming in early June along roadsides, in the low ground of open coniferous woods, in local swamps, and on dry sandy hillsides and rocky upland barrens, black chokeberries *(Aronia melanocarpa)* fill the air with a musky sweet scent. In these wild places they seldom exceed 3 feet in height, but in the garden, growing in full sunlight with their roots in compost-enriched soil, they reach a height of 6 feet.

Suckering profusely, each shrub consists of multiple slender stems held stiffly erect, the upper two-thirds covered in glossy dark-green leaves frosted with white flowers. The five petals of each half-inch flower surround a cluster of pink anthers held high on extended filaments.

The flowers are foraged by several pollinator species. Once, in a few minutes of close observation, I recognized two different species of bumblebee, two different fly species, a tiny wasp of unknown identity, and several different solitary bee species, all moving chokeberry pollen around as they went about their foraging.

From early September to late November, the shrubs bear loose clusters of glossy black berries, fruits that contain higher levels of antioxidants than any other temperate fruit including blueberries. This feature has prompted increasing interest in black chokeberries among small fruit growers in the United States. Whole berries are canned, the juice is used in making jelly or added to apple juice, and extracts of the berries are used as natural colorants in other foods.

The flowers of black chokeberry attract a variety of pollinators, including bumblebees.

In the wildlife garden, black chokeberries are eaten by grouse, black-capped chickadees, cedar waxwings, black bears, red foxes, rabbits, and white-footed mice. I read that the astringent taste of the berry (the characteristic responsible for its common name) makes it a food of last resort among winter birds. I have noticed that many berries do shrivel on the stems, but I have also watched robins feast on ripe berries when other fruits were still locally abundant.

As a landscape plant, the merits of black chokeberry have been sung since its introduction to Western gardens in the 1700s. In 1972, *Aronia melanocarpa* received the Royal Society's Award of Merit and was described as a "splendid shrub for naturalistic plantings, especially on the edge of woodlands." Others have recommended it for use in mass plantings, informal hedges, pond plantings, and as a spot of color in a mixed border.

## Meadowsweet

A denizen of meadows, pastures, and roadsides of New England, meadowsweet *(Spiraea alba* var. *latifolia)* begins to bloom in May and continues flowering through August. Its small, soft, pink flowers, borne in terminal branched clusters, are pollinator magnets throughout the summer. In autumn the leaves turn to tarnished gold, and in winter the pale brown to red-brown seed heads float shadows on the garden's blanket of snow.

The soft pink flowers of meadowsweet attract pollinators and other beneficial insects from May through August.

Wherever there is a little shade and acidic soil, bunchberry grows among the mosses.

In a comprehensive study of native plants conducted by Michigan State University, meadowsweet was the third most attractive plant to beneficial predatory insects and spiders, over four times as effective in attracting predators as a grass control. Beneficials attracted by meadowsweet included both crab and jumping spiders; soldier beetles that eat aphids and other insects; plant bugs that prey on leaf beetles; damsel bugs that prey on aphids, leafhoppers, mites, and caterpillars; ladybug beetles important in controlling aphid populations; and ichneumonid wasps, which are parasitic on beetles and caterpillars.

In the same study, meadowsweet attracted moderate numbers of bees, including bumblebees, sweat bees, and Andrenid bees, very common spring pollinators in Maine.

## Bunchberry

Growing only a few inches high, bunchberry *(Cornus canadensis)*, a native dogwood, is one of several companion plants of mossy areas. Along with lowbush blueberries and ferns, bunchberry helps fill in small niches where the moss languishes to create a tapestry of colors and textures. Like its tree-form relatives, the flowers of this dogwood are in tiny white clusters surrounded by four large bracts, giving the appearance of a single blossom.

In late July through autumn, each bunchberry plant bears a cluster of bright red fruits. This photo, taken in the garden of Dr. Charles Richards, Great Wass Island, Maine, shows a cultivated wild colony of *Cornus canadensis.*

The fruits, borne in clusters (or bunches, as indicated by the common name), are coral red.

Many New England gardeners are lucky to have bunchberry growing wild on their property, often in the garden proper. It grows most vigorously in partial shade, preferring soils that are moist but well drained and acidic.

## Elderberries

The bright red berries that give the red elder *(Sambucus racemosa)* its name are ripe by mid-June, and wood thrushes frequent the branches of several plants scattered about Marjorie's Garden. They are welcome to these berries, as they are toxic to humans.

In a wetter and slightly shadier bed close to the porch, several common elderberry shrubs *(S. canadensis)* are in full bloom, their small off-white flowers, often called elderblow, borne in flat-topped clusters. Over the years, as these plants have matured and spread, they have colonized the entire bed with pithy canes that sprout from underground stems. Old canes die back, but there are always young canes to take their place.

The berries of these plants will not ripen until late summer, when they become dark purple-black. We harvest those that the birds leave us and bake them into delicious muffins.

Red elders prefer dry soils in the wild, while common elders are more often found in moist, well-drained soil, but we have both species growing together in one area of the garden. The contrasts in color and texture between bright red berries and white elderblow are a highlight of our summer garden.

Flat-topped clusters of common elderberry flowers can be dipped in batter and deep-fried to make elderblow fritters.

The purple-black berries of common elderberry make delicious muffins.

When common elderberry blooms in Marjorie's Garden, the bright red fruits of the red elder are already fully ripe, and are quickly taken by thrushes that live in the surrounding woods. Growing both of these native elders in the garden can lead to a striking combination of flower and fruit.

# *Bringing Mountain Maple from Woods to Garden*

Several species of garden-worthy native trees, shrubs, and vines make their homes in the shade of taller trees. Included in this group are the pagoda dogwood *(Cornus alternifolia,* see Chapter 7), an understory tree with horizontally spreading branches that are trimmed in early June with upright flat-topped clusters of creamy-white flowers; Virginia creeper *(Parthenocissus quinquifolia),* an exuberant vine with bold scarlet autumn foliage; and New England's native honeysuckle *(Lonicera canadensis),* an early May-flowering shrub with lovely pale-yellow blossoms quickly followed by bright red fruits.

All three of these native woodies grow at the back of Marjorie's Garden under the shade of red oak and bird cherry. In early June, however, the dogwood must share center stage with a rarely cultivated native maple.

Known as mountain maple in the Great Smoky Mountains of Tennessee and North Carolina, where it grows to 30 feet, *Acer spicatum* is often reduced by deer and moose browsing to a large multi-stemmed shrub in New England forests, hence the alternate common names of moose maple—a name it shares with another native maple, *A. pensylvanicum*—and low maple. Yet another common name, water maple, refers to its mountain habitat, described by Donald Culross Peattie as "the neighborhood of white and singing water."

In Maine I have found examples of both growth habits, tree form and shrubby. My introduction to the species was a lovely small tree growing in the shade of tall pines near Boothbay, where a former student and I were collecting data for her research project. It was near dusk, and the small maple was in full flower, the upright spikes of greenish-yellow flowers turning horizontal branches into candelabras.

I was so enchanted by the tree that I returned later with the intent of collecting seed, only to find the tree nearly destroyed by timber harvesters dragging pine logs out of the woods. Only one of the original three trunks had survived to mature a handful of seeds on its branches. I collected these seeds and successfully produced seedlings, two of which now grow at the back of Marjorie's Garden. Mountain maple is easily grown from seed sown outside in fall or stratified in the refrigerator for three to four months followed by spring sowing. Considering the scarcity of this species in nurseries and garden centers, growing your own from seed may be the only way to bring this lovely maple from woods to garden.

The early June flowers of mountain maple brighten a shady corner of the garden.

Mountain maple deserves to be more frequently grown in shady gardens. In June, its shoot tips are graced with upright spikes of chartreuse flowers that glow like candles in the understory. Small two-winged samaras ripen through the summer to red or yellow before they are carried off on autumn winds as the tree's foliage turns to yellow, orange, and scarlet. In winter months, the tree's bright red young twigs add a touch of color to the snow-covered landscape.

An inhabitant of beech-maple-hemlock woods, hemlock ravines, and pine forests, mountain maple demands shade. Scorching of the leaves and the thin bark occurs when it is exposed to full sun, a trait which it shares with the striped maple, the other moosewood. A sheltered location protects the weak wood of both species from damage by wind.

Mountain maple is not tolerant of urban stresses such as soil compaction and pollution. It is intolerant of flooding, too, and its shallow roots, seldom more than a few inches below the soil surface, make it very susceptible to drought. On the plus side, it can be grown from USDA Zone 2 to the mountains of Zone 7, and it has no serious insect or disease pests. Both *A. spicatum* and *A. pensylvanicum* are among the most resistant of all maples to attack by the Gypsy moth.

Europeans have long recognized the garden worth of mountain maple, first introduced in 1775 and again in 1905. Like many gardeners in the United States today, they had a penchant for the exotic. For many of us, however, there is growing interest in sustainable managed landscapes that express the uniqueness of native flora. Plants like mountain maple have come into their own.

## Managing Garden Herbivores

Herbivores include the the lowly slug as well as the insects that eat our garden plants, that cut down seedlings during the night, chew holes in plant leaves, and suck the sap from tender young shoots. Whether we like it or not, all are integral members of the garden food web. As caretaker of a healthy garden ecosystem, the gardener understands that small populations of herbivores are necessary to ensure the presence of beneficial insect predators that feed on them. And occasionally, when the herbivore is an invasive species, the gardener must assume the role of chief predator, dispatching herbivores without the use of toxic chemicals.

## Slug Wars

In June 2009, I received a letter from a reader in Wesley, Maine, a response to a recent column on slugs in the garden. She had tried all of my suggestions for controlling slugs with minimal results, but had her own method that really worked. "I take an empty can, put a little salt in the bottom, and using a plastic teaspoon, I go around and pick them up the first thing in the morning. When I get done, I sprinkle some more salt on them and they are out of commission. They exude a liquid when they hit the salt. So I leave them in the can overnight, in that salty brine, and then go dump them under a tree in the woods."

I thought I had a slug problem until I read her body counts for the previous four years, led by a total of 5,651 slugs salted down in 2008. "So far this summer I've picked 2,608," she wrote, "so I guess it's going to be another big year. Now, that's a lot of slugs to get rid of. If I don't do that I might as well give up gardening."

A Tenants Harbor, Maine, reader, recently transplanted from Alaska where slugs are numerous and large, emailed her recommendation for slug control, a mixture of half water and half household ammonia. "We keep the mixture in a spray bottle ready to zap the critters whenever they appear," she emailed. "On contact, the slugs will sizzle and dissolve."

Are you beginning to feel the absolute loathing that New England gardeners have for garden slugs?

Also by email came good advice from a Town Hill, Maine, gardener: "I turned my chickens loose last fall, and I feel that I have a lot fewer slugs to contend with. Guinea hens will keep your garden slug- and bug-free without the damage to plants that accompanies chickens."

Marjorie, meanwhile, has come up with a way to keep her ripening strawberries out of the slugs' reach. Patrolling the four rows, she props each ripening berry off the ground with a recycled plastic fork, cradling the fruiting stem in the tines. We pick ripe strawberries free of slug bites, but the berries are in full view of every crow and jay perched on a garden post.

So go the slug battles. Weapons in the arsenal are numerous and varied, but the gardener wins skirmishes at best—never the war. The slugs keep sending reinforcements.

Most Maine gardeners are battling the gray garden slug, a destructive three-quarter-inch slimy villain varying in color from yellow to black with brown specks and mottling. They appear in hordes during wet, cool summers, mowing seedlings to the ground and climbing up stalks to suck the juice from ripe tomatoes, all under the cover of darkness. During the day they hide from the sun in the crevices of stones, under boards, or beneath the garden mulch.

In their hiding places, they—meaning just about all of them, since slugs are hermaphroditic, each with both male and female reproductive organs—lay eggs. And not just a few; each adult, over a life-span of nine to thirteen months, will lay between 300 and 500 eggs, clusters of clear, jelly-like eggs about an eighth of an inch in diameter.

Slug eggs are highly resistant to cold and drying and are often the only life stage to overwinter in the garden. Adults survive the winter only if they can find shelter from freezing temperatures.

At cold temperatures, 32° to 45° F, it may take 100 days for eggs to hatch. But in late May the eggs hatch in a mere 10 days. Newly hatched slugs resemble their parent, only much smaller.

Slugs young and old are very fond of just-emerging vegetable seedlings. For the gardener, it's a "now you see them, now you don't" act. In one night the tiny seedlings that you waited two weeks to see emerging from the ground have been rasped to the ground, leaving only the ragged bases of stems.

Slugs will occupy the top layer of the compost pile, feeding on discarded vegetable scraps. Frequent turning of the pile, burying the scraps deep in the middle, will minimize the pile's slug population.

Garden slugs take me to the brink of chemical control. The garden is host to very few toads, the primary predator of slugs, and we have provided the slugs with plenty of dark, cool crevices in which to reproduce. But in the end we refuse to use the baits and other chemical controls, fighting the battle with all the non-chemical weapons possible.

Unless you consider beer a chemical weapon. Beer traps, shallow containers set at ground level and covered loosely with a board, do work. We scatter traps wherever slugs feed and find several sunken slugs each morning.

Or save the beer and just dig a small hole in the garden bed, cover it with a board or piece of bark, and the next morning you will likely find slugs resting in the hole. Time to get out the empty can, spoon, and salt! Truthfully, I just fish them out of the hole and toss them far into the woods, hoping to make a toad happy.

Slugs will avoid crawling over anything scratchy, including wood ashes, coarse sawdust, gravel, and sand. I encircle every planting with wood ashes saved over the winter from the wood stove, and I apply ashes into the crevices between stones around the garden beds. These treatments have to be repeated after two or three heavy rains, and I always run out of ashes before July. And slugs will find any gap left in a ring of ashes. (Diatomaceous earth used to be on the list of scratchy slug deterrents, but we have stopped using it out of concern about its persistence in the soil and its impact on beneficial soil organisms, including earthworms.)

Sowings can be protected from slugs with a fence made from fly screen cut into 4-inch strips and placed on edge, partly embedded in the soil for support. The fence can be removed once the seedlings reach the five-leaf stage, when stems toughen and any slug feeding is usually superficial.

If you like to wander about the garden before sunrise, try baiting slugs with citrus fruits. Squeeze the juice from several oranges or grapefruits and scatter the halves around the garden before dark, leaving one inside edge close to the ground for easy access. Stroll though the garden before dawn, drinking the juice and picking up the "traps," disposing of the slugs by feeding them to your chickens and guinea hens.

Some gardeners swear by the copper tape sold to deter slugs from potted plants and raised beds. The tape has adhesive on one side to secure it to the pot rim or bed edges. Slugs trying to cross the copper get a small electric shock.

Finally, don't make it easy for the slugs to find daytime shelter in your garden. Remove logs, boards, and rocks from the garden and keep surrounding plants cut low to the ground.

## Japanese Beetles

The 2011 garden season may well be remembered as beetle summer in Marjorie's Garden and throughout Maine. Cucumber beetles in historic numbers caroused on the blooms and leaves of squash, pumpkins, and of course cucumbers, while Japanese beetles ran rampant among the roses, raspberries, grapes, and many other garden plants. The list of Japanese beetle host plants seems endless.

The previous winter had provided a thick blanket of snow to protect overwintering cucumber beetle adults snuggled beneath the forest floor litter, while Japanese beetle larvae hibernated peacefully deep underground. Fewer winter mortalities translated into more summer beetles to keep New England gardeners on their toes.

I needed a ladder to reach some of the Japanese beetles on our grape vine. It became a morning ritual: Take a pail of soapy water to the garden before the beetles emerge from their overnight torpor, position the pail under a leaf crawling with beetles, and knock the critters into the pail. Most of them will oblige you by slipping their hold on the leaf and tumbling to their end. My days were punctuated with beetle predation. At first the task has its own rhythm and does not seem so bad. After a few mornings, however, you begin to realize that you're fighting a rear-

Japanese beetles are easy to recognize and sluggish enough in the early morning to hand pick from leaves or fruits into a pail of soapy water.

guard action and would rather be starting your day some other way.

The bad news is that Japanese beetles will continue to occupy New England gardens for the foreseeable future. While annual fluctuations in summer populations will occur, nothing we do will eliminate this beetle from our gardens. Get used to it.

One piece of good news is that we are not the only creatures preying on Japanese beetles in our gardens. A small tachinid fly *(Istocheta aldrichi)*, imported from Asia in 1922 and released into the wild to combat agriculturally important herbivores including the Japanese beetle, is our ally (with assurance from the USDA that it is host specific).

The larva of this fly is an internal parasite of the adult Japanese beetle. The adult female fly produces up to 100 tiny (about 1mm) eggs over a two-week period, attaching one or more to the thorax of any adult beetle it can find. Upon hatching, the maggots bore into the beetle body, killing the beetle before it has a chance to reproduce.

So, if you find a Japanese beetle with one or more small whitish dots just behind its head, don't destroy it! Let it live out its short doomed existence so that the tachinid eggs will hatch and the larvae will consume the beetle on their way to becoming adult flies.

Reports on the effectiveness of tachinid fly parasitization of Japanese beetles in northern New England range from 20 to 40 percent. Sounds encouraging, but hold on, there are some interesting wrinkles preventing the fly from becoming the be-all and end-all.

First, the presence of the tachinid fly depends on the presence of the adult fly's major food source, the aphid secretions of Japanese knotweed, a non-native invasive plant that many of us are trying hard to eliminate. So, to combat the Japanese beetle we need to encourage an Asian fly which depends for its existence on an invasive plant species from Japan.

Also, the tachinid fly's life cycle is not well synchronized with that of the beetle. The flies emerge several weeks before the beetles and thus only lay eggs on the first emerging beetles, then disappear before the peak of beetle emergence.

Another ally in our fight against the Japanese beetle is an insect-eating nematode that seeks out beetle grubs in the soil during the fall. There are two such species of nematodes (microscopic round worms), but only one that is commercially available, *Heterorhabditis bacteriophora*.

This nematode forms a mutualistic symbiotic relationship with a species of bacteria. The nematode penetrates the beetle grub and inoculates the grub with the bacteria. The bacteria reproduce rapidly as they feed on grub tissue. The nematode feeds on the bacteria.

You can purchase the nematodes from lawn and garden shops or through biological mail-order catalogs. They are applied to the soil (typically lawns) with an ordinary sprayer. For best results, they should be applied during the last three weeks of August. Encourage your neighbors to treat their lawns as well.

This Japanese beetle carries one tachinid fly egg on its thorax (the white dot just behind its head).

A discouraging sight for a gardener. Japanese beetles arrived on this midcoast Maine grape vine in early July 2012 and soon started reducing the leaves to lace.

Pheromone traps are controversial, largely because of their misuse. They are intended for monitoring beetle populations, not for primary control. If placed within the garden, they actually attract Japanese beetles that will feed on your garden plants before finally ending up in the bottom of the trap. However, if you place the trap at least 50 feet from your garden plants, beetles will leave them alone and go for the trap.

Persistent hand-picking should remain a weapon in your arsenal, but check for white dots behind the head before dispatching a beetle. Also, susceptible vegetable crops can be covered with lightweight row covers to exclude beetles.

Don't even think about toxic chemical controls, even those recommended for Japanese beetle control. The beetle will develop resistance while the chemical destroys beneficial insects, including pollinators, and the life in your soil. Surely, by now, gardeners have learned this lesson.

Finally, gardeners should consider eliminating Japanese beetle magnets in their garden, plants such as rugosa rose and Norway maple. Both of these plants are invasive species, displacing native shrub and tree species in invaded natural areas. Eliminating them from the garden would benefit both the garden and surrounding natural areas.

In 2011, I found Japanese beetles on native birches surrounding our garden for the first time, more evidence that they had become firmly entrenched in our area. This was very disturbing, since birches are ranked second only to oaks as larval hosts for native caterpillars that are a primary food for garden birds. I know of no bird that eats the adult Japanese beetles, so their presence will only reduce the food source for important native herbivores and, ultimately, for our garden birds.

## Cucumber Beetles

There are gardening seasons in which slugs and Japanese beetles are the only really troublesome herbivores, and then there are seasons in which a specialist herbivore appears in plague proportions throughout New England. In 2010, for example, gardeners across the region were talking about the hoards of striped cucumber beetles feeding on cucumber and squash plants in their gardens.

I first heard about the beetle scourge from Eva Eicher and Dorcas Corrow, owners of Sweet Haven Farm on Mt. Desert Island, Maine, who grow food for local food pantries in deer-fenced plots (see Chapters 1 and 13). In the winter squash plot, hand-picking the beetles every early morning was necessary to keep them at tolerable levels. These beetles (and Japanese beetles too) are like me before morning coffee, lethargic and easier to subdue.

A day later, while visiting another gardener in her Bucksport garden, cucumber beetles entered the conversation as we walked past the pumpkin patch. She was using yellow sticky traps to control the beetles, but mentioned that sucking them up with a portable vacuum also works. Now there's a market that the Dust Buster folks have overlooked!

And then I received a reader's email with two attached photos, one of her vegetable garden's squash plants, the other a close-up of a single squash flower crawling with cucumber beetles. She wanted to know what they were and what to do about them. I immediately replied, giving her all the non-chemical remedies including vacuuming, hand-picking, and yellow sticky traps, then wished her luck.

Later that day I received a reply thanking me for my prompt response to her concern. She went on to say, "My husband ran out and bought a package of Sevin-5 (5% carbaryl) and got rid of those pesky bugs."

Sadly, cucumber beetles were not the only creatures eliminated by this errant act. Between 2 and 4 million pounds of carbaryl (typically in the form of Sevin) are used every year on U.S. lawns and gardens, despite the fact that it has been identified as a mutagen (causing genetic damage) in humans by the National Institute of Occupational Safety and Health. The U.S. Environmental Protection Agency likewise classifies carbaryl as carcinogenic in humans; it has been linked with cancer among farmers. Toxic to birds, fish, tadpoles, salamanders, shrimp, bees, and other non-target insects, it kills by inhibiting normal nervous system function.

Carbaryl is highly toxic to honeybees and native pollinators, including leaf-cutter bees, alkali bees, and bumblebees. So while my reader may very well have eliminated the cucumber beetles on her squash, she also minimized her squash harvest by killing off the essential pollinators.

Carbaryl also kills ladybug beetles and parasitic wasps, two very important beneficial predators in our gardens. How long will it be before species diversity returns to near normal after an application of carbaryl?

When an herbivore such as the cucumber beetle shows up in the garden, the first step is to identify it. Kudos to my reader for at least wanting to know the identity of her squash-eating bug before finding a remedy. There are still a lot of people who will reach for the Sevin dust or other toxic chemical without knowing whether an insect is friend or foe.

Once you have identified the herbivore as one that will need control, learn all you can about its life cycle. In the case of the striped cucumber beetle, unmated adults overwinter in wooded areas beneath the litter and under rotting logs, often as much as a mile from the garden. They leave their hibernating quarters in the spring when temperatures reach 55° F and initially feed on pollen, petals, and leaves of willow, apple, hawthorn, goldenrod, and asters. But as soon as cucurbit plants (cucumber, squash, pumpkin) appear in your garden, the beetles fly to these plants, often in large numbers.

The beetles soon mate and continue feeding throughout the season, laying eggs 8 to 25 days after mating. Each female deposits up to 800 orange-yellow eggs in small clusters or singly in soil cracks at the base of the cucurbit plants.

Eggs hatch within eight days, and the white larvae (⅓-inch long when full-grown) spend about 15 days feeding on the roots and fruit stems in contact with the soil. The pupal period then lasts about a week before the next generation of adults emerges. The total time from egg hatching to adult for this generation is about one month. Only one generation occurs each season in northern New England, but in southern New England there can be two generations per year.

Knowing the life cycle, we can call to mind non-chemical controls other than those already mentioned. Growing cucurbits on trellises should help reduce larval feeding on fruit stems. Removing goldenrod and aster plants from the immediate vicinity of cucurbit crops makes sense. Row covers supported over the cucurbit plants with wire hoops will exclude the beetles.

But indiscriminately killing off most of the insect life in your garden, including pollinators and beneficial predators, is not a good option. Toxic chemicals, including insecticides, herbicides, and fungicides, have no place in an ecologically functional garden.

### Leaf Beetles

Thirty percent of all animals on Earth are beetles, with 34 times more beetle species than bird species. Within this immense order of insects (Coleoptera) is the family Chrysomelidae, the leaf beetles, which feed exclusively on the leaves of their host plant or plants, ignoring other plant parts. It is a family of much interest to farmers and gardeners, as leaf beetles are very good at eating plants.

The list of leaf beetles includes the Colorado potato beetle, the cereal leaf beetle, the asparagus leaf beetle, the flea beetles that perforate the leaves of broccoli and eggplant, and the viburnum leaf beetle, a European beetle that has severely limited the use of several native viburnum species in Maine gardens. (Japanese beetles eat fruits as well as leaves and are not leaf beetles.) The most devastating species have been introduced to our gardens from other regions of the world.

## Viburnum Leaf Beetle

Invasive insects arrive in this country without their natural predators and consequently wreak havoc on native ecosystems, including our gardens. The viburnum leaf beetle, for several years now a major threat to several species of native viburnums, is no exception. We gardeners are its only predator.

I have found adults, larvae, or egg casings of this devastating Eurasian herbivore in gardens (and on wild viburnums) from Orono to Mt. Desert Island, Maine, and along the Maine coast as far as Eastport. We have several mapleleaf viburnums *(Viburnum acerifolium)* scattered about Marjorie's Garden, and it is one of the beetle's favorite hosts, along with arrowwood viburnum *(V. dentatum)* and cranberry viburnum *(V. trilobum)*, two other favorites of New England gardeners. I know of several large plants of the latter two species that were killed within two years, defoliated each summer by the adult beetles and their larvae.

Because the viburnum leaf beetle entered New England from earlier invasion sites in Canada, it has been in Maine longer than in other New England states. There was never any doubt, however, that it would eventually be feeding on viburnum leaves throughout the region. It entered Connecticut in 2004, and the reports of damage to native viburnums there, both in the wild and in gardens, sound like a replay of the earlier invasion of Maine.

Early May is a good time to play the role of predator. Scout the upper twigs of your viburnums for clusters of beetle egg casings. They appear as small raised "warts" on the surface of the twig, and often the portion of the twig above the casings is dead. If you scrape away the raised portion of a casing, you can see the yellowish eggs inside. When you find casings, prune off the infected twig with a cut just above a pair of leaves below the infected area. Gather all such prunings and burn them. Believe me, you don't want to let those eggs hatch!

We love the native viburnums in our garden. But they would not be there, adding the beauty of their summer flowers and fall foliage to our lives, if we were to cease our continuous efforts to monitor for and control the beetle.

## Lily Leaf Beetle

Native to Europe, the lily leaf beetle was discovered near Montreal, Canada, in 1945. For decades its damage was limited to the Montreal area, but in the summer of 1992 it was discovered in Cambridge, Massachusetts, apparently entering the U.S. on bulbs shipped from Europe.

Lily leaf beetles are now devouring lilies in gardens throughout New England. Lilies are their preference, although they will nibble on frittillaria, Solomon's seal, potato, hollyhock, hostas, and flowering tobacco *(Nicotiana)*. They lay eggs, however, only on true lilies *(Lilium)*; daylilies *(Hemerocallis)* are safe.

The adult is a striking creature, about ¼-inch long with a shiny scarlet body and black head and legs. They squeak when you squeeze them, a defense mechanism to deter predators, but don't let that deter you from hand-picking them from your plants, preferably in the early morning while they are sluggish. Crush them or throw them into a jar of soapy water, just as you treat Japanese beetles. Like the Japanese beetle, lily leaf beetles are able fliers, and some will escape, perhaps to a neighbor's garden.

Lily leaf beetles on their favorite plant.

The larvae resemble slugs with swollen orange, brown, yellowish, or greenish bodies and black heads. To deter their predators, including gardeners, they secrete and carry their excrement on their backs. Fascinating creatures!

The adults spend the winter in the soil or plant debris, often some distance from their host plants. They emerge from late March through June, mate, and the females lay their reddish-orange eggs on the undersides of leaves in an irregular line. Throughout the spring, routinely inspect your lilies for eggs and either crush them or remove and burn the affected leaves.

The eggs hatch in seven to ten days, and the larvae commence feeding on the undersides of the leaves for up to 24 days, causing more damage than the adults. The larvae can be hand-picked if you are not squeamish, or you can wear gloves.

The larvae pupate in the soil. After 16 to 22 days, new adults emerge and feed until fall, but they do not mate or lay eggs until the following spring. Look for these new adults and eliminate as many as possible.

University of Rhode Island scientists are working on biological controls for the lily leaf beetle, concentrating on parasitoids that control its populations in France and Switzerland. They hope eventually to release an effective control agent in this country.

## Colorado Potato Beetle

We've been growing potatoes in Marjorie's Garden for several years, and the Colorado potato beetle has yet to find us. The reason is a floating row cover over the potato bed from the moment sprouts emerge in spring until harvest.

Floating row covers are a chemical-free way of denying plant-eating insects such as the Colorado potato beetle access to your vegetable crops. They also exclude squash bugs, cucumber beetles, and squash vine borers from squash, cucumbers, and pumpkins. They keep cabbageworms and root maggots from finding your broccoli, and they will foil bean beetles, corn earworms, whiteflies, grasshoppers, spinach leafminers, aphids, and leafhoppers.

Most garden row covers are a polypropylene fabric of varying weights. For insect control, we prefer a lightweight row cover (0.45 ounce per square yard) that retains very little heat in the soil while transmitting 95 percent of available light. Water from rain or irrigation easily passes through the fabric.

Row covers are available in rolls of varying length from garden stores and online, and in widths ranging from 5½ to 8 feet; wider is always better. Be sure to buy a width that will accommodate the upward growth of the plants.

Installed with plenty of slack between bed edges, our potato bed row cover literally floats on top of the growing plants, providing a millimeter of hindrance to potato beetles. And because producing potatoes does not involve pollinating insects, the row cover can remain over the potato bed throughout the summer.

## Flea Beetle

Small "shotholes" in leaves are the work of flea beetles, tiny black or dark brown beetles that use their large rear legs to jump like fleas when disturbed. There are several different species of flea beetle ranging in size from 1/16 to 1/5 inch in length, each species showing a preference for certain crop families. Crops most likely to suffer attack include the cabbage family, potatoes, tomatoes, eggplants, beets, corn, grapes, and spinach.

Most flea beetle damage is done in spring. Overwintering adults begin feeding in May, attacking the leaves of seedlings and young transplants. They feed for several weeks, the females taking time out to lay eggs in soil cracks at the base of the plants. The growth of infested plants can be retarded, and heavily infested plants may even be killed from a combination of beetle feeding and disease transmission.

The worm-like larvae feed on small roots and root hairs with minimal effect on the host plant (with the exception of the tuber flea beetle's damage to potatoes), then pupate in the soil. The adults emerge in time to begin a second generation within the same year.

In my experience, infestations of flea beetles occur most often on plants already stressed. For example, tomatillos that we planted too early (late May) and that subsequently were subjected to a week of rain and cold soil temperatures were devastated by flea beetles.

Adult flea beetles feeding on the leaves of young transplants, such as this tomatillo seedling, can severely retard growth. Heavily infested plants may be killed.

Populations of flea beetles can be reduced with yellow sticky traps placed within the host crop. Other nonchemical controls include trap crops, such as radish, planted near the crops to be protected, and floating row covers that exclude beetles flying in from overwintering areas. Because adult flea beetles overwinter under leaves and soil clods in the garden bed, the effectiveness of row covers depends on crop rotation.

## Aphids: Indicators of a Healthy Garden

Also known as plant lice, aphids seek out the tender new growth of garden plants upon which they form colonies, eventually drawing the gardener's attention with their sheer numbers, A herd of sap-sucking insects crowding the stem tips of a favorite rose or herbaceous perennial or shrub is hard to miss. There are numerous species, each a different color, and each species typically feeds on one plant species or a group of related plant species. Colonies grow as females give birth to live young, all female; males enter the picture only when it is time to produce eggs for overwintering. In a typical colony, some aphids will be winged, others wingless.

I have known otherwise rational gardeners to drag out the big guns from the toolshed shelf upon spotting a single aphid on their roses. Some of the most toxic insecticides, including nicotine sulfate, malathion, diazinon, and dimethoate, have been used in the past to kill aphids, along with beneficial insects and other forms of garden life.

### Coming to Terms with Neem Oil

In the *Week-by-Week Vegetable Gardener's Handbook,* authors Ron and Jennifer Kujawski recommend using neem oil to control flea beetle infestations. I have always resisted the use of anything likely to kill non-target organisms, so I researched neem oil thoroughly before considering its use when a serious infestation of flea beetles threatened to destroy our young tomatillo seedlings.

Neem oil is a natural substance extracted from the seed of the tropical neem tree. The most active ingredient in neem oil, azadirachtin, reduces insect feeding and acts as a repellent. It also interferes with insect hormone systems that control growth and reproduction, resulting in death, albeit a slow one.

An insect must eat the oil to be killed. This is reassuring in that bees and insect predators are not herbivores. It is important, however, that neem oil not be sprayed on plants when bees are foraging on the treated plants, as they could eat contaminated pollen or nectar. A warning to this effect is on the various neem product labels.

I ended up making one application of neem oil to the tomatillos, spraying the foliage early in the morning when no bees were around. A day later the flea beetles were gone, and they did not reappear for about a month. By then the plants had grown enough to tolerate a little herbivory without impact on flowering and fruiting, so no additional neem was applied.

This is the organic gardener's dilemma: what to do when faced with loss of a crop unless you use some chemical to control the herbivore. Handpicking flea beetles is not an option, and there is no effective predator. The careful use of neem oil (or one of the other botanical remedies) is an option, but do your homework and read the product label.

Aphids—preyed upon by ladybugs, wasps, and other beneficial insects—are part of the garden food web.

A ladybug patrols the foliage of a red elder, laying eggs and hunting aphids. A population of adult and larval ladybug will consume hundreds of aphids per day.

### Aphids, Ants, and Sooty Mold

While leaving the porch by the back steps one June morning, I spotted a cluster of blue aphids on the tip of a red elder stem. At least a hundred aphids completely encircled the stem, tapping the sugar-rich sap just beneath the surface, while several winged females prepared to migrate, leaving to establish new colonies on nearby plants.

A dozen or so black-and-red ants were working at one end of the colony, milking the aphids for honeydew by stroking them with their antennae. Honeydew, excreted by the feeding aphids and rich in plant sugars, is highly valued by the ants as food.

Drops of honeydew missed by the ants had accumulated on leaves below the aphids and had started a growing colony of a fungus, commonly called sooty mold, on the upper leaf surfaces. The mold blocks sunlight from the leaf surface, rendering the few affected leaves useless for photosynthesis.

A single ladybug beetle larva approached the other end of the colony, intent on eating aphids. In the absence of the ants there might have been more of these larvae, but the ants protected their herd of aphids from predation by killing the lady beetle larvae.

Aphids and aphid-farming ants, predaceous beetle larvae, and sooty mold were characters in a drama unfolding within the terminal 6 inches of a single elderberry stem, a lesson in garden ecology available for viewing from the back steps.

I would plead the case that a few aphids are evidence of a healthy garden ecosystem. Aphids have many predators, including ladybugs, lacewings, parasitic wasps, and syrphid flies. Of course, to maintain populations of these beneficial insects, there needs to be a steady supply of aphids. If I see a few aphids in the garden along with numerous ladybugs, or when I see lots of aphid exoskeletons punctured with the emergence holes of adult parasitic wasps, I feel that all is right in the garden world.

Entomologists agree that aphids rarely do enough damage to warrant intervention by the gardener. And in exceptional situations, when predators cannot keep up with a heavy infestation on young plants or your prize roses, mechanical controls will work. The gardener can dislodge them with a strong stream of water or trap them with sticky cards, thin plastic cards painted yellow and coated with Tanglefoot.

## Cutworms

Cutworms, the larval (caterpillar) stage of several species of night-flying moths, are a major herbivore in Marjorie's Garden each spring, cutting down unprotected young transplants at or below the soil surface and devouring seedlings before they break through the soil. As with all garden herbivores, understanding the life cycle of the cutworm gives clues to effective controls.

Cutworms overwinter in the late-larval or pupal stage. The adults, brownish-gray moths, appear with the warm weather in spring, flying at night. They are attracted to weedy fields, particularly to mustard and quackgrass, and also lay eggs in weedy gardens during early spring.

Once gardens are planted, the young larvae feed on small roots until half-grown (about three-quarters of an inch long), at which point they become more likely to cut off plants at or just below the ground, often dragging parts of the plant into the soil where they hide during the day. Their favorite garden plants include tomatoes, peppers, beans, and corn.

Northern New England gardeners are fortunate in that most cutworm species have only one generation per year, although a few have two. In southern New England, some cutworm species may go through three generations per year. And because there are several cutworm species, the larvae will vary in color from gray to brown or black, striped or spotted. A mature cutworm larva can be up to 2 inches long and will curl into a tight ball if disturbed.

Management begins with keeping the garden as weed-free as possible. Unfortunately, egg-laying moths are also attracted to green manures and cover crops in spring, so getting these crops incorporated into the soil as soon as possible should be a priority. Using aged composted manure in lieu of green manures may be necessary if cutworms get out of hand.

Cutworm collars, properly installed, will deter damage to transplanted seedlings. We use newspaper collars because they are biodegradable, rolling a 2-inch-

## When and How to Use Floating Row Covers

For leaf and root crops, row covers can be kept on throughout the growing season. For crops that require pollination by insects for fruit production, however, row covers must be removed during flowering.

Some crops, such as tomatoes, peppers, and others with fragile growing tips, do better if the row cover is supported with hoops. Many gardeners use hoops made from 9-gauge wire cut into 6-foot-long pieces. The ends of the hoops are pushed into the ground. In raised beds framed with timbers, small holes can be drilled in the top timber to support the hoops.

Other options for hoops include inexpensive plastic pipe, the ends pushed into the soil or slipped over rebar stakes. Rebar stakes with plastic end caps work well for supporting row covers over tall plants.

Row covers can be used for two or more seasons if properly used and stored. Small rips in the fabric can be closed with staples or clothespins, and much of the soil can be removed at the end of the growing season by hanging the fabric on a clothesline and rinsing it with a gentle spray from a garden hose. Once the fabric is dry, fold it for storage indoors.

### *When Floating Row Covers Work (and When They Don't)*

Successful deployment of floating row covers requires knowledge of how insects overwinter. For example, some herbivores, such as the Colorado potato beetle, spend the winter as adults in the soil near the plants on which they fed as larvae. If potatoes are planted in the same bed the following spring and the bed is covered with fabric, these adults will emerge to find their favorite food handy beneath a cover that protects them from their natural enemies. Other herbivores that overwinter near last year's plant host include the onion maggot, corn rootworm, and flea beetle (which affects many vegetable seedlings). Clearly, crop rotation must be used along with row covers to foil such herbivores.

Some herbivores, such as slugs, cutworms, millipedes, and sowbugs, overwinter in scattered locations around the garden. These insects have the greatest potential for causing plant damage under row covers, since they could emerge anywhere. Frequent inspection is the key. If noticeable populations of these herbivores are found, the row cover should be removed to allow beneficial insects access to their prey.

Floating row covers should be used only to prevent the establishment of an herbivore capable of serious damage, such as the Colorado potato beetle or the cabbage worm caterpillar. They should not be used at the expense of building strong populations of beneficial insects. If you cover everything, the beneficials will disappear, and that is a recipe for disaster.

A floating row cover, used to exclude Colorado potato beetles, can be left on potato plants for the entire season.

wide strip several times around the seedling stem, positioned so that half of the collar will be buried beneath the soil after planting. We put these collars on every seedling transplanted to the garden.

Minimizing cutworm damage to direct-sown crops is trickier. Direct-sown beans, for example, may never make it above ground if cutworms sever the embryonic stem as it emerges from the seed. Eliminating all weeds from potential seed beds is a start, since the moth is unlikely to lay eggs in bare soil. Shallow raking and sifting of the soil before sowing is another precautionary measure, destroying any cutworms found by crushing or drowning in soapy water.

Once seedlings of crops with succulent stems—such as squash, cucumbers, and beans—have successfully emerged from the ground, I surround each seedling with a 2-inch tall collar cut from a plastic water bottle, pushing each collar an inch into the ground around the seedling. These crops, the ones with juicy stems, seem to be cutworm favorites, but only for the first week or so after emergence. The stems soon harden, and the collars can be removed.

Finally, get proactive. If you have cutworm damage, usually evidenced at the crack of dawn by a severed seedling or two lying on the ground, dig 2 or 3 inches into the soil around the damaged plant and you will likely find the culprit. And visit the garden at night with a flashlight, looking for cutworms on top of the soil.

## Cabbage Worm Caterpillars

A floating row cover is essential for growing broccoli, cauliflower, and other brassica crops. Without it, cabbage worm caterpillars, larvae of those ubiquitous white moths with black spots on their wings, will significantly reduce both the amount of harvest and its quality.

*Bacillus thuringiensis* (Bt), a naturally occurring bacteria found in the soil and gut of lepidopteran larvae, can be sprayed on target crops to kill caterpillars, but I choose not to use it. It has been shown to kill non-target butterfly and moth larvae, while some target species have developed resistance.

Stick with the row covers. Properly used, they are 100% effective and have no side effects (see sidebar).

# Container Madness

Space is at a premium in Marjorie's Garden, particularly for sun-loving annuals and vegetables. Over the years many of the vegetable garden's beds have been turned over to cultivation of raspberries, strawberries, grapes, and highbush blueberries. We still find space for garden peas, tomatoes, onions, a trellis or two of cucumbers and sweet pea, hills of summer squash, and a bed of tall sunflowers.

When all of the sunny beds are filled with plants or plans, we turn to containers. In a typical summer there

Out from winter storage, these pots are ready for their annual spring cleaning.

The bright orange and yellow flowers of potted cosmos look like butterflies in the summer air.

A large pot planted with nicotiana, 'Only the Lonely,' brightens up the perennial bed in July.

are twenty or more pots scattered about the garden. Container gardening is a madness without a cure. In October, as we put all the pots away for the winter, we pledge that never again will we lug the watering can about the garden on hot July afternoons. But every May they all come out from storage and are scattered across a patch of grass to be scrubbed clean for the new season. And every year they seem to multiply, their numbers augmented by Christmas gifts and such.

In early June, we buy a bale of potting soil, mix it with a little composted goat manure (three parts potting soil to one part compost), and fill half of the pots before our first visit to the nursery, promising to be conservative. The shopping begins with pansies for pots on the porch rail, a garden tradition. And there we probably should stop, but instead we take the grand tour through every greenhouse, envisioning beautiful combinations of color and texture, designing specific plantings for each of our favorite pots.

By the end of the day there are pots of basil and parsley on the porch steps. Joining the pansies on the porch rail are glazed bowls of petunias in full bloom and a large terra cotta pot of yellow daisies and deep red nasturtiums. In a small bed at the edge of the garden, beneath the fringe tree, sits a glazed pot painted with dragonflies and planted with seeds of a blue morning glory; in July the leafy branches of this small tree will support sky-blue flowers on slender, twining stems. Other containers of morning glory seedlings sit at the edge of the garden's deer fence and under the tall iron stake that holds the hummingbird feeders. In the sun of the perennial garden sits an old terra cotta pot, weathered to a patchwork of green paint and

A single copper-leaved sedge (*Carex* sp.) in a hand-painted pot provides textural contrast to the flowering summersweet clethra.

An old weathered terra cotta pot is the perfect container for this combination of twinspur, purple-leaved sweet potato, and an annual rush, Fiber Optic Grass *(Isolepis cernua)*.

raw red clay, planted with a combination of twinspur, purple-leaved sweet potato vine, and an annual grass with arching wiry leaves.

Other pots extend the vegetable garden into the perennial bed and up the porch steps, pots propped on rocks and rotting stumps, any level place in full sun. Container-grown vegetables become portable color in the garden. A large pot filled with a mix of ruby red and green lettuces is a feast for the eyes as well as the table.

If you are new to container gardening, know this: like children and pets, potted plants are demanding. You can't go on vacation without a sitter. On the other hand, they extend your time in the garden, always a good thing.

## Welcome Garter Snakes into the Garden Food Web

We first found Lucy, the garden garter snake, sleeping in tight loops atop a pile of woodchips. She was not disturbed when we pulled back her blanket, a tarp to keep the woodchips dry, and we watched her closely for several minutes before resuming the morning's work. When we returned several hours later to recover the pile, she was gone. Late in the afternoon we found her sunning atop one of the firewood logs used to hold the tarp down.

At dusk I went out to the garden with the camera, looking for Lucy. She was still coiled on the log, but as I crept closer she slowly unwound and slithered across the ground until the distance between us seemed safe. She stretched out in front of me, 3 feet long with a dark gray back, red-brown stripes along her sides, and a light gray belly. Her eyes were cloudy blue.

Lucy let me take her picture, several frames with long exposures, then several more with flash, before she slid away. "Watch me," she whispered, and I did, until she was out of sight.

Two days later, when the sun came out, we slowly pulled back the tarp, hoping to find Lucy sleeping among the woodchips. Instead we found her just-shed skin stuck to the bottom of the tarp. I now know that cloudy blue eyes mean a garter snake is about to shed.

Lucy, the resident garter snake in Marjorie's Garden

In my mind I carry a picture of the garden food web, and I'm always pleased to make room for another creature like Lucy, an Eastern garter snake, *Thamnophis sirtalis*. To fit her into the picture I had to do some research. I learned that she eats insects, primarily grasshoppers, as well as earthworms, small rodents, salamanders, frogs, and tadpoles.

She doesn't dig holes. Do you hear me, Reilly the Brittany?! She doesn't chew or damage any plants in the garden. And she avoids gardeners at all costs.

And what eats the garter snake? Birds of prey, including the sharp-shinned hawks and kestrels that lord over the garden from the top of an old spruce snag, are probably the major predators. Perhaps the skunks or raccoons that meander around the garden at night would make a meal of her. But Lucy is probably safe, sleeping under her tarp blanket.

We don't see Lucy often, but somehow I know she is around, watching me, seeing me far more often than I see her.

# *The New England Garden in June, Zone by Zone*

June is the busiest month in the New England garden. Bolting spinach is replaced with a summer crop as hardened seedlings of cucurbits and tomatoes go in the ground. Ripe strawberries are munched as you set pots of basil in the sun. And there are always weeds to keep you in the garden.

| IN THE GARDEN | June | Date by USDA Hardiness Zone | | | | | Notes |
|---|---|---|---|---|---|---|---|
| | | 3 | 4 | 5 | 6 | 7 | |
| **GENERAL MAINTENANCE** | Control Japanese beetles through the summer by hand-picking.<br><br>Keep weeding! | | | | | | Toss hand-picked beetles into a container of soapy water. It is their comeuppance.<br><br>Be a discriminating weeder. Call each plant by name before deciding whether it is a plant growing where you do not want it or a plant worth nurturing. |
| **THE COMPOST PILE** | Turn compost piles regularly. | | | | | | Monitor compost pile temperature with a compost thermometer and turn the pile when the middle begins to cool. |
| **VEGETABLE GARDEN** | Mulch around plants.<br><br>Protect planted seedlings from wind and sun.<br><br>Irrigate crops without wetting the leaves. | | | | | | Don't be in a hurry to mulch. Wait until mid-June, giving the soil plenty of time to warm.<br><br>Use cedar shakes or other thin boards to shield transplants.<br><br>Ditch the sprinkler! Wetting the leaves while watering increases foliar disease. |
| **VEGETABLE CROPS** | | | | | | | |
| Asparagus | Stop harvest for the season | | | | | | |
| Beans, Bush | Resow if first sowing failed.<br><br>Sow every two weeks for continued harvest. | June 29 | June 22 | June 15 | June 8 | June 1 | |
| Beans, Pole | Resow if first sowing failed. | | | | | | (Photo courtesy Charles Heaven) |
| Beets | | | | | | | |
| Broccoli | Harden-off transplants from second sowing. | June 22 | June 15 | June 8 | June 1 | May 25 | Harden plants gradually, extending outside time by one hour each day. |
| | Set out transplants from second sowing. | June 29 | June 22 | June 15 | June 8 | June 1 | |
| | Sow seeds indoors for fall crop. | June 29 | June 22 | June 15 | June 8 | June 1 | Transplants from this sowing will be planted in July for a fall crop. |

| IN THE GARDEN | June | Date by USDA Hardiness Zone | | | | | Notes |
|---|---|---|---|---|---|---|---|
| | | 3 | 4 | 5 | 6 | 7 | |
| Cabbage | Harden-off transplants from second sowing. | June 22 | June 15 | June 8 | June 1 | May 25 | Harden plants gradually, extending outside time by one hour each day. |
| | Set out transplants from second sowing. | June 29 | June 22 | June 15 | June 8 | June 1 | |
| | Sow seeds indoors for fall crop. | June 29 | June 22 | June 15 | June 8 | June 1 | Transplants from this sowing will be planted in July for a fall crop. |
| Carrots | Direct-sow now that soil has warmed. | | | | | | Carrots germinate best when soil temperature is above 50° F. Mix radish seeds with the carrot seeds to mark the rows. |
| Cauliflower | Harden-off transplants from second sowing. | June 22 | June 15 | June 8 | June 1 | May 25 | Harden plants gradually, extending outside time by one hour each day. |
| | Set out transplants from second sowing. | June 29 | June 22 | June 15 | June 8 | June 1 | |
| | Sow seeds indoors for fall crop. | June 29 | June 22 | June 15 | June 8 | June 1 | Transplants from this sowing will be planted in July for a fall crop. |
| Celery and Celeriac | Set out transplants. | June 29 | June 22 | June 15 | June 8 | June 1 | |
| Corn, Sweet | Make second sowing if necessary | June 29 | June 22 | June 15 | June 8 | June 1 | Consider hand-pollinating small plantings. |
| Cucumbers | Set out transplants. | June 29 | June 22 | June 15 | June 8 | June 1 | Wrap stems of transplants with cutworm collars. Dig a spadeful of aged manure, compost, or worm castings into each hill. Wait until late June to mulch, allowing time for the soil to continue warming. Support plants with a trellis to save garden space. |
| Eggplant | Begin hardening off transplants. | June 29 | June 22 | June 15 | June 8 | June 1 | Harden plants gradually, extending outside time by one hour each day. |
| | Set out transplants if soil is warm enough. | July 6 | June 29 | June 22 | June 15 | June 8 | Wait to plant until soil temperatures have been above 65° F for a week. Place a bamboo stake next to each plant for later support of heavy fruit load. |
| Garlic | Fertilize with organic nitrogen. Mulch with 1-inch layer of straw or compost to keep soil cool. Harvest scapes when they begin to curl. | | | | | | |

| IN THE GARDEN | June | Date by USDA Hardiness Zone | | | | | Notes |
|---|---|---|---|---|---|---|---|
| | | 3 | 4 | 5 | 6 | 7 | |
| Kale | Harden-off transplants from second sowing. | June 22 | June 15 | June 8 | June 1 | May 25 | Harden plants gradually, extending outside time by one hour each day. |
| | Set out transplants from second sowing. | June 29 | June 22 | June 15 | June 8 | June 1 | |
| | Sow seeds indoors for fall crop. | June 29 | June 22 | June 15 | June 8 | June 1 | Transplants from this sowing will be planted in July for a fall crop. |
| Muskmelon | Set out transplants. | June 22 | June 15 | June 8 | June 1 | May 25 | |
| Peppers | Begin hardening off transplants. | July 6 | Jun 29 | June 22 | June 15 | June 8 | Harden plants gradually, extending outside time by one hour each day. |
| | Set out transplants if soil is warm enough. (Photo courtesy Charles Heaven) | | | | | | Wait to plant until soil temperatures have been above 65° F for a week.<br>Place a bamboo stake next to each plant for later support of heavy fruit load. |
| Potatoes | Hill plants. | July 6 | Jun 29 | June 22 | June 15 | June 8 | Do the first hilling when the plants are about a foot tall, mounding soil against the lower half of each plant. Repeat once or twice more during the growing season as the plants grow taller. |
| Pumpkins | Set out transplants. | June 29 | June 22 | June 15 | June 8 | June 1 | |
| Rhubarb | Continue harvesting stems from 3-year-old and older plants. | | | | | | |
| Spinach | Replace a bolting spinach crop with basil, summer squash, or other summer crop. | | | | | | Make a second spinach sowing in August. |
| Squash, Summer | Set out transplants. | June 29 | June 22 | June 15 | June 8 | June 1 | Wrap stems of transplants with cutworm collars.<br>Dig a spadeful of aged manure, compost, or worm castings into each hill before planting.<br>Keep a continuous ring of wood ashes around each hill to deter slugs until several true leaves have formed on each plant. |
| Squash, Winter | Set out transplants. | June 29 | June 22 | June 15 | June 8 | June 1 | |
| Tomatillo | Begin hardening off transplants. | June 15 | June 8 | June 1 | May 25 | May 18 | Harden plants gradually, extending outside time by one hour each day. |
| | Set out transplants. | June 22 | June 15 | June 8 | June 1 | May 25 | Give plants plenty of room to sprawl. |

| IN THE GARDEN | June | Date by USDA Hardiness Zone | | | | | Notes |
|---|---|---|---|---|---|---|---|
| | | 3 | 4 | 5 | 6 | 7 | |
| Tomatoes | Begin hardening off transplants. | June 22 | June 15 | June 8 | June 1 | May 25 | Harden plants gradually, extending outside time by one hour each day. |
| | Set out transplants. | June 29 | June 22 | June 15 | June 8 | June 1 | Put a handful of aged manure, compost, or worm castings under each plant. |
| | Cage tomatoes at planting time. | June 29 | June 22 | June 15 | June 8 | June 1 | Using cages means less maintenance (minimal pruning), more (if slightly smaller) tomatoes, and less sunscald. |
| Watermelon | Set out transplants. | June 22 | June 15 | June 8 | June 1 | May 25 | |
| **SMALL FRUITS** | | | | | | | |
| Strawberries | Pinch off blossoms on new plants. Harvest as ready. | | | | | | |
| **HERBS** | | | | | | | |
| Basil | Set out transplants and keep a pot or two on the porch steps. | June 22 | June 15 | June 8 | June 1 | May 25 | |
| **FLOWERS** | | | | | | | |
| Cosmos | Set out transplants. | June 15 | June 8 | June 1 | May 25 | May 18 | |
| Sunflowers | Sow outdoors. | June 29 | June 22 | June 15 | June 8 | June 1 | |
| Zinnia | Sow outdoors. | June 29 | June 22 | June 15 | June 8 | June 1 | |
| **ROSES** | Keep soil moist through summer, providing an inch of irrigation per week if no rain. | | | | | | |

# Chapter 9

# The Garden in July

*"The sun has shone on the earth, and the goldenrod is his fruit."*

*—Henry David Thoreau, 1853*

***On a wall of our dining room is a photograph of a butterfly***, a Harris' checkerspot, its wings folded while it sips nectar from sulfur-yellow flowers. When I take the time to really see this image, I remember the day that I captured it.

I was in the garden of a friend, looking through a drift of metallic-blue globe-shaped flowers that filled an island bed to the golden-tasseled plants just beyond the garden's edge, blue and gold together, a classic color combination achieved by chance. The globe thistle *(Echinops ritro)* had been planted by the gardener, and the wild goldenrod *(Solidago* sp.) had been sown by the wind.

It was a blue-sky summer day without a breeze, but the stems holding blue and gold flowers to the sun swayed back and forth under the weight of bumblebees and butterflies, tiny wasps, native bees, beetles, and other pollinating insects. I spent the better part of the morning among them, trying to capture it all.

Why is it that, when there are goldenrods in a picture, they are usually in the background at the edge of the garden, seldom part of the border or bed, seldom on center stage? English gardeners have long recognized the garden worthiness of goldenrods, but it has been a hard sell to American gardeners, who think of them as weeds at best, the cause of hay fever at worst. But goldenrod suffers from guilt by association where the latter charge is concerned, flowering at the same time as ragweed, the true cause of hay fever. Goldenrod pollen is too heavy, too sticky, to be borne on the wind; hence the dependence on pollinating insects.

A Harris' checkerspot sipping goldenrod nectar.

*Facing page:* Sweet pea plants grow with abandon in July.

Among the more than two-dozen goldenrod species that grow throughout New England, most bloom from late summer into fall, but a few, such as *S. juncea* (early goldenrod) bloom in July, and in years with warmer-than-usual June temperatures, I have even seen the earliest goldenrods in flower during the last week of June. Thus, a gardener can enjoy goldenrod blooms throughout the summer. Unfortunately, because there is not (yet) great demand from gardeners for goldenrods, they are not widely stocked by commercial growers and garden centers, and the number of species available for purchase pales in comparison with those in the wild.

We owe to English hybridizers the existence of early cultivars such as 'Golden Baby,' a compact, clumping goldenrod about 2 feet high with upright sprays of golden flowers from August through October; 'Golden Dwarf,' with its yellow flowers on foot-high stems; 'Cloth of Gold,' with golden blossoms on 18-inch stems, flowering in late summer; and 'Golden Mosa,' with lemon yellow flowers on 30-inch stems.

While these early hybrids are still available, the list of goldenrod cultivars has grown substantially over the years. I am partial to the native species and their cultivars. One highly rated cultivar is 'Fireworks,' selected from *S. rugosa*, wrinkleleaf goldenrod, a species native to all of New England. It features tiny, bright yellow flowers borne in dense, plume-like panicles on the ends of stiff stems over 3 feet tall. In addition to attracting butterflies and other pollinating insects, the seeds are eaten by goldfinches and pine siskins. (See Chapter 10 for other recommended species of native goldenrod.)

Goldenrods are more than single-season perennials. Their dried stalks make handsome additions to winter bouquets. Choose stems with only about one-third of the blossoms open and hang them in a dark but well-ventilated room to air-dry. The flowers will remain in the condition they were in when picked.

Few winter scenes are more beautiful than a patch of goldenrods, their dry seedheads coated in ice or dusted with new snow. I look forward to viewing this scene from the family room window, my back to the wood stove.

Or perhaps I will go out to visit the goldenrods and look for galls, insect-caused swellings found on goldenrod stems that serve as winter homes for *Eurosta solidaginis*, a fruit fly. Thoreau contemplated this relationship between plant and animal, writing the following in July 1853: "*The animal signifies its wishes by a touch, and the plant, instead of going on to blossom and bear its normal fruit, devotes itself to the service of the insect and becomes its cradle and food. It suggests that Nature is a kind of gall, that the Creator stung her and man is the grub she is destined to house and feed.*"

## July in the Vegetable Garden

For the New England vegetable gardener, July can be as frenzied as June, but with a shift in priorities from planting to maintenance and harvest. Dry periods mean more time spent dragging the hose. Rainy spells bring mildew and botrytis. Beetles and hornworms reach population peaks. Weeds run rampant. Each day ends with a final trip to the garden, hod in hand, for harvest of new potatoes, green beans, broccoli, zucchini, a head of cabbage, a few green tomatoes. The day's work ends with a harvest meal, a reminder of why you do it all.

### Garlic

No matter how long the gardener keeps at it, the garden always has something to teach. Such was the case the first summer we grew garlic.

Marjorie planted the seed cloves the previous October, after the first good frost, and covered their bed with a thick layer of straw to prevent winter heaving. Roots grew until ice formed in the soil. In spring she pulled away the straw, making way for onion-like shoots to emerge from sun-warmed soil.

Through spring and early summer I paid scant attention to the growing garlic shoots, my gardener's mind on melons, tomatoes, and carrots. But in July, the garlic bed was transformed to center ring as each leafy plant sent up a sturdy 4-foot-tall scape with a twisting loop near its top, then a cluster of tiny bulbils followed by a long pointed tip. Looping and pointing their fingers in every direction, the garlic scapes were the clowns of our summer garden.

Experienced growers recommend removing the scapes early to promote larger bulb development, but we left them until late July, finding great pleasure in them. Marjorie remarked that the patch looked like a crowd of accusing fingers, each pointing at the other and shouting, "She did it!"

In July we found garlic scapes for sale at the Blue Hill Farmers' Market, baskets loosely stacked with scapes cut just below the loop, and wondered how they were used. A little Internet research turned up recipes for Garlic Scape Pesto (see sidebar), Lemon Scented Pasta with Garlic Scapes and Veggies, and Garlic Scape Soup, to name just a few. Adding sliced garlic scapes to a stir fry or sauce imparts a milder, more subtle garlic flavor than the cloves. I learned that scapes should be harvested while in full curl (they straighten somewhat as they mature), snapped like a bean rather than cut. As I harvested ours, albeit late, I noticed that they still snapped readily just below the curl, giving off a mild, delightful garlic odor. Removing the lower portion of the scape required pruners.

(Above) Garlic scapes in the July garden. "Which way did she go?" Our first harvest of garlic scapes (left).

We've learned that not all garlic types produce flowering scapes, only hardneck garlic, a type recommended for cold climates. It doesn't produce the largest heads, but the individual cloves are large and the flavor is preferred by true garlic lovers.

In late July, the garlic circus closed with the hardneck scapes removed and the remaining leaves slowly dying. Harvest time was near. I learned a lot about garlic that first summer. The next year I removed the scapes sooner and saved the looping tops for Marjorie's pesto.

## Harvesting Garlic

Sometime between late July and the end of August, depending on location and the season's weather, garlic leaves will begin to slowly die back, an indication that harvest time is near. When the leaves are gone or nearly so, dig the bulbs and brush off the soil, spread them out on the porch to dry for a week or so, and then braid them for winter storage. Don't forget to set aside some of the largest bulbs for planting in the fall.

### Mariellen Eaton's Garlic Scape Pesto

Makes 1½ cups of pesto

10 garlic scapes, chopped (I use about 8-10 inches of the stem as well)
½ cup grated Parmesan cheese
⅓ cup walnut pieces
½ cup olive oil
salt and pepper to taste
¼ cup basil or parsley (optional)

Put the chopped scapes, ⅓ cup of cheese, nuts, and half of the olive oil plus optional herbs in the bowl of a food processor. Process until everything is finely chopped, then add the rest of the oil and Parmesan and process until you have your desired consistency. Add more oil if you prefer looser pesto. Add salt and pepper to taste. Refrigerate.

Great over gnocchi or ravioli, but we also like it on roasted potatoes.

## Peppers

You will notice in "The New England Garden in July, Zone by Zone" at the end of this chapter that pepper transplants should not be planted until the first of July in Zone 5, and even later in Zones 4 and 3. In fact, experienced gardeners in Zones 3 and 4 often sow pepper seeds and transplant the seedlings into small pots at the same time as gardeners in more southern zones, but then move them into even larger pots and hold them indoors until soil temperatures have sufficiently warmed.

Peppers have no tolerance for soil temperatures below 60° F. They are a difficult crop to grow in regions with short, cool summers.

## Tomatoes

Watch for spots and yellowing on the lower leaves of your tomatoes. They are early signs of diseases such as septoria leaf spot and early blight. Preventive measures include removing the infected leaves (bag them for the trash or burn them, but do not put them on the compost pile) and spreading a straw mulch over the soil to minimize splashing of spores onto the leaves during rain or irrigation.

Some gardeners remove all of the leaves below the first flower, infected or not, in order to minimize these disease problems. This makes for an odd-looking tomato plant, but it is very effective, particularly when combined with the straw mulch.

### *Blossom-End Rot: a Physiological Scourge*

Another common problem of tomatoes, eggplants, and peppers is blossom-end rot, named for the dark, sunken, leathery blotches that develop on the fruit's blossom end (the end opposite the stem). It is not caused by a fungus or virus, but by a deficiency of calcium in the developing fruit that typically occurs during periods of stress, particularly drought stress. It can also result from wide fluctuations in soil moisture levels and when plant growth is overstimulated with too much nitrogen fertilizer. Also, heavily pruned tomato plants, such as those tied to stakes, often succumb to blossom end rot—another good reason to cage rather than stake your tomatoes.

There is no cure. Avoidance of this physiological stress involves watering during dry periods, applying mulch around plants to maintain consistent levels of soil moisture, and using moderate levels of nitrogen fertilizer.

Tomatoes planted in cold soil tend to develop blossom-end rot on the first fruits, with the problem disappearing as the soil warms. Wait until soil temperatures have settled above 60° before setting out transplants.

Cultivating too close to plants and too deep can damage water-absorbing roots. Pull weeds around tomatoes by hand when they first emerge.

Also, maintain the soil pH at 6.5. Liming to raise the pH (i.e., to reduce the acidity) will also supply calcium and increase the ratio of calcium ions to other competitive ions in the soil. Foliar applications of calcium have little effect due to poor uptake by the plant and minimal translocation to the fruit.

## Onions

Onions appreciate an organic nitrogen boost in July. Apply a handful of cottonseed meal or soybean meal to each 10 feet of row. This light feeding will result in larger bulbs. Too much nitrogen, however, will produce bulbs that do not store well through the winter.

## Summer Squash

As summer heat and humidity intensify, check summer squash fruits for blossom blight, fuzzy growth at the tips of fruits that leads to rotting of the fruit. Control this problem by improving air circulation, removing excess foliage and all weeds, and thinning overcrowded plants.

When the weather turns hot and humid, the powdery mildew fungus attacks the older leaves of cucumbers and squash. A weekly spraying of all leaves with a baking soda solution will prevent the infection from spreading.

You can prevent powdery mildew from infecting squash plants with weekly sprayings of a baking soda solution. Make the solution with one tablespoon of baking soda per gallon of water, adding a half teaspoon of liquid dish soap as a spreader-sticker. Apply once a week in midsummer and only on well-watered plants. Spray the plants early in the day, not in full sun. Discard any unused solution. Try the solution on a few leaves first to make sure your variety of squash is not super-sensitive.

## Edible Flowers

Make summer salads tastier and more colorful with a variety of edible flowers, including calendula petals, viola blossoms, nasturtium flowers, and daylily blooms.

## Dragging the Hose

When rain becomes elusive in July, I drag the hose around the vegetable garden. Often the water is turned on to a mere trickle and I move the hose end from spot to spot as I pull weeds, letting water seep deep into the soil. Meanwhile, a drip irrigation kit sits in its molding cardboard box under the porch. One of these days. . . .

The rules of watering are simple. First and foremost, when you water, water deeply, then allow the soil to dry at the surface before watering again. Your best measure of when to water is your index finger: Stick it in the soil, and if it doesn't find moisture, drag the hose.

Second, apply water at the feet of garden plants, keeping the foliage and fruits dry. This is critical to keeping tomato leaves blight-free and squash fruits from growing gray beards. A drip irrigation system, even a simple soaker hose stretched between plants, really pays off here.

Third, if you must use an overhead sprinkler—and we do when it gets really hot and everything is too dry at once—water early in the morning. This will allow the foliage to dry quickly. Water left on leaves at the end of the day is an invitation to fungal diseases, including blights and mildews.

Fourth, keep a layer of organic mulch on the soil to reduce evaporation of water from the soil. A 3- to 4-inch-thick layer of straw or shredded leaves works well and also prevents the rain, when it finally comes, from splashing fungal spores onto the lower leaves of plants.

Finally, weed, weed, weed. Unwanted plants compete with crop plants for water. Much of our garden time in July and August is spent pulling weeds, trying to get them out when they are small. Mulching makes this task less time consuming.

A July garden salad, complete with edible flowers.

Pulling weeds will keep you in touch with the soil's need for water. If dry soil is pulled up with the weed, it's time to water.

Containers scattered about the garden, as their plants become potbound, need watering every sunny summer day. I either drag the hose from pot to pot or, if some of the potted plants look hungry, I mix up a half-strength fish emulsion solution in a 2-gallon watering can and carry it around the garden. In either case, I water slowly until I see excess water leaking out of the drainage holes. Moving some of the potbound plants into deeper shade can lighten the load a bit.

Everything in its season. There is time in July to drag the hose or allow it to drip water into the soil while I pull weeds. It is contemplative work that puts me in close touch with the plants. Marjorie is likely there too, and Reilly, both good company. Perhaps this is why the drip irrigation system is still in the box.

## Intensify Your Scouting

As garden plants mature during July, herbivore populations can multiply to the point of standing room only on the undersides of leaves. The smart gardener will set aside time for scouting—inspecting plants for insects or the damage they have done.

Make your scouting trips early in the morning, when insects are sluggish. Check the undersides of bean leaves for Mexican bean beetles and inspect the leaves and flowers of cucumber and squash plants for striped cucumber beetles. Examine eggplant leaves for Colorado potato beetles. Inspect raspberry and grape leaves, as well as roses and other ornamentals, for Japanese beetles. (They like hawthorn trees too.) Carry a small pail of soapy water with you and pick or knock the beetles into it. I have dispatched entire leaves to the pail when they were heavily infested.

Yellow sticky traps, thin plastic cards painted yellow and coated with Tanglefoot or other sticky substance, are often used as monitoring tools in the garden. Insects are attracted to the yellow color and become permanently stuck to the cards. Mounted on bamboo stakes, these traps can be placed among a crop and frequently monitored for specific herbivores and their numbers.

I am ambivalent about the use of sticky traps, particularly when they are used for control rather than short-term monitoring. Beneficial insects, including herbivore predators, may fall victim to these traps as readily as the herbivores, so I recommend using them only as a last resort and only for a short period of time. For example, if you are faced with an explosion of striped cucumber beetles and need to monitor the effectiveness of hand-picking, place a few yellow sticky traps in the midst of the plants and closely monitor what is being trapped. Discontinue their use as soon as possible.

## Converting Lawn to Garden

Across the country, lawns are shrinking or disappearing entirely. Good riddance! Nothing is more wasteful, more ecologically damaging, than a wide expanse of turfgrass. The garden's ecosystem is thrown out of whack by the intensive chemical management of most lawns. And, the Environmental Protection Agency tells us that gasoline-powered lawn mowers are major polluters of air, and their operators annually spill more gasoline into the environment than all of the oil leaked by the *Exxon Valdez.*

There is definitely a wrong way to convert lawn to garden space: throwing out the topsoil by stripping off the sod with a spade or sod cutter, then obtaining (usually at a steep price) more topsoil, often sold as "loam," that may be contaminated with noxious perennial weeds and weed seeds. Often, purchased "topsoil" also contains a high percentage of subsoil. Following the procedure outlined below, you can avoid this expense and added work.

Plan on taking a full year to make the transition from lawn to garden as you follow these three steps.

### *Step 1. Test the soil*

Using a small trowel, take several soil samples from different spots in your lawn. Each sample should include the sod and the soil beneath it to a depth of 6 inches. Thoroughly mix the samples in a pail and place two cups of the composite sample in a clean plastic bag. Take the composite sample to your nearest County Extension office for processing. On the soil test order form, be sure to state that you are converting lawn to garden.

### *Step 2. Eliminate the lawn grass and other perennial weeds*

Eliminate the turfgrass and other perennial grasses by smothering them, leaving the topsoil intact. Begin by mowing the grass one last time, then cover the area with cardboard or several thicknesses of newspaper. Hold down this cover with several inches of finished compost or aged stable manure.

Plan on about two months of growing weather for the grass to be completely killed. For example, if you start in early July, the area should be ready for sowing a winter cover crop of oats by mid-September. Any soil amendments dictated by the soil test can be worked into the soil along with the compost before sowing the oats.

Winter temperatures will kill the oats, leaving a mulch of dead nutrient-rich foliage over the area through the winter. This mulch can be tilled into the soil as soon as the soil can be worked in spring.

### *Step 3. Reduce the annual weed seed bank.*

Now, at this point you have eliminated perennial weeds, including the lawn grass. No doubt, however, seeds of annual weeds still persist in the soil. If you plant your garden immediately, be prepared for some serious weed pulling.

Another option would be to use the spring to eliminate many of these weed seeds with repeated shallow

This native plant landscape was once a monoculture of turfgrass.

cultivation. Allow the seeds to germinate, undercut the seedlings with a hoe, then turn the soil over to bring more weed seeds to the surface. Add more finished compost or aged stable manure with each cultivation. Two or three rounds of this work and your new plot should be ready for planting in early June.

With this approach, there should be no need to bring in additional topsoil. You can grow vegetables or ornamentals in the ground or in raised beds constructed with the compost-enriched topsoil from walkways.

## *The Vegetable Garden's Second Season: Planning and Planting for Fall*

Mid to late July is the beginning of the vegetable garden's second season. In addition to planting seedlings of broccoli and the other brassica crops, including cauliflower and cabbage, this is the month to sow seeds of beets, peas, green onions, lettuce, Swiss chard, and turnips. And it is the time to plant leafy herbs such as basil, dill, and cilantro, fast-growing herbs that will be ready for harvest about a month after sowing the seed. You can harvest the young leaves as needed until the plants are killed by frost; basil is very frost sensitive, but cilantro will tolerate the first light frosts.

Leafy vegetables, such as spinach, Swiss chard, kale, mustard greens, and leaf lettuce are second-season crops that should be harvested before their leaves reach full size. The small leaves are often more tender and tastier than mature ones. These crops can be planted in succession every few weeks as small spaces open up in the garden to provide a steady supply of young leaves.

Remember that many of these second-season plants, including most of the leafy vegetables and turnips, can survive and even improve in flavor after a light frost. Beets, green onions, and peas will survive 28° F, while the hardiest varieties of Brussels sprouts, cabbage, and kale are cold hardy to 20° F.

In general, be sure to incorporate compost or organic fertilizer into the soil before starting any of these fall crops. If you need more seed for these second-season crops, buy it now while garden center racks are still stocked. Many mail-order seed companies are still filling orders as well.

In the following guidelines for planting your late-summer and fall vegetable garden, sowing and planting dates are for USDA Zone 5. Gardeners in other zones should check the spreadsheet at the end of the chapter.

### Cilantro and Dill

In the second week of July, sow seeds of cilantro and dill directly in the garden, taking advantage of spaces that have opened up as summer crops were harvested. By mid-

August, you will have plenty of fresh cilantro leaves and tender dill shoots for use in the kitchen.

By mid-July, earlier sowings of these two annual herbs will be flowering. Let a few of these plants go to seed, then either collect the seed for use in the kitchen or allow the plants to self-sow next year's crop.

## Basil

Basil plants grown from seeds sown in July, in the garden or in pots, will produce a first cutting by mid-August. Continue cutting through September, but remember that basil is very sensitive to frost, so be sure to get your last cutting of fresh leaves when that first frost of the season is imminent.

## Brussels Sprouts

Start this crop from seed indoors in the first week of July so that you will have four-week-old transplants for the garden by the first week of August. You should be able to harvest sprouts about 90 days from planting, after they have been kissed by a frost.

## Broccoli, Cauliflower, and Cabbage

Seeds of these brassicas should have been planted in June to produce garden transplants for mid-July. If you did not make this sowing, perhaps your local garden center did. When shopping for transplants, be sure to purchase young transplants produced for midsummer planting, not potbound, worn-out leftovers from the spring crop.

## Spinach

Because of problems with early bolting of spring-sown spinach, many gardeners in northern New England wait until late July to early August to sow spinach. Late-summer-sown spinach will continue to produce leaves until the plants succumb to freezing temperatures. Recommended varieties for fall sowing include Avon, Indian Summer, Melody, Razzle Dazzle, Olympia, and Tyee.

Summer-sown spinach seedlings will need shading through periods of hot weather and plenty of water. Spinach only needs 30 to 45 days from sowing to harvest, so you can continue sowing through late summer.

Use the "cut and come again" method of harvesting your spinach, removing the older, outer leaves of each

Basil transplants for early July planting can be started from seed sown six weeks earlier, or you can simply sow seeds directly in the garden and harvest the first basil leaves a month later.

### What Can We Do with All This Basil?

Most of our basil harvest goes into a classic basil pesto that Marjorie has made for years. The recipe below comes from *Pestos!, Cooking with Herb Pastes,* by Dorothy Rankin (The Crossing Press, 1985).

#### *Classic Basil Pesto*

2 cups fresh basil leaves
2 large garlic cloves
½ cup freshly grated Parmesan cheese
2 tablespoons freshly grated Pecorino Romano cheese
¼ cup pine nuts or walnuts
½ cup olive oil
Salt and freshly ground pepper

Combine the basil leaves, garlic, cheeses, and nuts in a food processor or blender. Process to mix. With the machine running, slowly add the olive oil. Season to taste with salt and pepper and process to the desired consistency. Let stand 5 minutes before serving. Yield: about 1 cup.

Marjorie makes this pesto in large quantities and freezes the surplus in small batches.

plant while allowing the young inner leaves to continue growing for a later harvest. If you need a lot of spinach, cut entire plants about an inch above the crowns; the plants will likely send out a new flush of leaves.

### Other Crops for Vacant Spots in the Garden

Seeds of bush beans, carrots, beets, kohlrabi, and turnips can all be directly sown starting in mid-July as space becomes available. If you have the garden space and leftover seed, start a fall crop of garden peas with a mid-July sowing. Success varies from year to year, but even a small crop of fresh peas in September is worth the effort.

## *Raspberries, the Queen of Summer Fruits*

As raspberries start to ripen we watch the extended weather forecast, hoping for a long string of dry sunny days. Even a short rainy period means raspberries molding on their canes. We hand-pick the fuzzy fruits to reduce the spread of disease, and we hope for sunny weather.

If the soil gets too dry during berry ripening, we set the end of the hose at the feet of the canes and soak the soil. No overhead irrigation allowed!

When the weather is with us, we pick raspberries as soon as the foliage has dried. I put one on my tongue and lift it to the roof of my mouth where it melts into sweetness. Some berries make it into the kitchen where they are immediately spread on a cookie sheet and quickly frozen, then transferred into small freezer boxes for later use in muffins and such.

You have to act quickly and carefully when handling ripe raspberries. Eat them or freeze them as soon as they're picked; let an hour go by and they've turned to mush. If you pile the berries too deep (more than three berries deep) while picking, the ones on the bottom get crushed. They are a fragile fruit.

## *Native Shrubs: The Scent of Crushed Leaves*

In a New England garden planted with native shrubs, the focus shifts in midsummer from flower to foliage, except, of course, for the soft pink blooms of meadowsweet and the bolder pink spires of steeplebush. Indeed, shrubs that had little to offer in terms of spring blossoms take center stage in July. Brush your hand across the leaves of a northern bayberry or walk through a colony of sweetfern and delight in the spicy scent of volatile oils warmed by the summer sun.

A handful of just-picked raspberries, the spirit of July in the garden.

### Northern Bayberry

Northern bayberry grows in Marjorie's Garden, and on a warm July afternoon I cannot pass by these shrubs without crushing a leaf between my fingers and savoring the spicy scent. This is why we planted them, and for the bold texture and dark green of their summer leaves, and for the waxy, bayberry-scented berries that cluster along the stems of the female plants.

Northern bayberry *(Myrica pensylvanica)* is a semi-evergreen native shrub found in the wild and in gardens from Newfoundland to Maryland. In the coastal regions of New England, it often grows within the reach of saltwater spray, where it forms immense rounded colonies due to its suckering nature. In cultivation it is often used in poor, sandy soils where few other plants will grow.

All parts of northern bayberry are aromatic when crushed. The waxy gray berries that appear in fall and may persist all winter are used in making bayberry

## An Imaginative Use of Bayberry in a Cape Cod Garden

When I think back on my visit to Patricia Crow's garden on Cape Cod, I recall the bayberry-lined drive winding up to the house and the imaginative way Patty used this native evergreen shrub as a foil for flowering perennials and native shrubs.

An informal bayberry hedge forms the perfect foil for the lilac flower spikes of butterfly bush *(Buddleia davidii)*, shasta daisies *(Leucanthemum x superbum 'Becky')*, and bold-textured flower clusters of oak-leaf hydrangea *(Hydrangea quercifolia)*.

Shasta daisy 'Becky' flowers within the bayberry. The seed heads, left for the birds, enhance the textural beauty of this planting.

A swamp milkweed, *Asclepias incarnata* 'Ice Palace,' adds a touch of color to the bayberry hedge while attracting a host of pollinators.

American cranberrybush viburnum *(Viburnum opulus* var. *americanum)* adds a splash of color to the bayberry hedge.

My favorite spot in Patty's bayberry hedge is an opening filled with oakleaf hydrangea *(Hydrangea quercifolia)* and inkberry holly *(Ilex glabra)*, both native plants to the eastern U.S. I had not seen the oakleaf hydrangea since leaving Georgia. Inkberry, however, is native across New England.

Grow northern bayberry for the bold texture of its summer leaves (inset) and for the bayberry-scented berries borne on female plants (above).

candles. The lustrous, leathery, green leaves make a gray-green dye.

For a striking year-round garden scene, interplant bayberry with one of the native roses, either the Carolina rose (*Rosa carolina*) or Virginia rose (*R. virginiana*). The dark green foliage of bayberry makes an excellent background for the simple pink flowers, deep red autumn leaves, and bright red hips of these roses. I cannot take credit for this design, however, as it is a common sight along the wild rocky coast of Maine.

## Sweetgale

A close relative of bayberry, sweetgale *(Myrica gale)* is a deciduous low-growing shrub, growing to 4 feet in height. Its suckering roots penetrate the wet muds of swamps and pond-sides throughout the higher latitudes of the northern hemisphere, and it is often found growing in dense thickets, its fragrant glossy blue-green leaves making the perfect background for wildflowers such as the cardinal flower, *Lobelia cardinalis.*

Sweetgale can be successfully grown in average garden soils with moderate moisture and plenty of sun. It forms an attractive natural hedge, either alone or in combination with other native shrubs such as mountain holly (*Ilex mucronatus*) and highbush blueberry (*Vaccinium corymbosum*).

Sweetfern gets its common name from its aromatic fernlike leaves.

## Sweetfern

Colonies of sweetfern *(Comptonia peregrina)*, consisting of low shrubs to 3 feet in height, grow in dry sandy soils along the New England coast, in old abandoned fields, and in woodland openings. Highly tolerant of shade, sweetfern grows best in poor, acidic soils. Not a true fern, its aromatic leaves are nevertheless fern-like in appearance, often remaining dried on the plant through the winter. As with sweetgale, the narrow-lobed leaves of sweetfern are covered with resin dots, the source of their spicy fragrance. During the Revolutionary War, American colonists used the leaves of sweetfern as a substitute for tea.

Many gardeners shy away from using sweetfern because of its vigorous colonizing habit, a characteristic that can be used to advantage, however, where a vigorous groundcover is needed. I recall a beautiful planting at the College of the Atlantic in Bar Harbor, Maine, sweetfern covering the ground beneath the canopy of a multi-trunk white birch.

### Steeplebush

There are two native species of *Spiraea* that have been largely passed over as garden worthy in modern times and are never seen in nurseries or garden centers. Meadowsweet *(S. alba* var. *latifolia)* was presented in the previous chapter, but steeplebush (also known as hardhack by haymakers for its hard, brittle stems), *S. tomentosa*, belongs in July, the month when New Englanders first see its terminal, spire-like clusters of rosy-pink flowers.

Steeplebush is a sun-loving small shrub, thriving in sterile, acidic, and rocky soils, both in moist and dry sites. We are lucky to have it growing on our property and have successfully transplanted several plants from driveway drainage ditches into the garden proper.

Steeplebush's terminal spire-like clusters of rosy-pink flowers bring much needed color to the July landscape.

Like meadowsweet, steeplebush attracts a host of pollinators. As the flowers on the central spire are pollinated, flowering side-shoots develop that extend the blooming season into August.

Charles Newhall, in his 1893 book *The Shrubs of Northeastern America*, describes steeplebush as "often cultivated for its pretty, steeple-like clusters of late-blooming, rosy flowers." It was pushed aside by our 20th century infatuation with exotic ornamentals, but perhaps American gardeners are on the cusp of a reawakening, a renewal of interest in steeplebush and other native shrubs with both ornamental and ecological value.

Meadowsweet and steeplebush growing together in a summer garden.

Bayberry, sweetgale, sweetfern, and native roses are among the finest of garden shrubs. Each provides cause to stop for a moment on summer strolls, to sniff the fragrance of a crushed leaf or cup a deep pink rose in your hand.

## Summer Perennials for Pollinators

Many summer mornings you can find me in the garden tickling blueberries for breakfast. Marjorie taught me the tickling method, the best way of harvesting each highbush blueberry at the peak of its sweetness.

I cup my hand around a cluster of berries, only some of which are fully ripe, and wiggle my fingers. The berries ready to slip their connection with pedicel will do so; the others will be there tomorrow.

As I tickle berries, I think about the bumblebees that pollinated blueberry flowers earlier in the summer. I watched them move from one white bell-shaped blossom to another, and I thanked them in advance for the coming harvest.

In the garden at harvest time, when I hear familiar buzzing in a nearby bed, I stop tickling berries long enough to watch bumblebees pollinate blossoms of sunflower, summer squash, and tomato. Unlike a honeybee, which prefers to forage in a large field of a single plant species, a

Tickling blueberries.

Catmint and lady's mantle meet in Marjorie's Garden.

bumblebee will move from one type of plant to another. It might start with a sunflower head, crawling over each tiny flower until it has filled its hairy hind-leg sacs with bright orange pollen, then dive into the throat of a male squash blossom, dusting its bristly body with bright yellow pollen, and then move on to a cluster of tomato flowers, grasping each blossom in turn with its legs and vibrating wing muscles at just the right frequency to release the pollen, a process called sonication ("buzz pollination") that is unique to bumblebees and essential to maximum tomato production.

I take a break from harvesting blueberries to watch bumblebees make their rounds, and I thank them for the squash and tomatoes.

One way a gardener can thank the bumblebees and other native pollinators is to help them build strong colonies within or near the garden by providing an abundance of blossoms for them to forage from early spring into fall. Native herbaceous perennials that flower in July and August, including goldenrods, milkweeds, and campanulas, will help sustain bumblebee colonies as vegetable flowers fade.

## The Catmint Patch

One of my favorite garden spots in summer is the perennial bed in the heart of Marjorie's Garden. In a corner of this bed, where the deep purple flower spikes of catmint *(Nepeta* sp.) meet and mingle with the chartreuse flowers of lady's mantle *(Alchemilla mollis),* bumblebees dance from dawn to dusk throughout July, the tall slender catmint spikes swaying back and forth under the weight of these tireless pollinators. Often in early morning I find a bumblebee asleep, or so it seems, having spent the night on a catmint flower, too tired at dark to carry its heavy load of pollen back to the nest. It awakens while I watch, warmed by a shaft of sunlight, and resumes foraging.

Both of these perennials are easy to grow. Nepeta thrives in lean, dry soils with little care. We fertilize ours with topdressings of compost or aged manure in early spring, before growth begins, taking care not to cover the plants themselves. In late summer, when the plants have

Lady's mantle in bloom after a summer rain.

These rudbeckias, growing beneath the peach tree in Marjorie's Garden, will produce seeds for goldfinches.

### Be a Deadheader

Deadheading, the removal of spent flowers after they start to fade, typically involves cutting off each old blossom and its stem as far back as the next healthy bud, blossom, or set of leaves. This induces the plant to allocate energy to producing more blooms rather than to seed production.

Removing the spent flowers of some annuals also reduces the spread of fungal diseases that attack decaying blooms. Petunia blossoms, for example, quickly succumb to gray mold after their one day in the sun; plantings require a little deadheading time every day, a simple matter of pinching off each spent blossom just as you would do with daylilies.

In some species, deadheading may encourage another flush of bloom. For plants that keep producing new flowers over a period of several weeks, including Shasta daisy, purple coneflower, peony, veronica, and garden phlox, cut back each spent flower or flower head to the next lateral flower bud, leaf bud, or healthy leaf. For plants that produce flowers on single stems, such as heuchera, hosta, pulmonaria, and lady's mantle, cut back each faded flower to the ground. Other plants, such as coreopsis, appreciate a good shearing after the first wave of bloom, rewarding you with another round of flowering later in the season.

Roses are kept floriferous and tidy with regular deadheading during summer. In early autumn, however, hips should be allowed to form on your roses, as their formation signals the onset of hardening for the coming winter.

Deadheading is often a matter of choice. If you are interested in attracting birds to the garden, you may choose to let purple coneflowers *(Echinacea)* and black-eyed susan *(Rudbeckia)* produce seed, knowing that any uneaten seeds will produce seedlings scattered about the garden the following year. Or you may enjoy seeing mature seedheads of sedum and coneflower dusted with winter's first snow.

Perhaps you want certain plants to produce seeds and scatter them to the wind, ensuring that their progeny will grace the garden next year. Such is the case with self-sowing annuals like pansies, calendulas, and Shirley poppies.

finished blooming, we shear them back to rejuvenate the foliage and keep them tidy.

Equally low in maintenance, lady's mantle requires only occasional tidying up, deadheading spent flowers and removing old, dried leaves, and an early spring topdressing with compost or aged manure. Plants overwinter best if the semi-evergreen foliage is left on the plant until spring.

Lady's mantle is something of a self-sower. Small clumps appear throughout the garden, started perhaps from seed in the compost pile where we toss the spent flower stalks in fall.

## Penstemon

In July, somewhere in the dry woods and rocky hillsides of Penobscot County, Maine, the rare hairy beardtongue *(Penstemon hirsutus)* blooms. At the same time and nearly statewide (except in Piscataquis and Washington counties), the uncommon foxglove penstemon *(P.*

*digitalis)* flowers in fields and woodland borders. And while I've done my share of botanizing where these herbaceous perennials grow, I've missed them, perhaps spending too much time looking up into the canopies of trees instead of down on the ground.

I know penstemons from gardens. Both species thrive in full sun at the University of Maine Cooperative Extension native plant garden in Ellsworth, and a cultivar of the foxglove penstemon with maroon-colored leaves, Husker Red, grows in Marjorie's Garden to the delight of ruby-throated hummingbirds.

The genus name Penstemon, from the Greek, means "five stamens." Four of the five are fertile, but the fifth is sterile with a tuft of small hairs. It is this hairy, sterile stamen that gives the plants their common name, beardtongue.

The hairy beardtongue is a woolly-stemmed plant growing 16 to 24 inches tall with open, stalked clusters of lavender, trumpet-shaped flowers, each about 1 inch long with a white tip. The foxglove penstemon is taller, growing from 3 to 5 feet in height with a spread of 2 feet. Its flowers are white, slightly longer than those of hairy beardtongue, and are borne in panicles atop erect, rigid stems. Both species have a clump-forming growth habit.

Best in full sun, penstemons will tolerate partial shade. They need well-drained soils and can tolerate periods of moderate drought.

More common in garden centers than in the wild, our native penstemons are ideal candidates for the pollinator garden. Both attract hummingbirds as well as bumblebees and butterflies. The hairy penstemon is a documented host for the Baltimore checkerspot butterfly, a species found in localized populations throughout New England. Beneficial insects such as ladybugs and parasitic wasps, whose larvae feed on aphids and other garden herbivores, require a source of pollen and nectar as adults. Native penstemons provide these essential foods.

Penstemons, including the hairy beardtongue, are ideal plants for the pollinator garden, attracting hummingbirds, bumblebees, and butterflies.

## Bluebell Bellflower

*Campanula rotundifolia*, the bluebell bellflower, blooms continuously from late spring through August. Native to dry, nutrient-poor grasslands in New England and throughout much of the United States, this rhizomatous perennial produces violet-blue, bell-shaped flowers in loose clusters on long, thin, graceful stems. It performs best in sandy, well-drained soils and in sun to partial shade and is perfect for the pollinator garden, attracting hummingbirds as well as bumblebees.

In search of nectar, bumblebees all but disappear as they crawl into the flowers of *Campanula rotundifolia*, the bluebell bellflower.

In order to reach the nectar at the base of the blossom, the bumblebee must crawl into the bell, disappearing except for the tip of its butt. It is not surprising that by the end of the flowering season the entire plant is bent over from the weight of bees.

## Swamp Milkweed

Although *Asclepias incarnata*, swamp milkweed, is native to swamps and wet meadows in most of the continental U.S., including New England, it is surprisingly tolerant of average well-drained soils in cultivation. Blooming in

### Swamp Milkweed and the Great Black Wasp

July asks the gardener to stop and observe the drama of life within the boundaries of the garden, and to pursue those observations to a deeper understanding of connections between plants, herbivores, predatory insects, birds, and the gardener.

Both wild carrot and swamp milkweed are pollinated by the giant black wasp, *Sphex pennsylvanicus,* a species of digger wasp found across North America. For its services, the wasp receives pollen and nectar. I took the time one hot August day to watch and photograph a female (recognizable by her larger size) foraging on swamp milkweed blossoms. For the most part she ignored me and the myriad other insects swarming around, completely absorbed in her work.

She is both beautiful and foreboding, an inch and a half long, black except for her wings, which reflect a shining metallic blue in sunlight. Her heavy-duty mandibles allow her to hang onto her prey, chiefly katydids and grasshoppers that are often larger than she. It is her larvae that feed on these captured orthopteran insects.

The nest, constructed underground by the female wasp, consists of several chambers, each of which hosts a single wasp larva. The female first provisions each chamber with one insect, which she has captured and paralyzed with three stings before gluing an egg to its underside. Although immobile, the prey will live until the egg hatches and the larva begins to feed. During its development, the larva will consume between two and six katydids or grasshoppers, so the adult female spends a good portion of her time provisioning each chamber of her nest. (Forget the male; he's just the sperm donor.)

Not every captured and paralyzed prey makes it to the nest. The female wasp can become a victim of kleptoparasitism (parasitism by theft) by house sparrows and gray catbirds as she drags her prey back to the nest.

A female giant black wasp pollinates the flowers of swamp milkweed as she forages for pollen and nectar.

Swamp milkweed (foreground) is a favorite of bumblebees and butterflies.

July and August, this erect, clump-forming herbaceous perennial grows 3 to 4 feet tall. It has a deep taproot and is best left undisturbed once established.

Swamp milkweed's flowers, ranging in color from pink to mauve, occur in tight clusters. The flowers are followed by seed pods (4 inches long) which split open at maturity, releasing silky-haired seeds on the wind.

## Enjoy Nasturtiums—In the Garden and On the Table

Planted at the end of May amid clouds of blackflies, potted nasturtiums are as much a part of summer in Marjorie's Garden as those pesky creatures. We have favorite varieties, including Night and Day, a mix of ivory, yellow, and mahogany flowers on bushy plants that grow from 16 to 20 inches high. We also like to grow a trailing nasturtium mix with flowers in red, rose, orange, and yellow, perfect for cascading from porch rails or baskets. Both of these varieties have typical nasturtium foliage, rounded leaves like those of water lilies, dark green with lighter veins. We also grow the variegated-leaved forms, including the bushy Alaska series and the trailing Jewel of Africa mix of yellow, cream, red, and peach-pink blooms.

Potted nasturtiums cascade down the porch steps.

Once the soil has warmed, nasturtiums *(Tropaeolum majus)* are also easy to grow from seeds sown directly in the garden or in containers. They will germinate quickly, in 10 days or less. Soak the seeds overnight, and then sow them ½ inch deep and 8 to 12 inches apart in the garden, a little closer in pots.

Nasturtiums love full sun, but not drought, so keep the soil moist. This is particularly important for plants in containers; allowing the soil to dry out will cause leaves to turn brown and the plants to stop flowering.

The soil should not be too rich or your plants will produce more leaves than flowers. Digging 3 or 4 inches of composted manure into the garden soil is perfect; no additional fertilizer should be needed throughout the season. For growing nasturtiums in containers, we make a mixture of two-thirds potting soil (Pro Mix) and one-third compost. Again, no additional fertilizer is required.

Deadheading fading flowers before they can form seedpods will stimulate your plants to continue flowering, as will picking the fresh flowers to eat. In fact, all parts of the nasturtium plant are edible. The flowers lend a sweet, spicy taste to salads, while the leaves, high in vitamin C, have a peppery tang. Pickled seedpods are an inexpensive substitute for capers.

Toward the end of the summer you can allow the seedpods to mature if you want to save seeds of a favorite variety for next year. Keep in mind, however, that if you are growing several varieties of nasturtiums in the same

A native solitary bee noses around a nasturtium flower.

garden, they will cross-pollinate and produce hybrid seed.

Those who enjoy nasturtiums in the garden and at the table are in good company. Beginning in 1774, Thomas Jefferson grew them as part of his Monticello vegetable garden, eating the pickled seeds. And Monet allowed large swaths of nasturtiums to ramble along the path at Giverny.

Nasturtiums will always grow in Marjorie's Garden. I cannot imagine a summer without trailing nasturtiums cascading down the porch steps, their bright blossoms poking out of masses of foliage, hummingbirds dusting their faces with pollen as they sip nectar from the long spur on the underside of each funnel-shaped flower.

Guttation, the production of small droplets of water at the leaf margins of tomato and other plants, adorns early-morning leaves with sparkling jewels.

Strawberry leaves with guttation droplets at the tips of conspicuous leaf veins.

## Guttation Adorns Even Common Weeds with Early-Morning Jewels

Before there were gardens, there was Dr. Bill Lenoir, my undergraduate botany professor. His classes kindled in me a life-long passion for plants. He inspired a desire to work beyond the syllabus, to explore questions that began in the lecture hall and ended with late night hours in the laboratory. I think of him often, recalling lectures and labs that deepened my understanding of observations made on garden walks.

If memory serves—it's been 45 years—Dr. Lenoir had us grow tomato plants to learn about guttation, the production of small droplets of xylem sap at the leaf margins of some plants. Not to be confused with dew, which covers the entire leaf, guttation fluid appears precisely where leaf vein tips meet the leaf edge, forming a ring of droplets that describes the outline of the leaf.

Guttation occurs when soil moisture levels are high and loss of water by transpiration through open stomates (pores in the leaf) is low. Since stomates of most plants close in the dark, we find the evidence of nocturnal guttation in the early morning light.

During the night, uptake and accumulation of salts by root cells leads to osmotic uptake of water into those cells. The increase in water leads to root pressures that can be relieved only by forcing of water out of specialized cells at the leaf margin, called hydathodes. The root pressures are minimal, soon equalized by atmospheric pressure, and thus the amount of water forced out of the leaf is minimal—just enough to adorn the early-morning leaf with sparkling drops.

Guttation droplets are ephemeral jewels, evaporating as the sun warms the leaf. A thin residue of dried salt on the leaf margin provides the only evidence that they were ever there.

A spell of cool wet weather is perfect for guttation mornings. On a sunny morning following several days of rain, I wander slowly around the garden, tripod-mounted camera in hand, Dr. Lenoir at my side as I photograph guttating leaves of radish, strawberry, sunflower, and, of course, tomato plants. Among my favorites are the potted nasturtiums, each leaf with a tiny, perfectly round drop of fluid expelled from the end of each conspicuous leaf vein. Garden weeds also reflect sunlight from sparkling drops of sap. The most beautiful jeweled leaves are those of

Guttation droplets, sparkling like faceted gemstones, adorn the margin of a mullein leaf.

When droplets are placed on foliage by a misty rain, not guttation—as here on alchemilla *(Alchemilla mollis)*—the effect is more general but no less lovely.

common mullein, each large flannel-covered frost-green leaf guttating droplets not only at vein tips along the margin but also from major veins within the leaf blade. Low-angled light gives the guttation droplets on mullein the appearance of faceted gemstones. A common weed becomes at those times the loveliest plant in the garden.

## *The New England Garden in July, Zone by Zone*

Scouting for insect herbivores becomes a daily garden activity in July for all New England gardeners. Set aside time for peering under leaves. Raspberries are ready for harvest throughout the region, and gardeners in southern New England may be harvesting garlic at the end of the month. In July, as vacant spots open in the garden, you can direct-sow summer squash for harvest in late summer and early fall.

| IN THE GARDEN | July | Date by USDA Hardiness Zone | | | | | Notes |
|---|---|---|---|---|---|---|---|
| | | 3 | 4 | 5 | 6 | 7 | |
| **GENERAL MAINTENANCE** | Keep Weeding | | | | | | |
| | Water as needed. | | | | | | When you water, water deeply, then allow the soil to dry at the surface before watering again. |
| | Keep a layer of organic mulch on the soil to reduce evaporation of water from the soil. | | | | | | A 3- to 4-inch layer of straw or shredded leaves works well. |
| | Replace the front lawn with a vegetable garden! | | | | | | Follow the three-step procedure explained in Chapter 9. |
| | Intensify scouting for herbivores. | | | | | | Set aside time specifically for scouting, inspecting plants for insects or the damage they have done. Make your scouting trips early in the morning when the insects are sluggish. |
| | Keep fresh water in birdbaths. | | | | | | |
| | Hand-pick Japanese beetles in the early morning and late evening. | | | | | | The beetles are sluggish at cooler temperatures, easier to capture. |
| **THE COMPOST PILE** | Monitor temperature and turn the pile when it starts to cool down. | | | | | | |
| **VEGETABLE GARDEN** | Sow beans, carrots, beets, or leaf lettuce in open garden areas. | | | | | | In mid-July, plant vacant spots with peas and summer squash for fall harvest. |
| | Plant warm-season cover crops in unused garden areas. | | | | | | |
| | Harvest daily. | | | | | | |
| | Contribute fresh vegetables to a local food pantry or soup kitchen. | | | | | | |
| | Keep after the slugs. | | | | | | |
| **VEGETABLE CROPS** | | | | | | | |
| Beans, Bush | Check underside of leaves for Mexican bean beetles and hand-pick. | July 1 | July 8 | July 15 | July 22 | July 29 | |
| | Sow in open spaces of the garden as space allows. | | | | | | |
| Beans, Pole | Check underside of leaves for Mexican bean beetles and hand-pick. | | | | | | |

| IN THE GARDEN | July | Date by USDA Hardiness Zone | | | | | Notes |
|---|---|---|---|---|---|---|---|
| | | 3 | 4 | 5 | 6 | 7 | |
| Beets | Direct-sow for fall crop. | July 1 | July 8 | July 15 | July 22 | July 29 | Sow seeds in open spots of garden. |
| Broccoli | Plant transplants under row cover for fall crop. | July 1 | July 8 | July 15 | July 22 | July 29 | |
| Brussels Sprouts | Sow seeds for fall crop. | Jun 18 | Jun 25 | July 1 | July 8 | July 15 | This sowing will produce 4-week-old transplants for late-summer planting. |
| | Transplant seedlings to garden. | July 15 | July 22 | July 29 | Aug 5 | Aug 12 | |
| Cabbage | Make a third sowing indoors for a continuous supply. | Jun 18 | Jun 25 | July 1 | July 8 | July 15 | |
| | Plant transplants under row cover for fall crop. | July 1 | July 8 | July 15 | July 22 | July 29 | |
| Carrots | Direct-sow for fall crop. | July 1 | July 8 | July 15 | July 22 | July 29 | Sow seeds in open spots of garden. |
| Cauliflower | Plant transplants for fall crop. | July 1 | July 8 | July 15 | July 22 | July 29 | |
| Chard, Swiss | Direct-sow for fall crop. | July 15 | July 22 | July 29 | Aug 5 | Aug 12 | |
| Cucumbers | Place yellow sticky traps around plants to control striped cucumber beetles. | | | | | | |
| Eggplant | Hand-pick Colorado potato beetles.<br>Water regularly to avoid blossom-end rot. | | | | | | Also, use mulch around plants to conserve soil moisture and avoid applying excessive nitrogen. |
| Garlic | Harvest scapes of hardneck varieties. | | | | | | Harvest the scapes when they are in full curl, cutting each one just below the "loop". |
| | Harvest bulbs when the leaves die back. | | | | | | Dig the bulbs and brush off the soil, spread them out on the porch to dry for a week or so, and then braid them for winter storage. Don't forget to set aside some of the largest bulbs for planting in fall. |
| Green Onions | Sow seeds for fall crop. | | | | | | |
| Kohlrabi | Direct-sow for fall crop. | July 1 | July 8 | July 15 | July 22 | July 29 | Sow seeds in open spots of garden. |
| Leek | Hill soil around plants at two week intervals. | | | | | | |
| | Apply organic nitrogen fertilizer. | July 1 | July 8 | July 15 | July 22 | July 29 | |

| IN THE GARDEN | July | Date by USDA Hardiness Zone | | | | | Notes |
|---|---|---|---|---|---|---|---|
| | | 3 | 4 | 5 | 6 | 7 | |
| Lettuce | Begin sowings for continuous fall harvest. Sow seeds in open spots of garden. | July 15 | July 22 | July 29 | Aug 5 | Aug 12 | |
| Muskmelon | Use baking soda solution to control powdery mildew. | | | | | | |
| Onions | Apply organic nitrogen fertilizer. | July 1 | July 8 | July 15 | July 22 | July 29 | Use cottonseed meal or soybean meal, a handful for each 10 feet of row. |
| Peas | Direct-sow for fall crop | July 1 | July 8 | July 15 | July 22 | July 29 | |
| Peppers | Set out transplants<br><br>Place a bamboo stake next to each plant for later support.<br><br>Water regularly to avoid blossom-end rot. | July 15 | July 8 | July 1 | June 22 | June 15 | Peppers' demand for warm soil (above 60° F) make them a difficult crop to grow in regions with short, cool summers.<br><br>Also use mulch around plants to conserve soil moisture and avoid applying excessive nitrogen. |
| Potatoes | Harvest a few new potatoes. | | | | | | |
| Spinach | In late July, begin sowings for continuous fall harvest. Sow seeds in open spots of garden as they become available. | July 15 | July 22 | July 29 | Aug 5 | Aug 12 | Recommended varieties for fall sowing include Avon, Indian Summer, Melody, Razzle Dazzle, Olympia, and Tyee.<br><br>Summer-sown spinach seedlings will need shading through periods of hot weather and plenty of water. |
| Squash, Summer | Sow seeds in open spots of garden.<br><br>Harvest fruits that are 3 to 4 inches long.<br><br>Use baking soda solution to control powdery mildew.<br><br>Check for blossom blight | | | | | | The flavor of zucchini and other summer types of summer squash is best when picked while the blossom is still attached.<br><br>See Chapter 9 for details.<br><br>See Chapter 9 for details. |
| Squash, Winter | Use baking soda solution to control powdery mildew. | | | | | | |
| Tomatoes | Remove suckers from tomatoes tied to stakes.<br><br>Watch for spots and yellowing on lower leaves, signs of leaf spot disease or early blight.<br><br>Water regularly to avoid blossom-end rot. | | | | | | Remove infected leaves and destroy. Spread straw over the soil to keep fungal spores from splashing on leaves during rain and irrigation.<br><br>Also use mulch around plants to conserve soil moisture and avoid applying excessive nitrogen. |
| Turnips | Direct-sow for fall crop. | July 1 | July 8 | July 15 | July 22 | July 29 | Sow seeds in open spots of garden. |

| IN THE GARDEN | July | Date by USDA Hardiness Zone | | | | | Notes |
|---|---|---|---|---|---|---|---|
| | | 3 | 4 | 5 | 6 | 7 | |
| **SMALL FRUITS** | | | | | | | |
| Highbush Blueberries | | | | | | | |
| Grapes | | | | | | | |
| Raspberries | July is harvest month for summer-fruiting raspberries. | | | | | | Keep the foliage dry and hope for clear skies! |
| Strawberries | Remove all but two or three primary runners from each new plant.<br><br>Renovate plantings late in month, after harvest is complete.<br><br>Water weekly if no rain. | | | | | | |
| **HERBS** | | | | | | | |
| Basil | Direct-sow for fall crop. | July 1 | July 8 | July 15 | July 22 | July 29 | Sow in pots or in open spaces of the garden. |
| Dill | Starting on the date for your zone, make small, successive sowings for a continuous supply of fresh leaves through the summer. | July 1 | July 8 | July 15 | July 22 | July 29 | Allow some flowering plants from earlier sowings to produce seed that you can either use in cooking or allow to self-sow for a new crop next year. |
| Cilantro | Starting on the date for your zone, make small, successive sowings for a continuous supply of fresh leaves through the summer. | July 1 | July 8 | July 15 | July 22 | July 29 | Allow some flowering plants from earlier sowings to produce seed that you can either use in cooking or allow to self-sow for a new crop next year. |
| **FLOWER BEDS AND BORDERS** | Deadhead those flowering plants that need it to keep blooming. | | | | | | |
| Geranium | Cut back hardy geraniums after first flush of flowers to encourage new growth. | | | | | | |
| Penstemon (Beard Tongue) | As flowers fade, cut back to just above a bud to encourage more flowers. | | | | | | |
| Snapdragon | Pinch back after flowering to promote new growth. | | | | | | |
| Sweet peas | Deadhead regularly to keep plants blooming.<br><br>Water daily in dry weather.<br><br>Move potted plants into more shade to encourage continued flowering. | | | | | | |
| **ROSES** | Do not deadhead if you want hips.<br><br>Cease deadheading at end of month to help plants harden for winter. | | | | | | |

# Chapter 10

# The Garden in August

*"Ripe vegetables were magic to me. Unharvested, the garden bristled with possibility. I would quicken at the sight of a ripe tomato, sounding its redness from deep amidst the undifferentiated green. To lift a bean plant's hood of heart-shaped leaves and discover a clutch of long slender pods hanging underneath could make me catch my breath."*

—Michael Pollan, *Second Nature: A Gardener's Education*, 2003

***August in Marjorie's Garden means ripe blueberries*** and ripening tomatoes, fresh cucumbers every day, the first harvest of basil, a river of orange and yellow self-sown calendulas flowing through the vegetable garden. August means stepping gingerly over elephant-ear leaves of winter squash, broccoli seedlings growing on the porch rail, goldfinches pecking at sunflower heads, the fragrant flowers of summersweet blossoms, oak trees with moth-eaten leaves, acorns in the grass.

In August the late goldenrod blooms appear along with wild carrot (Queen Anne's lace) and, in wetter spots, the flat-topped white aster. Together they form the heart of a natural insectary along the rough edges of the garden.

Reaching into the middle of the purple raspberries to pick one perfectly ripe berry, Marjorie says, "This is what August is all about, grazing on the fruits of our labor."

Indeed, much of our August harvest is eaten in the garden; picking berries hand to mouth is our way of entering and leaving a day's work. The strawberries of June and early July are followed in the first week of August by raspberries, both red and purple, then the highbush blueberries in the month's second week and bunches of table grapes ripening at month's end. When a friend asked if we planned to make wine, Marjorie said no, most of the grapes never make it into the house.

On peak blueberry days there are enough left for Lynne to make her famous blueberry buckle. Any surplus is frozen with thoughts of warm muffins in December.

*Facing page:* Garlic harvested in late August is hung to dry through September.

Bumblebees enjoy grazing on the silver-blue orb of a globe thistle.

Bumblebees are also grazers, and they join us in the August garden, buzzing from one type of flower to another. I followed one as it crawled over the silver-blue orb of a globe thistle, sipping randomly, then vanished within the folded petals of a monk's hood, finally taking a nip of nectar from a nearby goldenrod.

We cut stems of these three flowers, taking what the garden has to offer as a feast for the eyes; blues and yellow, a combination so appealing to the human eye. When I look at the arrangement of cut flowers, I am reminded of the bumblebee's delight in these August blooms.

## A Lesson from a Chipmunk Named Theodore

Marjorie's Garden is a clearing in the woods. The vegetable garden, perennial bed, and several native woody species that we have planted over the years are surrounded by a forest of mostly spruce, fir, and birch, a forest that provides protection for the garden's wildlife visitors, including birds, a family of red fox, deer, red squirrels, skunks, porcupines, and chipmunks.

In early August, the garden becomes a festival of birds fattening up for migrations south. The black-oil sunflower seed feeders on the porch empty at three times the rate of any other time of year as hordes of bright yellow goldfinches join the ever-present chickadees and nuthatches. The goldfinches split their time between the feeders and sunflower heads that tower over the vegetable garden.

Meanwhile, the pithy branches of common elderberry bow under the weight of white-throated sparrows feasting on purple berries. Treetops are filled with vireos and warblers searching for caterpillars, and juvenile hermit thrushes, the same youngsters that took every berry from the back-porch red elder last month, forage in the highbush blueberries.

An avid birder since youth, I enjoy this August bird frenzy and take particular delight in seeing rare garden visitors such as black-and-white warblers and northern parula warblers darting in and out of sight in the canopy of the old pin cherry.

On hot August afternoons, Reilly the Brittany sits at a corner of the porch watching red squirrels and chipmunks dart back and forth as they scavenge seeds dropped by nuthatches in the mysterious way these birds grade a seed's worth. Nothing goes to waste.

For me, this is the reason for gardening, knowing that our garden not only provides us fresh fruits and vegetables for half the year and the beauty of native plants in every season, but that it also nourishes a wide diversity of wildlife.

Coexistence with the garden's wildlife was tested one summer when I noticed a red squirrel's interest in our Reliance peach tree's immature fruits. As an old Georgia boy with fond memories of fresh peaches and homemade peach ice cream, I had been waiting three years for this tree to bear fruit. With only 20 young peaches starting to show color, I took offense at the squirrel's interest and decided to place a net around the lower half of the tree, securing it all around with stones to keep squirrels from reaching the trunk. I used the remaining netting to cover the two largest and most productive Patriot highbush blueberry bushes.

The next morning there were two sparrows trapped within the apron surrounding the peach tree, and when I approached they panicked and became tangled in the netting. After freeing them, I immediately took down the entire net and threw it away.

A day later, while harvesting blueberries, I nearly stepped on a chipmunk tangled in netting. It had rained during the night, and the poor animal looked more like a wet rag than anything alive, motionless until I tugged at the net.

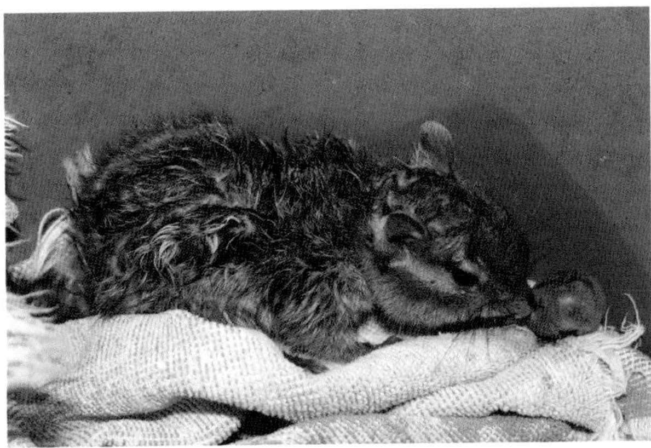

Theodore almost paid a dear price for a taste of blueberries.

I ran to the house for scissors and separated the chipmunk from the net, then worked for several minutes to carefully cut away rings of netting around its neck and front legs. I wrapped the chipmunk, now and forever named Theodore, in a towel and placed him in a large clay pot on the porch, adding a handful of blueberries and sunflower nuts.

Theodore dried in the sun, snuggled within folds of the towel, eating blueberries. Later that afternoon, he jumped out of his pot and joined his comrades in scavenging seeds. While he recovered, I removed the net from both blueberry plants and threw it away.

Lesson learned, twice. I regret my avarice and am forever content to share the garden with birds, chipmunks, and all other creatures that live there.

## *August in the Vegetable Garden*

At the beginning of August, summer crops in the vegetable gardens of southern New England are well ahead of those farther north and away from the coast. Gardeners in Zone 7 areas of Connecticut and Rhode Island are applying a nitrogen boost to sweet corn, eggplants, peppers, and tomatoes, a task that Zone 5 gardeners schedule for later in the month. (See "The Garden in August, Zone by Zone" at the end of this chapter.) Zone 7 tomatoes and peppers are ripening early in the month, while gardeners in Zones 4 and 5 wait anxiously for a blush of pink. And with their short summer growing season nearly half over, Zone 5 gardeners are already sowing seeds of kale, carrots, and spinach for harvest in late fall, something Zone 7 gardeners will not do until the last week of August. But before the month is out, gardeners throughout New England will have tasted the season's first cucumbers, summer squash, and beans.

### Carrots

Early-sown carrots may be ready for harvest by the end of August. Don't pull them up, as this often results in a handful of tops with the roots left behind. Instead, dig carrots with a spade or fork. Push the spade into the soil several inches from the row and push down on the handle, wedging the carrots out of the ground.

Carrots can be harvested when they reach finger size. Dig what you can use immediately and let the remaining roots continue growing. If you do harvest excess, store them in plastic bags in the vegetable crisper drawer of the refrigerator.

For a fall crop of carrots, sow seeds of a short-rooted variety in August, growing the crop in a raised bed. These midsummer plantings mature quickly in cool autumn weather, producing tender, sweet carrots that are delicious. Suggested varieties include Touchon, Baby Spike, Little Finger, Minicor, and Short'n Sweet.

Marjorie digs while Reilly exercises quality control.

With their tops starting to die back in mid-August, these onions are ready for harvest.

We dry our garlic bulbs on the porch, tying them in labeled bunches by variety and hanging them from the rafters close to the inside wall, out of blowing rain.

## Celery

Blanching celery in August will produce stalks that are tender and mild-flavored. Simply mound soil around the plants or, if you prefer, wrap the leaf stalks with paper or aluminum foil. Consider leaving a few plants unblanched, adding their stronger flavor to soups and stews.

## Onions

Onions should be pulled from the ground as soon as the tops start to die back, well before the plants start sending up flowering stalks. The harvested bulbs should be cured by spreading them out in a warm, dry, airy location, out of direct sun, until the tops and outer skins are completely dry and brittle.

Once cured, the bulbs can be stored in a well-ventilated, dry, cool (but not cold) location. Store the onions in mesh bags by variety so that air can circulate around the bulbs. Or braid the dry tops together, always keeping a few bunches of braided onions hanging in the kitchen, handy for the winter soup pot.

## Garlic

When garlic leaves start to turn yellow, stop watering. A dry spell prior to harvest will aid the curing process.

Some veteran garlic growers insist that garlic should be harvested when a third to half of the leaves have turned yellow. Wait longer and the cloves within the bulb start to separate, a condition that reduces the storage life of the bulbs. Other experts suggest waiting until the lower leaves start to turn brown. The only way to know for sure is to harvest a bulb when half the leaves have yellowed and cut it in half; if the cloves fill out the skin, it's ready.

Always dig the bulbs rather than pulling them up; they are too deep and too well-rooted for pulling. To minimize bulb damage, use a fork rather than a spade. Damaged bulbs will not store well and should be used right away.

After digging the garlic bulbs and brushing off the clinging soil, allow them to dry for three or four weeks in an airy location out of direct sunlight. Placing them on wire racks will improve air circulation. This "curing" process is essential to prolong the storage life of the bulbs. Once the tops and roots have dried, they can be cut off, unless you plan to braid the bulbs together.

Store your cured garlic bulbs in a cool (32 to 40° F, dry (60 to 70% relative humidity) dark place with some air circulation—not in a brightly lit kitchen.

Finally, consider setting aside a few top-quality bulbs for next season, storing them at room temperature with fairly high humidity to prevent desiccation.

## Summer Squash

Summer squash is one of my favorite summer vegetables, and I can't wait to transplant seedlings in the middle of June, as soon as the soil temperature settles above 60°. In recent years I have also direct-sown summer squash on the first of August for a fall crop. The plants reach reproductive stage before the month is out, and I pick squash two or three times a week through September.

### Squash Surgery

Sudden wilting of squash vines—summer squash, winter squash, and pumpkins—is the first symptom of squash vine borer invasion. A hole at the base of the vine that leaks a wet sawdust-like frass is conclusive evidence—this is where the fat grub-like caterpillar (the larva of a moth that looks like a wasp) made its entry. Your only recourse to save the patient is immediate surgery.

Starting at the entry hole, slit the stem longitudinally through the top epidermal layer with a sharp scalpel (a razor blade or knife will also work), extending the cut until you find the borer. Remove and dispatch the borer, then pack the damaged area of the stem with moist soil to promote root formation. With a little luck, the patient will live to bear fruit.

Late June (Zones 6 and 7) or early July (Zones 4 and 5) sowings of summer squash are good insurance against an outbreak of squash vine borers on earlier sowings. The female moth has stopped laying eggs by these later sowing dates. I've made early August sowings of summer squash and harvested borer-free fruits from mid September until first frost.

## Ripening Green Tomatoes, On and Off the Vine

A year or so ago, on August 6, I determined that there were only 60 days remaining until October 5, the middle of the date range (October 1– October 10) for the average first frost in USDA Hardiness Zone 5a. Marjorie's Garden is in Zone 5a.

This is sobering information for a gardener who measures success by the number (or poundage) of harvested ripe tomatoes, for if first frost arrives on schedule, tomato flowers formed after the middle of August in Zone 5a are unlikely to bear ripe fruits. Under the best of conditions, it takes about 60 days for tomatoes to go from blossoms to fully ripened fruit. In late summer, as days get shorter and nights get longer, it takes even longer.

If both pollination of the flower and fertilization of the ovules are successful, it takes 40 to 50 days for a tomato fruit to grow to the "mature green" stage. Florida tomato growers routinely pick tomatoes in this condition, load them on trucks and then transport them to large warehouses where they are gassed with ethylene, a fruit-ripening hormone that promotes changes in tomato fruit pigment from green to red, pink, yellow, or orange, depending on the variety. The end result is those tasteless tomato facsimiles that consumers across the country demand in order to add a touch of color to winter salads.

The garden-ripened tomatoes that we love so dearly depend on both temperature and naturally produced ethylene for ripening. In the garden, the optimum temperature for ripening lies between 68 and 77° F. The further temperatures stray from optimum, the slower the ripening process will be, and if temperatures are outside this range too long, the ripening process may halt completely.

Lycopene and carotene, the pigments responsible for tomato color, are not produced when the temperature exceeds 85° F. Thus, extended periods of heat can produce fruits that are typically yellow-green to yellow-orange instead of red.

Understanding this bit of botany related to tomato ripening, it is not surprising that gardeners in northern New England have yet to ripen a tomato by mid-August, other than Sungold and other cherry tomatoes that seem to play by other rules. Yet there is little the gardener can do except wait and hope.

By late August, I will be removing any new flowers that form on tomato plants, knowing that they are unlikely to produce even mature green tomatoes that can be ripened indoors. With their removal, the plant will divert more of its energy to ripening the fruits already formed.

Heavy fruit set late in the season can work against the gardener. Ripening many fruits at once takes a lot of energy from the plant and delays the entire crop from turning red. If only a few weeks remain until first frost and fruits are not ripening, try removing some of the mature green fruits to ripen what is left on the vine. You can readily identify the mature green tomatoes by their pale green, almost translucent appearance, perhaps with a blush of pink at the blossom end. These removed fruits can be ripened indoors as described below.

(Another diagnostic test for the mature green state is to cut a fruit in half and examine the tissues. If the tissue surrounding the seeds is yellowish and jelly-like or sticky, the fruit is at the mature green state. Any of the remaining fruits that have the same color are likely mature green as well.)

At some point, between late September and mid-October in Zone 5a, when first frost is in the forecast, the non-ripe tomatoes that have reached the mature green stage should be harvested and ripened indoors. Green tomatoes that have not reached maturity should be heaped on the compost pile.

Harvest mature green tomatoes before the first hard frost. If they are hit by a hard frost, use them up as soon as possible, for they will not ripen. Recipes for green tomatoes, including several for fried green tomatoes, can be found at http://www.grouprecipes.com/green-tomato.

When harvesting mature green tomatoes, clip the fruit off the plant, leaving a very short stem. Tearing the fruit off the vine will often create wounds that can quickly lead to rot in storage.

Wrap each mature green tomato in newspaper to help prevent bruising that leads to rot. Wrapping also provides the proper atmosphere for accumulation of ethylene. Place the wrapped fruits in single layers on shelving or in shallow boxes. Plan to check them frequently, at least once a week, to remove rotting fruits.

Store the tomatoes at between 55 and 70° in a location away from sunlight and not too humid. Possible storage areas include garages, cellars, porches, or pantries. Do not try to ripen tomatoes on a windowsill where temperatures are typically too hot. Despite popular thinking, light is not necessary for ripening green tomatoes.

The length of time needed for ripening will depend on the temperature. Ripening occurs in about 14 days at 70°, 28 days at 55°.

Once the fruits have ripened, store them between 45 and 50°, not in the refrigerator. The optimum relative humidity for storage is between 90 and 95%, but this is difficult to produce in most homes. Try to avoid extremely dry air, which will quickly dehydrate the fruits. Canning or freezing the ripened tomatoes may be the best approach.

## Grazing on Pineapple Tomatillos

Every gardener should plant one or two "grazing crops," plants bearing fruit to nibble on as you work in the August garden, fruits that never make it out of the garden. Cherry tomatoes often fill this role, particularly sweet 'Sungold,' but the queen of grazing crops in Marjorie's Garden is the pineapple tomatillo. The yellow fruits, the size of large peas, are picked off the ground still wrapped in their papery husks. They taste fruity, redolent of pineapple, and we munch them like popcorn as we work.

If you've already scarfed down all the pineapple tomatillos on the ground, look for those still on the plant that have bright yellow or brown husks. They are ripe enough!

## Tickling Blueberries

On a dewy August morning I walk through wet grass to the garden, one hand grasping a mug of steaming coffee, the other a bowl for berries. I set the mug on a rock to swing back the garden gate. For years we gardened without this fence, but then came a spring when deer ate more than their share of raspberry canes, and we fenced them out.

Opening the gate flushes eight blue jays from the garden. Until the blueberries ripen, there are never more than two.

I walk past the raspberry beds, ignoring the need to pick and toss moldy berries, the fate of many raspberries in a rain-soaked season. I make an early breakfast of ripe Sungold tomatoes and check to see if any cucumbers are long enough for harvest, but otherwise stay focused on the task at hand, beating the jays to the blueberries.

They are highbush blueberries, and this morning their branches bend under the weight of ripe fruit. We picked a few berries from these shrubs in July, but August is the peak harvest month.

We have anticipated this morning since early spring, when Marjorie pruned each dormant blueberry shrub, scrutinizing its potential for fruiting and form. She removed dead, damaged, and diseased branches as well as spindly side branches with few flower buds. She cut away the witches' brooms, dense masses of short, thick, twisted stems caused by a fungus that requires balsam fir—of which there are plenty in the woods around the garden—as its secondary host. She renewed the compost mulch around each shrub. All this before the leaf buds started to grow.

In June we watched native bees pollinate blueberry blossoms. Bumblebees will leave catnip flowers for blueberry nectar. They are a joy to watch as they forage from first light to dusk, stopping to rest only in a cold rain, when they seek refuge under a leaf or flower cluster. On chilly mornings we might find an immobile bumblebee that spent the night on the last flower visited, too cold at dusk to fly to its underground nest, and we watch as it finds its legs in the sun's warmth.

This morning I fill the bowl with blueberries—big, juicy, plump—each ripe berry gently tickled from its slender stalk. I hold my cupped hand beneath a cluster of berries—some further along toward full ripeness than others—and move my fingers over the berries as if tickling the bottom of a child's foot. Only the ripest berries break their fragile connection and fall into my hand, dark purple-black fruits bursting with sweetness.

With practiced tickling, only the ripest blueberries will fall into your palm. The rest will still be there tomorrow—unless the blue jays beat you to them.

I eat a few berries as I pick, some imperfect from the pecking of jays that now sit in the top of a nearby wild cherry, squawking at my interruption of their feast. The filled bowl goes to the kitchen for breakfast.

The harvest will last until mid-August. The joy of growing highbush blueberry shrubs does not end, however, with the harvest. In October their scarlet red and golden yellow leaves will draw us to the garden, autumn color at another level.

## Harvesting and Drying Basil

Early one August morning, Marjorie gives the basil plants a haircut, bringing a pile of leaves into the kitchen for microwave drying. She strips the leaves from their stems, divides them into small single-layer batches, each sandwiched between two paper towels, and zaps each batch on high for 2 minutes and 20 seconds. (The exact time will vary from one microwave to another. Starting with 2 minutes as the recommended minimum length of time, Marjorie determined the optimum time required to produce fully dried leaves that crumble when crushed. She watches each batch from start to finish, making sure all goes well.)

Once the precise microwave time is determined, the work goes quickly, producing a year's supply of dried basil leaves for soups and sauces. The house smells like basil all morning.

## *Exuberant Herbaceous Perennials*

In August our garden's border expands to take in plants growing along a curve where dirt road becomes driveway, for it is in August that this short stretch of "roadside weeds," including goldenrods, Queen Anne's lace, white campion, and meadowsweet bursts into bloom, a tapestry of color. This is a place where insects thrive, a natural insectary providing pollen and nectar during a time when these essential pollinator foods are scarce in the rest of the garden.

August also brings the flowering of exuberant perennials that we have planted in the garden, plants that bring rich color and bold texture to perennial beds or mixed borders. Some, such as Joe-pye weed, are best planted only in gardens with plenty of space. Their combined foliage makes a bold statement in the early summer garden, but they come into their own when flowering begins in August. They belong to late summer, to chilly nights and cloudless days, to ripening pumpkins, to the last bees and butterflies of the garden year.

The orange-belted bumblebee is but one of many pollinating insects that service goldenrods in August.

### Goldenrods

There are more than two-dozen goldenrod *(Solidago* sp.) species native to New England, each unique in size, leaf shape, or the form in which it displays its golden flowers in summer or early fall. Learning to identify each species, even in bloom, would be an ambitious project, a goal for my retirement years. At the moment I am more interested in the role of goldenrods in our gardens.

First, let me again dispel the notion that goldenrods cause hay fever; their pollen is too heavy to be carried on the wind. The tiny green flowers of common ragweed, an inconspicuous plant flowering at the same time as some goldenrods, are the main cause of hay fever.

Goldenrod pollen is dispersed by pollinating insects, including native solitary bees and bumblebees, butterflies, wasps, and beetles. Even spiders have been shown to move goldenrod pollen around as they prey on insects. For gardeners interested in bolstering pollinator populations in their garden, goldenrods are hard to beat. Their late-season nectar and protein-rich pollen attract pollinators in higher numbers than any other plant species.

For sunny dry gardens, New England gardeners should grow the tall goldenrod *(S. altissima),* a rare species that grows to 7 feet tall, and two shorter species, gray goldenrod *(S. nemoralis)* and elm-leaved goldenrod *(S. ulmifolia),* growing to 3 and 4 feet, respectively. All three species flower in August, with gray goldenrod and tall goldenrod continuing into September.

For wetter (though still well-drained) garden sites, use blue-stemmed goldenrod *(S. caesia),* which grows 4 feet tall, and smooth goldenrod *(S. gigantea),* which tops out at 7 feet. Both flower in the fall.

During the first week of August, New England roadsides and fields are filled with goldenrods growing side-by-side with a pollinator-attracting native shrub, meadowsweet *(Spiraea alba* var. *latifolia).* The soft pink of meadowsweet's small flowers, borne in terminal branched clusters, is a pleasing contrast to goldenrod's bolder bright yellow. Planting both species together in the garden represents the essence of bringing nature home. Regretfully, goldenrods are not yet widely available to New England gardeners. Hopefully that will change in

Gray goldenrod, shown here blooming with Joe-pye weed, grows best in sunny gardens. Once established, it can withstand periods of summer drought.

In this garden of exuberant perennials, sneezeweed is sandwiched between Joe-pye weed (rear left) and gray goldenrod (front).

the future. The New England Wildflower Society grows goldenrod species and sells them from their shop at Garden in the Woods in Framingham, Massachusetts, but they do not ship. There are also a few online sources for some of the cultivated varieties.

## Sneezeweed

Sneezeweed *(Helenium autumnale)* can reach 6 feet or more in height and is just as wide when grown in rich, moist soils. Its branched stems bear huge masses of 2-inch flowers in August and September. The common name has nothing to do with the plant's pollen, but can be traced to the use of the dried and powdered leaves as a snuff to cure the common cold.

Sneezeweed is another example of a native North American plant that was not popular in gardens until European breeders worked with them. Now there are several varieties in flower colors of gold, orange, rust, and red. A mix of gold and red heleniums creates a bright and cheerful garden scene.

Sneezeweed can get wild and woolly. You may want to stake the taller varieties or, to keep the taller types

Planted together, gold and red heleniums make a bold statement in the summer border.

Helenium continues to flower into the autumn, creating striking garden scenes when combined with the early fall foliage of native shrubs such as black chokeberry *(Aronia melanocarpa)*.

blooming on shorter, bushier stems, cut them back hard around July 4. Deadhead the plants after the flowers fade.

## Joe-Pye Weed

Joe-pye weed *(Eupatorium purpureum)* is a mammoth clump-forming perennial, reaching up to 9 feet tall in rich, moist soils. The species has loose clusters of small pink flowers, but many gardeners prefer the cultivar 'Atropurpureum' with violet purple flowers and dark burgundy stems. Everything about this plant is bold, including the lance-shaped, toothed leaves that form a dark green foil for early-blooming perennials. Flowering from early August through early autumn, Joe-pye weed is one of the best butterfly- and bee-attracting plants.

## Queen Anne's Lace

I realize that I am out on the end of a skinny branch here, but I am fond of Queen Anne's lace *(Daucus carota),* the wild carrot and ancestor of the garden carrot. I encourage its cultivation. Fully aware that it was not growing in North America in pre-colonial days, I do not believe it is an invasive plant species. Rather, it has gracefully inserted

Joe-pye weed (at far left), a mammoth perennial that towers over most other herbaceous plants, belongs in a garden of other exuberant perennials including tall goldenrods and sneezeweed.

The flower of Queen Anne's lace is actually a cluster (umbel) of several small flowers, each destined to produce a seed.

An adult hoverfly forages for nectar on Queen Anne's lace.

itself into the flora of New England without, as far as I know, outcompeting native species for resources. It has become naturalized.

Wild carrot is a biennial that flowers in August of its second year, the 3-inch-wide clusters of flowers, called umbels, borne a meter high on stems with ferny foliage. Before opening, the umbels are claret-colored or pale pink, turning bright white and rounded in full bloom. Finally, as flowers give way to seeds, the umbels contract and become concave, resembling birds' nests. Dried umbels ultimately detach as tumbleweeds.

Upon close inspection, you will notice that the round umbel is a multi-branched structure, each branch bearing clusters of tiny white flowers, the entire arrangement producing a lacy pattern reminiscent of an old-fashioned doily produced by the queen herself. And in the center of most umbels is a single red flower that some say represents a blood droplet where Queen Anne pricked herself with the needle. Now it serves to attract insects.

Wild carrot grows with goldenrod and meadowsweet on the edges of the dirt road leading to our driveway, forming a natural insectary within bee-reach of the garden. On a sunny August afternoon I find flowers covered with lacewings (whose larvae eat aphids and mites), ladybugs, hoverflies, parasitic wasps, and both bumblebees and solitary bees.

## *August-Flowering Native Shrubs*

Garden-worthy native woody plants that flower or fruit in August, like summersweet clethra and staghorn sumac, are rare. Both are found in the wild throughout New England, but only the clethra has found its way into the hearts of gardeners. Staghorn sumac is too exuberant for many gardeners, but perhaps I can convince those who shun it that it has merit and can be managed with success.

### Summersweet Clethra

Summersweet clethra, *Clethra alnifolia*, is a native plant success story, a favorite shrub among the many gardeners who grow it for its spicy fragrant summer flowers and golden yellow fall foliage. Also called sweet pepperbush for its peppercorn-like fruit, white alder for the similarity of its foliage to that of the true alders, and "poor man's soap" because the flowers produce lather when crushed in water, summersweet has been in cultivation for over

This spreading colony of 'Hokie Pink' summersweet was started a decade ago with three small plants. On a hot August day, its blooms fill the air with a spicy scent.

Individual flowers of summersweet open slowly, starting at the base of each spike. The result is a flowering period that lasts several weeks.

This female colony of staghorn sumac was likely started from a single bird-dispersed seed.

200 years. It is an essential plant in the pollinator garden, attracting butterflies, bees, and hummingbirds, and it is ignored by deer, a draw for many New England gardeners. Borne in dense narrow spikes, the blossoms can fill the summer air of the garden with a spicy scent for several weeks in late July and August. Following the bloom are small rounded seed capsules, each one-eighth inch in diameter and containing several seeds, all packed into the same dense spikes of their forebears. These tan-colored capsules persist into autumn, gradually darkening in color and adding textural depth to fall foliage that varies from light yellow to gold.

While the species has white blossoms, many new cultivars of summersweet have been introduced in recent years, including 'Hokie Pink,' the cultivar that grows in Marjorie's Garden. And while the species can reach heights up to 10 feet in the garden, newer cultivars selected for compact habits top out at 3 to 4 feet.

## Staghorn Sumac

> *"In summer, Staghorn Sumac lifts its immense panicles of vivid flowers among the great frond-like pinnate leaves, and in autumn the brilliant fruits, the most variously brilliant foliage, shout out their color to the dying year. Flaunting orange, war-paint vermilion, buttery yellow, or sometimes angry purple may be seen all together on a single tree. More, it commonly happens that half of a compound leaf, or even half of a leaflet, may retain its rich, deep, shining green, in calm contrast to the flaming autumnal hues. And at all times the lower surface of the foliage keeps its pallid, glaucus cast that, when early frost has brushed it, turns silver. Probably no tree in the country, perhaps in the world, may exhibit so many and such contrasting shades and tints, such frosty coolness with its fire."*
>
> —Donald Culross Peattie,
> *A Natural History of Trees of Eastern and Central North America*, 1948

You know this tree, the staghorn sumac *(Rhus typhina)*, its common name derived from the fine felt-like hairs on young stems, giving them the texture of a deer's antlers. You know it if only from the window of your car, those roadside colonies of tropical foliage with wine-red pyramidal fruit clusters encircled by long, dark green, pinnately compound leaves. If you are really observant, you've noticed that some colonies sport these showy fruit clusters while others lack them. Some colonies are female, some are male.

Each cone-shaped staghorn sumac fruit cluster consists of several berries, each covered with fine red hairs. These fruits, formed in summer, persist through winter, providing food for songbirds and game birds.

Actually, each colony can be considered a single multi-trunked tree, each trunk derived from a suckering shoot that likely originated from a single bird-dispersed seed. The shoot that started it all may have long since died, leaving behind a group of suckers that are all the same sex and that, in time, will produce more suckering shoots. And so the colony grows, old stems dying, a multitude of young suckering shoots taking their place.

Old colonies of staghorn sumac can cover an extensive area. I recall a two-acre hayfield divided in half by a colony of 20-foot-tall fruiting branches, a beautiful sight in August when the colony was fruiting, in October when the leaves were turning, and in winter when the persistent fruits were dusted with snow.

Staghorn sumac's vegetative growth habit makes it a difficult plant to bring into some gardens. When I recommend its use as both a lovely ornamental and a valuable wildlife plant, I'm likely to hear the term "invasive" tossed into the discussion. But no, a native plant, by definition, cannot be considered invasive. Aggressive it is, for sure. In the right place, in the right garden, I like "exuberant."

It comes down to a matter of placement. The suckering habit of staghorn sumac can be controlled by mowing, paving, and water. For example, I recall a colony of fruiting plants in Orono, Maine, growing between the banks of the Penobscot River and a paved road, their spread controlled by water on one side, asphalt on the other. In Orono, I lived next door to a colony of sumac in a neighbor's backyard, its spread limited by the lawn mower.

Staghorn sumac's shallow, wide-spreading roots make it ideal for soil stabilization along slopes, streams, or pond-side, wherever its suckering habit can be tolerated or controlled and drainage is good. Because of its tolerance of salt, it is also an excellent plant for seashore and roadside plantings.

The berries of staghorn sumac, small fleshy drupes covered with fine red hairs and borne in cone-shaped clusters, are eaten by ruffed grouse, eastern phoebe, common crow, northern mockingbird, gray catbird, American robin, wood thrush, hermit thrush, eastern bluebird, and over 30 other bird species. Because the fruit persists through the winter, it is an excellent emergency source of food for these creatures.

Staghorn sumac's spring flowers, greenish-yellow and borne in conical clusters, provide nectar for bees and several butterfly species, including banded and striped hairstreaks. It is also a larval host for the luna moth and the spring azure butterfly. In late August its leaves are riddled with the chewing of these caterpillars.

For those who can manage its exuberance, staghorn sumac belongs in the wildlife garden, where it will nourish a host of birds and insects. And it belongs in the ornamental garden, where the gardener can watch it change in texture and color through the seasons.

## Ripe Elderberries in August

The berries of common elderberry *(Sambucus nigra* ssp. *canadensis)* ripen in the second half of August. Birds perch on the pithy canes and pluck the berries one at a time, but we cut entire clusters of berries from the shrubs in our garden, take them inside to do the plucking, then fast-freeze the berries on cookie sheets before packing them in freezer boxes.

All winter we have elderberries for muffins, simply substituting them for blueberries in a favorite recipe. They provide a unique, crunchy texture to the muffins, and they are not as sweet as blueberries. We love them!

High in antioxidants, elderberries can be used to make jams, jellies, pies, and, of course, wine. Recipes abound on the Internet.

If you do not grow common elderberry in your garden, you can harvest berries from plants growing in the wild throughout New England. Just remember to tread lightly as you harvest, for the canes are easily broken, and leave plenty of berries for the birds.

The purple-black berries of common elderberry are a favorite of birds and gardeners.

## The Joy of Gardening in Tune with Nature

The greatest joys in gardening often arise not from careful planning or practice, but from working in tune with nature. For example, consider the joy brought to the garden by a weed not pulled.

One early June morning I decided not to pull a small sunflower seedling growing on the edge of a bed planted to tomatoes and summer squash, not to consider it a weed. I remembered the native sunflowers we had grown in that bed the year before and thought this little seedling might have grown from a seed missed by the goldfinches, though there is no way to know for sure.

By the end of June, the sunflower plant had grown taller than all of last year's possible parents, tall enough to require staking. The optimist in me reached for the longest pole I could find, a stout arrowwood stem of 8 feet, sinking it 2 feet into the ground.

By August this volunteer sunflower stood 9 feet tall, splitting at the top of the stake into several branches, each bearing several 6-inch flowers, each flower a dark center cluster of fertile disk flowers surrounded by golden yellow ray petals. At one point there were 15 flower heads attracting the attention of equally brilliant goldfinches.

Wherever we were in Marjorie's Garden, this sunflower towered over us; it was the center of the garden universe, with all other garden life revolving around it. In addition to the goldfinches, hummingbirds sipped nectar from the small disc flowers and bumblebees crawled across the sunlit landscapes in search of pollen.

I would look up from my garden work to see a goldfinch pecking at a seedhead and think, perhaps I should bag a head or two, save some seed of this magnificent plant for next year's garden. But no, this tall sunflower was a gift of joy to the birds, to the bees, to me, to all the creatures of this garden. The mystery of its appearance is part of that joy.

# The New England Garden in August, Zone by Zone

Throughout New England, gardeners in August search the undersides of leaves for beetles and try to stay ahead of the weeds. We harvest the last of spring-sown lettuce and the first of the summer's tomatoes. We drag the hose and spread compost between the garden rows. Gardeners in Zone 7 may harvest garlic toward the end of August. And many of us will sow seeds of fall crops as vacant spots open up in the summer garden.

| IN THE GARDEN | August | Date by USDA Hardiness Zone | | | | | Notes |
|---|---|---|---|---|---|---|---|
| | | 3 | 4 | 5 | 6 | 7 | |
| **GENERAL MAINTENANCE** | Continue battle against Japanese beetles. | | | | | | Hand-pick and toss beetles into soapy water. If you choose to use beetle traps, do not put them in your garden; put them upwind of your garden. |
| **VEGETABLE GARDEN** | Sow oats in unused garden areas. | | | | | | Sow 2 pounds per 1,000 sq. ft. |
| | Avoid applying heavy doses of nitrogen to fruiting tomatoes, peppers, and eggplants. | | | | | | Poor fruit set on these plants is not due to lack of nitrogen but to low night temperatures (below 60° F). |
| | Pull up and discard any diseased and insect-damaged plants. | | | | | | Keeping these plants around will perpetuate the problems. Do not compost diseased plants. |
| | Remove any cracked tomatoes or other overripe fruit to deter sap beetles. | | | | | | Sap beetles, also called picnic beetles, are attracted to the garden by overripe or damaged fruit. Once in the garden, they can damage raspberries and other fruits as they ripen. |
| | Buy straw if available. | | | | | | Straw can be scarce in spring, so stocking up in late summer makes sense if you have a place to keep it dry during the winter. |
| **VEGETABLE CROPS** | | | | | | | |
| Beans, Bush | Monitor for Mexican bean beetles.<br>Harvest every other day. | | | | | | Hand-pick beetles and crush yellow egg masses. |
| Beans, Pole | Monitor for Mexican bean beetles.<br>Harvest every other day. | | | | | | Hand-pick beetles and crush yellow egg masses. |
| Cabbage | Harden-off transplants from third sowing. | July 25 | Aug 1 | Aug 7 | Aug 14 | Aug 28 | |
| | Set out transplants from third sowing. | Aug 1 | Aug 7 | Aug 14 | Aug 28 | Sept 4 | Heads can split if they are left on the plant too long. Minimize splitting by twisting the head a quarter turn or shearing one side of the roots with a spade to reduce water flow into the head when close to harvest. |
| | Twist mature heads to prevent splitting until harvest. | | | | | | |

| IN THE GARDEN | August | Date by USDA Hardiness Zone | | | | | Notes |
|---|---|---|---|---|---|---|---|
| | | 3 | 4 | 5 | 6 | 7 | |
| Carrots | Keep plantings uniformly moist. | | | | | | Alternating dry and wet periods will produce carrots with splits and cracks. |
| | Harvest with a spade or trowel, not by hand. | | | | | | Pulling carrots often leaves the roots behind. Harvest with a small spade, pushing it into the soil a few inches from the plants and lifting the carrots out of the ground. See Chapter 10 for more information on harvesting and short-term storing of carrots. |
| | Try an August sowing of carrots for a late crop. | Aug 1 | Aug 7 | Aug 14 | Aug 21 | Aug 28 | Short-rooted varieties are your best bet for a late crop. See Chapter 10 for suggestions.. |
| Cauliflower | Blanch heads for 1-2 weeks before harvest. | Sept 4 | Aug 28 | Aug 21 | Aug 14 | Aug 7 | Tie leaves together above the head. |
| Celery and Celeriac | Blanch celery for a week before harvest. | Aug 28 | Aug 21 | Aug 14 | Aug 7 | Aug 1 | Blanching produces tender stalks with a milder flavor. |
| Corn, Sweet | Side-dress with compost or rotted manure. | Aug 28 | Aug 21 | Aug 14 | Aug 7 | Aug 1 | |
| | Harvest just before cooking for best flavor. | | | | | | If you can't pick just before use, harvest the ears early in the morning and store them in the refrigerator until needed. |
| Cucumbers | Monitor for striped cucumber beetles. | | | | | | Consider using yellow sticky traps placed just above the plants as a means of control. |
| | Keep soil consistently moist. | | | | | | Alternating dry and wet periods may cause fruits to taste bitter. |
| | Harvest fruits before they turn yellow. | | | | | | Once cucumbers get large and yellow, the plants stop producing and do not recover. |
| | Pick early in the morning when the fruits are still cool. | | | | | | |
| Eggplant | Side-dress with compost or well-rotted manure. | Aug 28 | Aug 21 | Aug 14 | Aug 7 | Aug 1 | (Photo courtesy Charles Heaven) |
| Garlic | When leaves start to yellow, stop watering. | | | | | | See Chapter 10 for more details on harvesting and curing bulbs. |
| | Harvest when half of the leaves turn yellow. | | | | | | |
| Kale | Sow seeds for fall crop. | Aug 1 | Aug 7 | Aug 14 | Aug 21 | Aug 28 | In hot weather, shade seedlings until they are several inches tall. Place a straw mulch around plants. |
| Lettuce | Make a final sowing of leaf lettuce in early August.. | | | | | | |

| IN THE GARDEN | August | Date by USDA Hardiness Zone | | | | | Notes |
|---|---|---|---|---|---|---|---|
| | | 3 | 4 | 5 | 6 | 7 | |
| Melons | Side-dress with compost or well-rotted manure. | Aug 28 | Aug 21 | Aug 14 | Aug 7 | Aug 1 | |
| | Keep ripening fruits off the ground. | | | | | | Use a coffee can or flower pot to support each melon. |
| | Avoid overwatering. | | | | | | Too much water at this point will reduce sweetness. |
| | Pinch off blossoms. | Aug 1 | Aug 7 | Aug 14 | Aug 21 | Aug 28 | There is not enough time left for fruits to mature. Pulling off the blossoms will speed ripening of remaining melons. |
| Onions | Harvest when tops bend over.<br>Keep the papery skins on bulbs when storing. | | | | | | Withhold water as tops start to die. This will harden bulbs for harvest and storage. |
| Peppers | Side-dress with compost or well-rotted manure. | Aug 28 | Aug 21 | Aug 14 | Aug 7 | Aug 1 | |
| | Harvest as needed. | | | | | | Leave peppers on the plant until needed, allowing some to turn red. |
| Potatoes | Harvest a few new potatoes. | | | | | | |
| Pumpkins | Begin pinching off new blossoms. | Aug 7 | Aug 14 | Aug 21 | Aug 28 | Sept 4 | This will promote faster development and larger size of existing fruits. |
| | Monitor for squash vine borer. | | | | | | The first symptom of squash vine borer is sudden wilting. See Chapter 10 for treatment. |
| | Side-dress with compost or rotted manure. | Aug 28 | Aug 21 | Aug 14 | Aug 7 | Aug 1 | |
| Spinach | Sow in open areas of garden for fall harvest.. | Aug 1 | Aug 7 | Aug 14 | Aug 21 | Aug 28 | See Chapter 9 for suggested varieties. |
| Squash, Summer | Monitor for striped cucumber beetles. | | | | | | Consider using yellow sticky traps placed just above the plants as a means of control. |
| | Monitor for squash vine borer. | | | | | | The first symptom of squash vine borer is sudden wilting. See Chapter 10 for treatment. |
| | Try a late July or early August sowing for late summer and early fall harvest. | July 28 | July 25 | Aug 1 | Aug 7 | Aug 14 | |

| IN THE GARDEN | August | Date by USDA Hardiness Zone | | | | | Notes |
|---|---|---|---|---|---|---|---|
| | | 3 | 4 | 5 | 6 | 7 | |
| Squash, Winter | Side-dress with compost or well-rotted manure. | Aug 28 | Aug 21 | Aug 14 | Aug 7 | Aug 1 | |
| | Begin pinching off new blossoms. | Aug 7 | Aug 14 | Aug 21 | Aug 28 | Sept 4 | This will promote faster development and larger size of existing fruits. |
| | Monitor for striped cucumber beetles. | | | | | | Consider using yellow sticky traps placed just above the plants as a means of control. |
| | Monitor for squash vine borer. | | | | | | The first symptom of squash vine borer is sudden wilting. See Chapter 10 for treatment. |
| Tomatoes | Side-dress with compost or well-rotted manure. | Aug 28 | Aug 21 | Aug 14 | Aug 7 | Aug 1 | |
| | Keep soil consistently moist. | | | | | | Uneven watering may lead to blossom-end rot and splitting of tomatoes as they ripen. |
| | Harvest split tomatoes and use them immediately. | | | | | | Split tomatoes will attract insects and promote decay-causing fungi. |
| (Photo courtesy Charles Heaven) | Pull out your favorite recipes for green tomatoes. | | | | | | See Chapter 10 for discussion of green tomatoes. |
| | Start removing flowers as they develop. | Aug 7 | Aug 14 | Aug 21 | Aug 28 | Sept 4 | Fruits initiated at this time have little chance of reaching the mature green stage by first frost. Removing flowers allows the plant to devote all energy to ripening existing fruits. |
| **SMALL FRUITS** | | | | | | | |
| Strawberries | Fertilize new plants if stunted or yellow. | | | | | | Apply an organic nitrogen fertilizer, one pound of nitrogen per 1,000 sq. ft. |
| | Give established plants a light application of nitrogen. | | | | | | Apply one pound of nitrogen per 1,000 sq. ft. |
| **HERBS** | | | | | | | |
| Basil | Harvest leaves through August. | | | | | | See Chapter 10 for details on drying basil leaves in the microwave. |
| **ROSES** | End applications of nitrogen at end of month. | | | | | | |

# Chapter 11

# The Garden in September

*"I grow old, I grow old,' the garden says. It is nearly October. The bean leaves grow paler, now lime, now yellow, now leprous, dissolving before my eyes. The pods curl and do not grow, turn limp and blacken. The potato vines wither and the tubers huddle underground in their rough weatherproof jackets, waiting to be dug. The last tomatoes ripen and split on the vine; it takes days for them to turn fully now, and a few of the green ones are beginning to fall off."*

—Robert Finch, *Common Ground: A Naturalist's Cape Cod,* 1994

***One day in September in Marjorie's Garden***—the exact day is a matter of the weather—the wheelbarrow path from woodpile to porch will be strewn with golden leaves of yellow birch. Only shaded leaves on the inside of the canopies will have fallen at this point, the outer leaves remaining on the trees, tattered and torn but still green, continuing to transform sunlight into sugar. Their day will come.

Tussock moth caterpillars continue to graze on leaves of oaks and birches. Every leaf is necrotic, riddled with holes and tears, and the caterpillars move slowly, crawling toward their winter sleep.

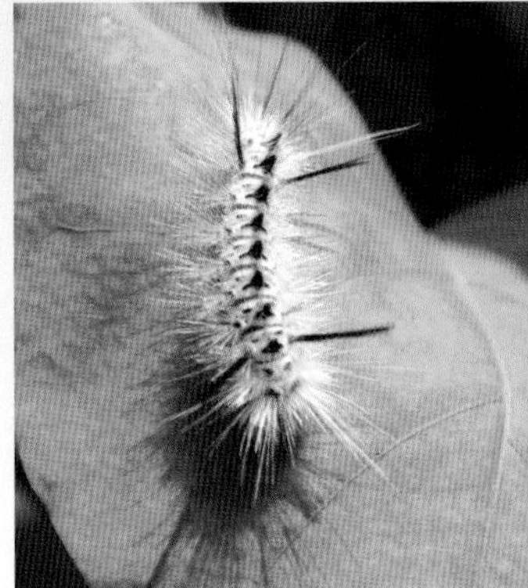

The hickory tussock moth caterpillar grazes on leaves of oaks, grapes, and a host of other garden plants. In September, the trees are alive with warblers and other birds feasting on these bristly creatures.

Deciduous trees and shrubs begin to shut down in September, while the vegetable garden's sunflowers, oblivious to the morning's chilly air, open new flower heads, even as goldfinches peck seeds from the ripe heads. A hard October freeze will soon put an end to all this, but for now the flowers' bright yellow faces tower over empty beds where peas and garlic spent the summer.

Along the edges of the garden, late-flowering goldenrods mingle with white and pale blue fall asters. The Queen Anne's lace flower clusters of August have turned to seedheads that look like birds' nests.

Summer's colors slowly fade from the September garden. Greens turn yellow and brown, branches thin toward bare. Potted hyacinth beans with yellow-brown paper-thin leaves would have been retired to the compost heap if not for the dark red pods clinging to their topmost branches, a spot of color in the early fall garden.

*Facing page:* In September, under the watchful eyes of thrushes, chipmunks, and red squirrels, Marjorie's grapes begin to ripen.

In early September, goldfinches keep watch on this bed of sunflowers, waiting for seeds to ripen.

In the garden insectary, late-blooming goldenrods and fall asters continue to provide fodder for bees and the last of summer's butterflies.

(Right) Among the earliest leaves to turn in our garden are those of maple-leaf viburnum *(Viburnum acerifolium)*. As soon as nights turn chilly, chlorophyll breaks down and a rosy-pink blush creeps into the margins of each leaf, a promise of what is to come.

In the same insectary, September colonies of Queen Anne's lace contain the last flowering plants and plenty of seedheads that look like birds' nests. Eventually the seedheads abscise, becoming tumbleweeds on the wind.

Look closely and you will find the first hints of fall color creeping into the leaves of garden plants. Look closely and you will find color in ripening wild fruits and seeds.

While vegetable gardens in northern New England are truly winding down in early September, those in southern New England are still verdant. The leaves of winter squash in Nate Atwater's garden on Rhode Island Sound (a garden that is featured in Chapter 13) show only a touch of mildew in the first week of September, while squash leaves in Marjorie's Garden, whitewashed with fungus, lie heaped on the compost pile. Green tomatoes on Nate's plants in early September have a shot at ripening, either on the vine or indoors. We may pick a few green fruits with a blush of pink in early September, hoping they will ripen off the vine, but most of the green fruits will be shared with friends who enjoy fried green tomatoes. Or they too end up on the compost pile. And Nate will still be picking green beans when our bean plants dissolve before our eyes.

## September in a Different Sort of Garden

As a boy growing up in rural Alabama, just across the Chattahoochee River from Columbus, Georgia, I often spent late summer afternoons following an English setter through a cornfield. We would go into the corn, Prissy and I, at the edge of the pasture that came with the house my parents rented, and stay in the corn for hours, walking the furrows between rows. A few feet in and the corn closed around us, endless walls of long green leaves that towered over my head.

It was a cornfield that went on forever in all directions, or so it felt to a boy of twelve. I never felt lost, but there were times when I had no idea where I was and didn't care. Following Prissy would eventually get me back home.

There was comfort in following the dog. My father would not let me go into the corn without her, for she could smell a rattlesnake long before I would see or hear it. He taught me the difference between her behavior trailing birds and when she smelled a rattler coiled among the stalks, and she kept me safe. I never had to use the snakebite kit that I carried in my pocket.

I remember sitting in the dusty red soil surrounded by corn and smelling rain, then hearing drops spattering the leaves at the edge of the field, then finally seeing the dust rise as raindrops hit the ground just ahead of me. Prissy would find me, lie down next to me, and we would wait out the storm.

These are memories of half a century ago, of a different time and place, both gone. But I have kept a fondness for cornfields and cannot ride past one without slowing down and remembering what it was like to be deep inside. And every autumn, Marjorie, Lynne, and I drive over to Levant, Maine, to a farm where you can pay to get lost in a cornfield.

I pay with a smile, for it brings back those distant memories. As I watch Lynne, now sixteen but still capable of running through the corn as she did at twelve, I realize that this may be the closest she will come, can come, to the experience I had at her age.

We exit the maze into a field of pumpkins, some round and orange, others flat and orange-red, pumpkins clinging to their leafless vines, and begin our private searches for the pumpkin each will carve, jack-o-lanterns to sit on the porch railing until hard freezes turn them to mush. I recall finding the perfect pumpkin one year only to discover that a field mouse had found it first, opening a door to the inside at ground level.

We fill a wagon with future jack-o-lanterns, maybe a pie or two. Back at the barn, I pay the farmer for letting me harvest his pumpkins, then join the line for free ice cream. While waiting, I watch children feeding grain to goats that scamper inside a fence from one small outstretched hand to another; some goats eat the grain, others nibble on ice cream and shirt sleeves. Marjorie and I sit in the sun with our ice cream, content to watch the host of people, old and young, embracing the farm at harvest time.

The last year we went to this farm, the corn maze took the shape of a rocking horse. We were given maps with our tickets, but I stuffed mine in my back pocket and followed Marjorie through the maze, preferring to feel lost in the corn, if only for a while. For one brief moment, as we turned a corner along the path, I saw Prissy running ahead, in and out of the stalks, her nose to the ground.

## Composting in Autumn

September begins the busiest composting season. Through the autumn months, one of our compost bins fills to overflowing with discarded plant material from every part of the garden, while the contents of another bin are harvested.

It begins when the first chilly nights finish off already-worn-out potted annuals. These plants are dumped into an empty compost bin, their tightly woven rootballs chopped to pieces with a sharp spade, and then a thin layer of finished compost from the adjacent bin is added to kick-start decomposition.

It is an inaugural event. Over the next several weekends the pile grows with uprooted potato vines, the baked skins of winter squash and apple peels from a weekend soup marathon, mildew-covered summer squash plants, shriveled sweet pea vines, thick-stemmed sunflower stalks, the rest of the potted plants, overlooked cucumbers the size of footballs, worn-out pole bean plants, retired tomato vines, and a legion of weeds.

Everything gets chopped with the spade as much as possible. Vegetable scraps from the kitchen get tossed in, and a few shovelfuls of finished compost or green grass clippings are added every so often to fuel the fire with their high nitrogen content. The growing pile is soaked with water at the end of each day's work.

Then in late September or early October, we make one or two trips to the goat farm for composted goat manure. While most of these nannyberries get stockpiled under tarps for the winter (they are almost impossible to acquire in spring when they are actually needed), some are set aside to feed the host of composting bacteria. We cover materials thrown in the compost pile with the manure, repeating the process layer after layer.

So the pile grows through October. A layer of garden debris, a layer of composted manure, another layer of garden debris, and so on. If I have time to harvest a bucket or two of seaweed, that goes into the pile, and the contents of the kitchen compost bucket are tossed into the mix. On cold late October mornings, steam rises from the heart of the pile where bacteria are still hard at work.

We don't bother to turn this autumn compost pile. At some point the fire goes out and the pile acquires a cap of ice and snow. If I wanted to keep those thermophilic bacteria working through winter in the center of the pile, a minimum size for the bin would be 5 feet by 5 feet by 5 feet (ours are a more standard 4 feet by 4 feet by 4 feet), and here in northern New England, I would still need to insulate the perimeter of the bin with straw bales or other suitable material. This sounds like a project for my retirement years!

We are careful not to toss dandelions, quackgrass, and other perennial weeds into the compost pile, nor any weedy plant that has gone to seed. The roots and stolons of perennial weeds, as well as many weed seeds, can survive the hottest compost pile temperatures to show up in the garden wherever the compost is spread.

On the other hand, we do not hesitate to compost the spent nasturtiums, calendulas, and other self-sowing annuals that we like to see pop up in the garden as volunteers year after year. By the time they are tossed on the pile, they've sown so many seeds through the garden that a few more surviving the composting process will not be noticed.

As one compost bins fills, the bin that contains finished compost empties as its contents are screened, then spread around the strawberry plants, highbush blueberry shrubs, and raspberry primocanes. If there is a surplus of finished compost, the grape vine and peach tree

We made our compost screen out of hardware cloth, attaching it to a wooden frame that fits snugly over the wheelbarrow.

Raking the compost over the screen with the back side of a garden rake produces a load of finished compost ready to spread wherever it is needed.

are next in line, followed by the garden's trees and shrubs. We give priority to these permanent plantings because digging composted manure into the soil around them would destroy roots. The finished compost that we spread over the roots of these plants is quickly incorporated into the soil come spring.

Screening finished compost is always necessary. Corn cobs, orange rinds, and sunflower stems take forever to decompose, so anything too large to pass through a ½-inch wire-mesh screen is recycled through the growing compost pile. A coconut half-shell spent three years in our compost piles before finally ending up as a bird feeder on the back porch.

# *The Vegetable Garden in September*

In many New England gardens, early September is when the harvest season begins in earnest. While August gardens supply a trickle of tomatoes, cucumbers, and summer squash, the first week of September turns the spigot wide open. Suddenly the garden overflows with these crops as well as tomatillos, carrots, onions, leeks, and the first potatoes. Cucumber vines crawl through rows of bush beans as they crank up their yield, and winter squashes grow on vines weaving through corn stalks with ripening ears.

Methods of dealing with September's surplus vary with crop type. Tomatoes can be canned or frozen, cucumbers pickled, and many crops, such as potatoes, onion, winter squash, leeks, and carrots, can be stored as harvested if you can meet their requirements.

## Potatoes

Potatoes to be stored should not be dug until their tops have died and dried. They can even be left in the ground for a few weeks after the tops have died, if necessary. Dig the tubers carefully to avoid bruises and cuts, setting any damaged potatoes aside for immediate use. Do not wash or scrub potatoes intended for storage, but carefully brush off the excess soil.

Once dug, potatoes need to be cured for a week or two in a warm (60 to 75° F), moist, dark location. We use a corner of our basement, laying the tubers in single layers on wire racks. Curing will help heal any minor wounds on the tubers.

Once cured, potatoes are best stored in a cooler location with temperatures near 45° F. This is difficult to achieve in most homes (unless you have an extra refrigerator), so pick the coolest corner of the basement, a location that is also humid and dark. The closer you get to these temperature and humidity requirements, the longer the potatoes will keep.

## Winter Squash and Pumpkins

Avoid frost on the pumpkins! If winter squash, including pumpkins, are to keep in storage, they should be harvested before being exposed to frost. Harvest them when their rinds have hardened and the fruits have developed a deep, solid color. Leave about 3 inches of stem attached to pumpkins and 2 inches attached to other winter squash. Do not try to store a squash if the stem has been completely removed.

Cure pumpkins and winter squash at 80 to 85° F for seven to ten days, then store in a dry, well-ventilated location with temperatures near 55° F (45° F for acorn squash). In olden days, gardeners would store winter squash beneath their beds.

## Carrots

Harvest carrots for storage in late fall, before the soil freezes, and while the soil is dry. Cut off the tops to within ½ inch of the root. Soil can be removed with a quick rinse, but the carrots should not be scrubbed.

Once dry, place the carrots in plastic bags perforated with small holes, and store them in a cold (32 to 40° F), humid location. Carrots can also be stored in the garden by placing a deep layer of straw mulch over the plantings as the weather gets cold but before the ground freezes.

## Leeks

Summer leek varieties that are intended for harvest in the fall, such as 'King Richard' and 'Tadorna Blue,' are best left in the ground and harvested as needed until the first frost. They can be kept in the ground even longer if they are covered with a thick layer of straw or shredded leaves. At some point, however, before a hard freeze, you will want to dig the leeks still in the garden bed and prepare them for indoor winter storage in the following manner.

Place 2 to 3 inches of a damp medium such as peat, clean sand, or sawdust in a 5-gallon bucket or large tub.

Do not get the medium too soggy, or it will cause the leeks to rot. Stand the leeks with their roots on the medium and push them down to establish good contact between the roots and medium. The roots do not need to be completely covered, just firmly in touch with the medium.

Stored in this manner, the leeks will continue to grow, very slowly, rather than going totally dormant. Trim the tops a bit and store the bucket or tub in a cool dark place with some humidity, checking the medium occasionally to make sure it stays moist. Do not remove any of the outer leaves until you use the leeks.

## Sow Oats Wherever Soil Is Bare

We prefer oats as a cover crop, sowing them in September wherever the soil would otherwise remain bare. The seeds quickly sprout, and by October the sown beds are covered in a green blanket. Roots of the oat plants grow deep into the soil, mining nutrients to feed the growing shoots.

Unlike winter rye (see "Cover Crops and Green Manures" in Chapter 3), oats will winterkill, and you can dig in the mat of dead leaves as soon as the soil can be worked in spring, then wait two weeks before planting. Or, if you are in a hurry to sow peas, you can move the mat of grass leaves aside, sow the seeds in rows, and use the oat leaves as mulch between the rows.

Sow oat seeds at the rate of 2 pounds per 1,000 square feet. Sow the seeds as early as possible, for the sooner a cover crop is planted, the more organic matter it will produce for incorporating into the soil in spring.

September sown oats will winterkill, leaving a mat of dead leaves on top of the soil when the snow melts. This mat is rich in nutrients mined by the oats as they were growing, nutrients that are quickly released when the mat is dug into the soil.

## Sunflowers Reign in the Late Summer Garden

September finds our garden looking for the most part tired and ragged. Spent nicotiana and nasturtium lie on top of the compost pile, and the lower leaves of tomato and bean plants are paper thin and yellow. Raspberry plants that were the focus of our attention a few weeks ago have become a tangle of sprawling brambles.

As I leave the back porch steps for my morning walk through the garden, the sun rising behind me, I am greeted by the painted faces of a tribe of annual

At the back of the garden, the happy faces of tall sunflowers greet the day. Some look hung over, their heads hanging heavy with ripe seeds.

sunflowers peering through and over those brambles. It is one of the few remaining spots in the garden where vigor and vitality reign.

In most years we plant several sunflower varieties ranging in height from roughly 4 feet tall to 12-foot giants. All have dark brown clusters of fertile disc flowers surrounded by ray petals in shades of red, gold, rust, and burgundy. Flower heads range in diameter from 4 inches to over a foot.

Sunflowers nod as they greet the morning sun and anyone who enters the garden with it. This nodding or drooping of heads as they mature has the practical value of reducing disease that might develop if water accumulated in the seedhead.

Our sunflowers are a far cry from their North American ancestors, small multi-branched plants with small flower heads and small seeds that can still be seen growing along roadsides in the western United States. Domestication of *Helianthus annuus* began around 1000 B.C. as Native Americans began using its seeds for food, the flower petals for dyes, and the stalks for winter fuel. Cultivation of the species by the Plains Indians eventually resulted in seeds 1,000 percent larger than those of wild sunflowers.

By the early 1500s, Spaniards had introduced the plant to Europe, where it was grown mostly as a garden ornamental. Sunflowers were not developed as an agricultural crop until their introduction to Russia in the late 1600s. By 1940, Americans were able to import domesticated varieties of their native plant with oil content much higher than home-grown varieties. Today well over two million acres of sunflowers are grown in the United States.

Hybrid sunflowers now dominate both agricultural and ornamental varieties. However, a few seed companies are striving to preserve open-pollinated varieties that represent the heritage of this North American species.

In Marjorie's Garden we plant our sunflowers for the goldfinches, planning to eat only a few seeds ourselves and perhaps save a few for next year's garden. The birds know the seeds are there long before they are ripe, and occasionally we see a few finches pecking at the heads, eating a few of the developing kernels. Is less work involved without the hard seed coat in the way? They leave before they are halfway through the head, returning to dine at the porch feeders. (I've tasted those immature kernels and found them similar to green peanuts just pulled from the ground. Perhaps the goldfinches agree with me that sunflower seeds taste much better when fully ripe.)

We plant sunflowers for the bees. On chilly September mornings we often find a bumblebee or native solitary bee motionless on a sunflower head, waiting for the warmth of sunlight to resume its foraging.

And we plant sunflowers for the dining room table, filling vases with their smiling faces. They last for a week or so, dusting the tabletop with pollen as they enrich our lives. I know, there are sterile sunflower varieties bred for use as cut flowers, varieties that do not produce pollen. What a sad thought!

## The Season's Harvest on Display at the County Fair

For our family, the end of summer is punctuated by the Blue Hill Fair, held every year on Labor Day weekend. On Friday afternoon we watch Lynne and a friend on all the rides and eat forbidden food. We all ride the Ferris wheel. On Saturday we take in the horticultural exhibits.

Hundreds of vegetable and cut flower entries representing the best of the season's harvest are displayed on long-tiered rows that stretch the length of the exhibit hall. From artichokes to zucchini, every type of vegetable that will grow in this part of New England is represented by at least one entry. Not surprisingly, tomatoes, both ripe and green, are most abundant.

On prominent display at the hall's entrance are the year's entries in giant pumpkins. I recall one year when the "winner"— there are no real winners and losers at the fair, with every entry that meets the standards receiving a first- or second-place ribbon— weighed in at 410 pounds. While photographing the huge ribbed squash, I wondered about its fate after the exhibit. Would it become a hundred pies? A world record jack-o-lantern? I thought about the "Giant Pumpkin Drop," an annual harvest event hosted by a local farm at which a huge pumpkin is dropped from the boom of a crane, an ignoble end for a prize-winning fruit. The annual Pumkinfest & Regatta in Damariscotta, farther west along the Maine coast, features "boat" races in hollowed giant pumpkins, some powered by tiny outboard motors.

Out of the corner of my eye I noticed that my attention to this pumpkin was being watched by a young boy. I detected the pride of ownership in his scrutiny and asked, "Is this your pumpkin? Are you the grower?"

He smiled broadly and told me that he was 10 years old and that indeed he had grown the giant pumpkin in his Sedgwick, Maine, garden. With little prodding he told me that it was an Atlantic Giant pumpkin/squash hybrid

Weighing in at 410 pounds, this pumpkin took First Prize at the county fair.

(Right) The wild fruits of September.

(Below) Stigmas, styles, and swelling ovaries, the essence of the season!

grown from seed, and that he had nourished it through the season with plenty of water and Miracle Grow fertilizer. And when I asked him about the pumpkin's fate, his smile widened as he told me that after the fair it would be on display at his school.

Pride of accomplishment was abundant in the great hall. I ran into Betty, a gardener who had submitted eight vegetable entries along with cut sunflowers from her garden. She showed me her sunflowers and grape tomatoes, both blue ribbon winners that year.

Gardeners like Betty enter only the best of their garden's produce, and thus the exhibit is always a reflection of the summer's weather and other more nebulous factors that determine a gardener's successes and failures. It was a good year for tomatoes, she told me, and a good year for onions and zucchini.

There is no taste-testing of vegetable entries; judging is based solely on appearance. A soft spot or blemish on one of your tomatoes will cost you the blue ribbon, as will lack of uniformity in size. If your tomatoes have not had time to ripen, you can submit them green, but make sure they are all the same size and spotless. Most entries are picked the morning of judgment day.

Everyone I talked with agreed that participating in the vegetable exhibit is serious fun. It is also part of the education of a gardener.

In late September or early October, arborvitae trees bear sprays of old scale-like needles in the shaded middle of each branch. The copper-brown color of these needles combines with the apple-green younger needles for a striking autumn scene. The old needles eventually fall through the interior of the canopy to the ground below, forming a light brown carpet.

## *Trees and Shrubs in the September Garden*

In September, demands of the vegetable garden ease and there is time to regain a sharp focus on the rest of the garden. I walk with the dogs down the drive of a chilly Saturday morning, and sunlight shining on the shaggy, honey-colored bark of a yellow birch greets me like an old friend. The rest of the walk is a reunion with trees, shrubs, grasses, and forbs that I have largely ignored for months.

I harvest samples of all the wild fruits that the garden has to offer: waxy blue-gray bayberries; the bright reds of winterberries, wild rose hips, and clustered mountain-ash fruits; purple-black wild raisins and elderberries; the two-winged samaras of mountain maple and single-winged fruits of white ash; the dried seedheads of grasses and sedges; beechnuts and their prickly husks.

As I collect, I recall a quote from Henry David Thoreau: "How little observed are the fruits which we do not use!"

Almost at the porch steps, I catch a glimpse of red within the summersweet clethra colony surrounding the old pine tree. On close inspection, the red belongs to thousands of tiny pistils attached to what were flower spikes but now are elongated clusters of developing seed pods. What an interesting and beautiful sight!

### The Tree of Life

Arborvitae *(Thuja occidentalis),* a tree called cedar or Eastern white cedar in parts of New England, can live 300 years and lift its horizontal branches 60 feet or more into the sky. Its roots are anchored firmly in New England's past.

In *The Maine Woods*, Thoreau described how Native Americans constructed a carrying harness for canoes from cedar shingles and bark. The frames of the canoes were also made from arborvitae wood for the same reason that all the old lumber camps of the North Woods had cedar shingles: the wood resists decay forever.

Arborvitae means "tree of life," a name conferred by the king of France when cedar tea, a drink made by Native Americans from the bark and needles of the tree, cured Jacques Cartier's sailors of scurvy during their voyage up the St. Lawrence in 1535 – 36. Arborvitae thus became the first North American conifer to be cultivated in Europe, introduced to Paris by Captain Cartier on his return.

Never as tall as its neighboring conifers, arborvitae is a compact tree with a buttressed trunk and shredding reddish or silver-gray bark. The soft yellow-green foliage, apple-scented when crushed, consists of tiny, scaly leaves borne in flat, filigree sprays that are a favorite of florists. In late summer the sprays of foliage bear clusters of oval, pea-sized cones that slowly ripen from green to warm brown.

Seedlings may persist for decades in the shade of taller trees, waiting for a gap in the canopy. Those trees growing on rocky upland sites remain small, growing as natural bonsai forms with twisted trunks and gnarly crowns.

For a brief moment in early autumn, the old needles on a white pine turn to gold.

We are fortunate to have several old arborvitae growing in Marjorie's Garden, as well as plenty of seedlings to replace the old trees in years to come. My favorite time of year with the larger trees is late September into October, when the older scale-like needles turn copper-brown.

## White Pines in the Garden

A towering Eastern white pine *(Pinus strobus)* grows in Marjorie's Garden only 10 feet from the porch steps, a tree 60 feet tall with a trunk diameter at breast height of 25 inches. During the reign of King George III, a tree of this size would barely make the cut for use in the hull of an English warship, but by modern standards it is a tall pine.

The lichen-stippled trunk is branchless for the first 12 feet, followed by several whorls of dead horizontal branches, broken to various lengths by ice and snow load, then a broad-spreading canopy of branches bearing needles and cones.

The section of dead branches, all we can see of this tree from the upstairs windows, is the stage for Daybreak Theater, complete with accompanying symphony. As the sun rises above the trees along the Union River, chickadees fly in from the porch feeder to crack open sunflower seeds, using a pine branch as an anvil. Gravity-defying nuthatches creep upside-down on the trunk or along the lower side of a branch. A hummingbird surveys the garden from a branch tip, its ruby throat sparkling. Out of sight in the canopy, red squirrels chortle as they play hide and seek around the bole, crows caw, mourning doves hoot— oo-wah-hoo-oo-oo.

And there is middle-of-the-night entertainment from the same stage. Dogs bark at porch noises, waking us in time to see raccoons scurry up the pine's furrowed bark to a safe perch on a dead branch, bright eyes shining back at us in the dark.

Another white pine grows in the garden among the blueberry and strawberry beds. Seven years old and 6 feet tall, it is clothed in long, soft, blue-green needles with only a few inches of smooth gray bark visible between each whorl of branches. One side of each needle is marked with a thin silver stomatal band, the location of stomates, pores in the leaf that allow for gas exchange.

If only this little pine would stay small, or grow only a few inches each year so it would always grace the garden with its lovely foliage without blocking the sun. We know better, and are making plans to move it.

In late September, after a week or two of chilly nights, old needles on white pines begin to lose their chlorophyll, slowly turning brown. At a point in this process, at the peak of fall foliage color in white pine, and only in morning sunlight, the color is golden.

Two-year-old cones of white pine fall from the tree in late summer and fall. We gather these resin-coated cones into boxes on the back porch and use them through the winter to kindle stove wood each morning. Nothing gets the fire going any quicker.

## The Wild Raisins of Eastport

September in Eastport, Maine, is a feast for the eyes. The native landscape cascades down granite escarpments into backyards and roadsides, and you are surrounded by color: bright orange-red berries of mountain ash, pink and blue wild raisins, sky-blue asters bunched among the lichen-crusted rocks and along the deer paths, carpets of dark green juniper and blueberry. And always the two bays, Cobscook and Passamaquoddy, sparkling in the sunlight.

There is a sense of place in Eastport in September. Like so many New England small towns, the landscape defines the place, and there is no other place like it.

And so on September afternoons I wander deer paths over the granite outcrop behind the elementary school, across the street from the high school where I teach. At the very top I might stop to watch the soccer team on the field below, but not for long. You can't stop for long in this place without the imported red ants finding you, grabbing hold of foot or leg. It is an encounter that you will not soon forget.

I try to stay on the rocks and avoid stepping on the groundcover of native blueberry, juniper, bunchberry, and rhodora. In pockets of soil between the rocks grow wild raisin viburnums *(Viburnum nudum* var. *cassinoides)*, large, bushy shrubs that are covered in mid-September with clusters of ripening fruits, berries that turn from pink to blue to black as they mature.

It is easy to miss this sudden display of color, for the transformation from fiery pink to dark purple is rapid. Thoreau described plucking cymes of pink berries and putting them into his hat for their beauty, half of them turning dark purple before he arrived home. "And, moreover, those which before were hard and bitter, as soon as they turn dark purple are soft and edible, having somewhat of a wild-cherry flavor— but a large seed. It is a singular and sudden chemical change."

# September Is for Planting Trees and Shrubs

A Chinese proverb tells us that the best time to plant a tree was 20 years ago, and the next best time is now. In September, as we enjoy trees planted decades ago, we can also take an opportunity to plant a new tree or two for enjoyment in future years.

## Planting Container-Grown Trees and Shrubs

Unlike the hardwearing daylily that can be uprooted time and again, woody plants should grace the garden space we give them for decades. Their planting should be approached thoughtfully and methodically.

At planting, a container-grown tree or shrub has less than 20% of the absorbing roots as the same size plant established in the garden. The gardener's goal at planting is to promote rapid root growth and reduce the water stress imposed by a limited root system.

The fruits of wild raisin do not all mature at the same time, even within a single cluster, producing a striking mix of color on every shrub.

New England soils are often compacted or poorly drained, conditions that give woody plant roots a hard time. Compaction of the soil prevents adequate aeration of the root zone, while too much water drowns roots. Neither of these conditions is remedied by planting in a hole barely larger than the root ball.

Roots of plants placed in small holes soon reach the compacted native soil and, unable to penetrate it, begin to circle in the hole, much like the circling that occurs when roots meet the impenetrable sides of a pot. Circling roots can become girdling roots, cutting off water flow to the plant like a crimp in the garden hose.

Small planting holes surrounded by compacted soil may also drain slowly after a hard rain. Roots die in the waterlogged soil.

A current trend designed to avoid these problems involves planting trees or shrubs in large beds. This technique provides roots with a larger area in which to grow before encountering native soil that might be too compacted or poorly aerated.

Planting day begins by outlining the bed's border with a section of garden hose. Make the bed at least ten times as wide as the root-ball, wider if possible, and tilled or dug no deeper than the depth of the root-ball. As you work, think about the roots that will soon be growing outward from the trunk in all directions, absorbing water and nutrients within the top 12 inches of soil.

For particularly clayey or sandy soils, increase the organic matter content by digging a 3-inch layer of compost into the top 12 inches of the soil. The compost should be fully decomposed, since bacteria working on unfinished compost tie up nitrogen in the soil. If a recent soil test indicates a need to adjust the pH, the needed lime or sulfur can be worked into the soil at this point.

Give the new plant a thorough watering before gently removing it from the pot, always handling the plant by the rootball, never by the trunk or stem. Carrying or lifting a tree by the trunk can sever young roots and root hairs.

If the plant has been in the pot too long, it may have roots circling both the sides and bottom of the rootball. Using the edge of the spade, slice off the bottom mat of circling roots and toss it on the compost pile. Then, using your fingers, gently tease the circling roots from the sides of the rootball so that they spread outward in all directions.

Now form a planting hole in the middle of the bed. The hole should be no deeper than the rootball but at least three times as wide. This is easy digging, and I often do it by hand for small plants, removing the loosened soil one handful at a time, breaking up clods, gently moving earthworms out of the way.

Slope the sides of the hole toward the bottom, then use the edge of the spade to score the sides of the hole; smooth, slick sides can act as physical barriers to root growth. And remember, the rootball should rest on undug soil to prevent the plant from sinking after it is planted, so tamp down any loose soil in the bottom of the hole.

Place the plant in the hole with the roots spreading outward and begin to backfill with the soil removed from the hole. When the hole is one-third full, check to make sure the plant is straight and at the proper depth, then resume adding soil until the hole is filled. The top of the rootball should be level with the soil surface. Water the new plant thoroughly to eliminate large air pockets in the soil.

The finishing touch is a 3-inch deep mulch of aged compost or shredded leaves over the entire bed. This mulch will break down over the course of a growing season, providing all the fertilizer the plant needs, and you will need to replace it each year. Avoid chunky bark mulches that take forever to break down and feed the soil.

Also, avoid "volcano mulching," piling mulch against the trunk, which traps moisture against the bark, causing disease and decay. You should always be able to see a ring of bare soil around the base of the plant.

Spend the better part of a day planting a single tree, working slowly with spade and hands. Then spend the rest of your life watching it grow.

## Planting Field-Grown Trees

There was a time when most trees were field-grown, dug by hand from long rows, then balled and burlapped in the field before being trucked to the nursery yard for sale. Less than two decades ago, I stood in a Massachusetts field and watched a crew of four migrant Mexicans dig and wrap a 6-inch-caliper tree with a 60-inch soil ball in two hours. They were artisans, beautiful to watch.

They were also among the last practitioners of this skill. Everywhere else the task had been handed to one or two men and a tractor-powered tree spade. And then it became clear that a grower could not keep giving away a portion of his topsoil with every tree sold. Field-growing gave way to tree production on top of the ground in plastic containers.

Most shrubs and small trees are now container grown, but larger trees are still dug from the field and sold balled and burlapped (B&B). In this process, less than 20% of the tree's feeder roots are retained in the ball. In my opinion, buying a B&B tree is a gamble, with success determined in considerable part by the time the gardener is willing to spend planting the tree and then caring for it during the first few years after planting.

Planting a B&B tree requires a planting hole wide enough to allow the gardener to remove the rootball wrappings *after* the tree has been positioned in the hole. The hole should be 1 to 2 inches shallower than the height of the rootball.

Once the hole is dug, remove the wrapping added for convenience in marketing, such as shrink wrap or other container, but *do not* remove the burlap, wire basket, and twine that hold the rootball together until the tree is set in place.

Set the tree in the hole, making sure that the top of the rootball rises 1 to 2 inches above grade. This compensates for the extra topsoil added over the top of the ball during the digging and wrapping operations. If the rootball is too deep in the hole, remove the tree and correct the hole's depth, firming any added soil at the bottom of the hole.

Make sure the tree is standing straight, then firm a shallow ring of soil around the bottom of the ball to stabilize the tree. Now remove all of the wrapping on the upper 12 inches or the upper two-thirds of the rootball, whichever is greater. Wrapping materials left under the rootball are not a concern, since new roots will grow outward, not downward.

At this point, I like to use my hands or a digging fork to carefully remove soil from the edges of the rootball until I expose roots. This gives me a chance to inspect the outside of the ball for circling roots and either tease them outward with my fingers or cut them away with pruners. Removing the outer inch or two of soil also puts the roots in immediate contact with the backfill soil, eliminating potential problems with root growth at the rootball-to-backfill interface.

Should the backfill soil be amended with organic matter? (Remember, you have already significantly modified the soil in the entire wide-bed area by digging or tilling.) Generally, the answer is no, unless the backfill is mostly clay or sand, in which case amending it with no more than 25% (by volume) aged compost is recommended. The organic matter should be thoroughly mixed with the backfill, not added in layers.

Otherwise, amending the backfill soil is fraught with problems. It may delay growth of new roots beyond the planting hole and even lead to roots circling within the hole. The excess organic matter increases soil water-holding capacity, which may lead to drowning roots. And, as the organic matter decomposes, the soil volume diminishes, allowing the tree to topple.

Now begin filling the hole with backfill soil. Add the backfill in increments and allow gentle watering to settle the soil around the rootball. Never walk or stomp on the backfill, as this compacts the soil and shears roots.

When you're done, no backfill soil should cover the top of the rootball; backfill soil should cover the rootball "knees," or edges, and taper gradually down to the original soil grade. This approach compensates for the added soil on the top of the ball and avoids planting the tree too deep.

As with container-grown trees, the final step is mulching the entire planting bed with 3 inches of aged compost. Avoid "volcano mulching," piling mulch against the trunk, which traps moisture against the bark, causing disease and decay. You should always be able to see a ring of bare soil around the base of the plant.

### Relocating Trees and Shrubs in the Garden

Fall transplanting of existing trees involves the loss of a substantial portion of the tree's root system. Your chances of success increase as the trunk diameter decreases; trees that are less than 2 inches in trunk diameter will transplant with less branch die-back than larger trees. Still, I have successfully transplanted larger trees (3 to 4 inches in trunk diameter) in fall by digging as big a rootball as possible and watering diligently the following spring, providing an inch of water every week for the first growing season.

## *Gardening with Reilly*

A few years back, Marjorie decided to redesign the perennial bed, the largest one in the center of the garden. This decision was actually made by Reilly, our Brittany, who was four years old at the time and spent the summer of 2006 excavating sections of this bed in hot pursuit of chipmunks. Reilly's picture on the cover of this book was taken at about that time.

I doubt that the chipmunks would have established residence in the garden if we had not invited them to an endless dinner of squirrel corn and sunflower seeds. Once they realized that they would never have to venture more than a few yards from the back porch, they looked around for suitable living quarters.

Early in the summer it was hard to say where the little rodents might be when not stuffing their cheeks with seeds. But Reilly knew. She and Dixie, an older black lab-German shepherd and Reilly's willing partner in crime, rooted them out of the woodpile so often that they were forced to move to the garden bed. We soon noticed small holes at the soil surface but gave little thought to the massive network of tunnels that lay below. Then Reilly started her own Big Dig.

Soon the perennial bed was a network of deep trenches. The chipmunks were gone, along with most of the perennials. Reilly would come to the back door panting, her normally pink snoot and white legs dirt-black. At night, as she slept on her half of the sofa, she would relive the day, her front legs moving in rapid digging strokes, her muzzle twitching.

Through the ensuing years, cultivation of the soil continued to be but one of Reilly's contributions to the work of the garden. She also helped with the harvest, using the instant-consumption approach that she learned by observing those around her. She worked by our sides, picking snow peas from the trellised vine, only the plumpest and sweetest. She supervised the carrot harvest.

Reilly, three years old in this photo, has been a constant companion in Marjorie's Garden, always interested in what the vegetable garden has to offer.

In late summer she liked to stretch out in the grassy walks with a fresh-picked tomato, devouring the Sungold cherry tomatoes at the peak of ripeness but only nibbling the green plum tomatoes, preferences she shared with Dixie. We would have our pick of leaky green tomatoes scattered around the garden and, occasionally, in the house.

Reilly also worked with hardscape. A rock hound, she would scatter an endless supply of stones for me to find while cutting the grass. There has always seemed to be a lot of spontaneity in this effort. Trotting purposefully across the garden on some errand, she would stop abruptly in front of a partially buried rock, or perhaps one rock among many carefully placed around a planted tree or shrub. After minute examination by sniffing and pawing, she would heft the stone by mouth and carry it off to a grassy spot for a little quality chewing time.

As I write this in 2012, Reilly remains a constant presence in Marjorie's Garden. She is the only member of the family that bothers to turn the compost pile, and she leaves a lasting impression on newly raked planting beds. I don't see how an earnest gardener could manage without a gardening companion like Reilly. But age has taken its toll. She is now, at nearly 10 years old, blind. The blindness came on suddenly over the past month, and we may never know why, other than old age. She still follows chipmunks and red squirrels around the garden with her nose and ears, occasionally bumping into a fallen branch or garden gatepost. And with the blindness came symptoms of Cushing's disease, a malfunction of the adrenal gland that results in a ravenous appetite (she gained 20 pounds in a month) and unquenchable thirst.

Reilly's life has changed, but she is remarkably active for a blind creature. She hasn't spent any time lamenting her loss, but simply makes the best of the faculties that remain intact. And she still goes to the garden with me.

## The New England Garden in September, Zone by Zone

Throughout New England, September brings the final harvests of sweet corn, cucumbers, potatoes, and winter squash. The stalks and vines are heaped on the compost pile, where they are chopped into pieces and mixed with aged manure or finished compost. When first frost arrives at the end of the month or early in October, you can see steam rising from the center of the compost pile. Before the snow flies, be sure to map the passing season's garden to help you with next year's crop rotations.

| IN THE GARDEN | September | Date by USDA Hardiness Zone | | | | | Notes |
|---|---|---|---|---|---|---|---|
| | | 3 | 4 | 5 | 6 | 7 | |
| **GENERAL MAINTENANCE** | | | | | | | |
| **THE COMPOST PILE** | Fill compost piles to overflowing with spent garden plants. | | | | | | See Chapter 11 for details on autumn composting. |
| **VEGETABLE GARDEN** | Map the vegetable garden for planning next year's crop rotations. (Photo courtesy Charles Heaven) | | | | | | |
| | Make notes on variety performance. | | | | | | |
| | Test soil for pH and add amendments as directed by the soil test results. | | | | | | |
| | Sow oats in unused garden areas, 2 pounds per 1,000 sq. ft. | | | | | | Sow as early as possible to maximize organic matter production. |
| | Pull weeds before they go to seed. | | | | | | |
| **VEGETABLE CROPS** | | | | | | | |
| Carrots | Harvest carrots for storage in late fall, before the soil freezes, and while the soil is dry. | | | | | | See Chapter 11 for details on harvest and storage. |
| Corn, Sweet | After harvest, chop up corn stalks with a sharp spade or machete before tossing them on the compost pile. The smaller the pieces, the faster they will break down. | | | | | | (Photo courtesy Rasbak) |

| IN THE GARDEN | September | Date by USDA Hardiness Zone | | | | | Notes |
|---|---|---|---|---|---|---|---|
| | | 3 | 4 | 5 | 6 | 7 | |
| Cucumbers | Pull up and discard diseased and damaged plants as needed. (Photo courtesy Charles Heaven) | | | | | | |
| Garlic | Select replanting stock from recently harvested bulbs. | | | | | | |
| Leek | Dig summer varieties after first frost but before hard freeze. | | | | | | See Chapter 11 for details on winter storage. |
| Potatoes | Dig up all tubers after tops have died down, destroying any infected with late blight. | | | | | | Dig the tubers carefully to avoid bruises and cuts, setting any damaged potatoes aside for immediate use.<br><br>Do not wash or scrub potatoes intended for storage but carefully brush off the excess soil.<br><br>Once dug, potatoes need to be cured for a week or two in a warm (60° to 75° F), moist, and dark location.<br><br>Once cured, potatoes are best stored in a cooler location with temperatures near 45° F. |
| Pumpkins | Harvest when ripe and cure for 1-2 weeks in a warm location. | | | | | | Harvest when rinds have hardened and the fruit have a deep solid color.<br><br>Leave about 3 inches of stem attached. Do not try to store if the stem has been completely removed.<br><br>Cure at 80° to 85° F for seven to ten days, then store in a dry, well-ventilated location with temperatures near 55° F. |
| Squash, Winter | Harvest when ripe and cure for 1-2 weeks in a warm location. | | | | | | Harvest when rinds have hardened and the fruit have a deep solid color.<br><br>Leave about two inches of stem attached. Do not try to store if the stem has been completely removed.<br><br>Cure at 80 to 85° F for seven to ten days, then store in a dry, well-ventilated location with temperatures near 55° F (45° F for acorn squash). |
| Tomatoes | Continue removing flowers as they develop. | | | | | | |

| IN THE GARDEN | September | Date by USDA Hardiness Zone | | | | | Notes |
|---|---|---|---|---|---|---|---|
| | | 3 | 4 | 5 | 6 | 7 | |
| **SMALL FRUITS** | | | | | | | |
| Strawberries | Plants are forming flower buds for next year's crop, so be sure to water when the soil is dry at any time during the month. | | | | | | |
| **HERBS** | | | | | | | |
| Basil | Make one last cutting before first frost. | | | | | | |
| Dill | Let seeds mature on plants, then fall to the ground to sprout next year. | | | | | | |
| Cilantro | Let seeds mature on plants, then fall to the ground to sprout next year. (Photo courtesy H. Zell) | | | | | | |
| Fennel | Let seeds mature on plants, then fall to the ground to sprout next year. | | | | | | |
| Oregano | Dig, divide, and replant. (Photo courtesy Thomas Then) | | | | | | |
| Mint | Dig, divide, and replant. | | | | | | |
| **FLOWER BEDS AND BORDERS** | Test soil. | | | | | | |
| | | | | | | | |
| **ROSES** | Reduce watering at beginning of month.<br>Cease deadheading at end of month and allow hips to develop. | | | | | | |

# Chapter 12

# The Garden in October

*"For man, autumn is a time of harvest, of gathering together. For nature, it is a time of sowing, of scattering abroad."*

—Edwin Way Teale, *Autumn Across America,* 1990

***In October the sun travels a low arc,*** barely making it above the tree line surrounding Marjorie's Garden. Long shadows crisscross the garden throughout the day.

In the wild border at the foot of the drive, all the goldenrods have gone to seed, leaving only small clouds of fall asters and a few white campion flowering amid the brown stalks and seedheads. The campion's bright white flowers were with us through the summer, and now most of the branch tips carry upright brown capsules, miniature urns filled with poppy-like seeds ready to spill out with the next strong wind.

In October, leaves and fruits color the garden. Winterberries sparkle in the early morning sunlight; crimson leaflets of Virginia creeper fall on golden pine needles in the garden footpaths.

In late October, long after most of the birch and maple leaves are on the ground, while oaks paint the hills with dark reds and browns, witchhazels bloom in a corner of the garden. Their yellow leaves persist, as do the leaves of blueberries and viburnums. It will take another rain to weigh them down, another wind to carry them off.

I am always saddened by it, all this color gone in one stormy night.

There is still plenty to do in the vegetable garden, tasks focused on either putting the garden to rest for the winter or preparing for the coming gardening year. If you have yet to get to it, now is a good time to make a map of where every vegetable crop was grown this year, a key tool for making next year's crop rotation plans.

And October is a fine month to have your soil tested. You can find instructions for testing your soil in the sidebar on "When and How to Test Garden Soil" in Chapter 3.

Continue to spend chilly mornings pulling out freeze-killed vegetable plants, chopping them up with a sharp spade before adding them to the compost pile. Gather up all the mushy fruits and add them to the pile; you don't want to be pulling renegade tomato and squash seedlings next

*Facing page:* In October, New England woods and gardens are painted with the rich browns and yellows of American beech *(Fagus grandifolia)*. Many of the leaves persist, giving voice to winter winds

## Give Hardworking Garden Tools a Good Cleaning before Putting Them Away

By the end of October, tools that have worked hard for you all year deserve a little respect.

My garden tools live in the garden through the summer, rain or shine. When not in use, garden rakes and scuffle hoes lean against spades or digging forks, each awaiting its turn. Wooden handles become rough and cracked, and working ends stay caked with soil and composted manure.

But at the end of the gardening year I atone for summer sins by cleaning and restoring the tools before putting them away. Despite the summer abuse, the following approach has kept our tools in service for years.

To clean the working end of a digging fork, shovel, trowel, rake, or hoe, first remove all soil and other debris with soap and water. A stiff wire brush or putty knife will help remove stubborn caked-on soil and much of the rust. Any remaining rust can be removed by rubbing with coarse steel wool. Finally, give the tool head a thorough wiping down with a dry cloth.

When all the dirt and rust have been removed, coat the metal heads with a light oil to prevent rust formation. Many gardeners apply this oil by rubbing the metal with an "oil sock," an old sock filled with sand and soaked in fresh engine oil, then squeezed out and stored in a ziplock bag when not in use.

Other gardeners prefer to use a large pot or wooden box filled with oil-saturated sand (again, fresh engine oil). The cleaned tools are coated with oil by plunging their heads into the sand. Some gardeners store their digging tools through winter with the metal ends buried in the sand. Either way, the oil-soaked sand will last "forever" if you use it only for clean tools.

spring. If you have some composted manure handy, add it in layers with the chopped plants and fruits.

To help control bacterial spot, canker, early blight, alternaria, and other tomato diseases that can survive a winter in the garden, tomato cages and stakes should be cleaned of soil and plant debris, then disinfected with a solution of one part chlorine bleach to nine parts water for five minutes. Rinse well and let them air-dry before storing them for the winter.

Unlike the above diseases, the organism that causes late blight on tomatoes and potatoes does not survive winter above ground. It is, however, carried through the winter on live plant tissue, so be sure to dig up and destroy any infected potato tubers, those with brownish purple spots that become a wet or dry rot. Start fresh next year with certified disease-free seed potatoes. Do not compost infected tubers, as some plant tissue could survive the winter in the center of the pile.

Keep weeding! Frost-tolerant winter annuals, such as henbit and chickweed, as well as perennial weeds such as dandelions, can be pulled now rather than waiting until spring. This is also a good time to tackle quackgrass and other persistent grasses that creep into garden beds from the edges during the growing season. Use a sharp spade

Don't forget to recondition the handles of your tools. If a handle is loose, tighten the essential screws and bolts. More than once I have had to replace a screw or nut lost in the garden—scuffle hoes are particularly needy in this way.

If the handle is broken, replace it. Handles can be purchased at most hardware stores, but you may have to reshape the replacement handle to fit your tool's head. This can be done with a wood rasp or sanding machine.

Clean each handle with a stiff brush, then sand away nicks and splinters with medium-grade sandpaper. Finally, slowly rub the handle with a rag soaked in boiled linseed oil. Repeat the application several times, allowing time for the oil to be absorbed into the wood between applications.

When it comes to cleaning and sharpening pruners and loppers, I defer to Marjorie's time-tested methods; she has never had to replace a blade on her pruning tools. To keep them clean, she regularly wipes the blades with rubbing alcohol, a solvent that will dissolve pitch while removing rust.

For sharpening a bypass pruner, the type that cuts like a pair of scissors, you should sharpen only the side of the cutting blade with a beveled edge. For an anvil pruner, the type with a cutting blade that strikes an anvil-like surface, both sides of the cutting blade should be sharpened. For either type, sharpening is done by holding the open pruner firmly in hand and slowly passing the sharpening stone across the blade, following the contour of the blade as if you were removing a thin layer of metal from the blade surface.

Marjorie recommends sharpening with a DiaSharp Diamond Mini-Hone Kit, available from on-line retailers. The kit contains three stones in extra fine, fine, and coarse grits.

Clean and sharpen your pruning tools at the end of the year. Before putting them away, oil the moving parts of each tool with 3-IN-ONE general-purpose oil.

If, like me, you often work the soil with a digging fork, you have probably experienced the frustration of bending one of the tines on a buried root or rock. To straighten the bent tine, often first noticed when cleaning and putting the fork away for the winter, I use a long galvanized 1-inch-diameter pipe driven into the ground with about 12 inches left above ground. Sticking the bent tine into the end of the pipe, I can usually straighten it as good as new, or nearly so. This works well for pitchforks, too.

With freezing temperatures imminent, be sure to keep your garden hoses drained when not in use; there is nothing more frustrating than trying to use a hose filled with ice. When you no longer need hoses in the garden, let them drain completely, then coil them for storage in the garage or basement. If you have several hoses scattered about the garden, you may want to label each one by location.

October's work will be rewarded in May, when you take your favorite digging tool down and feel the smoothness of its handle in your palm for the first time in months.

or an edger to cut a straight line, then pull out the grass, making sure to get all of the roots.

## Strawberries and Raspberries

Strawberry growers should use October to stockpile weed-free straw for a November mulching of the strawberry beds. Be ready to apply a 6-inch layer of straw before the snow flies, but not before the plants have acclimated to cold weather as indicated by the leaves laying flat. For most New England gardens, mid- to late-November is strawberry-mulching time.

Wheat straw is absolutely the best mulch, as it is resists compaction and holds the insulating snow in place, a real benefit for strawberries growing in raised beds where snowfalls are subject to drifting. If you find wheat straw hard to come by, any baled straw will do, but do not use hay as it is full of weed seeds.

Now is a good time to straighten and secure raspberry primocanes, the canes that grew this year and will bear next year's berries. By October, the primocanes are sprawling across the walkways in our garden. Marjorie lifts each one carefully and binds it to the lattice with velcro tape. She leaves the current year's fruiting canes intact until spring to buffer the primocanes from winter winds.

## Planting Garlic

Two broadly defined types of garlic grow well in Marjorie's Garden, hardneck and softneck. Along with many other New England gardeners, we prefer the hardnecks, noted for their stiff stalks and large cloves. They produce a scape, or flowering stem, that bears tiny aerial cloves called bulbils. These can be saved and planted but will take two years to produce a bulb.

Most hardneck growers prefer to cut the scapes as they develop and slice them into stir fries. This does not interfere with normal bulb development and some gardeners believe that removing the scapes actually diverts more energy to bulb growth.

The bulbs produced by a hardneck garlic variety are relatively few in number but huge in size. Hardneck varieties do not store as well as the softneck types, which is why some gardeners grow some of each. For garlic varieties that perform well in New England gardens, read Ron and Jennifer Kujawski's essay, "For the Savory Smell of Success, Grow Garlic," in Chapter 13.

As the name suggests, softneck garlics have a more pliable stalk. They produce smaller bulbs, each bearing 12 to 20 cloves. Since they do not produce a scape, they can be braided for storage.

Most garlic sold at the grocers is of the softneck type, though you should not use grocery-store garlic for planting as the varieties typically come from California or China and are not suited for growing in New England. Also, they may have been treated with a sprouting inhibitor to lengthen storage life.

On the other hand, if you see garlic for sale at a local farmers' market, ask the grower which variety they are growing and consider purchasing some for planting. Locally grown organic garlic will be a type hardy for the area and will not be treated with sprout inhibitor. Recommended softneck varieties for gardens throughout New England include New York White (the local favorite on Cape Cod), Artichoke, Idaho Silver, California Early, Red Toch, and Silverskin.

The best time to plant garlic is two weeks after the first killing frost, or so some experts say; others say anytime between October 1 and November 15 is good. Either way, the planted cloves will have time to develop some roots before going dormant for the winter.

It is possible to plant garlic too early. Rather than planting by the calendar, be sure to wait until after the first hard freeze. Cloves planted into warm soil will sprout and then be killed by a hard freeze. Dorcas Corrow, whose garden is featured in Chapter 13, always plants her garlic on Veterans Day.

Begin planting by preparing a well-groomed bed enriched with compost or composted manure. Break each bulb into individual cloves, then plant the cloves with the pointed end up, 4 to 6 inches apart, covering the tip with 2 to 4 inches of soil. If planting in rows, allow 12 to 18 inches between rows.

About four weeks after planting, as the ground begins to freeze, cover the planted area with 6 to 12 inches of straw. This will prevent heaving of the soil with freezing and thawing and ensure survival of the planted cloves through extreme cold.

As the ground thaws in the spring, look for green shoot tips beneath the straw. When they emerge, pull the straw back, but leave it in place between rows to smother weeds and retain water in the soil. If you have planted in a wide row or bed, completely remove the straw.

# *Herbaceous Perennials for the October Garden*

There are several herbaceous perennials that belong in the October garden. Some, such as heleniums, begin flowering as early as August and continue into autumn, while others wait until late September or early October to burst into bloom. While I have presented some of these plants in earlier chapters, I think it is fitting to bring all of these exuberant perennials together as part of a colorful autumn border.

## Smooth Blue Aster (*Symphyotrichum laeve*)

The smooth blue aster is a native fall-flowering plant throughout New England. It grows 2 to 3 feet tall with a central stem that produces a few flowering side shoots in its upper half. Each flowering stem produces panicles of numerous daisy-like flower heads, each about ½ to 1¼ inches across. As with most members of the sunflower family, each head has about 15 to 30 lavender or light blue-violet ray flowers surrounding a disk of yellow

## Bringing the Season's Harvest Together in a Soup Pot

Few of us have enough garden space to grow everything we want to freeze or can for winter meals. We rely on local farmers to fill the gap.

In early October, Marjorie and I visit a local farmer's roadside stand to stock up on delicata squash and red onions. Later in the month we travel a few miles down the road to a pick-your-own orchard and stock up on apples for cooking and eating. From these two growers we acquire everything we need to make Gingered Squash and Apple Soup.

Why delicata squash instead of Waltham butternut or any other type of winter squash? It comes down to flavor. We've used butternuts in a pinch, but the soup is not as creamy or rich in flavor.

And it comes down to the ease of working with delicata. A Japanese "pumpkin" squash (also called sweet potato, peanut, or Bohemian squash), delicata is smaller than a butternut and has a thin skin that is much easier to cut through than other types of winter squash. The skin is edible, and delicious when roasted.

At the farmstand, delicatas are stacked in a waist-high bin for easy picking. We take our time, filling boxes with fruits that have a deep yellow skin and no bruises or cuts that would shorten their storage life. We store most of the squash in the basement, placing them in single layers on stacked wire racks, but we always keep a few on hand in the kitchen.

Perhaps because of their thinner skin, delicatas will not store as long as butternuts and other winter squash. We can count on them to store well through November, giving us time to use them up.

Once we've managed to bring all the soup ingredients together, October and November weekends become squash-baking marathons. Containers of cooked squash and squash soup fill the basement freezer. We always time the last batch out of the oven for the evening meal.

### *Gingered Squash and Apple Soup*

3 cups baked delicata squash (about 2½ pounds fresh)
2½ tbsp. butter
2 medium red onions, coarsely chopped
1½ pounds sweet apples, peeled, cored, and sliced (salt to taste)
4½ cups vegetable broth
¾ cup dry white wine
1½ tbsp. minced fresh ginger
2 tbsp. chopped fresh cilantro (more for a garnish, if you like)
pepper to taste

Open the wine, set aside ¾ cup for the recipe, and pour yourself a glass.

Cut the squash in half (lengthwise), wipe the cut surface of each half with olive oil, and place the halves cut side down on a lightly oiled baking sheet. Roast in the oven at 375° for 50 to 60 minutes or until a fork will easily penetrate the flesh. Let it cool until you can handle it, then scoop out the soft flesh, discarding any seeds, and measure out 3 cups.

In a very large non-stick sauté pan, melt the butter and cook the onions in it over medium heat, stirring often, until they are very soft. Add the apple slices and a little salt and keep cooking for 15 minutes more, stirring frequently.

Add the baked squash, vegetable broth, wine, ginger, and chopped cilantro, and simmer another 15 minutes. Everything should be very soft.

Purée the soup in a blender in batches until perfectly smooth, then add salt and pepper to taste. Serve hot, sprinkled with cilantro leaves.

The essential ingredients for Gingered Squash and Apple Soup are gathered together from local growers.

In Patricia Crow's Cape Cod garden, the flowers of the smooth blue aster cultivar 'Bluebird' provide much-needed nectar for monarch butterflies about to embark on their long flights. The flowers also attract native bees, syrphid flies, and hoverflies. The caterpillars of the silvery checkerspot butterfly feed on the foliage along with caterpillars of many moth species. (Photo courtesy Patricia Crow)

flowers. These tiny central flowers turn reddish-yellow as they age.

The common name, smooth blue aster, reflects the lack of hairs on the stem and leaves.

Flowering begins in late September in Zone 5 and lasts three to four weeks. During October, the small fruits, called achenes, develop with small tufts of light brown hair that aid their dispersal by wind.

Smooth blue aster has many fine qualities, including adaptability to a variety of soil types, beautiful flowers, attractive foliage, and stems that remain erect during the blooming season. It performs best in full or partial sun and mesic soils, typically fertile loam or clay loam. Plants withstand drought fairly well.

## Swamp Milkweed *(Asclepias incarnata)*

By October, caterpillars of the monarch butterfly are munching on the leaves of swamp milkweed as the first ripe seed capsules are splitting open to release their seeds to the wind.

Milkweed seedpods open in the fall to release seeds that are scattered by the wind. Silky hairs at the end of each seed form a parachute-like tuft that aids in dispersal.

Swamp milkweed is a tall plant with fragrant clusters of pink and light purple flowers (see photograph in Chapter 9). As its name implies, it prefers moist to wet soils and is ideal for planting in a rain garden or along the edge of a pond. Best grown in full sun, it tolerates heavy clay soils and is very deer-resistant.

## Stonecrop *(Hylotelephium spectabile)*

Known by several common names, including showy stonecrop, showy orpine, ice plant, and butterfly stone crop, this plant (formerly named *Sedum spectabile)* is Asian in origin but has escaped cultivation to become naturalized in small areas of Connecticut and Massachusetts. It has an upright habit, reaching 18 inches in height and width with leaves that are bluish-green and semi-succulent. Clusters of pink flowers open in late summer and last until frost. A hybrid between this species and *H. telephium* led to the introduction of the very popular cultivar 'Autumn Joy.'

Stonecrops should be grown in full sun and well-drained, neutral to slightly alkaline soil that has been amended with plenty of compost. Divide the clumps every three or four years. Plants often flop late in the season and may need staking.

Beautiful in the October border, stonecrop is very popular among bees as a source of late-season nectar.

Cultivated forms of *Helenium autumnale* can be found in a wide array of rich colors from pale yellow to deep red and bronze.

## Sneezeweed *(Helenium autumnale)*

*Helenium autumnale,* common sneezeweed or dog-tooth daisy, occurs in wet meadows, thickets, swamps, and river margins throughout New England. Garden forms of this species (introduced in Chapter 10) also show a preference for damp conditions, although they will tolerate all but the driest of soils. They can be grown on heavy clay that is amended annually with compost.

## Giant Sunflower *(Helianthus giganteus)*

Native throughout New England, the giant sunflower lives up to its name, reaching 12 feet in height when grown in rich garden soil. Without sturdy staking, you will go to the garden the morning after an October storm and find some of its tall stems lying on the ground. Not a candidate for the perennial border, it is better suited to stand alone at a pond's edge or where woods and clearing meet.

Giant sunflower is not particular about soil type, growing well in sandy, loamy, or clayey soils as long as they are well-drained. It is cold hardy to USDA Zone 4.

Given its size and tendency to be flattened by wind, what gardener would grow this mammoth plant? Anyone interested in attracting wildlife, for one. The nectar and pollen of the flower heads attract bumblebees, hoverflies,

The flower heads of the giant sunflower are borne on numerous leafy branches in the top third of the main stem, each head measuring 2 to 3 inches across. The first heads appear in late September, but the main show is reserved for October.

butterflies, and other pollinators. Other insects feed on the foliage and stalks, including numerous species of beetles as well as caterpillars of the silvery checkerspot and painted lady butterflies. The seeds are eaten by mourning doves, white-winged crossbills, goldfinches, black-capped

### Tipping the Balance toward Native Trees and Shrubs

In a garden in tune with nature, the majority of woody plants should be native species of trees and shrubs that have co-evolved with the insects, birds, and other animals of the region. Such a garden grows as part of the local ecosystem and helps sustain local biodiversity.

But this idea of a garden should not preclude planting non-native trees and shrubs. It is a matter of balance.

Have you noticed that one of the strongest selling points used to market a non-native tree or shrub is the phrase "pest free"? And it's a fact. Non-native plants typically are not the target of native herbivores because they have no evolutionary connection with them. By the end of summer, most of the leaves on red maples and sugar maples are tattered and torn by the munching of native insects, while the leaves of nearby Norway maples remain intact.

I've noticed the same lack of herbivory on the red-vein enkianthus and katsura in Marjorie's Garden. Their autumn leaves are as clean and fresh as if new.

I have no misgivings about planting the few non-native trees and shrubs that grace our garden. None is invasive, and each has special significance. The redbud *(Cercis canadensis)* reminds me of my Georgia roots. The enkianthus, one of Marjorie's favorite small trees, enriches our lives in every season (the bumblebees treat it as a native plant when it is in bloom), and our Octobers would be poorer without the katsura.

If I had to guess, I would say that non-native woody plants make up less than one percent of the woody plants in the garden. Three red oaks and several yellow birches, native favorites of insect herbivores and predators, more than tip the scale, their canopies alive with birds throughout the year.

So, as a gardener in tune with nature, you can feel good about growing your favorite non-native trees and shrubs. Just do your homework (see the sidebar, "Screening for Invasive Potential," later in this chapter) to make sure none of your favorite non-natives is considered invasive (and thus a threat to local biodiversity), and keep the balance tipped toward native plant species.

chickadees, white-breasted nuthatches, tufted titmice, and various sparrows.

## *Native and Non-Native Trees in the Autumn Garden*

Marjorie and I prefer hardwoods over conifers, except for white pines, tamaracks, and arborvitae. In other words, out with the spruce and firs, particularly since the spruce in and around our garden are all towering black spruce that block the sun, and the firs are a secondary host to witch's broom on blueberries.

In October the hardwoods in Marjorie's Garden, both native and non-native, surround us with a procession of color that begins with the yellow birches and ends with the red oaks, all of which were mature trees before there was a garden. We transplanted a white ash that was struggling for existence at the foot of one of the oaks (birds and squirrels have no sense of garden design), moving it into one of the garden's beds. It is still a young tree, stretching to find its space in the sun, full of the promise of autumns to come.

We also planted a katsura *(Cercidiphyllum japonicum)* and a redvein enkianthus *(Enkianthus campanulatus)*, both non-native tree species that add their unique foliage colors to the October garden. There are other trees, both native and non-native, that we would have planted if only there were more room. In a small garden the struggle between a love of trees and a passion for growing vegetables is endless.

### Autumn Birches

I am fond of all New England's native birches, including paperbark birch *(Betula papyrifera)*, grey birch *(B. populifolia)*, river birch *(B. nigra)*, and yellow birch *(B. alleghaniensis)*. We have all but river birch growing in our garden, and we have visual ownership of several river birches in the area. In my opinion, the best of the bunch for year-to-year consistency in autumn foliage color are yellow birch and the 'Heritage' cultivar of river birch.

### Moose Maple

At the end of our driveway and a few yards into the woods, a moose maple *(Acer pensylvanicum)* has been growing for many years. It is crowded in there, competing with a black

The 'Heritage' cultivar of river birch combines exfoliating outer bark, salmon-colored inner bark, and yellow fall foliage for a striking autumn display.

Even after a dry summer, the leaves of yellow birch begin to turn golden yellow in late September, beginning with those closest to the trunk. By early October, foliage closer to the branch tips begins to turn until suddenly, while your back is turned, the entire tree turns golden.

A moose maple at the peak of fall color lights up the woodland garden.

cherry and several birches for every necessity of life. Its green-and-white striped trunk (another common name is striped maple) is contorted and branchless beneath a narrow one-sided canopy.

But for a few days every October, this maple stands alone, its large lemon-yellow leaves lighting up the woods like a beacon, a celebration of the season.

I hesitate to recommend moose maple to your garden, as it is favorite browse for moose and deer. I've only seen stately trees of this species on the northern end of Vinalhaven Island, off the coast of Maine, were there are no moose and deer are rare. Elsewhere, moosewood is almost always a multi-stemmed shrub.

If you have one growing unmolested in the nearby woods, clear it a space to grow. It will reward you in autumn with a short but lovely autumn scene. When I see one in the October woods, I think of a line from Robert Frost: "*Happiness makes up in height for what it lacks in length.*"

## Katsura

At times I think that we were foolish to plant a katsura tree *(Cercidiphyllum japonicum*, native to China, hardy throughout New England, a large shade tree with the potential to reach 60 feet or more in height) within 10 feet of the vegetable garden's eastern border. But I could not help myself, for I love the shape and autumn foliage of katsura, and Marjorie was no help—she was right there with me.

So while we cut down black spruce and balsam firs to bring more sun into the vegetable garden, we watch the katsura grow taller and stouter. We've limbed it up to the height of our tallest orchard ladder and we've trimmed its

Oh, but what a lovely tree in October when the round-oval leaves of the katsura tree, like those of a small redbud (*Cercis* = redbud genus and *phyllon* = Greek for leaf), turn yellow! And when it is time for the leaves to break the connection with their stems, the air nearby is filled with the scent of ripe apples and burnt sugar. How can you not want such a tree in your life?

In autumn the leaves on our enkianthus turn a mix of brilliant red and gold. Fall color is variable within the species, with some plants turning all red—a better red than the invasive burning bush *(Euonymus alatus)*—or all yellow. Cultivars have been selected for red fall foliage, others for deep red flowers.

sail, widening the spaces between scaffold branches. We'll grow lettuce in the shade of its spreading canopy.

## Red-Vein Enkianthus

The red-vein enkianthus in Marjorie's Garden *(Enkianthus campanulatus*, native to Japan, hardy throughout New England to Zone 5), now in its tenth year, flowers in early June (see page 134), clusters of creamy-yellow bells with deep red veins hanging below the whorl of leaves at each branch tip. The flowers are slightly larger than those of highbush blueberry but have the same drooping habit. The fruit is a dry seed capsule, and the tiny seeds are not dispersed by birds into natural areas.

It is now about 8 feet tall, and we have pruned this naturally shrubby plant into a small multi-trunk tree, highlighting its layered branches. It may eventually grow to 12 feet in height, the perfect small garden tree. Kept in shrubby form, red-vein enkianthus also makes a beautiful informal hedge.

At the beginning of color change, enkianthus leaves turn a bright golden yellow, with some leaves still showing a little green. The dark brown seed capsules provide a striking contrast in both color and texture.

## Screening for Invasive Potenial

Screening non-native plant species for invasive potential is the work of gardeners; no one else is going to do it for us. Growers and garden center managers have demonstrated, for the most part, a "buyer beware" operational philosophy. Many will eagerly sell you a Norway maple, Japanese barberry, burning bush, or any of several other known invasive species; all you have to do is ask.

Screening for invasiveness requires the gardener to do a little research, a process greatly facilitated by the Internet. Simply coupling the scientific name of a plant with the phrase "invasive species" in a search engine will bring up helpful links. For example, if you search "Acer platanoides invasive species," you will be inundated with links to sites that leave no question about the invasive potential of Norway maple.

Entering "Enkianthus campanulatus invasive species," you find sites that recommend the use of red-vein enkianthus as a substitute for the non-native invasive burning bush *(Euonymus alatus)*. You will find no evidence that enkianthus is an invasive threat anywhere in the United States.

There are more elaborate screening tools, including a decision-making model developed by Dr. Sarah Reichard of the University of Washington's School of Forest Resources. Dr. Reichard specializes in the biology of invasive species.

Her model is a set of questions, each answered "yes" or "no," and it starts with the question, "Does the species invade elsewhere, outside of North America?" For Norway maple, the answer would be an easily documented "yes."

The second question—"Is it in a family or genus with species that are already strongly invasive in North America"—would also be answered "yes" for Norway maple, since box elder *(Acer negundo)* has proven to be invasive outside its native region. This leads quickly to the decision to reject Norway maple as a candidate for North American landscapes. Unfortunately, Dr. Reichard's decision-making scheme was created long after the Norway maple was unleashed upon American landscapes.

Invasive species are available for sale in local garden centers not from lack of evidence regarding their invasive potential, but because there is a lack of concern by growers and retailers for the destruction they cause to ecosystem integrity and biodiversity. This means that it is up to gardeners, you and me, to stop the trade in invasive species with informed, intelligent choices. We have to screen non-native plants for invasive potential before buying.

The red-vein enkianthus in Marjorie's Garden is the highlight of our late autumn garden. But every year, about this time, I check to make sure *Enkianthus campanulatus* has not become an invasive weed somewhere in the world. It is a gardener's duty. See also this book's appendix.

A few days later, the golden enkianthus leaves are infused with red. A few more days and the ground around the little tree is littered with these colorful leaves.

When it comes to fall foliage, not all red oaks are created equal. The leaves of some trees turn yellow or yellow-brown, while the leaves of other trees, like this young oak in Marjorie's Garden, take on a rich red color.

## Red Oak

My life is richer for having watched the largest red oak in Marjorie's Garden grow over the last decade. I've seen it grow from immaturity into an annual producer of acorns, and now I can find seedlings from those acorns scattered about the garden.

In October the leaves of all the garden's red oaks are ragged and riddled with holes, yet they still put on quite an autumn show. The maples have shed their technicolor leaves, and only the red oaks remain in leaf, painting the garden in rich earthy tones of yellow-brown and russet red. And then one night a strong wind breaks the already weakened connection between petiole and twig, and rain-soaked oak leaves fall to earth, signaling the end of autumn.

## Tamarack

There are three times during the year when tamarack *(Larix laricina,* also northern larch or hackmatack) captures my attention, first in early spring when the soft, bright, light-green tufts of needles first appear along the twiggy branches, again in October when I come across a stand of dusky-gold tamaracks growing among dark green firs, and

A common sight from New England roadsides in October are mixed stands of dusky-gold tamarack and dark green conifers.

finally in the dead of winter when folks from away mistake these deciduous conifers for dead spruce as they drive by the frozen bogs where tamarack grow.

You would have to travel to South Carolina to see the only other deciduous conifer—bald cypress, *Taxodium distichum*—native to the eastern half of the United States. But tamarack is a common site in wetlands across New England, and it is quite happy in drier sites as well.

"Tamarack" is Algonquin for "wood used for snowshoes." Hackmatack was also prized by Maine's wooden-boat builders for use as highly rot-resistant knees and floor timbers.

We have several young trees growing in the thin rocky soil along our driveway, the parent trees growing a mile away as the crow flies, their roots in wetter soil. We keep the space around our tamaracks free of competing spruce, but we let a young fir or two grow nearby, imagining these two conifers growing side-by-side in an October yet to be.

# *New England Native Shrubs: Autumn Color Closer to the Ground*

I acquired my love for autumn as a boy hunting bobwhite quail in November, following my dad and our setter, Prissy, through Georgia cornfields surrounded by blazing red tupelos and multicolored sweetgums with green, red, and yellow leaves, all on the same tree. After shooting on the covey rise we would watch the singles sail into a bottom cane break, give the dog time to find the downed birds and the singles time to leave a scent, and then walk to the cane through oak-leaved hydrangeas with russet red leaves, large and lobed, autumn color at a more muted level.

As if its spring flowers and summer fruits were not enough, highbush blueberry rewards the gardener a third time with brilliant red autumn color.

On closer inspection, not every leaf is the same shade of red. Some are barely red at all.

Some of the blueberry leaves hang on long enough to be kissed by a late October freeze. Such a sight is truly a special moment in the autumn garden.

Beyond the vegetable garden, the bright red of highbush blueberry leaves is echoed in the autumn foliage of Virginia creeper *(Parthenocissus quinquifolia)*, a vine that will creep to the top of the tallest tree while covering the ground around it.

Dad is gone, Prissy followed by other dogs but never replaced, and I no longer go after wild birds with a shotgun. Autumn comes much earlier here in Maine, and the trees are golden-yellow birches that light up the woods and, of course, sugar maples.

But in October, in Marjorie's Garden, I still find autumn color at different levels. I find it in the bright reds of highbush blueberry leaves and the scarlet leaflets of Virginia creeper, in the sprawling hobblebush viburnum's deep reds and yellows, and in the mapleleaf viburnum's salmon pink and purple leaves. I find it in the brown-flecked yellow leaves of summersweet clethra and in bright red winterberries.

Virginia creeper, often called woodbine in New England, can be found on lists of vines that are seldom severely damaged by deer. Also recommending woodbine is its fast growth rate, once it is established in the garden. The berries, also ornamental, ripen in late summer, and most are quickly eaten by birds, mice, skunks, and chipmunks. I do recall snowy winters in Orono, Maine, when clusters of the dried blue fruits hung like ornaments from leafless stems that traced the outer walls of campus halls—places where no bird or rodent dared to go.

Over the years I have accumulated a photographic

Mapleleaf viburnum's fall leaves are painted with the colors of an October sunrise.

Following summersweet clethra's August flowers are small rounded seed capsules, each one-eighth inch in diameter and containing several seeds, all packed into dense spikes. These tan-colored capsules persist into autumn, gradually darkening in color and adding textural depth to the brassy fall foliage.

By late autumn, winterberry's leaves have dropped, setting the stage for a winter-long display of bright red fruits.

Winterberry *(Ilex verticillata)* fruits begin to ripen in early autumn, and in some years the fruits will turn red while the leaves are turning from green to yellow.

portfolio of Virginia creeper growing into tree canopies and upon walls, trellises, and high fences, always admiring its exuberance, a characteristic some label as invasiveness. A native plant, however, cannot be invasive, only aggressive or fast growing. And isn't this what we want when it comes to covering a fence?

I did not know mapleleaf viburnum *(Viburnum acerifolium)* before I came to the Maine woods and found it growing beneath a canopy of white pines, a colony of spindly plants that I took at first for red maple seedlings. In Marjorie's Garden, I've come to know it as a robust suckering shrub that can grow to 6 feet tall.

While it appears that each witchhazel flower is monoecious, equipped with both male and female flower parts, in fact each blossom is either functionally male or female, and cross-pollination by insects, chiefly small gnats and bees, is necessary. Botanists believe that this autumn flowering habit evolved as a means of reducing

Eventually, as October's nights grow longer, witchhazel leaves tarnish and drop but the flowers persist, clustered in threes along the stem where leaves were once attached. When temperatures are below freezing, the petals roll into tightly curled balls, extending the life of the flower to ensure pollination when the temperature rises.

competition for pollinators. It would appear that in the October garden, the common witchhazel has the stage all to itself.

The fruits of witchhazels, fuzzy two-beaked woody capsules, take a full year to ripen. The capsules explode violently, ejecting the shiny, hard, black seeds more than 30 feet away from the parent plant. After expelling their seed, the open capsules remain on the plant for yet another year.

## Proper Protection Can Help Hardy Roses Survive Winter

In my education as a gardener, I had a rose period. It was long ago, but I remember having a penchant for old English shrub roses. I don't remember ever worrying about winter protection for my roses, but then I lived in coastal South Carolina where, I now realize, there was no winter.

Non-native roses of all types, including hybrid teas, grandifloras, and floribundas, can be grown throughout New England if the gardener focuses on the more winter-hardy varieties. Some climbing roses and many old-fashioned shrub roses are hardy throughout New England as well, including the Explorer varieties developed in Canada for superior winter hardiness.

Among my favorite autumn shrubs is common witchhazel *(Hamamelis virginiana)*. You will find it growing in the forests of New England as a large shrub, 15 to 20 feet tall, with a full rounded crown and a vase-like habit. In the garden it can be pruned into a small multi-trunk tree with smooth gray bark.

Like the taller birches in the nearby forest, the brassy yellow fall foliage of witchhazel lights up the garden in October. Witchhazel stands alone among October shrubs in bearing small flowers, each with four ribbon-like petals of the same yellow as the leaves.

Zone 4 and 5 winters can damage even the hardiest of roses in several ways: rapid changes in temperature; root injury from desiccation as a result of plants being heaved by alternate freezing and thawing; gnawing by mice beneath the snow; and snow or ice breakage. Often, it is the rapid changes in temperature and the repeated freezing and thawing that do the most damage. The good news is that all these problems can be mitigated by proper winter protection.

Winter protection begins by ending nitrogen applications in late August. Nitrogen encourages the growth of new shoots, which will be less winter hardy than the older shoots. If you see any new shoots starting to grow from the base of the plant in September, remove them to prevent freeze-damage to the plant.

Many rose growers believe that you can increase the winter hardiness of your roses at least one zone by autumn fertilizing with potash. One formulation of potash, known as Sul-Po-Mag, also contains two other beneficial nutrients, sulfur and magnesium. Potash is also in organic materials such as manure, wood ashes, and seaweed.

Stop deadheading your roses (removing spent blossoms) after October 1, and allow them to develop hips (fruits). Fruit development promotes hardening of plants as they go into winter.

Beginning in early September, gradually reduce watering. This will also help initiate the process of hardening. Continue to monitor soil moisture through the fall, watering only as needed to avoid extremely dry soil. Stop all watering when the ground freezes.

Don't do any pruning during the fall except for removing dead, damaged, and diseased canes. Wait until the end of April, at the earliest, to prune your roses for summer growth and flower production.

Winter protection techniques are designed to keep rose plants uniformly frozen through the winter and to prevent the damaging effects of freeze-thaw cycles. Do not start too early! Wait until a hard killing frost has caused most of the leaves to fall, then clean up all dead leaves and other debris around the base of the roses. This eliminates the overwintering stages of fungal diseases and should result in far fewer disease problems next year. Throw the debris into the trash or fire rather than into the compost pile, where temperatures are not high enough during winter to kill the diseases.

In late October or early November, before winterizing your roses, remove all the old mulch from around the plants and put down new organic mulch such as composted manure or seaweed. This helps control diseases and will jump-start growth in the spring.

In mid- to late-November, a couple of weeks before the ground freezes and when the plants are fully hardy, bush roses (climbers will be discussed later) should be mounded with 10 to 12 inches of well-drained soil around the base of each plant. This soil should come from another location in the garden, not from around the roses. Then cover the mound with another 12 to 16 inches of mulching material such as leaf mold, straw, pine needles, or wood chips, holding the mulch in place with evergreen boughs or chicken wire fencing. This added mulch will help stabilize soil temperature and reduce heaving. If your garden has resident rodents, you may want to skip the addition of this mulch material as it will provide them with a winter home.

Remove the soil and mulch in April when you feel the worst of winter is over. If an extended period of freezing temperatures looms, you can always replace the mound of soil to protect the sensitive crown.

Climbing roses are best winterized by removing the canes from the fence or trellis, laying them on the ground, and allowing snow cover to protect them from extreme cold. If you cannot count on continuous snow cover during the winter, you can mound soil or mulch over the canes on the ground. The practice of leaving the stems attached to the trellis and covering them with burlap offers only a few degrees of winter protection at best.

The only roses growing in Marjorie's Garden were planted years ago by a bird, perhaps a thrush sitting on a high branch of the old yellow birch at the edge of the drive. The trunk of this tree is now skirted with a colony of native roses that bear simple summer flowers, each a single whorl of pink petals encircling golden stamens, and bright red autumn hips. I don't worry about their winter survival.

## *The End of a Season*

At the end of October, in Marjorie's Garden, the vegetable gardening season is over for the year. Gardeners in southern New England, particularly those on the coast,

have another few weeks, but for all of us it is a short growing season, ending too early.

It is difficult to turn my back on the vegetable garden, and I do so with reluctance. I still go there in winter, shoveling out the paths after each snow to walk among the naked blueberry shrubs, spindly raspberry canes, windblown sunflower stalks topped by heads pecked clean of seeds. And I am not alone. There are footprints of mice, squirrels, rabbits, and turkeys. If I stop crunching the snow with my boots, I can hear the winter wind rattling the last few leaves still clinging to the oak tree.

### *Spring and Fall*

to a young child

*Margaret, are you grieving*
*Over Goldengrove unleaving?*
*Leaves like the things of man, you*
*With your fresh thoughts care for, can you?*
*Ah! as the heart grows older*
*It will come to such sights colder*
*By and by, nor spare a sigh*
*Though worlds of wanwood leafmeal lie;*
*And yet you will weep and know why.*
*Now no matter, child, the name:*
*Sorrow's springs are the same.*
*Nor mouth had, no nor mind, expressed*
*What heart heard of, ghost guessed:*
*It is the blight man was born for,*
*It is Margaret you mourn for.*

—Gerard Manley Hopkins (1844 – 1889)

# Chapter 13

# Gardens in Tune with Nature

*"One of the pleasures of being a gardener comes from the enjoyment you get looking at other people's yards."*

—Thalassa Cruso, *To Everything There is a Season: The Gardening Year, 1973*

***I seldom go into someone's garden without learning something new:*** a new crop to grow or a new way to grow a familiar crop, a new variety of tree or shrub, a new tool, or a new technique. Gardeners, as a rule, love to share what they have learned with others. At work, in the grocers, or at the feed and seed store on a Saturday morning, if I bump into another gardener we drop everything and talk gardening. My idea of an afternoon off from working in the garden is to stroll through someone else's garden, picking their brain.

In this spirit, this chapter offers a glimpse of several New England gardens and the gardeners who tend them. While different in many respects, all of these gardens reflect the gardener's passion for gardening in tune with nature.

## *Nate and Berta Atwater's Garden in Little Compton, Rhode Island—Zone 7a*

Berta and Nate Atwater's ornamental garden provides numerous examples of striking garden scenes achieved by skillful pruning with an artist's eye for combining color and texture. Berta is the artist at work in this garden, her eye for form and contrasting textures evident in the placement of trees, shrubs, and herbaceous perennials. Nate's passions are his vegetable garden and the grove of American hollies that he has cultivated for decades.

I was in their garden in late August, just after a pruning crew had finished work on the large trees—an annual task that Berta had done herself for many years. She had also completed her pruning of the dwarf conifers in the rock gardens as well as the other small trees and shrubs that can be pruned with feet firmly on the ground.

In summer, the spreading canopy of a towering pagoda tree *(Sophora japonica)* casts deep shade on the west side of their home. Nearby, other large deciduous trees, including a kousa

*Facing page:* The path that wanders through Charlie Heaven's Connecticut vegetable garden begins here. (Photo courtesy Charles Heaven)

Pruned to reveal the architecture of its branches and its thin, papery, light-tan bark, a heptacodium grows next to the stout trunk of a pagoda tree.

Each of the tall trees along this shady path is annually pruned to highlight its branching habit and bark character.

dogwood *(Cornus kousa)*, a Japanese maple *(Acer palmatum)*, and a heptacodium *(Heptacodium miconiodes)* expand the shaded area into a cool, breezy oasis for shade-loving shrubs, ferns, and flowering perennials.

As we walked the paths in this section of the garden, I found several turkey feathers on the ground. Berta explained that turkeys are regular visitors to their garden, though the numbers have fallen off in recent years. They are her favorite animal visitors to the garden.

Deer also have free run of the property, four running through the garden while I was photographing. Other than the yews, the deer seem to leave the garden plants alone, no doubt content to graze in the open fields. I also noticed several white cedars, favorite winter browse, along the distant property line.

In a garden bed behind the pagoda tree, a well-established planting of yellow wax bells

Sunlight filters through the pagoda tree's canopy, playing with the shades of green in this bed.

The shredding dark red-brown bark of an old yew provides stark contrast to the light green leaves of yellow wax bells.

*(Kirengeshoma palmata)*, a herbaceous perennial native to Japan with large maple-leaf-shaped leaves, grows beneath an old yew *(Taxus* sp.). Berta's skill in creating beautiful garden scenes is evident in the juxtaposed colors and textures of these two plants.

Closer to the house, but still in the pagoda tree's shade, a small garden bed planted with ferns and broad-leaved hellebores is punctuated by a mushroom-shaped staddle stone. Berta explained that the stone and others scattered about the garden had once been used as supports for a granary in Europe. In this bed, the stone provides a stark contrast in texture to the foliage of ferns and hellebores.

While admiring this lovely garden scene, I thought to ask Berta how she maintained soil fertility in her garden to promote such verdant growth. Did she spread compost between the plants when they were dormant? No, she replied, just coarse bark mulch every year. I looked closer and could still see nearly decomposed bark shreds in an open space near the staddle stone.

When I asked her how she watered the garden during dry spells, having seen no sign of an irrigation system or even a hose, Berta smiled and mentioned a friend with a thousand-gallon water tank on the back of a truck. A true friend indeed, he came over whenever Berta called.

Shady and cool in summer, this same area of the garden is quite different in early spring before the leaf buds break dormancy. "I love to work in this part of the garden at the end of winter," Berta announced as we passed under the shade of the heptacodium. "It is the warmest part of the garden that time of year."

The rock gardens, bed, and borders that surround the Atwater home are planted with "dwarf" conifers (see the sidebar on page 260 for more about slow-growing conifers), deciduous shrubs, ornamental grasses, herbaceous perennials, and small deciduous trees such as Japanese maples. Berta's reliance on texture and color to create striking garden scenes is evident everywhere. "I'm not so much a flower person," she told me. "I prefer the textures and colors of leaves."

Berta Atwater pauses for a moment in the shade of a tall Japanese maple. This is one of her favorite garden spots, a microclimate in both summer and winter.

### What Is a Dwarf Conifer?

The term "dwarf conifer" is often used to describe a slow-growing form of a conifer species. For example, the white pine, *Pinus strobus*, can grow to over 100 feet tall. A form of white pine, *P. strobus* 'Nana,' will reach 18 feet tall after decades of growth, but it is still considered a dwarf form of the species because it remains so much smaller. And there is a weeping form of the white pine, *P. strobus* 'Pendula,' which also remains much smaller than the species.

The term "dwarf" can be misleading in that some slow-growing cultivars will, given enough time, reach the size of their species. I have seen so-called "dwarf" forms of conifers that have been around long enough to be indistinguishable from the species. For this reason, I often substitute the term "slow-growing conifer."

In this garden border scene, Berta framed a variegated form of purple moor grass, *Molinia caerulea* 'Variegata,' between slow-growing forms of white fir *(Abies concolor)* and purple leaf European beech *(Fagus sylvatica)*. The flowering spikes of the grass give this combination of plants a totally different look in summer.

Pruned to hug the rock as it grows, this slow-growing form of *Pinus parviflora* 'Glauca' caught my eye the moment we turned the corner.

A Japanese maple *(Acer palmatum,* center) grows among a variety of conifers in another rock garden planting.

This is one of my favorite spots in Berta's garden, a combination of evergreens, including a rhododendron (front left), a "cloud pruned" false cypress *(Chamaecyparis* sp.), weeping Japanese larch *(Larix kaempferi),* and Japanese maple. I can imagine this scene in winter with each chamaecyparis cloud dusted with snow.

One of Berta's favorite plantings is this combination of yellow wax bells *(Kirengeshoma koreana)* and Japanese forest grass *(Hakonechloa macra* 'Aureola'). The foliage in the foreground is a low-growing *Prunus* species.

Over the years, I have seen many of the plant species growing in Berta's garden—many, including the slow-growing conifers, in arboretum collections. But I have never seen them displayed with such a keen eye for combining texture and color or with such care and precision in pruning. Berta's garden is a reflection of her passion for the beauty of plants, a passion she has nurtured for over half a century.

Nate Atwater's passion is his vegetable garden, about 900 square feet of sandy soil enclosed by wire-reinforced rail fencing. In late August, the soil seemed too sandy, too loose, and yet the garden's plants were thriving. Nate explained that he top-dresses the garden with compost late in the year, lets it sit on top of the soil through the winter, then tills it into the soil in spring before planting. He used manure in the past, but now he uses a packaged seafood compost.

Berta has a special recipe for butternut squash. "It's to die for," Nate says, and he makes sure there is no shortage of squash for the kitchen. (See the sidebar for Berta's recipe.)

Nate Atwater rests on the rail of his vegetable garden.

From Nate's point of view, I had missed the best time of year in this garden. I should have been there in spring to see row after row of lettuce: Paris Island romaine, red sails, baby romaine, four seasons, and black-seeded Simpson, to name just a few of the varieties he grows, some every year, others less often.

By early August, the shallots are drying in the sun and the Walla Walla onions are ready for grilling. By late August, leeks are harvested as needed in the kitchen, tomatoes and cucumbers are ripening on the vines, and huge Waltham butternut squash cover the ground in a third of the garden's space.

Over in one corner, fingerling potatoes wait to be dug. "They're the only ones I grow," Nate explained, "Swedish peanuts, Russian Banana, and Rose Finn Apple, all fingerling potatoes. Stick with the tried and true."

Nate grows no beans. "It takes the deer about five seconds to wipe out an entire row," he explained.

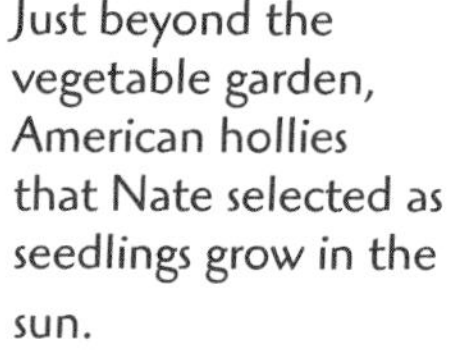

Just beyond the vegetable garden, American hollies that Nate selected as seedlings grow in the sun.

### Berta's Roasted Butternut Squash in Balsamic Glacé with Parmesan

**Ingredients**

2 medium butternut squash, peeled, seeded, and cut into 1-inch cubes
¾ cup chicken stock
¼ to ½ cup balsamic vinegar (di modena)
2 tbsp extra-virgin olive oil
pinch of salt
½ cup freshly grated parmesan cheese

Preheat oven to 350° F. Add the cubed squash to a shallow baking dish. Add the chicken stock, balsamic vinegar, olive oil, and toss. Sprinkle with the parmesan. Cover with foil and bake for about 50 to 60 minutes. Remove the foil and bake uncovered until all the juices have been absorbed. Serve hot. Serves 6.

When I asked him about planting for fall crops, he was quick to say, "No, by this time of the year (late August), I'm sick of this garden, ready to quit. Still, we get a lot of food from this garden." And he enumerated all that he grows, including onions, leeks, shallots, spinach, snow peas, chard, early beets, cabbage, tomatoes, peppers, summer squash, potatoes, and, of course, lettuce.

When Nate stops to rest in his garden, he can lean on his rake and gaze at the beautiful American hollies *(Ilex opaca)* that he has cultivated over the last half century. Each tree was selected as a small seedling, some transplanted to more favorable sites. Some are male, some are fruit-bearing females. No doubt these trees are one reason why numerous species of songbirds frequent the Atwater garden through the year.

## Ron and Jennifer Kujawski's Garden in West Stockbridge, Massachusetts—Zone 5a

What do two plant physiologists talk about when one visits the other in his vegetable garden? To a hoverfly on the garden shed wall, I imagine it sounded pretty much the same as any other conversation between two avid gardeners, tomatoes taking up a lot of our discussion what with the drought and another late blight epidemic unfolding across New England, and plenty of talk about flea beetles and cover crops. The discussion of colored plastic mulches, however, may not have sounded familiar.

Ron's interest in using colored plastic mulches to speed up production and increase crop yields is a good example of his approach to gardening. As he puts it, "If I learn one new thing, it has been a good day." "Retirement" means spending all day in the garden, experimenting, learning what works, then sharing what he has learned with readers of his gardening columns and with visitors to the 10,000-square-foot garden that he and his daughter, Jennifer, cultivate.

Ron had harvested their garlic crop just before my visit, leaving a sizable portion of the garden temporarily bare. Listening to Ron talk about growing and cooking with garlic, I realized that I was in the garden of a true garlic guru. The sidebar on page 266 says it all.

## Colored Plastic in the Vegetable Garden

When Ron mentioned in an email that he had been using red plastic mulch with remarkable success to speed up production and increase the yields of tomatoes, peppers, and eggplants, and that he was experimenting with using green plastic for cucumbers, I started packing for an early August road trip to the Berkshires. I had heard about this new gardening technique and knew that commercial vegetable growers are using it, but I had never seen plastic mulches in colors other than black in use.

Before visiting Ron's garden, I did my homework, reading up on colored plastic mulches. I learned that the color of a mulch determines its solar energy-radiating behavior and its influence on the microclimate around a plant. It affects the surface temperature of the mulch, and it affects the underlying soil temperature. The amount of soil warming is dependent on the degree of contact between the mulch and the soil; a rough soil surface will reduce the warming effectiveness of the mulch.

Black plastic mulch has been used by home gardeners and commercial growers to raise soil temperatures for many years. During the day, the soil temperature under black plastic in good contact with the soil surface can be 5° F higher than air at a 2-inch soil depth and 3° F higher at a 4-inch depth. New England growers of winter squash and pumpkins, crops that require a long growing season, transplant seedlings into beds warmed by black plastic in order to get the necessary early start.

Clear plastic mulch is even more effective in transmitting heat to the soil. Water droplets beneath the clear plastic trap heat, so daytime temperatures can reach 8 to 14° F higher at a 2-inch soil depth and 6 to 9° F higher at a depth of 4 inches. Commercial corn growers rely on clear plastic-covered soil to produce early crops. Because sunlight reaches the soil, weed growth can be a problem.

White plastic reduces soil temperature and is often used to establish crops in areas where uncovered soil temperatures are too high. Decreases in soil temperature of 2° F at a 1-inch soil depth can be achieved.

The newer IRT mulches (infrared transmitting mulches), typically blue-green or brown in color, are intermediate between black and clear plastics in terms of soil temperature increases. They absorb the photosynthetically active light, thus suppressing weed growth, but transmit the infrared energy to warm the soil. In other words, they have the weed control effectiveness of black

Ron and Jennifer are growing several tomato varieties in beds mulched with red plastic. Resulting yields and production times are encouraging.

mulch and are intermediate between black and clear plastic in their effect on soil temperatures. Commercial growers of cucurbits, including cucumbers, squash, melons, and pumpkins, are already using the IRT mulches, including green plastic, to promote growth of these crops.

Highly reflective silver plastic mulch is used to repel aphids on squash plants, effectively delaying the onset of virus symptoms in fall crops. Silver plastic is also very effective in potato production, since tuber formation is greater in cooler soils.

The use of red and green plastics to boost yields for home gardeners is very much in the testing phase. Some university research trials with tomatoes grown on red plastic mulch demonstrated benefits either of improved yield or enhanced ripening and fruit quality. Trials by other researchers produced no response. Some trials showed a potential for red plastic mulch to reduce severity of early blight on tomatoes. There is evidence that the orientation of production rows may be a factor in the effectiveness of red plastic mulching, with north-south orientation best.

How do red- and green-colored mulches work? The answer is still up for grabs. During our discussion, Ron speculated on the stimulation of phytochrome by far-red light reflected back into the plant canopy.

Even if we don't need to know *how* it works, Ron's success, and the success of other gardeners, in boosting yields of tomato, pepper, and eggplant with red plastic mulch is exciting, particularly for home gardeners with short growing seasons. There is already enough demand for red plastic for use as mulch for many garden centers to stock it.

The drawback to the use of plastic in the garden is, of course, disposal of the plastic when it is no longer usable. At the moment, this is a real problem for the environmentally conscious gardener, but there are possible solutions that may help. First, colored plastic mulches already on the market are durable enough to be used for more than one season if properly handled. Second, some states already have plastic mulch recycling centers and, if the popularity of mulches grows, more are likely to be developed. Finally, researchers are working on developing biodegradable plastic mulches in the appropriate colors.

Ron is also experimenting with the use of red plastic mulch on okra production. His garden and Marjorie's Garden are both in Zone 5a, but I have never considered growing okra, thinking of it as a Southern vegetable. Next year I'm giving it a try, red plastic and all.

Will green plastic mulch enhance production of cucumbers in the home garden?

## For the Savory Smell of Success, Grow Garlic *by Ron Kujawski and Jennifer Kujawski*

Is there anything that whets the appetite more than the fragrance of garlic-infused culinary creations? Garlic is a common ingredient in almost every cuisine and a mainstay for most home cooks, yet it is not commonly grown by home gardeners, which is a stinking shame. Okay, enough with the odiferous references. Our objective is to encourage you to grow garlic even if you have only a small garden. It is one of the easiest crops to grow.

Garlic differs from most other vegetables in that it is commonly planted in fall. As a rule of thumb, plant garlic within a few weeks after the first killing frost. Depending upon where you are in New England, that will mean anywhere from late September to late October. Why a fall planting? Garlic needs cold temperatures to initiate bulb and root development. Garlic can be planted in very early spring, but the results are usually disappointing. Stay with fall planting.

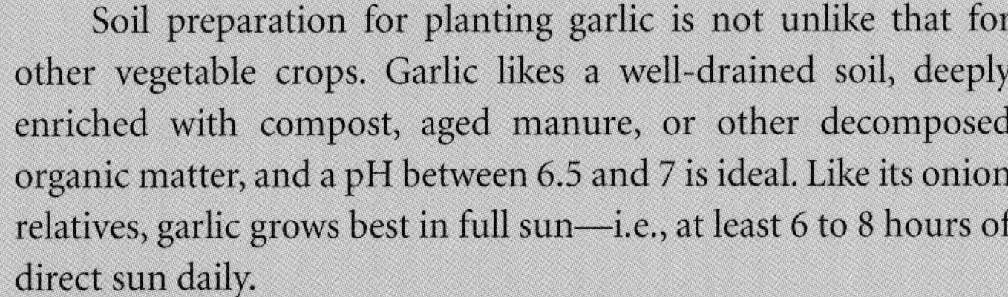

Soil preparation for planting garlic is not unlike that for other vegetable crops. Garlic likes a well-drained soil, deeply enriched with compost, aged manure, or other decomposed organic matter, and a pH between 6.5 and 7 is ideal. Like its onion relatives, garlic grows best in full sun—i.e., at least 6 to 8 hours of direct sun daily.

Once the soil is prepared, it's time to plant. You may be tempted to use garlic bought at the local grocery for planting, but we don't recommend that. Store-bought garlic was most likely grown in California or another mild region and is likely to be a variety that is ill-suited for a northern climates. Buy garlic for planting at local garden centers or farms, regional garlic festivals (which is where we seek out new varieties), or from on-line sources. When you're selecting bulbs for planting, bigger is better. Bulbs with the largest cloves have given us the largest bulbs at harvest time.

The hundreds of varieties of garlic can be grouped into two main types: hardneck and softneck. Hardneck varieties produce a stiff stalk, called a scape, in the middle of the plant. Softneck varieties do not produce a scape. We've grown about 35 varieties of garlic, both hardneck and softneck, over the years. Some we've discontinued because of their poor development, lack of hardiness, or inconsistent performance. Generally, hardneck varieties are best for the cold New England climate, though we've had some success with a few softneck types. Among our favorites are the hardneck varieties Music, Spanish Roja, Rieslig, French Red, Hnat, Polish Jenn, and Metechi and the softneck Inchelium Red. Each variety has a different flavor, some being rather spicy and strong while others are mild tasting. We recommend starting with two or three of these varieties, but keep in mind that what does best in our garden and soil may not be best somewhere else.

After buying garlic bulbs, keep them intact until just before planting. At that time, separate the cloves and select the largest for planting. Eat the rest for energy to complete the task at hand and also to repel vampires; no one needs vampires interfering with his or her gardening efforts. Plant the individual cloves 2 to 3 inches deep (2 inches in heavy soil, 3 inches in light sandy soil) and 6 inches apart. Additional rows can be spaced 12 inches apart, but we plant in double rows spaced 6 to 8 inches apart. Garlic will grow well in raised beds and in containers.

Many garlic growers cover their garlic with a mulch right after planting. The best mulch is a light, coarse material such as straw. If we mulch, we usually wait until the ground has frozen before application, since we are mostly concerned about preventing the alternate freezing and thawing of soil common in winters without snow cover. These cycles can damage roots of garlic. We have to admit, however, that there have been years in which we did not apply mulch and the garlic came through quite well. On the other hand, there have been some very wet winters in which many garlic bulbs rotted beneath the mulch. Inconsistent and unpredictable New England winters can be tough on gardeners.

In early spring we remove mulch but place it beside the rows for weed control and to facilitate soil moisture retention. During the growing season, weeds are a critical concern. The same can be said for any crop in the garden, of course, but because garlic is shallow rooted and does not compete well with weeds, regular weeding is a must. Also, for best development of your garlic plants, make sure they get plenty of water and an occasional side-dressing of an organic fertilizer that is high in nitrogen during the leaf development stage of growth—i.e., April, May, and June.

Hardneck varieties will begin to develop scapes at some point, usually in June. Research has shown that removing the scapes soon after they appear will result in the plant producing larger bulbs. Don't throw away the scapes. They have become a gourmet item in recent years and command hefty prices at farmer's markets. The young scapes are used in salads, stir fries, and a variety of other dishes. Older scapes, those that have curled before removal, can be a little tough. We use them to make a hearty garlic broth.

Garlic is ready to harvest when about a third of their leaves have turned brown. We dig up our plants using a garden fork rather than pulling them up. Keeping plants in the ground until the leaves have completely browned often results in the cloves separating within the bulbs. These bulbs are still usable, but they will not keep long in storage. If we see any bulbs with separated cloves, we use them first.

Garlic growers have various methods for handling their plants after lifting them from the soil. We hang small bunches of intact plants from the rafters in our garden shed for curing. The plants may also be spread out on screens or other surfaces in a dry, airy, warm place for 2 to 4 weeks. After the curing phase, we trim the roots and cut off the dried tops, leaving a 1-inch stem section attached to the bulbs. At that point we sort through the bulbs of each variety and pick some of the largest and healthiest for fall planting. The bulk of our crop is then stored in net bags in a cool, dark, dry spot in the basement.

The length of time that garlic bulbs keep in storage varies with the condition of a bulb at harvest, how well it was cured, storage conditions, and the variety. Some of our garlic bulbs begin to dry and shrivel by January, while others remain firm into spring.

While we prefer to use fresh garlic, we do dry a lot of garlic in a dehydrator. Individual cloves are peeled and sliced about 1/8 inch thick and then dried until hard. These garlic chips are then stored in airtight jars. Some of the dry garlic is ground in a spice grinder to make garlic powder as needed. Other chips are crumbled and used to flavor soups, sauces, stews, and other dishes. With fresh or dry garlic, those dishes will surely be a success and smell wonderful.

Ron and Jennifer's vegetable garden is characterized by wide rows that maximize growing space. Many of the rows are covered with plastic mulch (like the green plastic on the cucumber bed), and a clean straw mulch keeps weeds down between rows. Trellises are used for climbing crops such as cucumbers.

Ron grows a lot of tomatoes! In early August he was closely inspecting his plants for any sign of late blight, a devastating disease that often destroys entire crops of tomatoes and potatoes. In the epidemic of 2009, home gardeners throughout New England were forced to destroy their entire tomato crops. As an organic gardener, Ron recommends using the biofungicide Serenade, a suspension of bacteria, Bacillus subtilis, that controls spread of the late blight fungus. To be effective, however, Serenade must be sprayed before infection, with repeat applications at regular intervals.

The cabbage plant on the right has yet to lose its head, but the plant on the right, after its main head was harvested, proceeded to produce smaller lateral heads.

Broccoli growers know that when they harvest the large central head of florets, the plant responds by producing side shoots with smaller heads that can be harvested later in the season. To my knowledge, no one has ever experimented with other brassicas to see if they will respond in like fashion. During my early-August visit, Ron showed me several cabbage plants that were producing lateral heads after the main head had been harvested. Chinese cabbage plants were behaving in the same manner. From now on I won't be in such a hurry to pull up that cabbage plant after harvesting the main head.

Ron estimates that he and Jennifer harvest enough fresh produce from their garden to provide 80% of the meals for both families during the growing season and 60 to 75% of their meals during the winter. This translates into a lot of freezing, drying, and canning, a lot of work but worth it, says Ron, to eat healthy, delicious food year-round.

## Patricia Crow's Garden on Cape Cod—Zone 7a

> *"We have otter, foxes, deer, turtles, frogs, and countless butterflies, bees, wasps, birds, and dragonflies, as well as many small mammals. In a sense we feel that, in our house, we are the zoo animals, and the animals are the citizens."*
>
> *—Patricia Crow*

In Chapter 9, The Garden in July, I described with several photographs the bayberry-lined drive leading up to the Cape Cod home of Patricia Crow and James Hadley, and the imaginative way Patricia used this native evergreen shrub as a foil for flowering perennials and native shrubs.

Through seven years of hard work, Patricia has transformed a swampy collection of invasive species such as black locust *(Robinia pseudoacacia)*, catbriar *(Smilax* sp.), shrub honeysuckles *(Lonicera* sp.), and sycamore maple *(Acer pseudoplatanus)* into a garden of native wildflowers, herbaceous perennials, shrubs, and trees. In all, she has planted more than 60 species of trees and shrubs, four species of vines, and 60 herbaceous species.

As the work progressed, all of the plants removed from the site were chipped for use as mulch. While Patricia continues to add manure and compost to areas of the garden, she credits the use of the mulch to initially break up the hardpan soil as a critical element in her success.

A single specimen of American cranberrybush viburnum *(Viburnum opulus* var. *americanum)* asserts itself within the branches of northern bayberry. With plantings such as these, Patricia paints the natural world with an artist's touch.

In Patricia's own words, "My focus has been mainly native species, local genotypes where possible, with a few timeless non-natives included for my own pleasure. I feel strongly that habitat for native birds, insects, and mammals is disappearing rapidly here on Cape Cod, and I had the opportunity to address this concern in my own yard. The original matrix of arrowwood viburnum, oak, black cherry, red cedar, and highbush blueberry has been expanded to include major plantings of bayberry, holly, birch, oak, dogwoods, viburnums, swamp azalea, hydrangeas, magnolias, ferns, and native grasses. It seems to have worked, as we have encouraged New England cottontail, otter, fox, and many small mammals and birds to come to the garden."

What are those "timeless non-natives" that Patricia grows for her own pleasure? Among them are deciduous magnolias, including 'Leonard Messel' and 'Porcelain Dove.' And she has kept the old English oaks *(Quercus robur)* that were planted on the property many decades before it was hers.

Patricia defines nativity on a broad regional scale, and her garden contains many plant species that are native to the eastern United States outside the New England region. A good example is Carolina silverbell *(Halesia carolina),* a tree that is native to the piedmont and mountains of the Carolinas, eastern Tennessee, Georgia, and Alabama, with scattered distribution in small populations over a wide area as far north as Indiana and Ohio.

One of her objectives is to provide sanctuary for endangered plant species such as a rare species of *Pycnanthemum* (mountain mint) and the endangered great blue lobelia *(Lobelia siphylitica).* And sometimes a plant species is added to her garden without her help. Shortly after my visit, I received an email from Patricia with a photograph of Indian pipe, a parasitic plant that had simply appeared in her garden near the swamp, growing under arrowwood viburnum and highbush blueberry. The accompanying sidebar describes this unusual plant and how it ekes out a living.

### The Ghostly Indian Pipe

Lacking chlorophyll, the green pigment that gives the leaves of most higher plants their familiar summer color, Indian pipe is waxy white in appearance, turning black when it gets old. It grows only 4 to 10 inches tall, with scale-like leaves that droop. Typically, it appears from June to September, growing in shady woods with rich organic soils. You are likely to find it growing near a tree stump.

Lacking the ability to make its own food from photosynthesis, Indian pipe extracts nutrients from certain fungi that establish symbiotic relationships with tree roots. The fungus relies on the tree for its nourishment and, in return, provides the tree with essential nutrients and water—i.e., the fungus becomes an extension of the tree's root system. The Indian pipe taps into this relationship, taking nutrients from the fungus without giving anything in return.

Indian pipe is a parasitic plant in the garden, an oddity for sure, but also part of the garden ecosystem where it grows, no more or less important than any other plant or animal living there.

Indian pipe *(Monotropa uniflora)* is also known as "corpse plant" because of its ghostly appearance. Believe it or not, this unusual plant is in the Ericaceae, the plant family that includes rhododendrons and blueberries. (Photo courtesy Patricia Crow)

When I think back on my walk through Patricia's Cape Cod garden, I recall many spots along the path where wildness yielded to the gardener's creative touch. Not every plant species in her garden is native to New England. Like the majority of gardeners who strive to stay in tune with nature, Patricia has her short list of non-native plants that she simply must grow for the enchantment they provide.

I hope someday to make a return visit to Patricia's garden to see how her idea of a garden has evolved.

Joe-pye weed *(Eupatorium purpureum)* blooms in the curve of a garden path while, on the opposite side, lavender *(Lavandula angustifolia)* and tufted hairgrass *(Deschampsia caespitosa)* sway gently in the summer breeze.

When you get closer, you notice that Culver's root *(Veronicastrum virginicum)* and bee balm *(Monarda didyma* 'Jacob Cline'*)* are growing among the clumps of tufted hairgrass, an example of the gardener's creative touch. (Photo courtesy Patricia Crow)

(Far left) Through the summer, bees and butterflies forage the bright white flowers of 'Ice Palace,' a cultivar of swamp milkweed. (Left) Yellow foxglove *(Digitalis grandiflora)* is native to Eurasia from central Europe eastward to Turkey and Siberia. One of Patricia's favorite flowers, it looks at home in her garden. (Photos courtesy Patricia Crow)

In this section of her garden, Patricia brought together the golden yellow flowers of St. John's wort *(Hypericum x 'Hidcote')* with the soft blue of lavender. St. John's wort is a compact deciduous shrub that can grow to 4 feet in height in warm winter climates, about 2 or 3 feet tall on Cape Cod, where it is usually cut back to the ground in winter. (Photo courtesy Patricia Crow)

Among the native shrubs in Patricia's garden is one of my favorite rhododendrons, the swamp azalea *(Rhododendron viscosum)*. Unlike most deciduous azaleas, this one blooms in summer, its numerous white flowers filling the garden with their spicy, clove-like fragrance. The flowers attract butterflies and hummingbirds. Although found in swampy areas and tolerant of damp soils, swamp azalea does not like its roots submerged. In fact, it will tolerate some drought. Hardy from in Zones 3 through 9, it should be grown in full sun or partial shade. Like all ericaceous plants, it must have acidic soil. (Photo courtesy Patricia Crow)

The last plant that I expected to find in Patricia's garden was the southern magnolia *(Magnolia grandiflora)*, the native range of which is from the Deep South north to Maryland. It is cold hardy to Zone 7, so Patricia is giving it a try. From my days in Georgia and South Carolina, I remember this plant growing to 50 feet tall and almost as wide, its broad, dark green leaves coated with a soft brown pubescence on their lower sides, and its large, saucer-shaped white flowers filling the spring air with sweetness. It seemed out of place in a Cape Cod garden, like an old friend suddenly appearing out of the blue. The cultivar growing in Patricia's garden is 'Edith Bogue,' the most cold-hardy selection of the species. It grows to 30 feet tall and half as wide, with large white blooms. (Photo courtesy Patricia Crow)

## *Tom and Jan McIntyre's Garden on Mt. Desert Island, Maine—Zone 5b*

Text and Photographs by Jan McIntyre

Located on a beautiful island off the coast of Maine, our home consists of a log cabin, a pond and adjacent fen, surrounding gardens, and a moss-covered spruce/balsam forest. When Old Man winter gives way to the warmth of spring, the ice on the pond slowly recedes, plant life awakens, and an ever-changing parade of blossoms and wildlife begins. Marsh marigolds explode around the pond, and mallards arrive to establish their territory for courting and possible nesting.

As gardeners for a registered National Wildlife Federation backyard wildlife habitat, our objective is to provide the four basic habitat elements needed for wildlife to thrive: food, water, cover, and places to raise their young in a diverse and sustainable environment. Of all the elements

Marsh marigolds *(Caltha palustris)* are native to New England, erupting from the soil in early spring. By the middle of May (in Zone 5), they are loaded with buttercup-like flowers. After bloom, the seeds are dispersed, and the summer-dormant plants disappear.

The mallard pair will often arrive so early in spring that some ice is still present on the pond. Courtship displays between the male and female occur regularly, and the male will fiercely defend his territory against other males. Nests are usually constructed quite a distance from the pond. Once nesting begins, the male will arrive at the pond alone, with the female making short, occasional visits during the day.

The fragrant flowers of the water lily last three days, remaining open during the day and closing at night. Hybrids produce blossoms of white, yellow, and shades of pink.

When grown, this immature green frog will be smaller than a bullfrog. It will have two prominent ridges on its back and a voice similar to that of a loose banjo string.

Ground phlox *(Phlox subulata)*, Jacob's ladder *(Polemonium caeruleum)*, basket-of-gold *(Aurinia saxatalis)*, and lambs' ears *(Stachys byzantine)* spill onto a pathway.

needed to attract wildlife, water draws them in like a magnet. Each spring, a mallard pair arrives to court on the pond and laze on our homemade floating island.

A pond provides the most diversity when 50 to 80% of its surface is covered by emergent and submerged vegetation and when the shoreline is 90% vegetated. Shoreline plants provide nesting materials such as the soft fuzz from cinnamon ferns *(Osmunda cinnamomea)* used by chickadees and yellow warblers, food in the form of berries from red-osier dogwood *(Cornus sericea)* and other plants, and resting places on emergent plants such as fragrant water lilies *(Nymphaea odorata)* and pickerel weed *(Pontederia cordata)*. The submerged plants increase the oxygen level in the pond and provide shelter and habitat for small organisms that live in the pond.

The web of the black-and-yellow garden spider is about 2 feet in diameter and located in a spot that is protected from the wind. The stabilimentum may be useful in stabilizing the web, as camouflage for the spider, or in attracting insects. It may also help in preventing birds from flying into and ruining the web.

Green frogs spend a lot of time resting on lily pads, waiting for the next meal to come near. Some of our frogs travel up from the pond and hide in the perennial beds, where they hunt for prey such as slugs, snails, and grasshoppers. Covering the entire perennial garden with a 2-inch layer of compost in the early spring and 2 inches of chopped-up leaves in the fall creates a moist, rich soil, an ideal place for frogs to hide while feeding.

Diversity of plants in the perennial beds and around the yard encourages a diversity of insects, fodder for nesting birds. Herbivores that are feeding on the leaves of plants are high in protein and are primary food for birds feeding their young.

One such insect, the black-and-yellow garden spider, makes its presence known in the garden in late summer by building a large web that is attached to surrounding plants. In the middle of the web is a zigzag pattern called a stabilimentum, where the female spider rests with her head pointing toward the ground. When small insects hit the web, she encircles them with silk, often saving them for a midnight snack.

After mating she will lay egg cases off to the side of the stabilimentum. Come fall, as many as 1,400 eggs will hatch into tiny spiders that overwinter in their protective home. In spring, many of the young spiders become food for returning hummingbirds. It is important not to be too fastidious when cleaning up the garden in the autumn, so these egg cases remain throughout the winter.

Native plants in the gardens are especially attractive to hummingbirds, bees, butterflies, and moths. Along with many of our favorite non-native plants, we plant native species that have co-evolved with the local fauna. Single-petaled rather than double-petaled forms make it easier for the pollinators to access the nectar. Flowers of varied heights are planted, since some butterfly species like to feed near the ground and others like to feed atop tall stems.

Biodiversity also increases with the variety of flower morphology. Small beneficial insects prefer tiny open flowers, while hummingbirds favor long tubular flowers such as turtlehead *(Chelone obliqua)*. Flower color and fragrance are also important in the garden for both insects and gardeners, although insects do not see flower petals in the same colors that we do.

In the shade garden, young witchhazel *(Hamamelis virginia)*, serviceberry *(Amelanchier laevis)*, and flowering dogwood *(Cornus florida)*, along with the muted greens of other plants, offer a cool respite from the hot, hazy days of summer. The dark crevices of the stone wall offer places for chipmunks, snakes, and salamanders to rest.

In the woodland garden in July, rosebay rhododendron *(Rhododendron maximum)* and ferns line a pathway covered with Eastern white pine needles. The path leads down to the pond and surrounding gardens.

As the summer evolves, so does the garden. The color palette changes, and more native plants erupt into bloom. On the steep slope in front of the cabin, heathers *(Calluna vulgaris)* are ablaze with color in mid to late August.

The blossoms of summer will last into late autumn, and when winter arrives, the pond will be covered again with ice and snow. The mallards and warblers will be gone, but evidence of wildlife will still be present.

By mid-summer, the garden is bursting with color from non-native plants such as astilbe *(Astilbe x arendsii)*, English lavender *(Lavendula angustifolia)*, and clustered bellflower *(Campanula glomerata)*. Queen of the prairie *(Filipendula rubra)* and threadleaf tickseed *(Coreopsis verticillata)* are North American native plants.

In the background, Virginia creeper *(Parthenocissus quinquefolia)* climbs up an Eastern white pine *(Pinus strobus)*. Native to New England, the creeper's leaves turn a stunning red as fall approaches, and the purple-blue fruits are a favorite of wildlife.

Rosebay rhododendron is native to New England and blossoms in July, even in a fair amount of shade. It can reach heights of 20 feet and is often used for screening purposes.

New England natives, Joe-pye weed *(Eupatorium maculatum)*, black-eyed susan *(Rudbeckia hirta)*, purple coneflower *(Echinachea purpurea)*, and tall garden phlox *(Phlox paniculata)* are predominant plants in the late summer garden.

The lime-colored foliage of the heather 'Wickwar Flame' contrasts nicely with the light pink 'County Wicklow,' the purple 'Barnett Anley,' and the white 'Alba Erecta.'

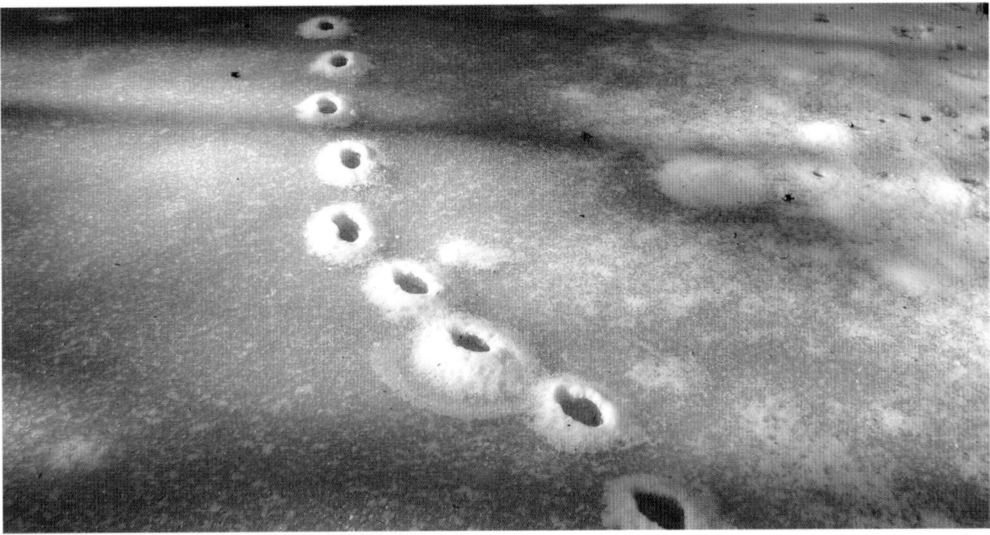

Deer tracks meander across the pond.

### Pond Diversity at Spruce Hollow *by Tom McIntyre*

Visitors at Spruce Hollow frequently ask when they see the pond, "What's in there"? The answer lies in where one looks.

When we had the pond dug in late summer, water entered through the sides and from the bottom of the surrounding clay layers, and we wondered what might be seeping into the pond with the muddy water. As fall passed and winter snows came, the pond froze over with brownish ice on the surface. The spring melt resulted in a less turbid water column, and the entire hole was filled to the brim with water running off from the surrounding fen. Within this runoff were organisms that formed the beginnings of complex food webs, creatures that would assure the success of this new corner of our wildlife habitat. These creatures included microscopic algae, zooplankton, a variety of insects and their larval forms, and a variety of snails and amphibians.

The pond filled with new concentrations of microbial life. These microbes were already present in the vernal water pockets of the fen environment, but in the pond, with a constant water column available, they flourished.

Also noteworthy was the creation of a new transition zone along the edges of the pond. This edge zone has allowed room for the natural secondary succession of native mosses, grasses, and shrubs, all of which have successfully taken up residence along the pond perimeter.

In August 2001, with the aid of a water-testing kit, we tested several aspects of the water quality, including dissolved oxygen levels, pH (which was 6.5), and temperature. The pond was in good shape, a healthy place for life to thrive.

Microbial organisms form the base of all food webs and thus are very important creatures in a healthy pond. On many occasions we have taken a bowl of edge water and spent many enjoyable hours with microscopes looking at the microbial life in the pond. Some of the more common species are diatoms, green algae, euglena, hydra, and colonial hydroids.

When we take water samples progressively farther from shore, the concentrations of organisms vary greatly. In our pond, the tannins (brown pigments) from the peat runoff in the surrounding fen seriously limit light at deeper levels. Algae life drops off to zero at a depth of one meter.

Of particular concern is the growth of filamentous algae. As the water warms in summer months, occasional pockets of this algae take up residence along the sunny shore of the pond. Helping control the filamentous algae are the pond snails, common "trapdoor" snails with gliding surfaces that grow to the diameter of a quarter in our pond. They feed on varied sources of detritus and are themselves harvested easily by raccoons, otters, and ducks.

Common shiners, some 5 to 6 inches long, constitute the pond's fish life. We don't know how they entered the pond, but they serve as food for otters and kingfishers. They also help to maintain a reasonable level of algae on the fringes of the pond throughout the year.

And we have trapped an eel in the pond, a juvenile about 8 inches long. We believe that eels wriggle their way through the marsh fen from a saltwater cove that is about a quarter-mile downstream of the pond.

Our local biodiversity has been significantly enhanced by the presence of our small pond.

## Theresa Guethler's Garden in Buckport, Maine—Zone 5b

There is beauty in wildness and in the combination of colors and textures that result when wildness is juxtaposed with a cultivated garden. Sometimes such garden scenes are planned and planted, but at other times they are the result of just letting wildness creep along and into the edges of the garden—of deciding not to pull what others would call a weed. Just let it grow and see what happens.

Theresa Guethler is a master of gardening with wildness. On her Bucksport, Maine, property bordering the Penobscot River, small cultivated patches of vegetables and flowers exist within an expanse of tall unmowed grasses and forbs, including goldenrods, Queen Anne's lace, and swamp milkweed.

Along the edge of this wildness, a long curving bed backed by a stone wall is planted with herbaceous perennials in the style of an English border. Tall staghorn sumacs, their branches loaded with bright red fruit clusters, arch over the bed to provide some relief from a scorching sun. By August, the time of my visit, many of the perennials had finished flowering, but a few late summer mainstays, including helenium and rudbeckias, were at their peak of bloom.

Surrounded by unmowed field, Theresa grows small patches of corn and strawberries (out of view), as well as an abundance of flowers for cutting in this small fenced-in plot.

Helenium (back) and rudbeckia (foreground) are part of late-summer sunny borders throughout New England.

Fruit-bearing persimmons are an uncommon sight in New England and even more rare in Maine.

Theresa likes to test the climate boundaries of her garden, finding microclimates to grow plants native to hardiness zones and habitats well south of Maine. Persimmon *(Diospyros virginiana),* for example, barely has a toe in New England, its native range extending only as far north as southern Connecticut. Most abundant in rich bottom lands and coastal river valleys of the southern states, the five trees growing in a grove on the edge of Theresa's open field seem truly out of place.

I first saw her persimmon grove in the spring of 2012, a year after they were planted. They had survived their first winter in Maine unscathed. When I visited her garden again in August, Theresa met me at the back fence grinning from ear to ear, eager to tell me that two of her persimmon trees were in fruit. I took the long walk down to the end of the field and, sure enough, found two trees loaded with green persimmons, a sight I had last seen in South Carolina 15 years before. Theresa credits their fruiting to the nearness of the Penobscot River, a large body of water that must create a warmer microclimate in nearby bottomlands.

In August, with many of the more domesticated perennials past their seasonal prime, Theresa's garden spots offer the visitor several examples of the union of wildness and cultivation.

Theresa's persimmon trees grow at the edge of an open, unmowed field. The Penobscot River flows just beyond the trees in the background.

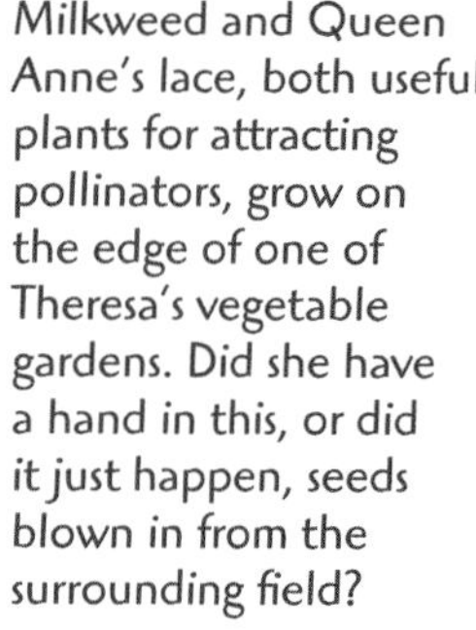

Milkweed and Queen Anne's lace, both useful plants for attracting pollinators, grow on the edge of one of Theresa's vegetable gardens. Did she have a hand in this, or did it just happen, seeds blown in from the surrounding field?

One of my favorite spots in Theresa's garden is the corner of a vegetable garden where (left to right) purple coneflower *(Echinacea purpurea)*, pink perennial sweet pea *(Lathyrus latifolius)*, and flowering tobacco *(Nicotiana alata)*, three pollinator magnets, bloom together in August.

There is no doubt that purple coneflower is one of Theresa's favorite perennial flowers. Here it mingles with an artemisia in a small bed by the driveway, a beautiful combination of color and texture.

By August, most herbaceous borders are well past the peak of spectacular color, particularly in a dry summer. Most plants look spent. Yet walking through some gardens at the end of summer can foster ideas of plant combinations that you want to use in your own late-summer garden, combinations of color and texture that stop you in your tracks. At each point you stop and ask, is this scene solely the product of the gardener's eye, or is it a fortunate stroke of serendipity? Theresa Guethler's August garden is a good example of both.

## *Dr. Charles Richards' Seacoast Garden—Zone 5b*

In 1965, a few years before his retirement as University of Maine's distinguished field botanist and plant taxonomist, Dr. Charles Richards purchased property on Great Wass Island, off the Downeast coast of Maine, and immediately began planting native trees in pockets of soil between the granite outcrops. While teaching taxonomy, dendrology, and plant geography to eager students, he found time to begin construction of a garden. He exposed even more of the granite, saving the peat for soil amendment, and filled in the depressions among rocks with loam and compost to create the

In this section of his garden, Dr. Richards uses foliage and flowers to create a summer scene rich in colors and textures. Gathered around the Japanese maple are a gold threadleaf sawara *(Chamaecyparis pisifera* 'Filifera Aurea Nana', left), a Japanese spirea *(Spiraea x bumalda,* front), and pink astilbes (right). Rhododendrons fill in the background of this colorful scene.

Along one garden path, a collection of rhododendrons fronted by heathers provides contrast to the bright colors of astilbes and daylilies just out of view.

future garden's foundation. He hauled stones by boat from outlying islands to form garden paths, a formidable task.

In the summer of 2012, Marjorie and I had the pleasure of meeting Dr. Richards and accompanying him on a stroll through his garden. Ninety-two years young, he led us along winding paths through an acre or more of planted beds. We were surrounded by the bright pinks, reds, and whites of astilbes and by daylilies, hostas, daisies, rhododendrons, dwarf conifers, Japanese maples, and many other plants, some native, some exotic. Native bees and other insects were everywhere, drawn to the abundance of nectar and pollen.

We were surrounded by a botanist's passion for plants.

As a child in Maryland, Charles learned to grow vegetables under the tutelage of his maternal grandfather, a truck farmer. As a university scientist in Orono, Dr. Richards had neither space nor time for an ornamental garden, but he did find enough of both for a vegetable garden. Since retirement, however, he has indulged his interest in plants of all kinds, including mosses, conifers, flowering shrubs, and herbaceous perennials.

"I enjoy just seeing what will grow here," he told us, "what will do well in a soil that is not conducive to vegetation. It is too shallow, too acidic." And yet he has turned the property surrounding his summer home into a botanical garden.

Even lichens have a place in Dr. Richards' garden. This native mountain ash *(Sorbus americana)* is festooned with a lichen commonly called "old man's beard."

Interesting plants are everywhere in Dr. Richards' garden. If you spend too much time looking up, you're likely to miss the native groundcovers that he nurtures in spots where they naturally take hold, such as this patch of bunchberry *(Cornus canadensis)*.

Nor should a visitor miss this scene of Canada mayflower *(Maianthemum canadense)* growing with lingonberry. The round greenish fruits of the Canada mayflower will eventually turn pale red.

"My goal," he stated, "is to integrate native vegetation with exotic species." And so it is that as you stroll along the winding paths you see astilbes, daylilies, and hostas growing alongside lingonberry, bunchberry, Canada mayflower, Japanese maples, catawba rhododendrons, and heathers beneath canopies of native birches and black spruce.

As we walked the garden paths, we talked about what it takes to grow such a beautiful garden under such challenging conditions. Deer are contained (most of the time) outside a perimeter fence, but slugs are the real challenge. "They love hostas," Dr. Richards told us, "and I've tried everything: wood ashes, diatomaceous earth, and solutions of yeast. In a bad year, nothing works!"

Dr. Richards and Marjorie stop to talk about nurturing moss in the garden. "All I do is pull out the occasional tree seedling," he told us. "Mother Nature takes it from there."

And what about that shallow, acidic soil? Dr. Richards adds lime to raise the pH where needed and also mineralizes the soil with rock phosphate as needed. To maintain fertility and organic content, he adds compost to each bed on a three-year rotation. This is accomplished by removing the plants from the bed, digging out the tree roots that have invaded over the past three years, then digging in compost made on site, and finally replanting.

He is learning what will grow in his garden and what will not. Astilbes will grow there, for sure (see sidebar).

We came to the edge of the sea of color and suddenly found ourselves in the cool shade of tall spruce, some of the trees planted by Dr. Richards over 40 years ago. The granite buttresses surrounding the trees were covered with a thick layer of sun-dappled moss that invited us to stop and rest a while.

From the moss-covered rocks, a woodland path took us down to the shoreline, then wound back into Dr. Richards' garden, a place where, in summer, astilbes prevail.

The path through Dr. Richards' garden ends at this shoreline scene.

## Astilbes in the Summer Garden

When Marjorie and I walked through the gate of Dr. Richards' garden for the first time, we were not prepared for the colorful scene that greeted us. A river of color flowed around tall spruce trunks and granite boulders, dappled sunlight brightening some sections of the stream, deep shade darkening others.

At first all I could see were the plume-like astilbe blossoms held high on tall, stiff stalks, the soft pinks, bright purples, and brilliant whites, but as my eyes adjusted I began to pick out other colors, the yellows and oranges of daylilies, the pink of spirea and deep burgundy red of Japanese maple foliage. So many astilbes!

Dr. Richards explains to Marjorie why he likes astilbes.

Accustomed to astilbes in small doses, I had to ask of Dr. Richards, why so many? The answer was simple and pragmatic: they will tolerate a lot of shade, they are relatively pest free—deer and slugs leave them alone—and they will tolerate the thin, acidic soil. "They do need water," he added. "In hot, dry weather, their foliage will burn." Dr. Richards drags the hose around his garden during dry spells.

Astilbes will bloom in the shade, but they need some direct sunlight to achieve full size. The dappled shade in Dr. Richards' garden moves across the garden in the course of each sunny day, allowing each plant a sufficient measure of full sun.

Adding to the list of astilbe virtues, he is quick to add that the plants stay in bloom for several weeks in summer, slowly fading as they dry. By early September, their dried brown seedheads give the garden a beautiful autumnal look.

Marjorie and I were both in awe at the swarms of pollinators foraging on the astilbe blooms. We walked through clouds of butterflies, bees, and hoverflies.

Pressed to name his favorite astilbe varieties, Dr. Richards said he was concentrating on the Vision series, a group of low-growing (12 to 18 inches tall) Chinese astilbes *(Astilbe chinensis)* with lacy foliage topped by dense upright plumes of lavender, red, or white flowers. He is also growing the Gloria series *(Astilbe arendsii)*, red and white varieties that he feels have exceptionally nice foliage after blooming. In general, he is working toward a garden with early, midseason, and late varieties, the latter coming largely from the *Astilbe chinensis* group of varieties.

(Left) A river of astilbe color flows around spruce trunks and boulders.

(Below) As the dappled shade moves around during the day, each plant gets its measure of full sun.

### Moss Gardening

I often receive letters and emails from gardeners frustrated by moss creeping into shady garden spots where they are trying to grow grass. I give it to them straight: There are only two choices. Eliminate shade and make sure the soil pH has not become too acidic for grass, or cultivate the moss.

Personally, I'll take moss over lawn grass any day.

My experience with moss gardening is limited to watching moss grow in Marjorie's Garden. Carpets of yellow-green sphagnum moss and gray foliose lichens begin at the edge of the woods and encroach into the paths around the garden beds wherever there is too much shade for grass. Other species of moss form dark green pincushions covering rocks and filling the spaces between surface tree roots, taking advantage of any small niche where other plants would fail to root.

Mosses like it cool, shady, and wet, thriving in thin, nutrient-poor, acidic soil, taking over wherever grasses wane. For a while it may seem as if the two groundcovers are waging a battle for the same spot of ground, but not really. Something has changed – more shade, more water – and the site is in transition. The mosses are destined to win.

Can this process be expedited? Can the gardener establish a moss carpet by encouraging mosses already present in a weakening grass lawn? This is the question posed by George Schenk in his book *Moss Gardening*. His advice: "Pluck out the wan remnants of grass and greet the moss as friend."

Acidification of the soil will encourage mosses while discouraging grass. This can be achieved by dusting the area with powdered sulfur, about 2½ pounds per 100 square feet, striving for a pH of 5.5. Or dust the ground with skimmed milk powder or aluminum sulfate, or sprinkle the area with rhododendron fertilizer. All of these materials will help acidify the soil. Be sure to lightly hose any of these powders into the soil, particularly if conditions are dry.

Aside from acidifying the soil, keeping the area groomed will help the moss become established. Pluck out weeds, including tree seedlings and grass plants, and keep the site raked free of tree leaves, pine needles, spruce cones, and other smothering debris. Use rakes with wire or bamboo tines, raking lightly to avoid disturbing the moss.

Once the moss carpet is established, I would be inclined to let nature take its course, to invite debris back into the picture. I enjoy coming across patches of moss strewn with newly fallen pine needles or colorful autumn leaves, and finding piles of spruce cone scales left by a hungry chipmunk or red squirrel – one could hardly find a better place to dine than a soft patch of sphagnum at the edge of a garden.

## The Vegetable Gardens of Dorcas Corrow and Eva Eicher—Zone 5b

As soon as I arrived at Sweet Haven Farm in Seal Cove, Maine, I went to work pulling weeds, joining a small group of volunteers helping farm owners Eva Eicher and Dorcas Corrow grow food for the hungry. It was the summer of 2011, and I had come to talk with both owners about their project, Sweet Haven Farm Harvest for the Hungry, but I felt compelled to pitch in and help Dorcas as she answered my questions.

Eva was up at the house growing seedlings under lights for later transplanting to the garden. This is the division of labor that the farm owners have developed, Dorcas manages the garden, Eva produces the starter plants. Dorcas and I would join Eva later for lunch on the porch.

As we worked our way down a row, Dorcas mentioned that an earlier group of volunteers had just left, having come in early to hand-pick cucumber beetles off the squash plants. Volunteers, including Master Gardener Volunteers from the University of Maine Cooperative Extension Master Gardener Program and community volunteers from all walks of life, are the backbone of Sweet Haven Farm's effort to provide good nutrition to seniors and others on limited incomes. "We try to provide as much healthy, fresh produce as possible to those who cannot either produce or purchase fresh vegetables," Dorcas explained.

The Project began in 2010 when Eva and Dorcas, working for the most part on their own, produced about 500 pounds of food for several low-income housing facilities. As of October, 2011, with an expanded force of volunteers, the farm delivered 1,000 pounds of vegetables, including 800 pounds of produce, 30 pounds of frozen tomato sauce, 150 pounds of winter squash, and fall crops of broccoli, beet greens, chard, and carrots.

To achieve this impressive increase in farm production, the amount of garden space committed to the project was increased to 1,800 square feet for the 2011 season. Second, succession planting and organic farming methods were used to maximize productivity. In addition, volunteers from the Master Gardner Program and the community at large came on board to work in the garden—planting, weeding, and harvesting.

"One thing that I am very proud of involves the success of the succession planting process," Dorcas says as she yanks a fistful of weeds from the middle of a bean row. "There were string beans available each week starting the first week in August until the last week of September, and a second crop of carrots, beets, chard, spinach, and broccoli is in progress."

Succession plantings extend the green bean harvest from the first week in August until the end of September.

## A Year-Round Labor of Love

Visiting Sweet Haven Farm amid the hustle and bustle of summer, I couldn't help wondering what went into planning such a large garden. I asked Dorcas and Eva to describe the planning behind the planting.

"Planning begins in January with a thorough review of seed catalogs," says Dorcas. "Eva takes an inventory of the seeds left over from the previous season, and together we compare notes on which varieties performed best and which we will not plant again. We determine which crops we will emphasize and how we will allocate the space.

"Allocation of space takes into account the feedback we get from our 'customers.' For example, in 2011 we dedicated a lot of space to string beans and they were very well received, so we allocated even more space to string beans in 2012."

By the end of January, Eva has selected the seeds and placed the orders. Dorcas has planned the crop rotation and garden layout for the coming year.

"In late February," Dorcas continues, "Eva begins to fill seed flats with germinating mix to start some of the crops that have long growing times, like onions, leeks, and shallots. These are grown under lights in the house until the weather is warm enough to transfer the operation to a hoop house and cold frames. Experience has taught us that we have much greater variety and better-quality seedlings when we grow our own seedlings from seed.

"As the onion plants grow, Eva clips the greens to about 2 inches to help the plants grow sturdy. Keeping in mind that some crops prefer cool weather, seeds of broccoli and other brassicas get started by mid March so they can get into the soil by early May.

"Soil tests are taken as early in spring as the frost leaves the ground. The soil is amended according to soil test results as the plants are placed in the soil. Specific crops may get additional additives such as epsom salts (a source of magnesium) for members of the tomato family and borax (a source of boron) for root crops.

"By April, the garlic that was planted the previous November is up. The first crop of peas is planted and the gardening season begins. Eva keeps very busy planting and transplanting the seedlings, getting them ready for me to plant when the season is right. Tomatoes and other nightshade crops like warm weather, so planting them outside too early only stresses the plants.

"When the volunteers show up to work, the garden plots have been tilled and are ready to be planted according to the plot plan developed in January. We maintain a four-year rotation plan unless there is some fungal disease that requires a longer period between replantings to burn out.

"Insects such as cabbage moth, cucumber beetle, and potato beetle are controlled by a combination of lightweight row covers and hand-picking the insects. We are finding that both early detection and planting the crops slightly after the peak insect season help reduce insect infestations.

"This garden project for feeding the hungry is a year-round labor of love. We have established a division of labor that utilizes the talents of each and keeps us busy and thinking about gardens all year."

Vegetables, including lettuce and beans, are all grown organically at Sweet Haven Farm.

Dorcas was also proud of their success in controlling several outbreaks of insect infestations without the use of insecticides. "Control of squash beetles was especially difficult this summer," she said. "The 100-plus winter squash plants were checked twice daily to control these pests."

But Dorcas was most proud of her volunteers. "I found the volunteers a joy to work with, and I was thrilled with the enthusiasm each brought to the project. These volunteers came with a strong work ethic, an eagerness to do whatever task was required, and ideas to share that helped make the project more successful. The goal of this project would not have been fulfilled without these dedicated volunteers."

The project was expanded in 2012 to 4,000 square feet of garden space, including field plots and raised beds. When I asked how long the project will run, Dorcas replied, "The project does not have a completion date. Hunger never stops. The need for good nutrition will always be there."

Dorcas and Eva are an inspiration to all gardeners, encouraging each of us to share our harvest with those in our community who need help.

# Chapter 14

# The Garden in Winter

*"As I write, snow is falling outside my Maine window, and indoors all around me half a hundred garden catalogues are in bloom."*

—Katherine S. White

***November brings the first hard freeze,*** the kind that forms ice needles on the bright red and yellow leaves of highbush blueberries and the still-green foliage of raspberries, the kind that rimes the tawny pappus of goldenrod and aster seedheads. In the woods at the edge of Marjorie's Garden, the tamaracks are golden.

The vegetable garden sleeps, all but the beds sown to winter oats. They look out of place, out of season, bright green swaths of grassy leaves dripping rainwater into the soil, their roots mining minerals leached beyond the reach of tomato or squash roots. In spring we will turn over the oats and return those minerals to the roots of summer vegetables.

Leaves have all fallen, except for the dry brown leaves of garden oaks and the still-green leaves of a peach tree that has no inkling how to behave in a Maine garden. Persistent winter fruits, berries and seed capsules of the garden's trees and shrubs, give reason to pause as I stroll around the November garden.

In December comes a brief interlude, lasting only a few hours, when snow works magic in the garden. Often it is early in the morning after the season's first real snowstorm. I awake to a landscape of stark contrasts, snow packed in branch forks, dark green fir boughs bending under their loads, brown seedheads wearing gnome-like hats of white, clusters of golden seed capsules crowned with snow at the tips of enkianthus twigs, and the north-facing side of the old pine's furrowed trunk whitewashed with wind-packed snow.

On such mornings the garden is mostly a blank canvas. The lines of the garden beds are buried, along with most of the herbaceous plants and smaller shrubs. Plants that catch my eye, like the enkianthus, do so because they offer contrast in color and texture to the whiteness. It is tempting to take credit for the siting of the enkianthus, to say that we framed it with the fireside window for mornings like this one, to pretend to have that much foresight.

Winter days can pull a gardener away from the fire. Trying to stay on the invisible garden paths, I visit some of my favorite trees, the yellow birches with their shaggy honey-gold bark, a

*Facing page:* On the morning after a winter storm, snow traces the branches of every tree in Marjorie's Garden.

Winter scenes like this make red-vein enkianthus truly a four-season tree.

sight that always warms my heart on a sunny winter morning, and the old white pine. I wish we had planted a beech tree for the dried paper-like leaves that hang on through the cold months, giving voice to the winter winds.

Wild turkey tracks emerge from the woods and cross the garden after surmounting an old canoe propped upside down on cinder blocks. I find the snow shovel and clear a few square yards to nearly bare ground, then throw down cracked corn, hoping the turkeys will check back later in the day.

Suddenly it is snowing again, a shower of feathery flakes floating down from the high branches of a yellow birch where a single black-capped bird pecks at a sunflower seed taken from the porch feeder. Snow drifts through blue sky. Chickadee snow.

I find other excuses to stay in the garden, absorbed by the magic of the place, until my knees start hurting and I begin to see the garden from Katharine White's point of view. A sizable stack of garden catalogs have arrived in the mail over the holidays. When tramping through the snow is no longer fun, it's time to sit in a rocker by the fire and repaint the canvas outside the window.

## Persistent Winter Fruits

From November until the midwinter thaw, the red berries of winterberry holly *(Ilex verticillata)*, a deciduous native shrub, will brighten both woods and garden, as will the larger red fruits of the American cranberry viburnum *(Viburnum opulus* var. *trilobum)*. Both of these provide late winter food for songbirds.

Some gardeners compete with the birds for the viburnum fruits, preserving them in jams or jellies with, I suspect, a lot of added sugar. After tasting these berries straight from the shrub, I understand why the birds eat them only as a last resort. I read that the winterberry fruits are also

### 'Donald Wyman' in the Winter Garden

When I was teaching woody plants at the University of Maine, Orono, I would take my classes to Littlefield Garden on the eastern edge of the campus and we would walk among the crabapples. My main purpose was to introduce the students to 'Donald Wyman,' one of the more than 100 crabapple varieties in the collection. This particular variety was named to honor Dr. Donald Wyman, a renowned horticulturist at the Arnold Arboretum.

Spring semester classes always ended before the majority of crabapples were in bloom, including 'Donald Wyman,' so I resorted to showing slides, first a close-up of the pink and red buds, then a shot of the entire tree, its wide-spreading branches layered in pure white flowers. And while students in spring would see new foliage of every variety, I made sure to tell them that by late August, particularly if the summer was dry, only the foliage of 'Donald Wyman' would still look fresh and clean, devoid of browning and spotting from the major crabapple diseases: fireblight, rust, and apple scab.

By fall, the majority of crabapple varieties in the collection had lost most of their leaves to diseases and insects, leaving little opportunity for a display of fall color. 'Donald Wyman' was the exception. At its October peak, it combined leaves of late-summer green and bright yellow with the glossy bright red of maturing small apples, each about ½ inch in diameter.

The fruits of 'Donald Wyman' persisted into winter, often still on the tree in late January, capped with snow or wrapped in ice. Resident robins, waxwings (both cedar and Bohemian), and pine grosbeaks waited for the midwinter thaw to soften the apples, then feasted on the fruits. They dropped bits of peel to the ground as they fed, creating a reddish-brown shadow of the tree on the snow.

Growing to 25 feet tall, 'Donald Wyman' is the perfect size for smaller gardens. And few other choices would compare in offering spring flowers, healthy summer foliage, fall color from both foliage and fruit, and winter color from the persistent apples. With over 600 crabapple types currently available, 'Donald Wyman' remains one of the best.

The bright red fruits of 'Donald Wyman' persist until the first midwinter thaw, when they are eagerly taken by robins, waxwings, and grosbeaks.

highly astringent and, as I think about it, I can recall winters in which the fruits of both plants were left to wither on the branches.

Not all persistent fruits are red and showy. The waxy gray berries of northern bayberry *(Myrica pensylvanica)* hug its twigs through the winter, eventually to be eaten by songbirds, waterfowl, and shorebirds. These are the same berries that we harvest for scenting of bayberry candles.

Northern bayberry leaves are evergreen in southern New England but take a beating in Maine winters. The waxy gray berries, still on the plant in late January, are eventually eaten by birds.

Not all persistent fruits are berries. The pale brown to red-brown seedheads of meadowsweet *(Spiraea latifolia)* persist through winter, extending the usefulness of this native shrub in the garden. And I love to watch the snow build up around the summersweet clethra *(Clethra alnifolia)* in Marjorie's Garden until only the uppermost dried seedheads remain exposed. I imagine a field mouse beneath the snow, snuggled close to the ground with a cache of seed, waiting for the thaw.

Snow builds up around summersweet clethra until only the dried seedheads are visible.

## *Forcing Paperwhites*

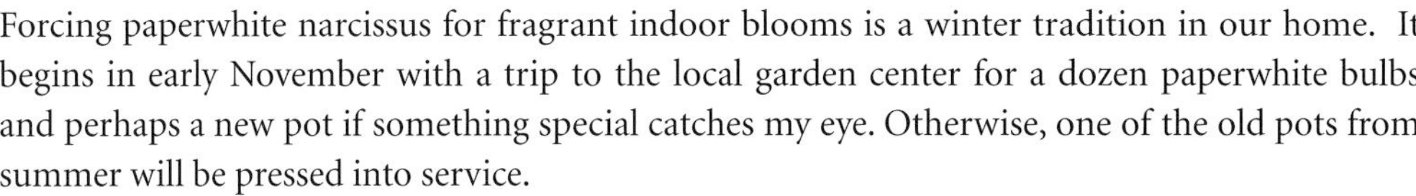

The fragrance of paperwhites forced into bloom in late December or January is evocative of spring.

Forcing paperwhite narcissus for fragrant indoor blooms is a winter tradition in our home. It begins in early November with a trip to the local garden center for a dozen paperwhite bulbs and perhaps a new pot if something special catches my eye. Otherwise, one of the old pots from summer will be pressed into service.

To plant a dozen good bulbs, I fill a 12-inch-wide pot with enough potting soil so that the tops of the bulbs will be just below the rim of the pot when planted. The bulbs are then placed shoulder to shoulder on top of the soil, pointed tip up, and enough soil is added to bury all but the tips.

The potted bulbs are watered thoroughly and placed in the basement, where it is both cool (50 to 55° F) and dark, perfect conditions to encourage root growth. I check the pot every few days to make sure the soil remains damp. When the shoots reach a height of about 3 inches, I move the plants to a sunny upstairs window where the temperature is usually between 60 and 70° F.

The plants begin to flower after about a month in the window, during which time the stems elongate to the point of requiring staking. Marjorie inserts slender bamboo stakes among the stems and then weaves green jute twine through them to form a nearly invisible supporting lattice.

Paperwhite varieties include 'Bethlehem' (creamy white petals with a yellow cup), 'Galilee' (pure white), 'Israel' (creamy yellow petals with a sulfur yellow cup), 'Jerusalem' (pure white), 'Nazareth' (soft yellow petals with a bright yellow cup), and 'Ziva' (pure white), all of which have a musky fragrance. 'Grand Soleil d'Or' (yellow petals with an orange cup) takes one to two weeks longer to force and does not bloom as heavily as other varieties, but it has a sweet, fruity fragrance. We are partial to the white varieties such as 'Ziva,' often adding a branch or two of bright red winterberries to the arrangement at Christmas.

Once the flowers are spent, the bulbs should be discarded. Paperwhites are not winter hardy in New England.

## *Protecting Trees and Shrubs from the Ravages of Winter*

The garden is nearly in order, ready for the blanket of snow that all gardeners hope will soon come and grow ever deeper through the months ahead, protecting roots and crowns from the bitter bite of January, February, and even March. While we wait, there are still a few loose ends. Winter plays havoc with the garden's trees and shrubs. Winter sun, wind, and cold temperatures can bleach and desiccate evergreen foliage, damage bark, and injure or kill branches, flowerbuds, and roots. Hungry mice burrow beneath the snow to feed on bark and twigs while deer and rabbits nosh on flowerbuds and foliage.

What can the gardener do to mitigate this damage?

### Protecting against Sunscald

On cold sunny days, the bark exposed to direct sunlight (usually the south and southwestern sides of the tree) heats up to the point that living cells beneath the bark become active. These cells, called cambial cells, are responsible for producing new water and food conduction tissues within the trunk. When the sun becomes blocked by a cloud or building, the bark temperature drops precipitously, killing the cambial cells. The resulting damage is called sunscald.

Sunscald is characterized by sunken, dried, or cracked areas of dead bark. Young and newly planted trees are highly susceptible, as are thin-barked trees such as cherries, crabapples, maples, birches, and mountain ash. Also, pruning evergreen trees or shrubs in late summer or fall to remove lower branches may expose previously shaded trunk tissue to direct winter sun, resulting in potential sunscald injury.

Protect sensitive trees by wrapping the trunk with a light-colored material that will reflect sunlight, keeping the bark temperature more constant. Commercial tree wrap, a polyurethane spiral wrap that expands as the tree grows, or any light-colored material will work. Wrap the tree in early November and remove the wrap in April. Newly planted trees should be wrapped each winter for at least the first two years, and thin-barked species should be wrapped for five years or more.

There is no remedy for sunscald after it has occurred other than to carefully cut away the damaged bark with a sharp pruning knife and hope that the tree's natural wound-healing capacity will work. Do make damaged trees a priority for wrapping in subsequent winters.

### Protecting Evergreens from Browning and Bleaching of Foliage

Whenever winter sun warms conifer needles, transpiration occurs. Water is lost from the needles while the roots are frozen, and this results in desiccation of the needles and destruction of chlorophyll, followed by needle browning or bleaching. Browning or bleaching of broad-leafed evergreens such as rhododendrons occurs in the same manner.

Among the conifers, the most susceptible types are yews, arborvitae, and hemlock. All conifers, however, can be affected.

The last of the kale (top) and sage (above) persists in this Maine garden (Zone 5b) in a mild early December. Like Brussels sprouts, beets, carrots, and other season extenders, they give the New England vegetable gardener a late-in-the-year bounty.

Solutions to this problem begin with proper placement of conifers and broad-leaved evergreens in the landscape. They are best planted on the east sides of buildings, certainly not on the south or southwest sides or in windy, sunny sites.

To protect low-growing conifers from winter wind and sun, prop pine boughs against or over the plants once the ground has frozen. The boughs will act as a windbreak as well as catch insulating snow.

For larger conifers and sensitive rhododendrons, burlap wind barriers can be constructed on the south, southwest, and windward sides of plantings. These barriers, if tall enough, may also protect against salt-spray damage to plants near driveways and roads.

Stakes for the barriers should be installed in early November, before the ground freezes. Later in the month, attach the burlap sheets to the stakes with staples or sturdy twine. Make the enclosure as tall as feasible to block wind from hitting the uppermost branches, and leave the top of the enclosure open.

Water-stressed trees and shrubs are ill-prepared for winter winds and cold. Throughout the growing season, your trees should receive an inch of water per week, either from rain or irrigation. Beginning in late autumn until freeze-up, they should receive an inch of water per month by rain or irrigation. Waiting until October to begin watering as needed will not maximize stress resistance.

Some gardeners spray evergreens with anti-desiccants or anti-transpirants to reduce winter damage. Save your money. Most studies show these materials to be ineffective.

### Rabbits and Mice and Deer, Oh My!

Most of our garden mice spend the winter in the woodpile below the porch sunflower feeders. In a really hard winter, however, we have experienced mice damage on the lower trunks of newly planted shrubs and trees, enough to induce us to start placing cylinders of ¼-inch hardware cloth around the bases of sensitive plants. To be effective, these wire cylinders must extend 2 to 3 inches below ground.

Cylinders made of the same wire will deter the garden's rabbits from feeding on specific shrubs or trees, but they should extend at least 18 to 24 inches above the ground to deter nibbling of tender lower branches. In all cases, these wire barricades can be left in place all year, but be sure to enlarge them as the plant trunks grow larger.

As for noshing deer, we built a fence to keep them away from the blueberries and raspberries in Marjorie's Garden. Beyond that solution, you're on your own. Deer at the edges of the garden are part of the joy of gardening in New England.

## *Hunkering Down, Waiting for April*

What a great snow! The garden is now covered with a foot-deep insulating blanket that will protect plant roots from killing temperatures, at least until the next thaw, and birds, including goldfinches, nuthatches, chickadees, a male cardinal, and an American tree sparrow, are in a feeding frenzy at the porch feeder.

The Christmas tree is now in the garden, propped up by the root system of a fallen spruce, close to the spot where I clear away the snow and scatter cracked corn for the blue jays, mourning doves, crows, and wild turkeys. It was a good tree, a fir that Lynne chose on a street corner lot the day after Thanksgiving. It spent more than a month inside our home, presents wrapped in colorful paper accumulating under its branches. On weekends and during the holiday break,

Marjorie and I sipped pre-dawn coffee by the woodstove and the light of this tree, listening to carols playing softly in the background.

Taking down the tree always saddens me. We remove the ornaments collected over the years, carefully wrapping each one in paper before packing them all away in boxes, then unwind the strings of lights, fir needles dropping at our feet as we circle the tree. Suddenly there is only the small tree, its trunk propped up in water that it no longer uses, and it drops a trail of needles as I lift it from its stand and carry it outside. For the rest of the day, there is the faint smell of balsam in a corner of the room.

If I lived in a city, I would never throw out my Christmas tree, never leave it at the curb with cardboard and wrapping paper. I would cart it into the closest woods, where birds could seek shelter among its branches, at least for one winter.

This is the message of Brad Kessler's tale, *The Woodcutter's Christmas.* A small book perfect for a winter evening read, it tells the story of a night in New York City when abandoned Christmas trees cried out and a woodcutter's life was changed forever. Read it before you take down your tree.

After Christmas, the tree becomes part of the winter garden, a haven for sparrows and mice.

Despite the cold and the whiteness of the landscape, there are still tangible connections to the garden. Buckets of compost and wood ashes need to be emptied, and this means shoveling a long path through new snow to garden beds where the ashes are spread and then on to compost piles at the back of the garden. The piles are brick hard, and all I can do to cover fresh compost is throw on straw and cover it with snow.

So now it begins, the long wait for the start of the new garden year. Hunker down, place your seed orders, read a good book or two, take care of the garden's birds. April will be here before you know it!

So much depends upon. . . . (Photo courtesy Patricia Crow)

# Appendix

## *Non-Native Invasive Woody Plants and Suggested Native Alternatives for New England Gardens*

As mentioned in Chapter 2, invasive species are second only to habitat destruction as a major threat to global biodiversity, and 80% of the invasive woody plants (trees, shrubs, and vines) now undermining the biodiversity of woodland ecosystems in the United States were introduced as ornamentals for our gardens. Many are still sold as garden and landscape plants by nurseries. The following list identifies some of these plant species and offers native alternatives to their use. Hardiness zones listed are for the New England region. Native alternatives include species native to the eastern United States but not to New England.

### Trees

| Invasive Species | Native Alternatives |
|---|---|
| Norway Maple *(Acer platanoides)* | Black Gum *(Nyssa sylvatica)*, Zones 4-7<br>Red Maple *(Acer rubrum)*, Zones 3-7 |
| Princess Tree *(Paulownia tomentosa)* | Northern Catalpa *(Catalpa speciosa)*, Zones 4-7 |
| Callery Pear *(Pyrus calleryana)* | Allegheny Serviceberry *(Amelanchier laevis)*, Zones 4-7<br>Fringe Tree *(Chionanthus virginicus)*, Zones 4-7 |
| Black Locust *(Robinia pseudoacacia)* | Kentucky Coffeetree *(Gymnocladus dioica)*, Zones 4-7<br>Quaking Aspen *(Populus tremuloides)*, Zones 3-7 |
| European Mountain Ash (Sorbus aucuparia) | American Mountain Ash *(Sorbus americana)*, Zones 3-7 |

Fringe Tree *(Chionanthus virginicus)*

## Shrubs

| | |
|---|---|
| Japanese Barberry *(Berberis thunbergii)* | Bush Honeysuckle *(Diervilla lonicera)*, Zones 3-7<br>Virginia Sweetspire *(Itea virginica)*, Zones 5-7<br>Witch Alder *(Fothergilla gardenii)*, Zones 5-7 |
| Butterfly Bush *(Buddleja daviddii)* | Buttonbush *(Cephalanthus occidentalis)*, Zones 4-7<br>Summersweet *(Clethra alternifolia)*, Zones 4-7 |
| English Hawthorn *(Crataegus monogyna)* | Cock-Spur Hawthorn *(Crataegus crus-galli)*, Zones 3-7 |
| Scotch Broom *(Cytisus scoparius)* | Bayberry *(Myrica pensylvanica)*, Zones 4-7 |
| Winged Euonymus *(Burning Bush)* *(Euonymus alatus)* | Black Chokeberry *(Aronia melanocarpa)*, Zones 3-7<br>Highbush Blueberry *(Vaccinium corymbosum)*, Zones 3-7<br>Fragrant Sumac *(Rhus aromatica)*, Zones 4-7 |

Highbush Blueberry *(Vaccinium corymbosum)*

## Vines

| | |
|---|---|
| Oriental Bittersweet* | Virginia Creeper *(Parthenocissus quinquefolia)*, *(Celastrus orbiculatus)* Zones 3-7 (Photo USDA) |

**Note: One of the main dispersers of this invasive species are people who harvest the fruiting vines for wreaths and other decoration.*

For more information and a more complete listing, I highly recommend *Native Alternatives to Invasive Species* by C. Colston Burrell (Janet Marinelli and Bonnie Harper-Lore, Editors), Brooklyn Botanic Gardens Handbook #185, 2006, Brooklyn Botanic Garden (ISBN 13:978-1-889538-74-7).

Virginia Creeper *(Parthenocissus quinquefolia)*

# Index

Page numbers in bold print refer to the tables of monthly activities at the ends of Chapters 5 through 11.

# Index of Scientific Names

# Acknowledgments

The scope of this book was enhanced by the help of several New England gardeners who opened their garden gates and answered countless questions. Many thanks to Ron and Jennifer Kujawski, Berta and Nate Atwater, Trip Millikin, Dora Atwater Millikin, Patricia Crow, James Hadley, Tom and Jan McIntyre, Theresa Guethler, Dr. Charles Richards, Dorcas Corrow, and Eva Eicher. Thanks also to Charlie Heaven, whose photos of his Woodbury, Connecticut vegetable garden grace numerous pages in this book.

Reeser extends special thanks to Tom McIntyre for flying him low over the coast of Maine to take photographs in a Rhode Island garden, and to Dan DeLong, avid gardener and faithful reader of Reeser's column, who for years prodded, "When are you going to write a book?"

We thank Janet Robbins for her many hours of work on cover and text design and page layout and Tristram Coburn of Cadent Publishing for his efforts in promoting the book. Jon Eaton, our editor and publisher, planted the seed that grew into *The New England Gardener's Year.* Watching the book grow under his insight and instruction has been an extraordinary experience for which we will always be grateful.

# Dedication

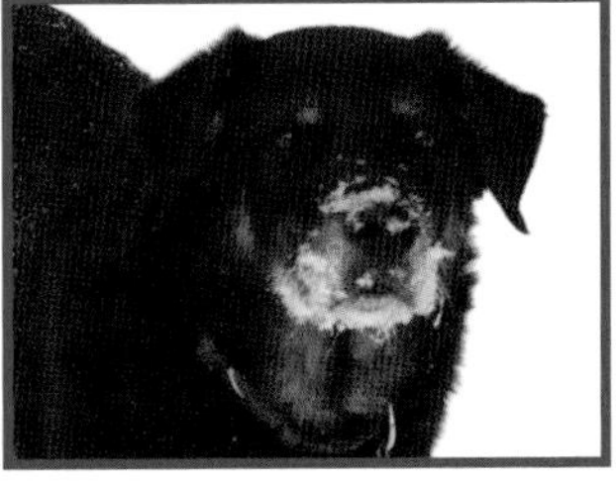

On December 23, 2012, we had to say goodbye to Dixie. She was Marjorie's first dog, rescued from a shelter in 2000, two years old. She loved playing in the snow, finding treasures in the compost pile, pursuing porcupines, and singing along with Lynne's French horn. We dedicate this book to her memory. Rest in peace dear one.

# About the Authors

Marjorie and Reeser

**Reeser Manley** has gardened in South Carolina, Washington state (while earning a Ph.D. in Horticultural Science), Massachusetts, and, for the last 12 years, in Maine. He also writes about the garden in a weekly column and online blog for the *Bangor Daily News.* Over a span of four decades he has taught horticulture at technical colleges and universities, including the University of Massachusetts, Amherst, and the University of Maine, Orono. These days he teaches chemistry and physics at a small high school on the coast of Maine and botany for the University of Maine Cooperative Extension Master Gardener Volunteer Program.

**Marjorie Peronto** received her M.S. in Environmental Education from the University of Wisconsin. Between college degrees she spent 2½ years in Togo, West Africa, as a Peace Corps Volunteer, followed by three years as Community Garden Consultant with the Save the Children Federation. She is currently a University of Maine professor with 20 years' experience teaching courses in ornamental gardening, ecological landscaping, and home food production. She trains Master Gardener Volunteers to conduct community outreach projects that promote sustainable gardening and food security. For the past nine years Marjorie has been conducting research trials on native trees and shrubs for Maine landscapes.

For updates and tips, visit Reeser's gardening community on Facebook at:
http://www.facebook.com/negardener